ANTHROPOLOGICAL STUDIES
IN THE EASTERN HIGHLANDS OF NEW GUINEA

James B. Watson, *Editor*

Volume V: Tairora Culture: Contingency and Pragmatism

Anthropological Studies
in the Eastern Highlands of New Guinea

James B. Watson, *Editor*

VOLUMES PUBLISHED:

TAIRORA CULTURE

Contingency and Pragmatism

JAMES B. WATSON

UNIVERSITY OF WASHINGTON PRESS
SEATTLE AND LONDON

This book is published with the assistance of a grant from
the National Science Foundation

Library of Congress Cataloging in Publication Data

Watson, James B. (James Bennett), 1918-
  Tairora culture.
  (Anthropological studies in the eastern highlands of
New Guinea; v. 5)
  Bibliography: p.
  Includes index.
  1. Tairora (Papua New Guinea people)   I. Title.
II. Series.
DU740.42.W37   1983   306'.0899912   82-23776
ISBN 0-295-95799-9

To Fred Eggan
who initiated me into the field

Preface

This monograph is the sixth volume to be published in a multidisciplinary study of a continuous small region of the Eastern Highlands of New Guinea, now Papua New Guinea, inhabited by four adjacent and linguistically related peoples: the Gadsup, the Auyana, the Awa, and the Tairora. Each volume reports one aspect of the four study peoples or, as in the present case, the culture of one of them. In the forewords to each of the other five volumes, as the general editor of the series, I sketched the design and purpose of the Micro-evolution Project,* as the collective enterprise is known, with a comment on how the aims of the Project in each case oriented the study in question. My preface here will follow precedent in commenting on the Project's overall aims and the relevance of this work to those larger aims.

In this monograph I depict the local variability of organization, beliefs, and practice between and within two Tairora-speaking communities. The chapters that follow document in some detail a fluidity and variation of cultural form and social organization, which are accounted for as the pragmatic response of people to the contingencies of their lives. The two groups studied are small autonomous societies living within close reach of numerous others much like themselves. These they largely replicate—regardless of other differences, such as language or ethnic identity—in the basics of coping both with resources and with each other. The variability of the two communities through time is seen to arise from the circumstances of their smallness, crowding, and widely shared coping patterns. Theirs is a turbulent field in which coping with neighbors, to be successful, must be flexible and pragmatic. If these circumstances have indeed the consequences I suggest, one would predict comparable contingencies and similar pragmatism and local variability, accompanied by frequent and rapid changes, wherever else such circumstances are found.[†]

---

*See also Watson 1963a.
[†]For a more detailed discussion, see Watson 1981.

The emphasis on fluidity and change is at odds with some of the views of people like the Tairora: preliterate, history-less, kinship-oriented, acephalous, isolated, and small. Changelessness has often been supposed to accompany such conditions. Is it possible that the present emphasis on change is an artifact of the research aims of the larger project? There is no question that change and variation were central to its aims, which were based on the premise that differences, even if minute, would be found to justify the comparison of two similar communities. Differences were deliberately sought by using the *Outline of Cultural Materials* (Murdock et al. 1950) as a checklist or standard descriptive inventory.

As the chapters to follow make clear, numerous differences were indeed found, some of which could only be described as minute, not easily assigned a broad implication. The Abiera use of cooking-cylinders made from hollowed sections of tree trunk, a custom the Batainabura know of but do not practice, would illustrate differences of this limited sort. But other differences seem to strike at more fundamental contrasts between these two communities, which after all use the same language, are located a scant half-day's walk apart, and are even linked to each other through the kinship of some of their members. Differences in the organization of society, in kinship nomenclature, in endogamy, in military prowess, in concepts of ghosts, in familiarity with forest powers, and in a more mythological founding (Batainabura) illustrate this latter group.

Granted the part played by the Project's specific emphasis on differences and change, the fact remains that some fairly substantial differences were found. Are they then perhaps a peculiarity of the Tairora? Or would such variation also be found in comparing other small autonomous societies of generally Neolithic character? Admittedly I ascribe the turbulence of Tairora life and the pragmatism that seems an essential response to it to their being small-sized groups, crowded, and replicative of their neighbors, who are, like themselves, village horticulturists. I therefore suppose that the circumstances in which the Tairora live would broadly characterize representative other Neolithic folk, who also would experience fluidity and frequent change.

It seems a mistake, in any case, to believe that peoples like the precontact Tairora typify a stable and "traditional" way of life. They lack the conditions for true traditionalism, which are surely confined to the slow eddies of civilization. Traditionalism best takes root in large, long-stratified societies where the comforts and privileges of one class depend on keeping a tight reign on another, usually much larger, subpopulation. There "tradition" may well become an ideological commitment because it protects the means of the few for reining in the many, once such means are successfully devised. It is hard to imagine how a people like the Tairora, lacking an efficient elite to devise and exercise superordinate control, could consciously defend their beliefs, practices, or institutions in such a manner—or why they would find it advantageous to do so. Only where the affluence of a few depends continuously on such efficacy do high stakes steadily support the beneficiaries in building and defending tradition. Only there does continuity become a positive and conscious value requiring and receiving skillful orchestration by those who best understand it, a literate minority who can record and read the record, who have much to gain from the defense and much at risk from losing control of continuity.

This familiar version of tradition, or indeed of civilization, has little relevance to peoples like Tairora. Thanks to isolation, to limited and monotonous communication, the rate of change will appear relatively slow in such societies, the changes themselves perhaps minor, especially when judged by the standards of alien observers familiar with recorded histories. The narrow scope for change can easily be mistaken as a justification for seeing such societies as stable— "traditional." That is tradition-by-default, however, not traditionalism, or tradition-by-design. Default does not argue for any innate conservatism of either the people or institutions in question.

If the views expressed in the present monograph are sound, the fluidity and variability of Tairora society and culture and the mobility of the people are ascribable to certain basic and prevalent circumstances of their existence. To find oddity or unrepresentativeness in their characteristics, thus, is presumably to find it also in their circumstances. It may be that some Neolithic societies did not consist of small autonomous village communities closely surrounded by numerous others of much the same size and coping capacity. Between any such Neolithic peoples and the Tairora there should therefore be a marked difference. Between the Tairora and peoples who face these same conditions, on the other hand, there should be a significant resemblance, probably in some of the very features that may to certain eyes make the Tairora and their neighbors as reported here seem exceptional.

Research aims and methods might discover but could hardly predict such findings. A general knowledge of the regional landscape at large showed a mosaic of languages, pockets of particular peoples and customs, set against rather uniform outward lineaments of local life. These seemed to invite a study in detail of local variation, and they supported the expectation that in such variability one could discern process and pattern.

The study area for the Project's linguist (McKaughan 1973), geographer (Pataki-Schweizer 1980), physical anthropologist (Littlewood 1972), and archaeologists (Watson and Cole 1977) was in each case the whole study area, while four ethnographers were needed to represent the cultures of that same area. The ethnographers—to date Robbins (1982) and myself (1983)—must lay our respective findings side-by-side to produce a picture comparable to that of our collaborators. That larger picture may yet be drawn. Meanwhile, in one small corner of an area already small in comparison to the land mass of which it is a part, it can be shown that being small and highly localized, and projecting timeless indigenous depth and changeless uniformity do not in reality betoken a stable insularity. That there are no such stable islands, however, is less remarkable than that the Tairora and their neighbors, against considerable odds, are obliged to create the semblance of eternal islands, and recurrently do so. The same exigencies of coping with outsiders that require endless improvisation evidently also require the assertion of fidelity. If this is the traditionalism of the Tairora and others like them, it is nonetheless a mask for change.

I am indebted to more people than there is space here to name for help in carrying out the following study. Were I also to attempt to list those who helped me on a previous field trip, when I was new in the area, the list would be double again as long. No mere thanks can repay Jim Dean and other members of the Summer Institute of Linguistics for the hospitality of their base at Ukarumpa and for many acts of kindness and assistance extended to me and members of my family. In particular I would like to acknowledge the help of Alex and Lois Vincent. As missionary linguists, they have lived among Tairora almost continuously since 1959, and in giving generously of their knowledge, they added to mine. My collaborators of the Micro-evolution Project, I hope, have profited as much from the collaboration as I have. They will surely see evidence here of their influence, but they are not to blame for shortcomings. For the maps used in this volume, thanks are due to Professor John C. Sherman and his students, Department of Geography, University of Washington, and to Dr. K. J. Pataki-Schweizer, University of Papua New Guinea.

Most of all I am indebted to the people of Abiera and Batainabura, whose involvement with this work is reflected on nearly every page. Amata was my friend as well as my landlord at Abiera—perhaps a "first" for him. That he fixed the roof when it leaked was the least of his help. Ihube, a tireless companion during my stay at Abiera, later accompanied me to Batainabura, where he learned some things that surprised him, too. Aukwa of Batainabura was second to none in his effort to see that I understood what he and others showed me or told me about. The mention of a few particular friends falls far short of a list of personal debts in both communities.

As an ethnographer, my wife, Virginia, shared both the work and the adventure of this field trip, and was later involved in preparing the archaeological volume of this series (Watson and Cole 1977).

The National Science Foundation supported both the field work and the publication of this report, for which I am most grateful.

Contents

Illustrations

TABLES

FIGURES

TAIRORA CULTURE
Contingency and Pragmatism

1. Introduction

It is largely since World War II that residents of the Central Highlands of New Guinea have become well known to the outside world. A score or so of Central Highlands peoples have been reported on, some of them at length. The explicit and public aspects of life are now familiar. As far as documentation is concerned, it is increasingly the finer details that remain to be known, and local and intraregional variations recognized. Apart from special topics and policy-oriented studies, which presumably will always find a place, there are in my opinion three outstanding ways to improve understanding of the cultures and peoples of the region: first, as mentioned, through ethnography in depth, the fuller detail of intraregional variation; second, through a better recognition of the aspects of life that are least visible, the underlying assumptions and premises; and, third, through a richer historical perspective. A good deal of the ethnographic attention given to the Central Highlands has been devoted to the organization of society, its overt living arrangements. Much less is known about Central Highlands religions, and some ethnographers profess to find the subject of religion so elusive as to discourage investigation, if they do not indeed doubt its existence. With respect to history, most of what we know about Central Highlands peoples floats in a timeless ethnographic present, a quiet sea without wind or waves. We have little insight into long-term change. This is understandable given the recency of Central Highlands studies and the infancy of prehistoric research in the area. More often than not, however, we lack even a sense of recent and recurrent fluctuations—the cyclic changes that shape and condition the social forms and beliefs of the immediate present. Thus, though in some respects progress has been outstanding in recording the contemporary or recent life of the area, other questions remain to be resolved. Some doubtless remain to be recognized.

The pages that follow are written in the conviction that the best exploration of a country not fully known is one uncommitted to previous routes. In

ining the information given to me by my friends and hosts of Northern Tairora, therefore, I have thought it more important to consider the material in its own right, sometimes refusing the easy chance to draw wider parallels, even where they might not seem premature. While broad categories are ultimately necessary and beneficial to a general description of mankind, students of the Central Highlands have already written their own cautionary tale with respect to the misleading use of old labels for new facts (Barnes 1962; Langness 1964). Every people, as well as every ethnographer, no doubt has eccentricities; but one is initially on poor ground to discriminate between the purely parochial and eccentric and those local features that, once recognized, may prove more widely relevant. If Northern Tairora is not the world, then equally the world is not Northern Tairora. The best manner of recognizing the world in Tairora is at the outset to pursue the implications of local detail, as far as possible uninhibited by extraneous formulations. The approach of this study is not as radical as such a statement suggests. The emphasis is less on rejecting the use of every familiar rubric than on considering fully and at length local circumstances and detail. Such an emphasis calls for suppressing, as it were, the "Oh, yes" reaction.

At the time of its writing the present monograph is the first attempt at a comprehensive account of any Tairora-speaking group. The two communities treated here are less pristine, however, than many that could still be found in New Guinea, some of them in fact in Tairora. The emphasis is not on reporting the pristine state of a New Guinea people, however, as a means of juxtaposing the exotic with the familiar. In probing certain qualities of Tairora life and organization that prevailed under pre-European circumstances, the purpose is to recognize in the undoubtedly exotic neither a singular contrast nor a sentimental identity with other people but an understandable human reality.

A central theme can be claimed for this study: the ecology of culture. The phrase refers to the coping patterns of a personnel and its definition of environment. Human personnels must adapt to more than the habitat they perceive. The adaptive requirements of their culture greatly exceed a use of natural resources for provisioning. Human beings are sustained as personnels—coresident groups cooperatively provisioning and competitively protecting themselves. Their environment invariably includes other groups, moreover, whose impingement is not limited to their number, demographic profiles, location in space, or pressure on local resources. Coping with other groups, furthermore, goes well beyond the question of how similar or different their cultures are or how much diffusion occurs or could occur among them.

A group is a personnel existing in and adapting to a social or intersocietal field, quite as much as it is a population occupying and exploiting a particular habitat. Its culture evolves in this intersocial field. Some fields, like that of Northern Tairora, are fields of small-scale societies. The culture of a small group is not the same as the culture of a large group. Neither kind of personnel could be sustained by the other kind of culture. Nor can a closed corporate community in a stable social field employ the culture of a fluctuating membership of open groups in a fluid social field. The genealogical metaphor, to take an obvious case, can hardly be developed in the same way in both cultures. A culture organized for autarky (producers and consumers principally of the same personnel) will not support a system of multicentric provisioning in which one group is crucial for another. Small, large, closed, open, uni- or multicentric—these characteristics, specifiable for human beings in quite concrete terms, are directly and substantially related to the cultural means a personnel possesses for adapting to the field it shares with other personnels.

The physical habitat is a major part of the environmental stage in which coping occurs. In the study of coping groups in their environment the importance of habitat and population has been made clear (Steward 1955; Vayda 1969; Vayda and Rappaport 1968; Rappaport 1967). Besides the undeniable relevance, certain methodological advantages may also justify an emphasis on the physical use of the physical habitat. There is no quarrel, moreover, with a provisioning emphasis that is presented not as an exhaustive and encompassing orientation but as a valuable index, or when provisioning is used, not as necessarily defining the most significant facts about a people—the heart of their culture—but as a facet of human existence that has much to recommend it for insight and manageability, especially in the susceptibility of some material factors to measurement.

No one should suppose, however, that the full measurement of energy inputs and outputs is an easy assignment in a human community. What then is to be done for places, like the Northern Tairora of this study, where some of the most significant energy flows move in or out on two legs? Where they speak a language like one's own, possess great skill or ability to learn, can work prodigiously for decades, and are capable of advancing or obstructing in varying forms and degrees the enterprises of others? Here is an energy flow of some magnitude. How should it be counted? (How much greater is the flow of energy in the migration of skilled and talented Europeans, Africans, and Asians to the New World, or the capture of slave energies?)

If a personnel is reduced to a "population," then perhaps to a collective belly of certain dimensions, needing to be filled with certain kinds of caloric stuff, and if it is recognized simply as a collective head to be kept dry or a collective back to be kept warm, then the calculation can possibly be limited to the energy expended in exploiting relevant habitat resources and that obtained from doing so. Such a model, however, might fit equally well the grazing efficiencies of a given number of cattle in a given acreage of pasture with a certain growth of herbage. The "cattle" of such a model, in any case, do not defend the carrying capacity of their pasture against other herds that would share or preempt it. Their pasture is in effect an island—but no more insular, to be sure, than many ethnographically specified habitat islands. The "cattle" do not assert or sustain a conviction that where they live is especially desirable; nor rationalize that their companions deserve preference over other animals; nor embellish the belief that how they graze and chew is uniquely right for them if not for other cattle. They have no need to contend for the loyalty of animals who might consider joining or departing their ranks, since that neither occurs nor would affect the herd at large in its tenancy of the pasture, or change its ability to exploit the habitat's potential.

For the purposes of studying change or evolution, the ecology of human habitats must face the question of how dynamic an aspect habitat is in human adaptation. One must ask whether, indeed, the evolution of human societies does not depend more directly and extensively on the interplay of society than on the interplay of producer and resources. This is not to revive the banal charge of habitat determinism but simply to raise the question whether societies and their cultures are stressed as much by the scarcity of provisions or the inadequacies of production as they are stressed by other societies or by elements within their own. If no single answer fits every society, at least this will caution us about limiting our consideration of human adaptation to a singular emphasis on the physical utilization of a given habitat for provisioning.

Some anthropologists have lately been impressed with the extent to which peoples of supposedly meager supplies do not in fact suffer the stress of inadequate provisioning. Sahlins, in reviewing the case of many primitive economies, sees fit to speak of the "original affluent society" (1972). Even if generally applicable, this view does not deny the central importance of production and provisioning in the shaping and evolution of human activities and codes. It does suggest, however, that the ease of provisioning frees many producers from the need to be mobilized to the utter limits of their talents and strength. There may be ample slack. Their manpower and institutions are not always maximally deployed, much less distorted, on behalf of provisioning. Their adaptation may require, on the other hand, that they retain control of the resources that suit them so well, or defend their compatible arrangements for using resources perhaps against some demand of other groups on one or both counts.

Not all intersocietal fields, to be sure, are highly stressful. Distance, barriers of various kinds, ample resources, a state of peace, and cultures either undifferentiated or tolerably—even desirably—distinct may combine in various ways to permit a group a smaller preoccupation with their nearest neighbors. They may have little concern to represent themselves in special ways to other groups, to obtain goods or women from them, or either to hold them at bay or to invite them in—by force of arms, by feasting and gifts, or by magic or other threats or benefits. While one need not suppose that provisioning is always at some peak of urgency, neither do external relations hover perpetually near the brink of survival. Being a significant source of influence for change, however, does not depend on being perennially critical for survival. Survival stress is influential indeed in changing (or immobilizing) peoples; but people are susceptible to the influence of their neighbors—

for change or for fixity—without recognizing in the neighbors a threat to survival.

For personnels in the intersocietal field of the Northern Tairora, as it happens, the struggle for social survival is keen. The continuity of a personnel or its dissolution is no mere hypothetical alternative but an option frequently faced by the region's peoples. Between the maximum size of a cohesive group and the minimum size for defending a territory the ultimate balance is critical. The limited means of recruiting and holding the loyalties of a local personnel are not equal to every challenge. The balance may tip, the group disappear as an autonomous social entity, for a time or forever. More often, apparently, some continuity of personnel is achieved but at the price of reconstituting the membership, that is, at the price of some discontinuity.

In a system capable of weathering such conditions, the means of producing essential goods and provisioning people may still be said to be its core (Steward 1955). If "core" is taken to encompass all major, crucial, or sufficient strategies of group continuity or survival, however, this is hardly useful. Production is indeed a key part of surviving in the Northern Tairora field. Yet all the pigs and sweet potatoes they could possibly produce by working on nothing else would not permit many if any Northern Tairora groups in their own name to continue to work the land they claim, to obtain as brides the women to work it, or to keep as allies the friends to help support their hold on essential personnel and territory.

If the ecology of culture refers to culture in its adaptive role, culture as environmental coping, then surely it refers to the intersocietal field and to external relations as well as to habitat and provisioning. Whatever the justification for a materialist focus in the ecology of human communities, even a "social physics" or a "societal technology" must consider security. Or say, if need be, that enemies and friends are "material," too; and outside women to wed and work, as well as gifts to give or receive, spears and arrows to discharge or dodge—all are substantial. These material considerations also represent very large flows of energy. They have extensive costs and benefits for a personnel and its individual members; and their strategic use is surely critical to coping and survival. The management of such "resources" is, in fact, far more critical in the perception of Northern Tairora than is sheer production in the sense of horticultural techniques or the pattern of productive work. The managerial males take this view if only because essential techniques and work patterns are considered perennial and fixed. By comparison with recruitment and alliance or war, work lacks the anxious demand for constant, adroit, and flexible adjustment.

If only in personnels is provisioning practicable and security possible in Northern Tairora, then the means for creating and sustaining personnels must be considered in the ecology of Northern Tairora culture. If a fluid membership is the only feasible form of personnels in the Northern Tairora field, then the need of local groups to keep channels open to the societal field must be a part of its ability to exist. If belief, value, and symbol—as I think is shown—are vital in sustaining a credible identity and creating effective loyalty among a changing personnel, then the adaptiveness and coping of personnels must be traced in part to the beliefs, values, and symbols that serve this purpose. Whether or not fluidity is seen as the failure of culture to support a more continuous membership in local personnels, the fact of fluidity is an aspect of the ecology of local cultures just as is their adaptation to intermittently changing membership. The circumstances of the intersocietal field of Northern Tairora, to put it differently, are as much a part of the environment of local peoples as the sources of salt, stone, or shell, or the supply of soil and sunshine suitable for growing sweet potatoes.

Like all their intermediate neighbors and much of the rest of mainland New Guinea, the Northern Tairora are horticulturists—gardeners oriented to the production of root-crop staples, with supplementary bananas, legumes, and leafy greens for subsistence and exchange. They are also competitive swine-keepers whose pigs, a highly concentrated form of wealth, depend on a combination of fodder and forage. The people dwell in small settlements, usually paired or clustered into larger complexes that jointly claim and defend a common territory. The aboriginal technology includes an array of implements of stone, bone, clay and other earths, wood, bamboo, and other vegetal materials (See Watson and Cole 1977), all of which, taken together, admit of the loose characterization "simple." A hand-tooled population of hard-working producers, the Northern Tairora are organized into households or linked households for the purpose of day-in-day-out production, distribution, and consumption.

In their own perception, as apparently in fact, vital resources, like garden land and water, are sufficient if not ample for most local groups. Through inequities of distribution among grassland peoples there are local shortages of such material as firewood and timber for constructing houses, garden fences, and defensive palisades. Grasslanders must also make do with less hunting, or hunt with permission in the forests of friendly neighbors. They may compensate with prowess and vigilance for their lack of palisades. No community is self-sufficient in all materials or goods, however, and such items as salt, fine-grained stone for adzes, shell, choice plumes, black palm staves for making bows and arrow foreshafts, wooden bowls, or clay pots are imports almost everywhere in the immediate area, coming in some cases from a considerable distance.

Local groups are diffusely and consensually organized for community decisions and actions, the more effective sphere being external affairs such as peace and war, ceremony, and exchange. Decisions affecting the internal order—above all, social control—are generally less easily reached, and less well coordinated, especially when compared with the galvanic unity the community is able to mobilize against outside threat.

Lacking formalized offices, Northern Tairora society also lacks a sure means of providing effective candidates for its informal positions of authority and power. Such positions are universally understood, however, and their incumbents are readily recognizable in name and comportment; and from time to time very powerful figures indeed emerge to hold sway over a local group or a fragile network of friendships and alliances connected—usually with the strong man as the link—to the community. Indeed the linkages of the community members themselves to the strong man sometimes seem only slightly less provisional and expedient than those of the outside network.

Northern Tairora communities are familistic. They are "kinship-oriented" in the sense of using a genealogical model or metaphor in the rhetoric and the etiquette of a majority of their most frequent—especially their collective—relationships. The familial metaphors are widely extended between individuals in the ranks of one's own personnel. These metaphors pervade the symbolism of place, surroundings, and the furniture of local life. They are deeply ingrained in the formulation of individual and collective origins and social histories that trace the unity and separation of groups. A kinship metaphor is used preclusively in stating and rationalizing local identity and the distinct indentities of others.

Small as they are, local groups or phratric clusters are in several respects truly akin to *peoples*, their territories akin to *countries*. Each people, like its country, is distinct from and often has a partly complementary relationship to others. Not infrequently the differences, or some of them, are explicitly recognized. They may be developed in the form of specialized trade, marriage, or other exchanges. Whether recognized or not, and whether developed or not through exchanges, such distinctness appears always to be implicit, however limited or obscure its basis may seem to the outsider. The tacit distinctness of each land and people is anticipated in local cosmology. The magical aspects of the Northern Tairora world view are relevant, as is developed especially in chapter 8. Efficacy originates in founders and in the environment, becoming transitive when competently manipulated by later generations of men or by spirits. Efficacy and competence ultimately shape individual personality and group character.

The following characteristics of their society seem to me most striking among the features that make the Northern Tairora peoples interesting. The openness of local personnels pervades local life. Individually or in blocs, people fairly often join or leave local groups for shorter or longer lengths of time (Watson 1970). Whether intended or not, their departure is often permanent. The reasons vary, as do the consequences. The regional flow of refugees begins or completes a shift in the membership of the social units they depart, when not indeed leaving them stripped of members sufficient to remain viable. One consequence of this fluidity is to qualify the sense of kinship and descent in local personnels. The accepted terms in which personnels are figured include their founding, kinship, and descent. These must be so phrased, therefore, as to become or remain credible in the absence of literal genealogy and with little fixity of lineage and local residence. A second consequence of the fluidity of membership is a special need for means of creating and maintaining identity and unity. These must be sufficient to counteract or compensate for the mixed or shallow loyalties that accompany a continuous splitting, shifting, and moving about of personnels.

The need for unity and local identity is especially critical in the face of a precarious life and livelihood. Internal security is jeopardized by the lack of nearly all means of social control beyond appeals to sentiment, good name, or the threat of partisan retaliation. Disruption threatens in the form of cliques surrounding rivalrous strong men. The diverse and shallow loyalties that often characterize local group members are an insufficient brake. External security can be managed only as a transitory balance of adversaries and allies. Neighbors continually threaten each other's wives, livestock, welfare, or very lives.

Confronting these conditions of existence, most Northern Tairora local groups develop—or perhaps succumb to—as much leadership as they are capable of developing and are able to tolerate, or are unable to avoid. The value of a strong man's leadership is most easily seen in his management of external affairs and the strength he gives the group through his political skill, his renown, and his influence in attracting and holding allies. Perhaps to a degree, at his career's outset, his values reflect his actual physical prowess in fighting or ambush.

A second means of confronting the internal needs and external challenges is the profound localism of Northern Tairora ideology. It is nothing less than a belief in a direct, transitive effect of the land and the locality on social identity. Those who live in and subsist from a land receive from it a common character. Conjoined with their ancestry, particular qualities of the very land itself pass over into the inhabitants, making them the people they are. Their collective identity and their common loyalties, in a word, are marked by the country they live in. The process is a part of magic, in keeping with one of the deepest assumptions of Northern Tairora thought.

The sense in which descent is taken by the Northern Tairora is quite congruent with both the shifting personnels of local groups and the active effect of country on peoples. Familism as descent thus makes of residence both test and validation of pedigree as well as of identity and mutuality. If a people are who they are in significant part because of where they are or where their forebears have been, and if partly by this process common residence promotes a convention of common descent, then a descent ideology is able to accommodate and survive the unstable membership of the groupings said to be formed by descent, whose identity and loyalty are said to arise from a common descent.

Even together, the will to unity and a credible focus for loyalty are not enough. A local group must also have the sheer power to survive in a precarious field. Local manpower must be sufficient to maintain production, sustain marital and other exchange relationships, and offer to the outside enough of a fighting force to be attractive to possible allies and give pause to potential enemies. Masculine prowess and aggressiveness must be emphasized, supported, and underwritten by a form of male cult widely familiar in the region. A rigorous initiation of youths is felt to be necessary. There is a corresponding opposition of a masculine principle stressing prowess to the feminine one stressing production.

Power also requires political skill and pragmatism, and a quickness in judging and reacting to the changing realities of the local field. These attributes of acuteness and situational responsiveness leave little room for deathless loyalties or irredentism. The heroism of the last-ditch stand has low priority compared with survival. While sudden shifts in allegiance may be denounced in others as treachery, such shifts are the common adroitness of a successful group. Flight and asylum, accompanied by the possibility of merging kinship and identity with an erstwhile unrelated host group, are but the ultimate consequence of war and political pragmatism.

In life at large there is a profound acceptance of adventitious and arbitrary interventions. Plans well laid and executed may misfire for reasons only fathomable after the fact. The apparently well person may be suddenly ill or dying. The certainty and completeness of subsequent explanation quite belie the absence of anticipation. Explanation is generally magical. With sorcery or adverse auspices as extraneous elements—"wild cards," in effect—the full and certain recognition of cause only in the outcome is understandable.

A similar unpredictability of change pervades the political affairs of Northern Tairora peoples. Sudden shifts of advantage make adversaries out of erstwhile friends. The very multiplicity of friends and enemies, and the varying devoutness of their relationships, are often in precarious balance. Crossed with sudden major shifts, politics take on the unpredictability of individual affairs and magical interventions.

Little wonder that strength, friendship, and the bonds of fraternity are emphasized. For all that friends may be fickle and family lines intermittently redrawn, they remain, together with strength, not merely the best but the only recognized means of coping in the social field. There seems little need to hesitate in calling this an embattled position, with the outside as the potential enemy. Yet the openness of the inside to the outside increases some of the risks while lessening some of the dangers. If few friendships or ties of kin are forever proof against cooling, few enmities if any are forever implacable. For any given present the effect is contingency, sometimes of radical proportions.

The foregoing characteristics, it seems to me after many months of living in the area, are central threads of the precontact existence of Northern Tairora personnels. The local peoples of this area live distinctly uninsular lives. Though each is styled as unique in its formative local and magical auspices, communities are not enclosed. Nor are they unique in their quotidian activities; and even quite alien immigrants suffer little handicap in adapting to production, etiquette, or ritual activities. Relative unboundedness is a main condition of individual and communal welfare. The tensions of openness mark the activity of Northern Tairora personnels in forming and reforming. Opposition provides the shifting boundary. Among the factors that are foremost in making Northern Tairora peoples, these seem the obvious themes to emphasize.

Certain points of emphasis reflected in these pages arise from the larger New Guinea Micro-evolution Project. As a part of this project a study of Northern Tairora groups, earlier begun, was continued. The context and the design of the project are described elsewhere (Watson 1963a). The intent of the project is comparative, both as between the various local peoples studied in each of four ethnolinguistic congeries and, within peoples, as between variables—geno- and phenotypic, linguistic, cultural, and environmental. This strategy was designed to measure the extent to which facts of communication (diffusion) or chance affected local variation in "race," language, and culture as distinct from the effects of inheritance and habitat.

In the fieldwork that underlies the present monograph, particular attention was paid to minute variations within more general and regional patterns. Intraregional or local variation was a preoccupation of all the project team. All manner of variation was of interest, not merely variation whose adaptive significance was apparent. We were also interested in variation that might seem arbitrary or fortuitous. Such variation was potentially significant (1) as an index of aspects in which peoples or local groups might be most variable and (2) as an index of degrees of freedom from adaptive pressure and hence an index of the play of chance.

The prominent concern of the monograph with the field of each local group noted is an especially appropriate emphasis in understanding the evolution of open societies like Northern Tairora. How much and in what ways is a local group a reflex of its external relations and larger situation? Might that situation ultimately be as large as New Guinea itself?

To suggest a situation as large as New Guinea requires more than some simple analogy, like a water level that will rise only as water is added somewhere within the pool. It is not enough, that is, to take the level as having a purely diffusional or additive limitation. If Northern Tairora has a wider, "New Guinea" character, it is in some degree because, in adapting and adjusting to given neighbors, each group in turn is constrained. It must be and must remain competitive in some viable terms. Except where complementary differentiation is favored, this produces what I have only half jocularly elsewhere called the Jones Effect (Watson 1965b: 442). It is the symmetrical effect of one group on another, specifically those adaptations, modifications, or characteristics in which a given group can only be, or can most parsimoniously or most securely be, competitive with relevant other groups.

A group must not only be as competitive as the terms of local relationships require, but it must demonstrate—that is, communicate—its proposition of power and competence to the relevant others in terms recognizable and credible to them. This need not mean absolutely identical terms, to be sure, for some terms of this intersocietal communication must be distinct, in keeping with the need for local identity. As Sumner pointed out, groups tend inevitably to be distinct, to have more or less impressive exploits or qualities to proclaim, more valorous strong men or doughtier allies to boast about, or a greater reputation for prosperity and hospitality, or for magic, or for astuteness in trade, or for whatever is praiseworthy or auspicious or only distinct (Sumner 1906). Thus, in a way, the Jones Effect is in operation here, too, in selecting for a certain degree of identity, or communicability of behavior and display. Given the theoretical concern of the larger project, it would be a point of interest to determine what degree of local variation is possible in social fields like those of this area; in other words, how profound is the Jones Effect, how detailed its consequences?

A further characteristic in which this monograph reflects the larger project is a holism of ethnographic perspective. This is not, in the present case, a simple reflex of anthropological tradition. It rather arises out of the spirit and purpose of the ecological question that largely described the project. In taking stock of the cultural answer, one needs to see a system at large with its particular strengths, stress points, and other limitations. Thus the central issue: what shape does the whole have, and on account of what problems or situational needs? In this light one may hope to determine what efficiencies are achieved in the culture, as well as how they are achieved.

Whether these horizons and limits justify a broadly ethnographic monograph in a world of special problems, of current research themes, topicality, even trendiness, the reader must judge from the pages that follow. For the writer, the greatest honor would be for children or grandchildren whose parents and grandparents befriended him and helped make this book possible to recognize here some part of their heritage, and obtain from it a heightened sense of their legacy. Here the heritage is mediated by an immigrant, to be sure, a sojourner. But immigrants and sojourners have ever been welcomed, often to become a vehicle of the tradition of their hosts, now a part of their own. *Arigaiba?a tigaiba?iro,* "Your forebears are mine."

2. The Northern Tairora Cosmos

A synthetic version of the precontact world of the Northern Tairora will be more abstract and orderly than the original beliefs it purports to encapsulate. To represent faithfully the cosmological particularizations of Northern Tairora would require something more like a recitation of the various and numerous contexts in which each individual association or idea tends to occur. It is not that individuals frequently or grossly contradict themselves in speaking about the world. Rather they express their beliefs piecemeal. Seemingly they are able—or at least are accustomed—to call forth these beliefs only in a singular and fairly specific manner, as a given context evokes or makes a given idea relevant. That being so, the present effort at synthesis, even if it were accurate in all particulars, can be considered a kind of misrepresentation or distortion. It is unfairly biased toward both economy and the specification of the implicit. As an observer's inference, it is a novel and hence alien codification of the beliefs that exist. With that caveat, I shall proceed to a synthesis of the Northern Tairora cosmos as well as I have been able to observe or infer it.

The surface of the world is entirely terrestrial, without seas, oceans, or other great bodies of water. There are watercourses, to be sure, both large and small; and here and there small ponds or pools are known. Those that I saw were few in number and were usually considered remarkable in some way if not treated with awe. Water from a pool below Batainabura, for example, is said to have special properties for the health and growth of pigs and to be much sought by friends of the group for this purpose. This same pool is also said to be the remnant of a much larger pond or lake whose waters escaped when a landslide breached the natural dike containing it. Before that, water monsters or supernaturals (now sometimes identified with lowland crocodiles, as there are no indigenous ones) are thought to have inhabited the lake. One can only guess whether what are now remembered as monsters were in fact natural creatures, perhaps crocodiles.

It could surely be added that *waters* are generally considered to be of especial importance, not just impounded still waters. Each stream or body tends to have some virtue, whether well specified or not, peculiar to itself.

One's native waters—certain ones—are especially salubrious, and wading or bathing in such a stream is often a healthful antidote to adverse magical exposure. While as a whole waters may seem more salient in the qualities ascribed to them than are other surface features, the terrain of any given group is minutely discriminated, and different features possess quite distinct names and histories. Each potentially offers favorable or unfavorable auspices for settlement, gardening, pigkeeping, or other activities.

As in all or nearly all of the Central Highlands of New Guinea, there was no indigenous idea of the world as an island surrounded by seas, no concept of "sea." In recent years, the visual experience of the sea or reports of it have typically been astonishing and exciting. The newly discovered sea is often associated with fabulous versions of postcontact events, the surprise of its very existence tending to give weight to the magical portents of "cargo" myths," which offer the apocalyptical expectancy to cult followers that spirits of the dead will return one day with large cargoes of modern European goods to distribute to adherents.

Within the terrestrial world, the portion believed to be inhabited by human beings is surrounded entirely by other territory in which no people live. Some of these peripheral lands are inhabited by supernatural beings. Perhaps the most often mentioned is the afterworld, or abode of ghosts, to the northeast of Northern Tairora country and clearly visible except when under cloud. It corresponds roughly to the Saruwaged Range (sometimes lumped with the Finisterres), rising from the far or northern side of the Markham Valley. From Nothern Tairora elevations of 5,000 feet above sea level and higher, these mountains across the Markham indeed seem a different country, and clouds floating up from the valley floor make a credible boundary between the land of the living and *bánamáqa*, that of the dead. In the afterworld the ghosts are thought to replicate human life in all respects except for mortality. The ethnography of spectral life, however, is rather general.

No other part of the nonhuman periphery is as prominent as *bánamáqa* from Northern Tairora, and some parts of it can only be identified by general direction or vaguely by reference to the distant skyline. There are nonetheless clear associations of other parts of the periphery with cosmic or mythic events, as well as with nonhuman denizens. The dying moons descend into an unseen valley to the west, where they expire to be replaced by new ones in the east. The ancestral founders of humankind, a sister and her younger brother, entered the present anthroposphere from the southwestern part of the periphery. (It is perhaps of interest, thus, that the northeasterly route of these founders is continued in the northeasterly passage of their descendants from the land of the living to that of the dead.) Stopping at numerous points on their journey, they gave a name to each, incorporating it at the same time into the tradition perpetuated in the *hakóri* song cycle.

Some of the nonhuman periphery, however, is less clearly assigned or is empty of known occupants. To the south are small-size anthropomorphs of fierce custom. Suggesting a people somewhat like the Anga (formerly "Ku-

kukuku"), they are, though monsters, not necessarily supernatural; but they have never been seen by most living informants (if by any), and these, hence, are vague about their status. Depending on location within Northern Tairora, other assignments of the nonhuman periphery are made. The Batainabura (but less so the Abiera) consider the Markham Valley to the east of them to be inhabited by naked, incestuous anthropomorphs who nest in trees, subsist entirely on bananas, and are probably indifferent to pollution by menstrual blood or other female contaminants.

The emptiness of other edges of the anthroposphere is not so much asserted as suggested by a lack of assertion. Indeed, pressing the point, one may be told, for example, that the pine forest far to the southwest, an area barely known and only by report, must surely be a dangerous place and that, even though unknown, it probably harbors evil spirits. Since few areas of the Northern Tairora cosmos are without denizens of some kind, it is likely that similar guesses would be made about other "empty" areas.

Forests more than grassland are apt to contain places of awe or danger. It is true that forests abound at the edge of the cosmos while a number of Northern Tairora groups live in grassland. Yet it seems wrong to suppose that it is forests alone that make the edges awesome. More to the point, probably, is that the edge of the cosmos is empty of humans though the home of ghosts, supernatural beings, or anthropomorphic monsters.

The center of the human sphere is the local community, though this is simply tacit. It is surrounded—indeed, the local territory is defined—by the territories of neighbors, whose lands in turn are bordered by those of their neighbors, and so on, until, for most members of the local community, one is speaking of scarcely more than place names, or of groups unnamed and unknown though believed to exist. While this description may suggest a neatly concentric array, a local map of social space is rather apt to be irregular, with a greater extension in some directions than in others. There are frequently holes in the field, moreover, where a void exists that Read (1952) has termed a no man's land. No man's lands are usually not areas that have never been occupied or even ones unoccupied within local memory. When not empty for some physical or supernatural reason, they are probably empty because of their character as battlegrounds or buffer zones. In an intricate network of amity and enmity, local history often juxtaposes hard and fast enemies with no mitigating conditions of terrain or neutral alliance to provide a tenable boundary. Holes or no man's lands usually occur, moreover, at the boundary between phratries, or what are sometimes called "tribes." The boundaries of phratries and local groups will be discussed at greater length in chapter 4, in which these personnels are themselves considered. Suffice it for now to say that in Northern Tairora a phratric territory usually includes smaller personnels who have a common name and loosely share a common tradition, and who do not make war on each other but intermarry, though they will not make common cause against every conceivable adversary of each of them.

It is necessary here to speak of phratries and at closer range of local groups, for in Northern Tairora the names of these personnels are generally the same as the names given to the land. In effect they are the names of the countries and peoples into which the human world is divided. To groups at a distance, thus, a people's phratric name is the same as the name of their territory, and it can be used interchangeably for land or people. At greater distance from the given local group, countries are apt to be less sharply distinguished, being called instead by names that designate the ethnolinguistic categories of the inhabitants, such as Agarabi, Gadsup, and so forth—though in no such case is the modern name used indigenous to Northern Tairora.

It is within the active social field of a group that distinctions between "bush" and *kunai* or grassland are most often made. Indeed, the Northern Tairora, probably like other ethnolinguistic congeries of the region, sometimes distinguish themselves or their neighbors as either "bush" people or *kunai* people, according to the preponderant character of their territory and the related orientation of their culture. The word "bush" carries a number of cultural connotations, including a greater emphasis on hunting; access to a greater quantity and variety of materials, such as firewood and construction materials for houses, tools, ornaments, and weapons; a more intimate knowledge of magical substances, largely botanical in nature; and greater awareness of or immunity to the dangers of the forest, often perilous to the ignorant or alien grasslander. Grassland peoples not utterly bereft of woods to supply firewood, posts, or palings, however, do not think of themselves as handicapped, much less as a second-class people. While acknowledging most of these attributes of bush people, they aver that grassland gardens yield better, and they assert their greater prosperity in pigs and boast of their fighting prowess. There is indeed some reason to consider these claims.

"Bush" and *kunai* designations cut across Northern Tairora society, which has local groups of either kind. Even in the heart of the grassland, however, there are only a few phratries consisting entirely of *kunai* people, although to the south one can find numerous phratries almost entirely of bush people.

The designation of a human sphere and a nonhuman perimeter does not imply that human beings and their animals have this sphere entirely to themselves. Indeed, populated space is shared with a remarkable number and variety of supernatural beings, most of them so local (and some so unique) in character as to be little known beyond a short distance from their accustomed places. For Abiera residents ghosts are prevalent, either as visitors, haunts, or occasional transients. Although like the Batainabura in believing in an afterworld where ghosts normally take up their permanent abode, Abiera folklore has numerous incidents of frightening encounters with ghosts returned temporarily to the midst of their kinsmen. Some ghosts, perhaps distant or unrelated ones, seem to frequent certain places— not always known—which are thereby dangerous for the living to stir about in or even to pass. The possibility is also acknowledged of encountering a new ghost on its way to *bánamáqa*, though the possibility of this peril seems greater at Batainabura. There people say that the main path to *bánamáqa*, especially the routes followed by the ghosts of the *pore* (modern Auyana) ethnolinguistic group, crosses their very lands. The thought of meeting one of these ghosts is especially frightening to the Batainabura. Not only are they uncanny, like ghosts in general, but *pore* ghosts are physically distinct, wearing or possessing some sort of wide yoke or appendage at the shoulders. Besides making the ghost grotesque, the appendage creates disturbing sounds as it loudly brushes the vegetation as the ghost passes along its way. The Batainabura, on the other hand, in marked contrast to the Abiera, do not otherwise think of their country as frequented by ghosts whom they are likely to meet. Nor are Batainabura informants readily able to describe a ghost from personal experience or reports of encounters—as can the Abiera.

In the bush there are various place spirits or demons—loosely *masalai* in Neo-Melanesian (New Guinea Pidgin). Though doubtless multiform, they seem to share several traits that may therefore be generic: they are anthropomorphs but usually small, hence are sometimes called "little men." They are associated often or always with outcrops or boulders, especially inhabiting holes or caves in rocks. They abide more often if not principally in forested places. They are neutral or friendly to the legitimate owners of the territory they inhabit but hostile to the stranger, hence dangerous to the unwary. Their common mode of attack suggests human exuvial sorcery, for it is often said to be bad to permit one's urine to fall into their hands; but here demon power differs from human sorcery in that urine is of little or no consequence (probably because of being "water") as a *materia prima* of human sorcery. The consequences of a local demon's magic, finally, seem to involve illness, specifically a loss of reason, mental confusion, or losing one's way in the forest and becoming hysterical, perhaps resulting in death through injury or starvation.

Another type or set of beings, the *wera*, also inhabit the bush. Described as zoomorphic, with a radiant pelage, these creatures are a source of awe but seem either not specifically malevolent or (perhaps because of visibility) can usually be avoided. Hunters in particular see *wera* but do not intentionally shoot at them. The Batainabura, being more nearly a bush people, know more of *wera* than the Abiera, though they are not unknown to the latter.

The *naabu* is still another kind of being, the denizen of certain waters. I heard so much less of *naabu* at Abiera than at Batainabura, presumably because one of their reported haunts is near the territory of the latter. These beings are said to resemble the crocodiles reported by indentured laborers returning from the coasts of New Guinea. This description is quite likely as recent as the reports of crocodiles.

The Batainabura also seem to make more than the Abiera of one or a pair of hermaphrodite guardians who lie in wait by the road to the afterworld. Perhaps this greater emphasis only reflects in their view the intersection of the road itself with Batainabura territory. The supernatural hermaphrodites, in any case, accost and sexually assault new ghosts en route to *bánamáqa*, the "female" guardian raping newly dead male ghosts, the "male" raping females. Or in the case of the single guardian, his/her hermaphroditic flexibility could adjust to intercourse with ghosts of either sex. Informants seemed unsure whether it was possible for a ghost to evade the guardian(s), or whether, indeed, it was desirable to try. A sexual encounter might be relished but perhaps not with so awesome a partner. There seemed in any case no question of the ghost's eventual arrival at his or her destination.

Well within the human sphere are various places associated with mythological or ancestral beings and deeds. The mountain known to maps as Erandora, in south Tairora, is called in the vernacular by a name that is both a play on kinship terms (alternatively "mother" or "father") and onomatopoetic. The pun is significant in that the peak of this mountain was inhabited by a mythological female, the original and once the only possessor of all the sacred knowledge and paraphernalia of Northern Tairora culture. Both knowledge and paraphernalia are now the exclusive property of men, while women, disfranchised, are kept from openly admitting knowledge of any such things, oblivious to the smirking secret of original theft. The onomatopoeia of the mountain's name connotes the sound of the *kundu* or waisted drum, a principal part of the treasure stolen by the ancestral benefactor to provide a ritual core for male domination. It was the sound of the waisted drum, indeed, which first drew the male intruder to the mountain top and there to the discovery of the sacred instruments. The hooked peak of Erandora is prominent on the southern skyline from many points in Northern Tairora. In noticing it, the outsider readily evokes a reference to this significant myth—if he is speaking to a man.

The territory of Batainabura is singular in including a primary mythological site where a fracas took place between two ancestral brothers. The names of these two brothers and their story are widely known in Northern Tairora. The site of the altercation is known as Airina after one of the brothers, and the same name, both territorial and eponymously ancestral, is given to one of the main sibs of Batainabura. The inclusion of this place in Batainabura territory is noteworthy, since the peoples of the vicinity are generally aware of the association though not necessarily of the eponymous sib.

A myth of more limited significance attaches to the other main sib of Batainabura, the Hararúnx. Like Airina, Hararuna is both territorially and ancestrally eponymous. An ancestor of that name emerged from the top of a casuarina tree said to be the one still growing on the site, and thus the people who trace their origin to that ground are known as Hararúnx (or sometimes as Baqe-Hararúnx, if one is adverting to the composite character of the modern sib's personnel). This landmark is for the most part meaningful only to the Batainabura themselves or to other peoples closely connected to them.

Abiera, though not lacking a terrain full of meaning, appears to have no sites as singular as either Airina or Hararuna. A particular pandanus tree has a quasi-totemic connotation for members of the local group—perhaps comparable to the casuarina Hararúnx. But I could uncover no claim that it was itself ancestral or the origin site of an ancestor. Incidentally, this difference between the two local groups would logically suggest that the Batainabura have lived longer in their present territory than the Abiera. For what it may be worth, such a difference is precisely what ethnohistorical data available to me suggest.

The human sphere is also visited or affected from time to time by nonlocalized supernaturals such as the earth-bearer, whose shifting of his burden from shoulder to shoulder produces the earthquakes so common in this part of the world. There are also lightning beings, though I am not sure whether it is one or many, and suspect a similar vagueness on the part of no few of the Northern Tairora. The presence of such a being is signaled, in any case, by a lightning bolt or by the hole it produces where it emerges from the ground, as the Tairora see it.

The skies, too, are inhabited by certain supernaturals, though in numbers that account for only a tiny fraction of the stars or planets. The sun and moon have personality or may be the abode of supernatural personages. They are sexually distinct as male and female, respectively, an antinomy carried further into the symbolism of sex, season, and activity (sun: heat: masculinity: forcefulness: dry season: fighting), as well as of physiological processes (moon: cold: femininity: passivity: antimale: menstruation). Some stars and constellations, such as the Pleiades, are tenuously associated with the abode of supernaturals in the view of some but not all informants. It is not clear what their character may be. Clouds, especially thunder clouds, have for some a vague personification. Some informants also speak of a "sky being" (or beings), *nárubabainti*, capable of visiting a human being with dream revelations; but I have little evidence of a well-developed belief, unaffected by possible Christian syncretism.

The extraterrestrial cosmos seems, then, sparsely populated. Apart from sun and moon, the various heavenly bodies are in only a few cases discriminated, and then but poorly. It could be said, however, that the *proposition* exists, despite this emptiness. The sky is at least known as the abode of some beings or symbolic forces. Knowing this, individuals may make more or less use of it in extending the proposition, as they seem to do at present. How much their projections may further be stimulated by Christian missions is only a guess, but the possibility of such an influence is surely considerable. *Tiyárafenu*, a sky being of the neighboring Agarabi, is reminiscent of *nárubabainti*. Wycliffe Bible Translators have selected the word *tiyárafenu* to convey "God" in the Agarabi version of the scriptures.

The content of the Northern Tairora cosmos is not fully stated, certainly, in locating, naming, and identifying the human, extrahuman, and superhuman beings or forces that can be assigned particular place, personality, or name. No simple map or catalogue will do, for—terrestrial or celestial—the elements of this cosmic field are far from exhausted by beings, whether symbolic or phenomenal. Some of the most important forces within the Northern Tairora cosmos are amorphous and lack generic name, so far as I know, let alone any collective or particular personification. Here I am speaking abstractly of magic and concretely of its kinds. If one were to take the latter by their various expressions or efficacies, the kinds of magic are exceedingly numerous as well as variform. This circumstance might well persuade one not to attempt generalization or abstraction about "magic." It is these classes or subclasses of efficacy, in any case, that the Northern Tairora typically name—for example, pig health magic, garden magic, strangulation magic, and so forth. Neither the field of forces at large nor its components are localizable. The component kinds of magic are multilocal, however, rather than ubiquitous or uniformly dispersed. Magical forces are characteristically covert, as distinct from substances that contain or embody them, hidden as distinct from their visible effects. The field of magic is only known in parts to any given man or to men at large. There is, in a word, more magical force or potential—or better, there are more *kinds* of force in the world—than anyone specifically knows about.

The few fairly overt forms of force, like the sun, that are localized and personified—potential deities—differ in a number of ways from magical forces and forms. Assignable to place and symbolized in beings—anthropomorphic or zoomorphic—they are characteristically fixed and ineluctable. In the cosmic field of forces these are the parts least subject to human intervention or control. Nor are they much subject to aberration beyond the established character of the beings symbolizing them. The sun is not merely potential heat but is hot, a fact that is established and one which can be reversed by neither the efforts of men nor probably by the intentions of the sun being itself. The moon is cold, invariably so. Neither men nor the moon being could make it hot. Local demons act as they are wont to do, despite any attempts their victims or familiars may make to direct them. Ghosts are ghosts and behave as such, scarcely serving as human agents. Their very inaccessibility to human purpose is perhaps a part of what is most frightening about them. Avoidance is the principal recourse for mortals.

It would be difficult to make a precise quantitative comparison of the proportion of the cosmic field assignable to magical forces with that pertaining to localized and symbolized forces. The Northern Tairora cosmos, in any case, is suffused with magical force. Many different kinds of experience of the people are potentially subject to magical influence. In principle, magical forces are at least as invariable as those symbolized by beings. Indeed, they may even be loosely compared to physiochemical processes. But those forces or efficacies that are fully known can be bent to human purpose—not thwarted, to be sure, but employed and deployed. They can be manipulated by anyone with a sufficient knowledge of source and process, whenever the requisite materials are available. The unpredictability of magical forces arises not from some inherent capriciousness of magic but is simply the reflex of human ignorance or inattention. Or it is one's unawareness of the intentions of other humans—that is, manipulators. Limited control reflects not an essentially uncontrollable order of force but, either human error or the simple limits of human knowledge of this vast realm. Humans are enormously powerful, indeed, in what they profess to control.

The overt force of magic is evident in the variable outcomes that people publicly witness or themselves experience. The proof or test and the measure of magical efficacy is in things like pigs or people or stones or trees, each one of which might otherwise be like all others of its kind but which over and over again turns out to be different. Gardens are gardens, but while some fail, others yield abundantly. Pigs are always pigs, to be sure, but only some die or grow large and prolific. Men are men, but only some are strong. These facts define the visible face of an invisible field of force: the vitality, competence, vigor, motive, power, or fertility—or the antitheses of these qualities—such as are perceived by all men but are of benefit or detriment only

A monolith in lower village, Abiera. Said to be ancestral and to have fine writing on it, it was brought to the village from the previous village site. By rubbing themselves on a monolith that, like this one, has power, pigs will prosper.

to some. The visible face of experience reflects the uneven distribution, or the unequal impingement, or the unusual impact of the invisible field of magic within the cosmos. It is where knowledge and the control of relevant material permit that humans can intervene in this impingement of magical forces upon experience, making it possible in some degree to encourage or forestall—in effect, to redistribute—the consequences. By intervening, a practitioner or sorcerer rearranges in some small part the forces at play on the visible cosmos. Typically he does so, to be sure, only in those magical parts of the cosmos that he has some hope of controlling and which he thinks may press upon him, favorably or unfavorably; and these parts might seem to be the minutest fraction of the cosmos. That is presumably a matter of perspective . The urban reader needs to be reminded that the Northern Tairora sun shines on a very small world indeed, with only a few thousand inhabitants. Moons wax and wane within a few miles of one's own country. In so tiny a cosmos the sphere of magical forces, even that smaller sphere of the manageable forces, may well seem great. As it is so pervasive of the cosmos, moreover, it must especially seem great.

On a relative scale, man must also loom large in this small cosmos. Indeed, for a long time before I could speak of Northern Tairora cosmology even as imperfectly as I do now, I had some intimation that their world was much more nearly man-size, so to speak, than mine. A flash flood that heavily damaged streamside gardens at Abiera in 1964 was considered immediately the magical work of humans living by the mountain headwaters of that stream. Such a world seems intimate—even if perhaps more frightening than one of cold fronts, moisture-bearing winds, and updrafts. Frightening or not, it is a world where human agents, often through magical means, produce or control events that to moderns are not easily subject to human control.

If it is correct to suggest that the Northern Tairora cosmos has a human magnitude, it seems at least consistent with that idea that living space is so densely and intensively a "humanized landscape." The marks of human activity are everywhere, above all in the grassland and just beyond its margin. The physical marks are perceptible even to the outsider, but to the inhabitants, tradition further richly fills their space with meaning far beyond the palpable traces of the human presence. Even the forest is neither trackless nor wanting in human imprint. The land itself is legendary—nothing less than a mnemonic grid into which is written the useful and remembered portions of the past. Toponymy is exceedingly minute, the more so the closer one is to the hearth of the given group. And to most of these many sites at least some slight domestic remembrance attaches: the location of a former boundary, a clump of cordylines someone planted, the floor of a house or pig shelter, the rooted canes of an old fence, the favorite resting place or viewpoint of a deceased kinsman, or the crevice in which he requested his bones to be put—or where they repose. At broader focus one picks up former village sites, garden trenches, battlegrounds, pig killing spots, burial places, or watch stations. And still more broadly there are, as we have noted, features of mythological significance well known to others beyond the occupants of the little country that contains them.

Most of all it is the designations of the inhabitants that imprint inhabited space. Though correct, it is one-sided simply to note that the names of Northern Tairora personnels are so often place names. What needs to be noted also is that people name places. The landscape is not, therefore, some powerful and immovable influence overarching the inhabitants, its eternal designations serving as well for theirs. People name places, moreover, not merely in the original sense of calling some spot this or that but in the larger sense of giving their names—because of their movements and their presence—to whole countries. When a country is occupied by a given group, that act often transforms a name once specific and minutely local, conferring it on the much larger territory that they now claim and defend. It is the presence of the people—their present or former residence on the specific local site of the given name—that produces the current designation of the territory. In this sense further, then, does the cognition of the anthroposphere reflect its deep "humanization." The names of the land are such as they are because of what people have done there and who they were.

So far in this synopsis of the Northern Tairora cosmos I have spoken more of space than of time. But what of time? It is oversimple to say that the Northern Tairora live in a timeless, ahistorical world, a world eternally like the present. When people answer questions about the past by saying that life then was like life now, they are most apt to do so with reference to the stage and its props, so to speak, than with reference to the actors. Even with respect to things like crops and ceremonies, however, one can frequently elicit comments seeming to contradict the idea that everything was always as it is; for, if "everything" is traditional, some things, at least, seem more traditional still. It would be overintellectualization to suggest that the "more" and the "less" traditional are indigenously translated into some composite historical scheme in which all things new and old can be placed with accurate temporal relativity. The Northern Tairora confront an assortment of historical facts, which, if abstracted and ordered, could produce a much clearer sense of history. A sense of history, in other words, may not be completely lacking but is largely inchoate.

In any case, the present facts of Northern Tairora history seem largely if not entirely mapped onto space. Among the markers of the anthroposphere, as previously noted, the sites where events occurred are prominent and numerous. Thus, while we have so far been speaking primarily in a space frame, there is in fact a fusion of space with an embryonic time frame, all the more, perhaps, since there is so little development of a spaceless frame for time.

The *hakóri* song cycle known to Abiera (but less familiar to Batainabura) details the journey of a mythical Elder Sister and her Younger Brother. It is a passage in which—like all journeys, of course—space marks time: the succession of movement and episode is linked to a succession of sites. Without becoming metaphysical, perhaps one need say only that (1) it would be impossible for space to be as little realized or recognized as time appears to be in Northern Tairora cultures; (2) events do occur at one place and not at another as well as occurring before, during, or after other events; and (3) in a cosmos in which the basic ordering of space is well developed relative to the ordering of history, events gain greater salience in the developed frame of space while helping fill the frame and give it a general aura of meaningfulness as well as many specific and local meanings.

Nor is it just the *hakóri* travels of Elder Sister and Younger Brother for which spatial references help in plotting time. The ethnic grid of space-and-peoples, or countries, serves also to plot the ethnic histories of migrant personnels. As people leave one country for another or return, the tracks across the landscape not only mark their vicissitudes but describe their identities and predict or define their loyalties, especially if their loyalties are considered complex or moot.

In stating who they were or why they then acted as they did, the more elderly repositories of lore and legend therefore tend to refer to where a person or group was living at some particular time. With the passage of time, of course, the immediacy and relevance of residence and origin become vague and general. The Abiera are by now less concerned with the specific place of origin of their ancestors in the Phratry Tairora, of which they are a part, than once they must have been. They still have a general belief about the direction the immigrants followed, and, using modern names, they can indicate the putative origin point. But they do not imply that their forebears are clearly (or even necessarily) connected with those present peoples or countries—or at least that anything could now be made of the connection. A sense of transience is present, thus, however uncodified.

3. The Development of Resources

A discussion of a people's use of resources can be terse or lengthy, plati-tudinously brief or tediously exhaustive. It can particularize quantity or focus on form and technique. It can be purely descriptive or insightful and synop-tic. It can seek to descry cultural overtones or recognize implicit values, for example, in form and style. And so on.

The numerous materials and manufactures of peoples like the Northern Tairora have always beckoned to the taxonomist who hopes to discover for-mal order. Several qualities of material culture, moreover, are convenient. Consider the discreteness of each artifact type: a house is not a bow; nor is a dwelling a pig stable (despite similarity of form and use). Consider the dis-creteness of each raw material or substance employed: shells are not teeth, are not bones, are not stone, are not wood, and so on. Each artifact is made of distinct materials, by particular techniques, by given makers, for specific but different purposes; each has a local label, more or less singular connota-tions of its own, its own technology or use of materials. This is undeniably an inviting terrain for sheer classification.

The question for the ethnographer, however, is not whether a compre-hensive or elegant taxonomy can be devised, for several have been de-veloped that comprehend much of the subject. He must rather consider what facets of indigenous life or thought can be reflected with any clarity by a given approach or scheme. Some of the more systematic and exhaustive schemes reflect an order that is probably the taxonomist's or simply the or-der of the physical world far more than it is indigenous to the makers and users of the resources under consideration. While needing to understand the physical limits of an environment for those who use it, the ethnographer also wants to understand their choices.

The divisions of this chapter on the Northern Tairora use of resources are more pragmatic than elegant, relating first to the several broad techniques of foodgetting (gardening, husbandry, hunting, and gathering), with all other resource uses, such as shelter and clothing, tools, weapons, furniture, and so on, treated as an additional large category, *instrumentarium*—to revive a use-ful Latin word. Since it will probably reduce the need for repetition, I shall present first a sketch of the Northern Tairora *instrumentarium*, which will be done in part by means of the list below of artifacts aboriginally known and used or made by the Northern Tairora.

Over a dozen classes of materials are involved in producing the Northern Tairora *instrumentarium:*

stone	teeth	shell
wood	grasses	skin and fur
bark	leaves and flowers	feathers
bone	bamboo	canes, reeds
human hair	earthen pigments	clay

On completing this list my initial reaction was that, of the principal sorts of raw materials present in the Eastern Highlands of New Guinea, almost nothing is lacking here. Even more broadly, only metal is missing. As to metal, indeed, I vaguely recall a conversation with someone in which what seemed a piece of meteorite had been collected by an inhabitant of the area and was kept in his house, chunks of it from time to time being hacked off for purposes no longer recalled. Pieces of aluminum from a fallen aircraft will perhaps come to the reader's mind, since they closely resemble in circumstance the legendary meteorite.

Such a list as the one above, of course, tells more about the extent of resource discovery and application than it does about the particular uses made of resources. In speaking of "canes," for example, one might have in mind the coiled rattan "cummerbunds" once worn by initiated males and used to induce male-cult purgation by vomiting; the canes used as arrow shafts; the canes cut for light fencing, which often take root to produce a living hedge; or the thorny canes three or more of which are sometimes used to tip an arrow made for fowling. The canes in question are not all the same plant, and these various applications are surely quite distinct from one another.

Over three score artifacts are listed below, grouped under eight general headings: (1) dwellings and public architecture, (2) furniture, (3) weapons, (4) tools, (5) clothing, (6) accouterments, (7) ceremonial paraphernalia, including musical instruments and special costumes, and (8) toys. No account is taken here of the fact that some artifacts are known in various styles. Arrows are perhaps the most notable example in Northern Tairora, running to somewhere in the vicinity of eighty to one hundred distinct, named varieties, some differentiated by use as well as by material, pattern, or manner of construction. A *Bogenkultur* indeed—to revive that Melanesian cachet of the *Kulturkreislehre.*

1. *Dwellings and Public Architecture*

Men's houses
Women's and children's houses
Huts for menstruation and giving birth
Fences: (a) village and pig run, made of light canes
          (b) garden, made of split palings lashed to stringers

Palisades of heavy posts
Trenches, especially garden, but others within the village site
Earth ovens, with cooking stones
Settlement ground, with the sod stripped off to expose tan subsoil
Beehive-shaped grass shelters in gardens
Pig houses
Sing-sing arbor
Rubbing stones for pigs, especially at Abiera
Sacred, "ancestral" stone in village, at Abiera

2. *Furniture*

Pots of clay (imported)
Wooden bowls (imported or local)
Bamboo tubes for
   (a) storage of seed, small objects, arrow cases
   (b) carrying, keeping water
   (c) cooking, disposable
Large cooking drums of tree sections (not at Batainabura)
Headrests, men's for sleeping; with slight zoomorphic modification; three-
   or four-legged.

3. *Weapons*

Bows
Arrows, many kinds, tipped with bone, various woods, bamboo, or barbed
   cane
Clubs, or "fighting sticks"
Thrusting spear
Sling (probably exotic or marginal)
Shields with attached net quivers and plumage sprays and bobbers

4. *Tools*

Digging stick, women's
Flat-bladed, paddle-shaped "spade" of wood, for turning sod (Watson,
   1967b)
Grass knife of bamboo, for initial clearing of garden (Watson 1967b)
Adze, widely varied in size and use
Scrapers, stone
Whetstones for sharpening adzes
Cassowary bone "dagger," for spearing and opening hot roast tubers from
   fire
Stone tips for small, bloodletting arrows
Bamboo blade for butchering (disposable)
Pig tethers
Small bamboo bow, for bloodletting

5. *Clothing*

Bark skirts, female: (a) unmarried, (b) married
Bark girdle and breech clout, male
Bark sash, women's
Wooden codpiece, men's, various patterns
Bark cape ("blanket")
Rush skirts, women's (especially at Batainabura), for festive occasions

6. *Accouterments*

Net bags, men's, women's
Dyes for net-bag decoration
Shell ornaments
Smoking pipes, bamboo
Lime gourd
Lime spatula
Nose bones or stones
Pig tusk ornaments
Cowrie-shell necklaces
Dog-teeth necklaces
Pandanus mat, for shelter from sun or rain and for sleeping
Amulets, for countersorcery
Rattan (cane) cummerbund, initiated man's
Walking stick, elderly person's

7. *Ceremonial paraphernalia, including musical instruments and special costumes*

Kundu (waisted drum)
Flutes, sacred, paired
Panpipes
Jew's-harp, bamboo
Stamping tube, bamboo
Small musical bow, held in mouth
Large musical bow
Food display post, ceremonial
Food display table, ceremonial
Pigments, earthen, for body paint and implements
Feather coronets, especially cassowary
Dancing frames, with feathers
Woven bracelets
Foliage for bracelets
Funeral litter, for interment (or also suspension?) of corpse
Stone rings and other prehistoric stone artifacts used in various sacred, magical contexts

Hollow tree trunk "chimney" for magical smoke in *hampu* ritual (Abiera)
Grass-armed sticks for nose-bleeding ritual, especially male
Anthropomorphic figures carved from tree fern

8. *Toys*

Woven grass figures, various
Cat's cradle, various patterns
Small bamboo bow for boys (e.g., for shooting insects, lizards)
Stiff grass or reed arrows
Balls of leaves, stuffed with grass, for games
Spinning tops of nutshells, and bamboo husk platform
Pig bladders, inflated

   This inventory is not likely to be exhaustive. Outside of cultigens, however, it probably lists the majority of indigenous Northern Tairora artifacts
that were in use or still remembered in the 1950s. The list also reflects local
variation in artifacts, even between such nearby groups as Abiera and Batainabura. Were one to consider styles and varieties within artifact types,
such as arrows, local variation might further be indicated.
   A list of artifacts can take us only a certain distance toward understanding
their living context in Northern Tairora society. This one is meant to serve as
background for the discussion that follows.
   Whatever success may eventually attend a formal integration of technological theory into some larger theory of culture, one can for now at least regard
the artifacts of Northern Tairora society as the furniture and equipment of
their activities, the props with which their stage is supplied, the means and
devices with which they work and around which their lives unfold. One can
look upon these artifacts as establishing the scope of Northern Tairora activities, for example, in the use of energy. The artifacts can be assessed in calculating the energy required to produce houses of the size and design required
by Northern Tairora, or in calculating how much work can be performed,
say, with an adze in cutting wood, or a digging stick in tilling soil. I can offer
no time-and-motion data to make this more precise, but there is nonetheless
some advantage even in an impressionistic "energetics."

GARDENING

   It is easy to become expansive in speaking of the garden sphere in Northern Tairora. These are profoundly horticultural people. The Northern
Tairora landscape reflects the present and past inhabitants in large expanses
of nearly unbroken grassland, which are considered to be the by-product of
cultivation (Robbins 1960, 1963). Even where there are no gardens now,
much if not all of the open country is crisscrossed with partly unfillled
trenches of old gardens, many of them still quite perceptible to the eye—or

the foot—of the traveler in walking the grassland. Footpaths, in fact, often incorporate stretches of old garden trench or the ridges running beside them. Sunlight aslant a distant slope gives further evidence in revealing in the form of a shadowy grid the miles of trenches with which, it almost seems, the entire grassland is latticed.

From afar nearly every settlement is first detected in its adjacent gardens, etched in shades of brown into the prevailing khaki green *kunai*. Or in the bush it is indicated by a thinning of the trees and a brightening of the light thus admitted. The aerial prospect of Northern Tairora gardening is less dramatic, however, than that of the valley floor gardens Heider (1970:37) observed among the Dani of Irian Jaya. In their drier, sloping terrain Northern Tairora trenches are narrower and shallower, only occasionally contain water, and thus lack the heavy garden margins engraved into the swampy ground of the Grand Valley.

The lives of Northern Tairora people reflect their gardening in too many ways to count. Working in gardens, sitting in the earth, and getting soil onto the body are claimed as a source of satisfaction by the women, who do most of the steady work of gardening. Little girls who accompany their mothers and elder sisters try to take part whenever possible and are a source of delight and approval when they take up an adult's spade or digging stick and commence to move it vigorously in childish imitation of the stiff-backed, bent-at-the-hips, arm-swinging movements they have witnessed in elder models.

The garden is evidently a pleasant place to be, in some respects a second home—as well it might be, given the hours spent there by mothers and children or by entire families. A fire is usually kindled somewhere nearby and smolders throughout the day, giving testimony even at a distance to the presence of people. The children play about. Women shout to others in neighboring plots or join them for smoking and gossip. Light meals are cooked and eaten, babies are nursed, firewood is collected from nearby trees. Some gardens have grass shelters, beehive-shaped, constructed against the rain or for bedding down an infant out of the hot sun. If an age-group gang has activities to pursue in private, the empty garden of a parent or relative is a favorite place. Pork that is not to be shared, such as a stolen pig or one's own that is to be eaten because it has died, may be cooked and consumed by a small gathering in the garden. Some gardens offer a privacy not available in the village, where words and other sounds are quite audible between adjacent houses. Isolated gardens are for these same reasons favorite spots for assignation. A stock illustration, furnished often by men, is of a woman announcing within earshot of her lover that she is going to be working in such and such a garden, one that is remote or isolated.

In precontact times, to be sure, a favorite target of enemy ambushers was a man or a woman alone in a garden. This danger made it more necessary then than now for the constant watchfulness of armed men, situated at traditional vantage points, usually ridges, hilltops, or other stations commanding a good sweep of a garden area. Watchtowers like those of the Grand Valley (Heider 1970) were evidently not constructed, perhaps in part because the Northern Tairora terrain has more relief than the floor of the Grand Valley. On the one hand, the hills and ridges would have blocked the view from lower watchtowers; on the other, vantage points on the land itself were high enough. Formerly it was considered necessary, more than now, for the people with gardens in the same area to visit and tend them as much as possible together. Since successful ambushes were carried out in the past, however, it seems that isolated gardens or solitary gardeners were not unknown. To-day, still, it is quite common to find people at work simultaneously in several adjacent gardens. Indeed, as of yore, on fine sunny days, one often finds an entire settlement devoid of people—except perhaps for the sick or senile— because they have all gone to their gardens. No doubt the garden has its urgent work, but it also clearly has a strong attraction for the Northern Tairora. Departing the settlement in unison early on a sunny morning, the group is spirited and gay.

One may well hesitate to offer a full crop inventory for Northern Tairora. The list of crops in use has evidently been changing through time ever since horticulture was first introduced to the area. Especially since the recent en-try of Europeans into the Southwest Pacific, new crops have been added at a

Yam gardens being planted at Burauta. Notably rich in associated ritual and belief (compared, e.g., to sweet potatoes), yams are likened to male sex organs, are bespelled in being planted, and may be accompanied by "yam rocks" that resemble the tuber and are likewise "planted' in setting out the new garden.

(*Above*) Young woman returning from the garden well-laden with firewood, stoppered bamboo tube of drinking water, and cooking tin. (*Below*) Three small girls emulate their elders in carrying firewood, cooking tin, and bamboo tube of drinking water.

great rate, even if old ones drop out less rapidly. Precontact crops such as tobacco, "wet taro" (*Xanthosoma*), maize, squash or pumpkin, and cassava (*Manihot* sp.) are earlier in Northern Tairora than the arrival of the first Europeans, though evidently these are plants of European introduction into the Pacific. The following list is presented, in any case, as including the main cultivated food or fiber sources and probably a majority of the subsidiary ones. "Aboriginal" is taken here as roughly the time of first outside contact, say the 1920s.

MAIN PLANTS CULTIVATED IN PRECONTACT NORTHERN TAIRORA

Garden Crops
Tubers: sweet potato, kudzu (*Pueraria lobata*), taro, yams (*Dioscorea* sp.),
    cassava, wet taro or "taro kongkong" (*Xanthosoma*)
winged bean (*Psophocarpus tetragonolobus*)
pitpit (two kinds: *Setaria palmifolia* and *Saccharum edule*)
leafy greens (several kinds)
tobacco
sugar cane
ginger
cucumber
gourd
pumpkin
pepper leaf (*Piper mythisticum*, for use with betel chewing)
dyestuff plants (2 or more)
maize

Tree Crops (grown singly or in groves and often if not typically apart from
    gardens)
bananas (closest to a garden crop)
nut pandanus
areca palm (for betel nuts)
bamboo
casuarina (one of two local species is that principally cultivated)
Cordyline terminalis (for boundary markers and a range of special uses of the
    foliage, including magical)
fence pitpit or reeds

Most of the foregoing crops will be familiar to anyone acquainted with the region. Some will be known to others as well. The six types of tubers are grouped at the head of the list, as seems fitting for the crop inventory of a people of this "root crop" region. (In precontact times rice did not reach beyond Indonesia.) The sweet potato is the preeminent food source and constitutes by far the largest garden acreage, though apparently much newer in the area than taro, yams, or kudzu. Estimates run as high as 90 percent for the proportional contribution to Central Highlands of New Guinea diets of this single crop. The eating of sweet potatoes is, as far as I know, a daily occurrence, probably at nearly every meal. No such statement can be made of any other present crop. Thus in dietary importance the sweet potato is comparable to rice in the Orient or to porridge or gruel in the agrarian West.

Kudzu appears to be an old crop in Melanesia (Watson, 1964a, 1968), and although it is little grown today, its lore gives hints of a greater importance at one time. Taro and yams both seem much older than sweet potatoes, and each figures in ritual usages in a fashion unmatched by the economically more significant crop. Taro is said to be a man's crop, for example, and the eating of a piece of raw taro by the father marks the birth of a first child or son. Yam lore is perhaps the most elaborate of all Northern Tairora crops, as far as actual cropping is concerned, though sugar cane is symbolically developed—again as a crop of masculine significance. Yams are likened to human bones, penises, and sometimes testicles, and ideally they should be placed in well-prepared ground with spells and other procedures. This often, or in principle, calls for the advice of a knowledgeable older male who officiates at the planting. Cassava and wet taro are later additions from the New World. The former has not become very important in Northern Tairora as yet, while wet taro, "taro kongkong," well suited to damp ground, is quite popular in certain localities.

Sugar cane and leafy greens both figure significantly in the local diet, as do bananas. Ginger is considered to have strong, medicinal properties rather more than those of a condiment; it is used to masticate and spit upon pork, other feast food, the bodies of the ill or ailing, and in other contexts where magical power is thought necessary.

The two kinds of pitpit, sometimes called "native asparagus," are much prized additions to the local cuisine. But probably because they are more suitably cooked by steaming than by roasting in an open fire (which suits tubers handsomely), they tend to be held back, used especially as feast foods, or eaten at other times when an earth oven is employed or when food is cooked in green sections of bamboo.

What I have called tree crops are several plants treated as distinct from garden crops. These Northern Tairora crops are not planted in broad expanses of prepared ground or gardens. This applies even to bananas, which, like garden crops, are not perennial like the remaining "trees." The trees are located in different places, often singly rather than in large areas of prepared ground. Except again for bananas, they stand for a relatively long time, the harvested kinds being recurrently harvested. Fast-growing casuarinas are grown for firewood and construction material, and perhaps receive special emphasis among grassland peoples, like many of the Northern Tairora, who are short of forest resources. There is at least some understanding, too, of the soil improvement effected by the casuarina (Brookfield 1962). I was told at Abiera, for example, that the ground where a fairly large grove of casuarina had been planted would some day make a good place for gardens. It had

been planted, however, to provide shade and to give distinction to a government "rest house." This does not suggest to me any regular application of
knowledge to improvement of the soil, for social and horticultural cycles
have tended to be shorter in recent years than the casuarina cycle.

Bamboo, cordylines, and fence canes—like the casuarina—are grown for
purposes other than food. Bamboo is a material much used for implements
(knives for butchering or for severing the umbilical cord, arrow tips, special
bows, and grass cutters) and for containers for cooking, carrying, and storage. Cordylines (the ubiquitous *tanket* of Neo-Melanesian) are important in
quite distinct ways—for marking corners of fences and boundaries (lately for
bounding the "government road"), for adornment, for binding wounds, and
for other magicomedicinal and ritual purposes. One sort of cordyline is carried as an emblem of peaceful intentions by a cautious enemy group arriving
for a peace ceremony. The green leaves of one cordyline are folded or bitten
to make a child's plaything. The cooked use of the root of the cordyline as a
foodstuff (Hawaiian *ti*) is not known. The symbolism of this plant stresses its
great vitality, such as its ability to grow up again from the root if the top is
destroyed in a grass fire. The suitability of the plant as a fairly permanent
boundary marker is perhaps thus in part explained, since grass fires would
be less likely to erase such markers.

Wild areca palms are probably more often claimed than they are actually
planted or grown from seedlings, but the latter practice is said to occur. Nut
pandanus, as far as I can tell, are found and claimed as seedlings, though it is
asserted that very young trees may sometimes be transplanted by an owner
to a more desirable location. But trees are, on the whole, forest-zone rather
than grassland crops.

KINDS OF GARDENS

The largest gardens are made high on slopes or flats or in the lower slopes
and bottoms of valleys and ravines. For the basic sweet potato gardens,
drainage appears to favor ground that is either high enough to be dry or
sloped enough to be drainable. The concave slopes of a wide basin just below
the settled ridges of Batainabura constitute an almost unbroken zone of gardens, though others are made in nearby bush or bush-margin situations. The
Batainabura told me, however, that they recognized no special advantage of
bush soils over those of the grassland—nor any disadvantage, other than initial labor, perhaps. But removing the sod of a grassland fallow is hard work,
too, with no incidental firewood as a reward.

The soil of sweet potato gardens is brought to a fairly fine tilth. Since the
tubers are planted in mounds, the soil must be sufficiently friable and free of
trash to lend itself easily to being moved about. The flying point of a woman's
digging stick, swung in a sidewise, dipping arc, seems to find and tear out
most of the larger roots and runners; but she also uses her hands a great deal
in separating the rooty trash from the soil that is to remain in the garden.

The most finely tilled gardens are those in which yams or winged beans are planted, and these two crops tend to be planted, like sweet potatoes, in a regularly spaced pattern. The winged beans are not usually, if ever, individually mounded, however, but are set out in long beds with small trenches between them. Both yams and winged beans are staked with sticks or poles,

Planting yams in ordered rows.

but sweet potato vines spread out across the ground, eventually all but ob-
scuring the clean, sharp mounds in which they were first set out.

Yams and winged beans more than sweet potatoes are grown without the
interspacing of other plants. A sense of symbolic exclusiveness may attend
the yam garden, but in the case of winged beans I would guess it is more the
technical requirements of the crop, with its climbing vines. Sweet potato
gardens are apt to begin as fairly extensive plantings of the one crop—
though usually in more than one variety. But almost at once the margins of
the garden begin to sport various other plants that are grown in lesser quantity. Gradually the sweet potato garden becomes more diverse as other
plants are sown or stuck into the ground wherever space affords. Old gardens tend to be recognizable from new ones, in part, because of this diversity. There is a great sense of practicality and little of ritual constraint about
sweet potatoes, albeit they are the staple foodstuff of the region.

The initial preparation of what might be called "dry gardens" consists in
cutting tall grass or thinning or removing a heavy growth of trees. The grass
or small trash of trees is then burnt, the ash to benefit the soil of the garden.
Larger trunks, if not left standing, are usually left lying if too big to remove;
the rest tends to be used for fences or firewood. Next comes trenching, the
extent and depth of which depends on the need for drainage. Some trenches
are a scant foot or less in depth, while in mucky, soggy ground trenches are
cut both wider and deeper—sometimes in bottom land up to several feet
deep.

The earth or spoil removed from a trench—at least the top layer of it if the
trench is deep—is usually thrown on the garden area itself. This may slightly
raise the bed of the planting area—again an advantage for drainage—but in
grassland gardens the immediate utility of the practice is said to be to help
rot the remaining stems and roots of the sod, more quickly permitting tillage
and planting.

Fencing follows, though in fact bundles of palings and coils of vines for
lashing them to horizontal stringers often begin to appear on the site long
before the fence is actually begun. Both materials are cut and the palings also
split in the forest, often a considerable distance from the garden site. Fencing is needed to keep pigs out of a garden, hence must be stout because pigs
are persistent and are said to smell the sweet potatoes that will be growing
there. Fencing is sometimes less formidably pigproof in the bush than the
grassland, but stout pig fence is also sometimes required there. It is, of
course, less laborious to build a fence in the bush, close to the supply of raw
materials.

A practice sometimes said to be modern is the communal fence, so to
speak, which encloses the gardens of a number of separate owners with a
single, continuous run of pig barrier. Batainabura has such a fenced enclosure. This scheme works best at the beginning, before the fence is old
enough to become weathered or breached by pigs. Then all garden owners
pay the costs of any owner's neglect. In 1954 a Phratry Tairora district suf-

fered a severe shortage of food in just such a case. As a modern experiment, it is claimed, a single run of several miles of fencing was built, linking each Phratry Tairora local group to its neighboring territories and splitting each territory into pig grounds on one side of the fence and ground for gardens on the opposite side. This scheme failed massively at Hapárira, resulting in a temporary but quite embarrassing shortage of food. More modern still is the now relatively safe practice of ranging pigs at a great enough distance from village and gardens that their depredations are less likely.

Once trenched and fenced, the garden becomes more nearly the exclusive domain of women, for it is mainly the "engineering" phases that the men manage. Men still, in theory at least, play the primary role in certain crops, especially sugar cane, yams, and bananas. In crops other than these, once the garden is made, the women's digging stick replaces the man's adze and paddle-shaped wooden "spade" as the main implement. Nowadays the steel spade has supplanted the wooden one and greatly supplements the digging stick in working the soil of the garden.

Besides the foregoing dry gardens, with subtypes for sweet potatoes and mixed gardens, yam gardens, and winged-bean plots, there are several other kinds of cultivation in Northern Tairora. The traditional taro is sometimes called dry taro, presumably to distinguish it from *Xanthosoma* or wet taro. Yet traditional taro is often specially planted in separate small beds in places chosen for moisture and fertility. These plantings are usually small, and numerous little pockets of from several to a score or two of taro cuttings are tucked into odd places, like the depression left by a disused latrine pit, a sunken grave at the forest margin, or a cul-de-sac where run-off and erosion from two sloping paths collect moisture and topsoil. Taro is also sometimes planted in tiny gardens near an owner's dwelling, within the settlement—a situation it frequently shares with a few tobacco plants or perhaps some stalks of sugar cane. At Abiera a single man may have up to a dozen or more separate taro plots like these, none of them resembling the laying out of a large area to a single crop such as sweet potatoes, yams, or winged beans. The planting of taro a few cuttings at a time is explained by some informants as reflecting that they have only a few cuttings to plant and these only when they have harvested and eaten some mature taro. The use of small, scattered patches of ground is thus apparently a matching of the intermittent availability of propagating material in typically small amounts to locations well suited to the habit of the plant but not to large plantings.

Wet taro, or *Xanthosoma* sp., is an introduced, American plant now well established in the Northern Tairora area. True to its name, it tends to be planted in valley bottoms with plentiful moisture. Often these plots are primarily given to "wet taro," suggesting that other crops might not fare as well in the dampness. Wet taro is something of an optional crop, however, and not every gardener plants it. There are interdistrict differences in the use of this crop, like some others.

Maize seems well established. It has found a special place in Northern

Tairora use as a snack and trail food—cooked ears being light and handy to carry in a net bag on a trip to the garden or a journey to another territory.

Within a settlement, sites where houses have stood are considered excellent for small gardens, especially for growing tobacco. This is sometimes jokingly attributed to the habit of women or children, afraid to leave their houses at night, of urinating on the floor inside. Tobacco is typically a plant grown in small amounts tucked in among other plants; and it is often grown within the village, perhaps in part because the availability of ripe leaves in outlying gardens would too strongly tempt the passerby to help himself.

Tobacco is only smoked, not chewed, in Northern Tairora—a use that predates contact by some years but allegedly does not predate the memory of some older men. Indeed, some said they recall the use of another— wild—plant for smoking before tobacco became known for the purpose.

Kudzu (*Pueraria lobata* or *P. thunbergiana*) is, in most Northern Tairora areas, grown very little at present, and it is not uncommon to have a villager deny that any is grown in his settlement, unaware that two or three people may have dooryard vines or have them growing against trees at the edge of a distant garden. The crop in any case lends itself to opportunistic planting, so to speak—wherever a favorable spot occurs. An old anthill was once described to me as a good place for kudzu. (I am using the Anglicized Japanese name for the plant, by the way, since there is no general regional name in use, a fact that doubtless reflects the present obscurity of the plant.) Kudzu is apt to be left growing for two or three years, because the root grows slowly but can in time become very large—the largest cultivated tuber known in Northern Tairora. The grassland Abiera say that kudzu is more important to bush peoples with their distinct type of soil than to themselves, but the bush people of Batainabura, at least, did not bear them out. Kudzu nomenclature suggests that it may once have been far more important in the region than it is at present (Watson 1964, 1968; Strathern 1969). If so, it was presumably dislodged when other crops became available to fill the same dietary niche— crops that grow faster or yield more generously.

Bananas, an important Northern Tairora food source, are planted singly or sometimes in small groves of from several to a score or so of plants. They are planted inside the settlement, near houses, in or at the edge of other gardens, or in stands apart. Fruit bats, or flying foxes, are a main predator of bananas and cause much damage—perhaps one reason for planting them close at hand. In some varieties, stalks of maturing bananas are usually wrapped well before harvesting, in part probably to protect against the bats. But more emphasis is given in Northern Tairora to keeping the fruit from being burnt by the sun or becoming spotted, because the bright, unblemished yellow of wrapped bananas is much appreciated and the flavor is said to be better. A number of varieties of banana are known in the Northern Tairora area, including one that is green and hard at maturity and which is roasted before being eaten. Exotic varieties are also known to Northern Tairora; one in particular is imported from certain Agarabi or Gadsup peoples to the northeast as a central incident of an annual renewal-fertility ritual called *órana*. This Agarabi word refers to a ritual sometimes identified with the seemingly more indigenous Northern Tairora *ihálabu*, now (like *órana* as well) rapidly falling into disuse. It was locally alleged that this variety of banana would not grow in any Northern Tairora country, hence had to be procured from its native situation in Agarabi and Gadsup territory, to which it properly belonged. My impression was that ritual propriety may have reinforced whatever ecological propriety was involved.

There are fairly clear differences from one locality to another in the degree of emphasis given to certain crops. Although sweet potatoes are everywhere in Northern Tairora the first in importance, the intensity of planting, which could be expressed as a ratio of yield per capita of local residents, doubtless varies. Variation reflects factors such as the quantities of *other* crops grown and the proportional size of the pig herd, since sweet potatoes are the primary fodder for swine besides being the foremost human staple. Among the crops whose use varies noticeably within the region are *Xanthosoma*, yams, winged beans, and possibly taro. (*Pueraria* varies, as already noted, but nowhere in Northern Tairora, I believe, achieves the former importance its lore suggests.) Yams are grown more at Abiera than at Batainabura, while the latter maintain that they are preeminent in the vicinity in the quality and amount of winged beans. (I noted that the cultivation of these crops varied appreciably between other peoples of the region as well.) In some degree such variation is probably a long-term matter, not simply annual fluctuation. The winged-bean lore at Batainabura suggests a traditional emphasis, and local traditions of other groups would suggest as much for additional crops, including a number of postcontact crops not considered here. In any case, through differences of local tradition perhaps as much as adaptation to environmental differences, the emphasis on individual items of the crop inventory is not uniform. This suggests, among other things, that percentages purporting to indicate the dietary significance of one foodstuff or another (e.g., that sweet potatoes constitute a certain percentage of the diet), if not merely impressionistic, are averages that may fluctuate from season to season and vary from group to group.

Seen broadly, this spatial and temporal variation in crop intensity is understandable. Northern Tairora is a region with a number of horticultural and dietary options. There is a certain nutritional (not to say caloric) redundancy, for example, among the six tubers and the bananas of the region. (This is to speak just of the species, moreover, and not of their numerous clones.) Palate and taste were evidently not strong enough to keep a single exotic tuber, sweet potatoes, from becoming paramount and dislodging previous staples. They may equally be incapable of guaranteeing a place to every crop of the region in every group and every generation.

Harvesting naturally varies with the crop. Sweet potatoes are harvested throughout the year, usually a day's supply at a time. The mounds where ripe potatoes may be found are recurrently opened and recovered to collect only the tubers large enough for human use, or to gather excess tubers or stunted ones for pig fodder. Other tubers, except for yams, are treated in much the same way, but, since they are less used, are not apt to be harvested daily.

Winged beans in Northern Tairora furnish three sorts of food: young leaves for greens, the seeds and fleshy parts of the pods, and finally the leguminous root nodules. The nodules are a fairly substantial seasonal food— each measuring an inch-and-a-half or two in length and perhaps an inch or more in diameter. Their importance is reflected in the familiar Neo-Melanesian name of the crop, *asbin* ("root bean"). The bean plot is on an annual cycle, in contrast to tubers, with planting and harvesting both falling within a short span of time.

Fallowing is an establishing practice, but no fixed cycle seems to be recognized. Gardens newly planted in sweet potatoes would normally run for two years or more to complete the harvesting, even if no new plantings were made. The lowering of yields guides the gardener in deciding whether to continue to replant or to run the harvest out while making a new garden elsewhere. The timing of a new garden may also affect the abandonment of an existing garden. As far as I could see, the scheduling of these several events is pragmatic and variable.

In completing the cycle of a garden it may be decided to admit pigs after the crop has been harvested. They will find whatever food remains, as a part of their fodder; and their rooting about for grubs and worms will be of benefit in tilling the soil, especially if a new garden is soon to be planted in the same ground. Whether pigs can be used as a part of cultivation, however, depends on whether the garden in question is fenced off from other plots that are still in active use. This employment of pigs may therefore be ruled out if a number of different gardens share a single fence but are not all fallowed simultaneously.

A given domestic unit or gardener ideally requires several gardens—not just several kinds—each probably in a slightly different stage of readiness or production. While palings are being cut and split and collected on the intended site of a new garden, the culmination of a man's mature garden is probably already being anticipated. The mature garden is perhaps already declining in yield even if some sweet potatoes are still harvestable or remnants of other crops remain to be harvested.

A given household's or gardener's plots may be widely scattered. The need for a different soil or situation for different crops partly accounts for this fact, but having gardens in various stages of the garden cycle is also a reason for separating gardens—namely, the practice of letting pigs root in a garden at its terminal stage. Still another factor is polygyny, in which different wives will tend to manage different gardens, even when resident in the same territory. And sometimes a man has gardens, whether or not wives, in different local territories, because of claims or connections there, through affinal or lineal kinsmen or through his own former residence in that group. The location of a given garden is also dictated sometimes by the need to supply a pig-feeding station. There is in addition an element of experiment—nowadays, at least—in which enterprising gardeners, especially those with a number of pigs to feed, seek out new ranges to improve their pigs. If the range is distant from existing gardens, good conditions are needed nearby for planting sweet potatoes. A new garden location may also presage a new settlement, for ideally colonizing is not precipitate or unforeseen. As a recurrent process, first a pig station, then gardens, then residences are established in an unused part of the parent group's territory. Perhaps this is coincident with the ambition of a dissident strong man, or some dissension within the existing group that is approaching the breaking point. A similar process may exist, perhaps with a more salient exploratory or experimental element, in zones of pioneer settlement (Sorenson 1972).

What consciousness there may be of the lessening of risk by establishing scattered plots, I do not know. The reasons adduced above, in any case, seem sufficient to insure a scattered tenancy of numerous gardeners; and whatever gain accrues to them solely because of a reduced risk may be theirs unwittingly. The amount of scatter, like the number of gardens, varies considerably from one person or household to another, for reasons such as polygyny, the size of a man's pig herd, his obligations, or age and health. (See Lawrence's study of Garia land tenure for an interesting comparison, 1955.)

The spatial oscillation and flow of humans and their activities seems continuous in Northern Tairora gardens, pig-feeding stations, and settlements. Unchanneled by other factors, the scatter of a group's gardens in theory might eventuate in the optimal use of available soil, moisture, and sunlight and the minimization of such factors as flooding or the costs of distance in tending a garden or transporting produce. But gardeners face a more complex array of considerations. Besides the distance from residence to garden and from garden to the presumed distribution points of harvest crops (e.g., dwelling, pig station, location of cooking sites and significant prestations of foodstuffs), there is initially the distance from the bush source of fencing materials to the garden site. The distance from a garden to potential garden predators—unfriendly peoples or pigs—is also to be considered and is a factor that may override the rest. Other constraints include land rights and accessibility, or the need to affirm or establish connections with one personnel or another. A man with cowives often needs to acknowledge the rights and separate standing of each of them by providing each a separate garden or gardens.

Such multiple needs, compounded by the variety of individuals, each with his own array of options, cannot produce a perfect match between everyone's garden locations and the requirements of crops for soil, sunlight, and moisture. The latter are more constant, certainly, than are the sentiments of gardeners, or people of the same or adjacent districts, toward one another;

and so the channelization and the fluidity of locational decisions seem to reflect gardeners' expectations about each other as much as the agronomical basics of plant and habitat.

The aggregate clustering of a group's garden locations, as would be expected, probably approximates more closely a simple match between plants and good growing conditions than do the garden locations of individual gardeners. Even so, if the traces of past gardens are considered, it seems reasonable to believe that gardens may feasibly be located in a great many places besides those in which they happen at present to be located. In other words, as in choosing which crops to grow, the physical options are quite broad.

LAND OWNERSHIP

The ownership of garden land is most simply stated as "usufruct." The basic entitlement to land is that of membership in or acceptance by a group as a coresident within their territory. Since there is no other basis in Northern Tairora on which coresidents could subsist, being a coresident necessarily entails the right of access to the basic resources of life, above all garden land. Land currently or recently under cultivation, however, belongs to the cultivator as long as he wishes to assert his right. Since the preparation of a garden involves an investment in fencing, tilling, and other care, it is understandable that ownership rights would not lapse immediately with the harvesting of a plot. How long such rights last varies greatly once the ground is unused for a period of years and after fencing rots or is removed. In theory, and often enough in practice, a remembered owner-user must be asked to cede his rights to someone wishing to assume them. Often enough he will do so. It is not unheard of, however, for someone without prior arrangement to commence a garden in grassland long disused, prompting a second party to observe that the land in question is actually his, through a father or some other claimed kinsman; but he may also decline to press the alleged case as an exclusionary right, saying that there is land enough for all.

Not all claimed rights are transferred so readily. Some plots of land can easily be matched, and claims to such land may be easily relinquished. Garden claims in the best bowls or bottom-land flats, on the other hand, are not so likely to lapse. Garden activity is nearly continuous there, with shorter fallow cycles. Here, too, other active gardens closely abut any section of fallow ground, tending to make clear boundaries; and a claimant thus can easily specify his claim to the ground through the independent testimony of adjacent gardeners.

Like other peoples of the vicinity, the Abiera think there is sufficient unused land and see no need for dispute. Whether in fact this optimism is justified, especially with the amount of ground now being committed to long-term cash crops like coffee, is for the moment beside the point. The sentiment is surely one of long standing. Batainabura feels more pressed for garden land, since much of its most accessible and best grassland is not considered safe to use for gardening or even for ranging pigs. It is too close to the Tuntuqirx, a hated enemy group regarded as encroachers. Batainabura has ample bush, which is said to be suitable for gardens, but much of it has to be developed at considerable cost, unlike the threatened and disused sections of grassland. The latter have been gardened within memory and appear to be *par excellence* the sort of situations presently favored in Northern Tairora for growing crops.

Usufruct rights endure as long as rights to residence endure. That is, wherever one has been a resident, or where one would in principle be welcomed or welcomed back as a resident—for example, in the territory of one's mother or her brother, or one's brother-in-law through a wife—a potential access to land exists that may be exercised at some time during the individual's life. Thus a Batainabura man has had a garden for a long time, he says, at Arau. He himself was once a resident there as a refugee, and a wife of his still lives there whom he visits fairly often. Whose garden this is, is perhaps moot, since the man's right to use the land could depend more on his daughter, native and still resident at Arau, than on his own status as former Arau resident or affinal kinsman. Practically speaking, it matters little. However, were a cash settlement to arise, as it might if some Arau land were alienated to government or private hands, it is doubtful if this former refugee would receive a share in his own right. His Arau wife should receive one, however, since she is herself still resident there.

Phratry Tairora—unlike Batainabura, which is a single territory—consists of a number of closely linked local groups and their respective territories. A significant minority of Tairora persons have gardens in more than one local territory, through former residence there themselves or through mothers, fathers, or wives. I see no essential exception here to the principle already stated: one may fairly seek garden land wherever one is admitted, has previously been admitted, or could readily be admitted (or readmitted) to residence. Since this applies to women as well as to men, men can and sometimes do exercise such claims to residence or usufruct through wives or mothers.

The strength or priority of a claim to land usufruct is, like the claim to ownership of a garden, a contingent and relative issue. The longer and more immediate, or the more continuous one's residence, the stronger the claim to a resident's land rights. The same principle seems to parallel one's rights to a former garden; and of course it parallels Cibber's classic aphorism, "Possession is eleven points in the law" (1697, *Woman's Wit*, act 1). In a conflict of interests, it is unlikely that the claim of a new resident, without numerous close or supportive kinsmen residents, could prevail over that of a current and long-term resident unless some split within the community were impending. Such a split is more than a matter for speculation, however, for the issue must often have become acute in the past when a bloc of refugees were admitted as residents. If their rights as newly established residents were vouchsafed by a strong man, their presence no doubt strengthened him; but it sometimes increased the disaffection of long-term residents of the community. If they were adversaries of the strong man, his sponsorship of the rights of the refugees sometimes therefore led to the withdrawal of the disaffected older residents from the community in favor of the newcomers—an outcome, incidentally, perhaps agreeable to the strong man (Watson 1967a).

Sections of forest land have direct and important uses apart from the possibility of making gardens. Rights to these are claimed by individual users, their rights inherited or sustained by the continuous cutting of trees for firewood or construction, the hunting of marsupials in certain trees there, and the collection of other forest resources, such as botanicals and excellent water. Claims to forest land may seem vague, since boundaries only exceptionally have the definition of a garden and much larger areas are involved. Yet in one respect, at least, forest claims are less apt than grassland gardens to lapse or become vague from long disuse. What they lack in definition they may gain in continuity of use.

Forest ownership, moreover, sometimes has a sanction that, as far as I know, does not apply to grassland gardens. This is the belief that the legitimate owner and his kinsmen are exempt from malice of spirits resident in their own forest area. They may claim their exception, it is sometimes said, by announcing themselves audibly upon entering the supposed vicinity of the *masalai*. The legitimate owners are quite literally familiar with the territory they claim. They know it and are thus far less likely than an interloper, let alone a stranger, to blunder into unsuspected danger. For those familiar with them the forest and its denizens are not as perilous as for others. A folktale well known at Batainabura, and probably known at least by some persons at Abiera, has to do with a grassland man visiting a bush-group kinsman. He meets death through ill-advised and ignorant contact with a snake. The same contact, asserts the story, would not be lethal to the bush-group man. While this tale immediately deals with the specific issue of the differences between bush and *kunai*, it also more generally states the immunity of the indigenous person in his forest as contrasted with the vulnerability of the alien.

Broadly speaking, a resident group owns its entire territory in common with such portions as I have mentioned being specifically and temporarily the assigned property of individual owners or their immediate heirs. Still, much is held in common, such as paths, water sources, dance grounds, and the area in and about a settlement: the fences, the palisade, and the footbridges and stiles. The pig range has also a sense of common property, though here again the establishment of a pig-feeding station in some part of the range undeniably preempts—just as establishing a garden does—the chance of someone else to put his station there or even to put one close by. Trees planted or claimed by individual owners stand at scattered locations about the common area, in the forest, or, in the case of bananas, in the grassland. The ownership of the ground in which such trees stand, it seems fair to say, has not been a question that strongly exercised the local mind. It seems clear, however, that the modern commercial development in this region of large stands of perennial crops, notably coffee, now gives an edge to this question that it never had before.

DIVISION OF LABOR

As already indicated, in the traditional division of garden labor men were basically in charge of preparing gardens—the "engineering," as we have called it—while women were in charge of planting and maintaining them, above all of operating the centrally important sweet potato gardens and managing the other crops customarily intermixed with sweet potatoes. The men thus fenced and trenched and broke the sod, or felled the trees and burned the trash; and women fine-tilled, planted, weeded, tended, and harvested the daily rations of greens and tubers that fed the family.

To this description it is necessary only to add that certain crops are primarily and some most exclusively in the male domain. These include bananas and other tree crops, sugar cane, and in principle, at least, yams and perhaps more vaguely taro. Judging only from contemporary observation, the masculine imperative seems to be met in the case of yams or taro by the presence of a male gardener, while no male need be present, for example, for planting or harvesting sweet potatoes. I observed that female gardeners were not excluded from the handling or planting of taro cuttings, nor (one Abiera case) even of yams. The exclusion of women, however, was more rigorously asserted and observed for sugar cane.

With the cessation of warfare, men are probably involved more than ever in gardening. Yet some men have always been much involved in garden work. "Garden man" is an epithet that can still produce a smile on older faces, reminiscent of the past when this phrase described the man with little heart for fighting. His stereotyped alibi is still readily volunteered—namely, that he could not join his mates in battle because his garden needed attention. A conflict of interest between horticulture and warfare seems clear, and informants often refer to the sad state into which their gardens sometimes fell in consequence of fighting. They are explicit that the care of gardens was a brake to the fighting of even the bitterest foes. "Garden man," moreover, seems to have been a somewhat ambivalent label. Such a man, although a loss to fighting, was nevertheless also an asset to the group. A part of the remembered stereotype, in fact, has the garden man proposing to help the fighter by doing work that the latter in his absence cannot do for himself, work such as fetching fencing and firewood from the forest. Today there is no need for such arrangements between garden men and fighters, since the defense of the group does not require neglecting garden work. The advent of cash crops such as cinchona, citrus, passion fruit, white potatoes, truck gardening, coffee, tea, and pyrethrum (in approximately this sequence) and the rising demand for cash have further led to the more intensive involvement of men with crops and cultivation.

Women's roles in gardening may have changed less than men's, but they, too, may now work more in gardening than formerly. If polygyny has declined, as it appears to have done, more women now find themselves the sole or main female producer in a domestic unit. The disappearance of the men's house, with its frequently shared meals, has eliminated a form of pooling of cooked food, in which some of a woman's responsibilities were merged with those of other women. There is now, moreover, much less need for women to move to and from the gardens in coordination with others under the watchful guard of their armed husbands, fathers, or brothers-in-law. Not only does this relieve the male guardians for other work and give women more freedom to pick and choose their work on any given day, but it probably permits a household to develop larger garden sites at remoter or more widely scattered locations than in the past. At the same time, the pig herd has probably also been increasing, with the availability of more time for tending pigs, less risk of loss of pigs to enemy capture, and a wider and safer pig range. This means for women, as the principal producers and transporters of fodder, more distant porterage as well as more pigs to feed.

Local Northern Tairora perception widely depicts the precontact past as a time of lusher vegetation, larger gardens, more numerous and bigger pigs, and taller, stronger, more forceful and productive people, as well as in general a more eventful and grander scale of life. This image of precontact times appears to be widespread in the immediate region. Many older Northern Tairora know of an event they date at about 1880 (Watson 1963b), when the air was filled with falling "sand," the ground was covered with the stuff, and the sun blotted out by it for several ("three") days. Some informants today rationalize that event as having produced a "cooling" of the earth, including especially the soil of gardens and the crops themselves, as well as the "heat" or strength of men. "Now we are cold; the pigs are cold; the crops are cold; the very ground is cold," a man told me, "and so we are small." Cold is negative in relation to vigor or potency, which heat symbolizes or typifies. This presumably modern myth is thus a way of viewing the alleged diminution of the Northern Tairora as people and the loss of strength-giving virtues in their most basic resources. The rationalization hence reinforces the more general belief that the life of people today is less in quality and magnitude than formerly.

It seems on the whole more accurate to ascribe the modern sense of powerlessness, in contrast to their vaunted precontact potency, to the contact of the Northern Tairora with Europeans and their fairly rapid pacification. Inherent in this development was a suppression of local initiative and the loss of sovereignty. The local version of the past is poetically correct, in the sense of an erstwhile autonomy replaced by a demeaning clientage. It cannot be taken, however, to represent literally the intensity or extent of resource exploitation before the white man, or before the falling "sand"—in all likelihood a fall of volcanic ash. Thus I think the assumption I have expressed here—of an expanding postcontact productivity and intensified use of resources, specifically in horticulture—is valid. Despite the contradiction of a common local view, I am confident in arguing that people—both men and women—work harder and produce more agriculturally today than they did in the past.

The use of steel tools to replace stone has sometimes been noted as an asset to productivity (e.g., Salisbury 1962), and indeed older men today stress how laborious, even painful, it was in the past to cut and split wood, for long periods, with a heavy stone adze. Since gardens require fencing that was formerly made with this tool, it is likely that the availability of steel axes, spades, and machetes has also been an impetus to modern horticulture in Northern Tairora.

HUSBANDRY

Of the several animals kept by the Northern Tairora, pigs and dogs are by far the most numerous and economically significant. Among the grassland peoples it is only the occasional cassowary that is brought into a village as a chick and allowed to reach maturity, when it will normally be eaten. Sulphur-crested cockatoos, while more common than cassowaries, are kept primarily for their ornamental white feathers and as amusing pets. Occasional wild birds other than these are taken captive by some peoples of the region, but this is more characteristic of peoples living in forested country than of Northern Tairora. Both cockatoos and cassowaries in time become tame enough not to require caging or tethering and move freely about the village. Since the cassowary is a formidable bird, stories are told about their occasional attacks on villagers, especially children. This is not seen as an argument against raising captured cassowaries, however, perhaps because it would also be an argument against raising pigs!

Dogs, to be sure, are eaten, but they are not kept mainly for food. They serve rather to warn their masters, for use in hunting, and for companionship. Though a good dog is much sought and may be an object of spirited trading, dogs are neither kept in such numbers as pigs nor are they fed or cared for as well as pigs. Dog teeth were an object of some value in precontact times, but they are not commonly seen or sought at present. I cannot say how much the precontact use of the teeth may have contributed to the utility or value of dogs.

PIG RAISING AND DISTRIBUTION

In the past more than now, pigs were an ever-present adjunct of the human household. They were commonly kept in a section of the house of a wife of their owner, where they spent the night. It would not be inaccurate, therefore, to consider that the woman's houses of Northern Tairora were also stables for this, the major livestock. Pigs are still led about when small on leashes, or are occasionally carried in a woman's net bag, like a small child.

Young nursing pigs are sometimes suckled by a woman when necessary for their survival, and pigs are frequently groomed and deloused by humans, the small ones usually being cradled in the lap during this procedure. The relationship between humans and their animals, in a word, is easy and intimate. An owner will frequently describe to an observer just what the pigs are thinking about at a given moment—statements that imply a high degree of empathy and anthropomorphism.

Partly because of what people understand to be the government's injunction against stabling pigs under the same roof with humans, and partly because it is now safer than formerly to keep pigs outside the village, even on distant ranges, the domestically domiciled animal is today rarer if not entirely gone from every settlement. Yet people not only remain close to the animals but feel that intimacy is a necessary part of their domestication and control. For they must not wander away and become wild. A sow with a litter that she delivers in the forest or canebrake is a particular concern lest the piglets remain at large. The presence of wild pigs in the vicinity is said to make this danger more acute, especially since the relation between the wild boar and the domestic sow is essential to the breeding of Northern Tairora herds. The young boars of domestic litters are castrated as soon as possible in order to control them. Thus pigs are not only fed a substantial part of their diet—enough so that they will remain dependent on it and will come promptly when called for feeding—but the food may even be cooked for them. Some portion of it is commonly premasticated by the owner or a member of the family (this is also done for weaning children) in order to foster an attachment between the pig and the owner of his family. The male or female owner of a pig may be referred to as its "father" or "mother," respectively, and a sense of soliticousness and sympathy, if not affection, is evident. People confidently speak of a pig's reactions, considering themselves in effect capable of feeling as a pig does. The pigs are trained to come at the call of their own keepers—a characteristic gutteral call that is standard in this area. Magical practices are also used in habituating young pigs to their keepers and their feeding places.

The preoccupation with establishing and keeping control over pigs is not unreasonable. Lost or stolen pigs are as commonplace as the wounded pig that escapes capture on the intended day of its slaughter, to flee, perhaps die, in the forest or a canebrake. Hours or days may be spent, often fruitlessly, to retrieve such animals. It is not only the native independence of the pig that creates the risk of loss, or even the attraction of neighboring wild pigs, but the fact that fodder supplied by human keepers constitutes only a portion—albeit substantial—of the average pig's diet. The rest is obtained by the pig through foraging where it can freely range, so the pig is on its own a good deal of the time, without constant herding.

Pigs from time to time break an old or poorly made fence and root up garden crops. Such pig depredations, as is widely the case in New Guinea, are a significant source of disputes within a community. Custom holds that the pig may be shot (though not used) if seen by an owner in his garden. But custom does not guarantee that the settlement of such disputes is accomplished without rancor. One frequent issue is whether the garden owner actually shot the pig in his garden. Trusting to his own ability to identify the invading pig, he may have killed it somewhere else, leaving open to debate whether the dead pig was indeed the culprit. For his part the garden owner may feel less than compensated for the loss he has suffered.

There is normally little difficulty in identifying pigs or in establishing ownership. Not only are the natural markings of pigs different, but their size and body configuration are generally distinct to persons familiar with them. The ears of many if not all animals are also clipped. One purpose of ear-clipping—and tail-docking—is to make a pig obedient and responsive to its owner. Informants differ over whether this or identification is the main point of the practice. Pigs can usually be identified without reference to the cutting of ears or tails; thus it is called upon only to resolve the occasional difficult case.

Where pigs are ranged varies with different keepers, from areas immediately adjacent to a settlement to ranges that in some cases nowadays are several miles distant from the dwellings of their owners. Some men of Abiera range their pigs in Urara, another territory, where residents take care of them for a share of the increase. For the owners of larger herds, the reasons for seeking less-used range include a concern for the health of pigs that are too crowded. They recognize a shortage of forage in overused ground; but they also claim a magical etiology where many pigs of many owners are found and pigs fare poorly. It may be said that there is too much sorcery being used in the vicinity. Whether or not directed against one's own herd, the magical fallout, as it were, can become so potent that unintended pigs sicken or fail to grow.

Thus strong efforts are made to locate pigs where they will fatten fastest and be healthy, not necessarily the grounds most accessible to their owners. The cost of farther ranges, however, is obvious. Except for an arrangement such as that between the Abiera men and the Urara herders, an owner must travel and his wife must carry pig fodder longer distances the farther away from settlement or garden he ranges his animals. The only alternative is to develop gardens in that area—near the pig station.

A shelter is usually provided for the pigs of a given owner at a strategic point within their range. The commonest sort of shelter resembles the round, conical-roofed dwellings of Northern Tairora in all respects except for being open-walled or partly so. Pig shelters vary considerably, however, in size, refinement, and upkeep. Some are little more than dilapidated lean-tos. A pig-feeding station that has been used for a long time will usually be recognizable by the trampled bare ground.

If the pig range is far away, the pig house may be built to protect the owners themselves from rain or cold or permit them to stay overnight. Between proximity to the settlement and the optimum range conditions for pigs, the tug is constant. Occasionally owners spend large amounts of time at their distant pig stations, and this sometimes leads to the construction there of fairly adequate houses. Even in the past this tug was evident. An Abiera story relates the fate of two local pig keepers, proud of the fine range they found for their pigs. Disregarding the warnings of their kinsmen, they proceeded with plans for a house and garden and commenced living at this place. All went well and the pigs prospered, seemingly vindicating the stubbornness of the pair, until one day when smoke was seen and the exultant singing of a marauding enemy party was heard. The rescuers who ran to the site found the two trussed-up bodies of the owners swinging from the ceiling inside their burning house.

Northern Tairora does not boast the massive festivals and pig slaughters of certain other parts of the Central Highlands (Luzbetak 1954), in which hundreds of animals, sometimes thousands, are gathered at a single time and place, representing a large number of communities. In Northern Tairora the pigs used on any given occasion usually were contributed mainly by the owners of a single community. Perhaps one or two others came from close kinsmen nearby.

I cannot speak for precontact distributions of pigs. Consistent with the views previously mentioned, these are represented by some informants as having been much greater in scale than at present. From my observations, however, an exchange involving the slaughter of as many as five to ten pigs would be outstanding in Northern Tairora. Certain modern governmental or mission-related ceremonies nowadays bring to bear the efforts of numerous local groups at a single time and place. Baptisms, the "kiap's Christmas," and a 1964 pre-election sing-sing represent such novel forms of participation. Although they are greater than any known traditionally, the numbers of pigs killed still do not reach those known in the Western Highlands.

Given this frequent but small-scale slaughter of pigs, largely limited to the animals contributed by one locality, it is hard to estimate the size of local pig herds in the past. An enumeration of the pig herds of Abiera was made in 1963, those of Batainabura were enumerated a few months later. The results are shown in table 1.

Several observations can now be made. First, the number of pigs per

TABLE 1
PIG HERDS OF ABIERA (1963) AND BATAINABURA (1964)

Category	Abiera	Batainabura
Male	60	38
Castrates	34	Not specified
Female	124	83
Piglets	232	Not specified
Total	450	121

owner varies appreciably within a single community. Second, the number of pigs per territory—judging from these two territories alone—may also vary significantly. For what it may be worth, the intergroup variation in this case matches the impression of some Central Highlands of New Guinea ethnographers that grassland communities like Abiera have larger pig herds than bush-oriented groups, taking Batainabura to represent the latter. (The bush status of Batainabura probably applies more to some of the elements of its composite personnel, such as the members of the Airina sib, than to others.) The people of Batainabura themselves, incidentally, claim a source of salubrious water within their territory with outstanding virtues for producing large and healthy pigs.

Differences in size of individual pig herds may reflect a number of factors, such as the age of the individual owner. Young men tend to have smaller herds than older men, especially if they have been away from the village on a labor contract or are just starting a herd. Elderly men, on the other hand, or men in poor health, may have few pigs or none. A man with two or more wives may have more pigs than a bachelor or a monogamously married man, since the polygynist has more hands to raise food as well as to carry it to the pigs and to tend them. But there are doubtless also differences of sheer entrepreneurial drive and skill, though these of course presuppose health and vigor, if not additional wives.

Since pigs require fodder in addition to forage, and fodder requires garden yield, individual as well as interterritorial differences in garden production must accompany differences in the size of a pig herd. The main fodder for pigs being sweet potatoes, the herding of pigs putatively bears on the intensity of cultivation of the staple regional crop, by individuals and by local groups.

In the view of the Northern Tairora, individuals differ also in their ability or capacity to raise pigs that survive, grow large, or have large, healthy litters. This concept implies innate, ultimately magical differences from one individual to another. It also presumes a certain fixed and irremediable competence—or lack of it—between different men and women. The notion is parallel to that of a person's competence in other important activities, such as bearing children, gardening, being knowledgeable, or having the power to fight or to influence other people. Thus, informants say, in lending out pigs to be raised by others, with a sharing of any resulting litter, their experience makes them readier to lend pigs to the husbands of women known to be competent in caring for pigs.

Pigs are in principle raised to be presented to others for consumption. It is usually thought improper to consume the pork of a pig one has raised by one's own hand. This custom has clear overtones of the close identification or intimacy of the owner and the animal. Indeed, a woman who has cared for a pig may show grief at its death. It is denied, however, that this response should be taken seriously, for it is, after all, the purpose of raising pigs to kill them for presentation.

Despite evidence of the sentimental attachment of owners to their pigs, the use of pork as a key component in exchange and presentation may be more fundamental in the etiquette of ownership and disposition. Most keepers of pigs at any time find themselves in a web of prior obligations as well as plans for establishing or strengthening future social relationships. Few or none of these intentions can be realized without some use of pork. And pigs may be unexpectedly needed quite apart from one's deliberate plans or foresight, as in the case of the illness or death of a kinsman or the visit of a trading partner or other significant person. Available pork, like its owner, tends to be committed to certain persons and certain purposes. The purposes already known may be more than enough to account for all the pigs an owner has. Indeed, an owner may speak of having designated given pigs for given purposes or persons, and an expectant recipient may also speak of it. It is a point of pride, a declaration of a significant relationship, and an assertion of an obligation. In such a context, the use of the marked pig for any other purpose than an obviously urgent one must seem grave, a possible affront. Thus, quite apart from any feelings of an owner or his wife about consuming pigs they have raised, there is ample reason for them to adhere strictly to the rule that pigs are for presentation to others, even to specific, declared persons.

The comment is sometimes made that pigs, as a storage of food and exchange value, are to be likened to money or to a bank account. No matter how much greater the energy cost of raising a pig than what it will return as food, in many societies like Northern Tairora pigs are among the largest units of value that can be deployed on short notice. The modern cash value of pigs in Northern Tairora is in fact very high, but it sometimes seemed to me more reasonable to say that a pig was simply not to be had for any feasible sum of money. This is probably because most pigs are virtually bespoken.

Pigs in Northern Tairora are only partly to be understood through the analogy of a bank account. Unlike money on deposit in a bank, they cannot conveniently or profitably be used as capital for all conceivable purposes. Pigs are special-purpose capital, the only exchange capable of use for certain purposes, and they are not reciprocally convertible into other values. This makes it unrewarding or harmful to use pork indiscriminately for various other sorts of utility.

Seen as an element in one of several "spheres of exchange" (Salisbury 1962), pork does not move against other sorts of food. Nor does it even move readily against money in a new, increasingly monetized Northern Tairora economy. It moves against ritual and social utilities, most of which are obligatory in form, even if variable in the quantity of pork required or exchanged.

What of an owner with pigs enough for all possible presentations? Would he boggle at using his own pigs for food, or for other purposes outside the system of presentations? A quick rejoinder is that, for most pig owners (omitting men who have no pigs), the hypothetical case is contrary to fact. Even the most enterprising pig breeders often continue to be energetic in increasing their herds because the imperatives and opportunities for exchanging pork are almost endless. The need for presentations is relative to the prestige and ambition of a given owner, that is, so that no point of diminishing returns is easily imagined, let alone reached by any pig breeder. The large operator, finally, least of all needs to use his own pigs for food. Widely and intensively involved in exchanges of pork with other men, he and his dependents can eat pork given him by his exchange partners far more often than can men having fewer pigs and making fewer presentations.

Eating one's own pigs, and to a lesser degree converting them directly to one's own benefit by means other than those traditionally recognized, is antisocial behavior. Denying the pork to others is more broadly and more directly disruptive, I suggest, than is the offense of propriety or sentiment in consuming one's own creatures. The traditional means of converting pigs to one's own benefit, presentations to other men, affirms mutual obligations. The traditional context of these presentations, moreover, is ritualized in a collective frame and has connotations of broad social purpose like community well-being. Thus withholding pork for private use may be doubly offensive: it denies the pork to individuals to whom it may be owed, in the public form of presentations, and it denies the pork to the community, thereby weakening their univocal statement of strength and solidarity in the presence of outsiders whose opinions matter.

A qualified use of pigs is the market. Sale of pork at least places the meat in the hands of other persons, sometimes perhaps members of the community who might expect presentations. I observed such a market (called by that name in Neo-Melanesian) in 1964 at Batainabura and was told that the practice was not new. A man who had butchered and cooked a small pig was offering cuts of the meat for sale within the community. He had set up shop by a footpath that ran near his house. Most of the sales were for cash, but he was ready also to consider trade goods in barter. I have no evidence that the practice is very old and incline to doubt it. Resident vendors were practically unknown in the village. Others professed to recognize no great novelty in the arrangement, however, when I queried them. My immediate concern is not to establish whether the "market" for pork is of long standing or rather a development that has occurred only since contact and nascent commercialism. Precontact or not, it seems to bear out that, while the deliberate private consumption of one's own pigs is said to be egregious, a public distribution of the meat, even if not a traditional presentation, escapes some of the opprobrium. Channeling the pork to others, doing so publicly, and permitting consumption to be determined by them, the so-called market escapes being the selfish decision of the owner himself.

In public presentations of pork the meat is generally cooked; or it has at least been butchered and exposed to a cooking process, whether or not it will be further cooked elsewhere before finally being consumed. Informants state that it is not uncommon for the recipient of a cut of cooked pork to take it home and cook it further, at least by way of heating it before eating.

Northern Tairora pigs are typically shot with arrows, having first been called by their owner or mistress to the feeding ground, or kept enclosed within a fenced yard overnight to be available in the morning for slaughter. More often than not the first arrow only wounds the animal, which bolts for freedom and must then be tracked until it drops, or stalked and shot again until it can flee no more. Some pigs escape for long periods; some are found dead days later, the meat spoiled; and some are never found.

The Northern Tairora pig slaughter closely resembles hunting. This raises the question why the animals are not clubbed, tied, or caged before shooting. I do not know the answer, if there is a simple one, other than tradition. In time and lost pigs the cost of the customary method is not negligible, though clearly many men enjoy the excitement of the chase and the chance to shoot their bows, track the quarry, and display their prowess. Shooting was still, in the 1960s, a significant preoccupation of many men, and a visual and aural pantomine of archery was as vivid as it was commonplace. Cutting the throat of a pig, in any case, was an unappealing technique because of the loss of blood. Blood is valued both as food and as a potent protective or curative substance sometimes used to smear on people who are ill or on possessions thought to be imperiled by magical forces.

Pigs are generally butchered to be cooked in a single piece except for the organs of the body cavity. First the body is singed of its hair. The process of butchering then consists in opening the belly and taking out the various organs for separate treatment, some by roasting, some by cooking—steaming—in a green bamboo tube. Smaller bits are often collected in a wooden bowl filled with edible leafy greens, then cooked together with the greens in a freshly cut section of bamboo. A bamboo knife is the preferred implement of butchery, being easily made and very sharp, as well as quickly re-edged. Following disembowelment the carcass and head are converted into a single flat slab. This is done by chopping the ribs and pelvic girdle from within the body, along both sides of the backbone. What results can be compared to a bearskin rug, a flattened sheet of meat with the head and legs splayed, ready now to be layed out for cooking in an earth oven.

The Northern Tairora earth oven is a shallow pit filled with heated stones. One or more such pits with suitable stones are to be found in nearly every settlement. The stones are heated by being stacked atop a large quantity of long sticks of firewood crisscrossed above the empty pit. As the wood is burned, the sticks break under the weight and the now heated stones fall into the pit below. When nearly all the wood is burned and the hot stones are ready, a thick blanket of grass is laid on the stones and around the earthen sides of the pit, in effect an envelope to contain the tubers and other foods to be cooked. The placement of stones, grass liner, tubers, greens, and, on top of all, the pig carcasses is the joint business of a number of the men and women of the host group, the donors of the food and other presentations.

With the pigs in place, the grass blanket is drawn over the whole mass of cooking foodstuffs and the oven is sealed by heaping earth over it, creating a mound within which the edible contents will be steamed. The juices of the cooking pork are expected to impart a good flavor to the vegetables, just as the wild greens are intended to flavor the meat. When the oven is opened after some hours, the food is apportioned to the guests and cuts of pork are distributed to key recipients among them, generally something to everyone or with the implication that the further apportionment of meat will achieve that result.

HUNTING AND GATHERING

In turning now to the sphere of hunting and gathering one can speak of each of the previous sectors of activity, gardening and pig herding, in a kind of synoptic comparison. Doing so may highlight in part what each means in Northern Tairora culture. With due allowance for the grossness of the following synopses, then, one might say of the gardening of these peoples that it represents a sphere of steady, satsifying, and surely essential activity in which the element of human control over outcome is at its local maximum. It is a very domestic activity, moreover, since for one thing the garden product is routinely handled by mothers, sisters, or wives, and is routinely destined, day by day, meal by meal, for the sustenance of the members of the household. Whatever may be done with any additional production, these needs come first, because the members of the household cannot live without food from the garden. Gardening is a comfortable sphere of activity, as well as the most familial and feminine of all in light of the prominence of its participants. It seems no exaggeration to speak of the garden, as I earlier did, as a second home. The physical site of many familial and pleasant activities besides the care and management of crops, the garden, like the house, is for everyone, not just members of one sex or age. It is a part of what it means to be a member of a family in Northern Tairora. Gardening activity is less fraught with anxiety or uncertainty than most other productive activities. Being a gardener does not, like being a pig breeder, expose one directly to the invidious rivalries of Northern Tairora life. One's sweet potato plot is not to any such degree as one's pigs threatened with magic, theft, illness, or simply acrimony over the disposition one may make of the product. In the past, the more a man engaged in gardening, the less he took part in the most rivalrous activity, fighting. Not for nothing, then, did the epithet "garden man" constitute an antithesis to fighting, prominence, or strength. To be successful as a gardener a man need not excel as a husband with several wives. Nor does gardening to the same degree as pig breeding place people in a position of dependence on each other. While there is undeniably a division of labor for gardening, with males complementing females, a gardener can be a bachelor or widower. And a woman, with the occasional help of a male relative in fencing and trenching, can be a sufficient gardener in her capacity as a widow or divorcée. Thus while the garden serves so well as the site of domesticity, it can also be a solitary and private undertaking, permitting the individual thus to pursue his tasks without the stress or need to depend constantly on others.

Pig breeding contrasts with gardening in a number of ways. Both by the nature of the activity and the destination of the product, pig breeding is much more of a high-stakes, high-risk business. Pigs frequently get lost or stolen, or fall ill and die. Feeding and tending pigs is a laborious business, and even on the day of slaughter, one's entire efforts can be wiped out if the pig escapes and is not recovered. Even as the pigs are growing, the owner is always potentially subject to accusation and strife if his animals are thought to be responsible for garden damage. It is at least symbolically fitting that the killing of the pig by the most violent and exciting means known—shooting—should be prescribed both for ritual slaughter and for resolving the grievances of an outraged gardener.

In many respects, keeping pigs is a costly, luxury undertaking entered into only by those already possessed of health and ambition as well as ample means, such as a productive wife or wives, kinsmen to furnish breeding stock, and thriving gardens. Ultimately pig breeding is entered into for purposes of competing in the prestige economy. While one cannot live without a garden or access to the product, he can live without pigs—as precious and desirable as ownership or the eating of exchanged pork may be. Some men do live without pigs (or wives), albeit as "rubbish men." It may be possible to keep pigs, as well as a garden from which to feed them, if one is a solitary male or is married to an infirm woman; but the strain would be great and the limits severe. No man in such a position would be apt to challenge the standing of anyone high on the ladder of prestige exchange. Indeed, a very high correlation is to be found between the owners of the largest herds and those with more than one wife. The dependence factor, in a word, is much higher in pig keeping than in gardening. One need only recall that pigs are for presentation to be reminded of another facet of the intense dependence of the pig breeder. He is perforce a public man, the more so the more pigs he has.

Hunting and gathering fall into a distinct third category, quite apart from any postulates about this form of activity as being more ancient or traditional than gardening or husbandry. Hunting at any rate is a quintessentially masculine activity and as such enjoys an approbation that is quite unambiguous. The activity is solitary or may be carried out by small parties of men only. Yet this activity or its product is not directly related to a competitive purpose like the prestige exchange of pork. The product of hunting and gathering is directly consumed or shared, or—in the case of certain kinds of game—is ritually required for the celebration of childbirth and other events in which sets of affinal kinsmen are mutually linked. Although hunting may be said, quite as much as keeping pigs, to be subject to conditions of risk and scarcity, scarcity does not make the participant dependent on the whim of his fellows, as in starting a pig herd, or the collaboration of wives, as in maintaining one. Except for the ritual requirement of certain forms of game, hunting—probably less so gathering—can be considered optional most of the time. The energetic and skillful man may avidly pursue hunting alone if his group has access to a suitable forest, but he seldom uses his energies in that direction if he does not wish. Thus marked differences are seen in the amount of hunting done by men in grassland and bush territories, perhaps just the reverse of their respective concern with pigs. Eeling is also an option for those with eel waters.

Nutritionally, hunting and trapping, and to a degree even gathering (namely eggs, grubs, larvae, insects, and certain plants), provide luxury elements for the diet that are rich in protein or fat, and bring welcome variety. These qualities doubtless insure that the product of the hunter and the collector will continue to be esteemed relative to garden products and even to pork.

Perhaps the single most distinctive aspect of hunting is that it brings the participant into direct contact with the wild. In addition to the salience thereby given to judgment and skill, as well as to chance, this places the hunter and even the gatherer in a more intense communion with the supernatural than does either gardening or pig breeding. It is not just the difference between wild and domesticated resources. The element of human will and management is undeniable in the case of crops and livestock. Pig stations and gardens are located at the wish of their owner while game birds, eels, and marsupials are to be found if and where forces beyond the hunter deem. In addition, however, the pursuit of game takes the hunter—as collecting also takes the gatherer—into the forest, the haunt at once not only of game and wild food plants but of supernaturals and a multitude of magical plant sources as well. It is therefore perhaps not going too far to suggest that hunting, even gathering, is a more awesome and sacred activity than gardening or pig herding—or at least that there is more awe and sacredness incident to it.

WILD RESOURCES

The wild resources of the Northern Tairora region vary greatly from one local territory to another. Here, above all, the contrast between bush and *kunai* is relevant, for the largest amount as well as the greatest variety of resources—plant food, magicomedicinal material, game, bark for slaking lime, construction and craft material, firewood, or luxury items such as feathers—undoubtedly belong to the forest sphere. Access to a forest, however small, is considered a prime possession.

As far as wild foods are concerned, a simple listing will suggest the regional range and variety. Birds and marsupials are taken from both grassland and forest, but the forest has more as well as more kinds. The forest has the litter incubators containing the eggs of bush fowl. It has cassowaries, opossums, tree kangaroos, many birds, lizards, and pythons. The grassland has

wild pigs in a few places (such as canebrakes), rats, and a few small marsupials, some native birds, and such forest-dwelling birds as occasionally cross
open country. The bush has numerous wild plant foods, such as leafy greens,
pandanus nuts, insects and grubs, various kinds of edible fungus, betel nuts,
and wild fruits.

It seems safe to say that for many of the modern peoples of Northern
Tairora, wild foods, especially wild game, have a traditional and ritual significance quite outweighing their caloric value. Small marsupial game is collected for presentation on several ritual occasions such as the celebration of
the birth of a man's first child. In grassland and even bush margin communities in Northern Tairora, hunting is discussed, esteemed, and celebrated out
of proportion to the time spent in hunting, and out of proportion to the
catch. The techniques and lore of hunting, in other words, are a living tradition however small its practice. The sudden appearance of a single small
game bird among the trees of a grassland community will galvanize the energies of several hunters until a lucky arrow finds it or it moves out of range.
Dogs, which are used in certain forms of forest hunting, especially for marsupials, are touted and sought for their ability. Eels, which are trapped in some
of the local streams, are a highly prized catch, and traps and trapping a lively
topic of conversation. Incidentally, the bones of eels must be carefully disposed of, particularly to avoid their being gnawed by dogs or other animals.
This particular custom is widespread in my reading of New Guinea ethnography, suggesting a time when hunting and gathering activities were more important than now and when they perhaps involved other such observances
once more widely shared.

One could surmise that the taking of wild food, especially game, eels,
snakes, and eggs, is emphasized for its recreational significance—that is, as
an exciting diversion from horticultural routines and diets, and one perhaps
even more valued now that warfare no longer supplies excitement. It could
also be suggested that these foods and activities were not long ago substantially more significant than they are now in grassland areas—at least as significant as they seem still to be for peoples with easy access to forests and
relatively abundant wild resources.

Batainabura surely does not have the highest intensity of exploitation of
forest resources in the region, but it illustrates the contrast between a bush
and a grassland people like the Abiera. Bush fowl eggs were a fairly familiar
although irregular item in the local diet. There was much talk of finding cassowary trails and a request was made to me for steel wire to make snares.
Forest marsupials were brought into the village from time to time, and a
twenty-foot python was captured and cooked. The python, by the way, was
extremely repugnant to an Abiera companion of mine, to the keen amusement of local youths who made sport of him by chasing and slapping him
with the snake's carcass. He later absolutely refused to taste the meat. His
traditional stamping ground, Phratry Tairora, lying just a few miles to the

west of Batainabura, differs but slightly in dialect, and even has affinal ties with Batainabura. But the Tairora lead the life of the grasslands.

Batainabura men were frequently absent from the village to cruise the forest, not solely for the purpose of hunting, to be sure, but generally with that among their purposes. Indeed, several men, two in particular, were known to spend more time in the bush than their fellows. This kind of specialization—perhaps idiosyncrasy—could be compared to the more intensive eel trapping or gardening or trading and visiting patterns of other individuals. At Batainabura the forest's edge meets the settlement on one side, so that a day spent in the forest need not take one far away. Other than visiting a small patch of woods at the crest of the hill behind their settlement, Abiera hunters and collectors would have to cross several miles of grassland to reach a forest of the same size. It belongs to a Kamáno-speaking group, moreover, although they say they enjoy rights of access and use. Sizable closer forests belong to unfriendly groups.

As to techniques, birds are hunted with arrows specially tipped with knobs or with barbed prongs for fowling. Forest marsupials are generally taken in trees, often by climbing to bring the animal or its hole into view as well as into range. Dogs scent the animals and help find the trees. Cassowaries are shot with arows or caught in snares set where the hunter thinks the bird is accustomed to pass. Pythons are shot or clubbed.

In the grassland, rats and small marsupials are caught in box traps made of sections of a hollow limb or in open snares set in the animal's pathway. Sometimes simple baits are set with an attached, tasseled stalk to signal by its movement the presence of the animals at the bait. Then the watching hunter shoots where he knows the game must be. Small bows of bamboo and stiff straw or bamboo arrows are used by boys in stalking rats, or the animals are caught in the hand and roasted whole. Rat hunting is said to be for children and women, though I have seen a middle-aged man hunting rats that he said he would be willing to eat. The Abiera are aware that in nearby Agarabi large rat hunts or drives organized by children are held at night in the full of the moon; but this practice was not observed in Northern Tairora.

Eels are caught in box traps made of the hollow section of a tree and baited. Once inside, the eel is held prisoner by a trap door. As with nearly all of the foregoing practices of hunting and trapping, there is marked variation among individuals in how much time they devote to eeling. Some men pursue the activity fairly often, others apparently rarely or never. Certain eeling streams and places are well known, but I am unaware of any sense of ownership attaching to them. My impression is that the different concern of individuals with eeling, as with hunting and other forms of trapping, is attributable to other reasons, including personal preference. Just as the breeding of pigs was recognized as requiring the proclivities of a public man, these activities seem the opposite.

The largest game and perhaps the most desirable (though that would be

hard to establish in proportion to the quantity of food represented by different quarry) is the wild pig. I did not observe the organization of any wild pig
hunt nor gather detailed information. My impression is that it would differ
little from the tracking and killing of a wounded domestic pig, except for the
initial lack of a blood trail, and the wild boar is doubtless a fiercer quarry.
Indeed, the wild pigs that came to notice at Abiera seemed to be former
domestic animals that had gone wild, and the line might be thin or arbitrary
between hunting a totally strange *wild* pig and one that had been "known."
In Northern Tairora, wild pigs seem less likely to be deliberately hunted
than other game unless they are thought to be invading gardens or lurking
close to settlements. It may therefore be that the hunting of this quarry is in
part defensive. Wild pigs are considered dangerous as well as wily game,
though their habits are basically the same as those of the domestic pig,
whose genes they presumably always share.

SHELTER AND CLOTHING

The basic environmental consideration of shelter in Northern Tairora, as
in all of the Central Highlands of New Guinea, is the range of temperatures.
While daytime temperatures may reach the upper 80s on sunny days, nights
can be extremely chilly, with temperatures down to the 40s. Yet people
were lightly clad and did not possess substantial covering or body insulation
even for sleeping. The bark cape, sometimes described as the indigenous
"blanket," was doubtless a help and is said to have been used to control the
body heat of sleepers as well as to protect the traveler against the elements.
But the pivotal adaptive response of Northern Tairora and many other Central Highlands peoples was in the design of compact, tight, windowless, and
well-insulated houses, with earthen floors. Their roofs were low to the
ground except at the center, and the interior thus was easily kept at a comfortable temperature by use of a modest source of heat, the fire on the
hearth, which was also used for cooking.

Basically similar to the house style prevalent over much or all of the Eastern Highlands of New Guinea, the modern and immediate precontact
houses of Northern Tairora have circular floor plans, low walls, and conical
roofs with a sufficient overhang of eaves to keep the roof drip away from the
base of the wall, and enough of a peak to permit the smoke inside to rise to
the center and escape through the thatch. Whether or not these houses are
admirable from the standpoint of smoke pollution or communicable diseases,
they are efficient from the standpoint of heating. Their low doorways, easily
barred by wooden slats against both intruders and the cold; their tight, insulated walls made of grass-lined bark or split palings; and their roofs thickly
enough thatched to contain the heat, though not the smoke—these make it
possible for nearly naked sleepers to spend a frosty night in comfort, stirring
only as the fire dies down. Indeed, a major hazard for the sleepers, especially children, is that as the fire dies down or the night grows cold, they

crowd their bodies closer to the hearth and sometimes roll over in their sleep and are burned. A significant fraction of the population has heavy burn scars, most of them apparently from childhood and from this cause.

Northern Tairora dwellings were of two kinds, the most obvious difference being size. The larger, men's house, however, differed in several other ways, both in its site and in its construction. The men's house stood apart from the other dwellings of a settlement, in a private precinct sacred to the initiated males of the group. On a sloping site the men's house probably occupied high ground. Its separation was probably defined by some means such as a log, or row of logs, that made it impossible to ignore the zone forbidden to females and uninitiated boys. Within this zone was a special latrine for the exclusive use of the resident men or their male visitors. One of its purposes was to safeguard the feces of the resident males. Like those of women or children, vulnerable to exuvial sorcery, feces must not fall into hostile or irresponsible hands. Quite possibly another purpose of the men's latrine was to keep men's feces uncontaminated by the feces and other exuviae of women, since magical contamination does not depend on the intention of a manipulator. A special plant was said to have been grown around the men's latrine, quite likely only one of a number of special—and probably variable—practices, all of which served to define or defend the separation and significance of the men and their special site. In some descriptions there is also an indication that a part of the men's precinct may have been screened off by vegetation, to constitute a symbolic barrier between the masculine quarter and the rest of the settlement. Certain secret activities of the men took place in their private precinct, which, since they should not be witnessed by women or children, might require a screen.

The men's house itself was round with a low, conical roof; but probably in part because of its larger span, the roof had a center pole, unlike the roof of

The old and the new: round men's house with centerpost protruding skyward, and, in right foreground, rectangular modern structure with walls of woven bamboo.

the women's house, to support the radially deployed light beams and circular stringers upon which was laid the thatch. The center pole typically protruded through the thatch and rose high above it. This pole was sometimes garlanded with magical leaves for the protection of the occupants. The symbolism of the center pole of a men's house is suggested in its name. It is called "our grandfather" (or "ancestor") because, like him, "it supports everything else." In the belief of some peoples of the area, when fiery arrows are discharged from the hilltop by a group seeking to discover the perpetrators of a recent death of one of their members, the tracer arrow wings its way and strikes the center pole of the men's house of the sorcerer's group. Whether or not the house can be seen by the archer, the direction taken by the arrow is a divination of sorcery—one of quite a number of forms of divination.

The men's house had wider eaves than women's houses. Indeed, a kind of low, narrow porch surrounded all or a part of its perimeter, especially in the front. This area served to store firewood out of the rain, and it was also sometimes used as a place for the men to sit and smoke or observe the community, for which they held themselves responsible as its owners and heirs.

The entry to a men's house was treated in a special manner, with two unbroken rows of posts leading from the door to the interior of the structure, in effect making a narrow passageway along which one must proceed before gaining admittance to the main space within. This arrangement is said to have been defensive, making it dangerous for an intruder to reach the occupants within, since he would be both exposed to their notice and vulnerable to their arrows if need be. The remainder of the interior space of the men's house was usually unpartitioned, but a number of hearths, spaced in a roughly circular array about the center, divided the floor into several areas. Each was used for sitting, eating, and sleeping by particular men. The existence of several hearths within the same dwelling, each requiring firewood, helps explain the need for the porch-storage area. With its higher roof, the men's house might also require larger or more constant fires for comfort than would the women's house, with its single hearth.

The men's house had only its one usual entrance, as described, with the palisaded passageway. It is generally asserted that emergency means of escape were also usually provided. By building a part of the rear wall so that an opening could readily be made, the occupants improved their chances of avoiding entrapment in a burning house, its main entrance sealed off by enemy men with drawn bows. To catch your foe in this predicament was considered the ultimate victory for attackers. It meant successfully breaching (or perhaps scaling) the palisade of the settlement and surrounding the men's house without awakening either the occupants or the village dogs. As a countermeasure against such a danger, one informant said, the floor of a men's house was normally left littered with trash, especially the husks and chewed pulp of sugar canes. Harboring large numbers of fleas that prevented the men from sleeping too heavily, the litter decreased the chances of a surprise night incursion by an enemy. Whether the fleas were equally cultivated during the wet season, when fighting was at an ebb, I did not learn.

The defensive concern expressed in the design of the men's house is seen in a number of other features of the Northern Tairora settlement. Sites were selected for their defensibility or commanding view of the terrain. Many, but allegedly not all, settlements were palisaded with heavy timbers stood on end and lashed strongly together with stout vines from the forest. Such a palisade would surely be beyond the resources of some grassland groups, however, and indeed the Abiera deny they had any palisade around their precontact settlements. This is a point of pride for them, moreover, and they say their fathers boasted of it in taunting enemy neighbors, daring them to retaliate for an attack inflicted on them: "You are angry now. So come tomorrow and attack us! We have no palisade and no one will be there to defend Abiera but old men and women. So come!" There was no retaliation, the informant tersely added. Lighter fencing of pitpit canes can be used in place of a true palisade, but while this would hold or exclude pigs if they were not too determined, it would only briefly impede an enemy.

Women's houses were more numerous than men's houses, as well as smaller. If the site was not level, the women's houses were situated below the men's house. Women's houses evidently had no interior passageway or any real porch beneath the eaves. The small size of the structure if nothing else probably made such features incompatible. Instead, the interior was most often divided by a single partition. This produced an outer apartment by the door, where pigs could be stabled, and an inner apartment for the woman, her children, and any other members of the household group.

Normally a man's wives had separate houses. Some even lived in different settlements, but several combinations and variations were possible, to judge from reports and from the present. The one fairly constant fact was the regular residence of men not with their women but in a men's house. It is hard to say how often—or when—the men visited their wives. Evidently a man might occasionally spend a night with his wife.

It is also hard today to gauge what force of conviction underlay the segregation of the sexes or the various beliefs—some still readily stated today—about the pollution of women and the contamination of their houses by their body functions and substances. One modern assertion is that women's houses were dangerous to men not merely because women lived in them but because they did not scrupulously go to the menstrual hut or even go outside to urinate at night—from fear of prowling ghosts or sorcerers. Northern Tairora seems no obvious exception to what has been reported elsewhere in the Central Highlands of New Guinea regarding the elaborations of sexuality and pollution (Meggitt 1964; Langness 1967; Allen 1967). Yet one must note with what speed the residential separation of sexes has broken down and men's houses have disappeared as a functioning institution, soon to be followed, no doubt, by their disappearance as an architectural form. Indeed, by the mid-1960s, some Northern Tairora settlements had no structure on the plan of a men's house, let alone any that served residentially as such. There was a growing number of what might be called family houses, distinctly larger than the small women's houses of yore, many of which were still being built, yet not as large as nor laid out like the men's houses of the past. They might have center poles, for example, but usually lacked the palisaded entryway.

The menstrual hut is also used for the delivery of babies and a lying-in period of several days' duration. It tends to be a smaller version of a women's house, round in ground plan and conically roofed. Less care is exercised, however, in constructing these shelters. Menstrual huts are located away from main footpaths or where they can be partially concealed, usually down the slope from a ridge or hilltop settlement and not rarely, therefore, near a stream. Normally more than one woman uses the same menstrual hut, so that one or two, several at most, are sufficient for a settlement.

CLOTHING

To generalize at the outset about the Northern Tairora costume, it consists for both sexes of bare legs and a bare torso and arms, no footgear, and no headgear other than that worn for festive occasions. Such a pattern of dress will probably raise no eyebrows in tropical New Guinea, and it could easily be duplicated in many other parts of the tropical world. One should bear in mind, however, that the Northern Tairora live at altitudes of from around five to six thousand feet, in a country that can be quite chilly at times. Perhaps the most obvious single adaptation of costume to climate was a short, plain bark cape, used by both sexes, hung from the shoulders and tied around the neck. The cape hung to the knees or just slightly above. Large net bags are also used by both sexes to cover most of the back, making a substantial supplement to the basic, lowland-tropical garb of the Northern Tairora and their neighbors.

The material from which nearly all clothing is made, including the cape, is bark stripped from a certain small tree. This is beaten to felt together overlapping strips and produce wider sheets. For festive attire another style of female skirt is made of rushes specially cultivated in swampy plots and imported by the Northern Tairora. These skirts are used particularly by women at Batainabura. Since the skirts are long and the rushes are light though voluminous, they amplify the movements of a dancing woman's body and emit a rhythmic rustling sound in time with her steps.

There are only two styles of the basic bark girdle and skirt of bark strips used by women. One is for unmarried girls, the other for women who are or have been married. The unmarried female's skirt is open at the sides, showing hips and legs, with panels of strips only at the front and rear. As a feature of the betrothal ceremony this skirt is exchanged for several, each with strips that form a skirt that completely encircles the body. When new, the strips of

(*Above*) Village woman with much-worn ''utility'' skirt of bark strips softened with pig grease. Light fence serves to demarcate the dooryard or to enclose small children. (*Below*) The net bag is worn over the back for carrying heavy loads.

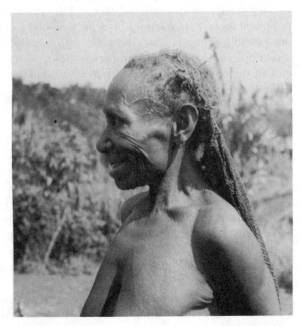

the married woman's skirt reach to just above the knee, and since up to four of these skirts are worn, one over the other, modesty is normally assured. Modesty in female attire was several times mentioned by Northern Tairora men in commenting adversely on the allegedly provocative dress of neighboring Gadsup women. Their skirts were supposedly worn too low, exposing the lower belly, even the pubic area; or they were said to be too short. Even the long Northern Tairora skirt becomes shorter with wear, as the bottoms of the bark strips abrade each other, are sat upon, or brush the ground when the woman works in the garden. When an outer skirt becomes too thin or short, a new skirt is simply added over it.

A kind of bark sash is considered necessary to complete the woman's costume. It is easily overlooked by the outside observer, and I omitted this item from a drawing I made for use in a projective test. The omission gave unintended poignance to the stories told by subjects concerning the woman depicted in what I meant to be a normal Northern Tairora costume. She must be so distraught that she has fled her house in a great hurry, some informants related, else she would not have left off her sash.

The range of styles in the men's basic bark girdle is greater than in the women's costume. All men, married or not, wear a girdle holding up a panel of strips of bark to cover a man's pubes from the front, though not necessarily from the side. A few long strips of bark hang down from the girdle at the rear but scarcely enough to conceal the buttocks. Here the basic pattern ends in a series of options, for the girdle or waistband may be more or less elaborate and colorful, as well as larger or smaller in the diameter of its cross section. The breech strips may be hung directly from the girdle or from holes in a wooden "codpiece" set into the center of the girdle in front. This "codpiece," to term it loosely, also comes in more than one design. Thus, through various possible combinations, the male costume yields something over a half dozen different styles, not to mention the opportunity for purely individual embellishment in connection with some or all of them. The contrast between male options and female uniformity is thus quite marked. To make them pliable, the bark strips of both men's and women's skirts are treated with pig grease, which is also considered an unguent.

The cape appears to have been the same in pattern for either sex, although my impression is that it may have been more often used by men than women. If this is true, perhaps it was only because men more often journeyed abroad, at which time they might wear capes. When new, the bark of a cape was brown to russet in color, but the surface of the tapa was not ornamented in any deliberate way, such as with paint or stain. It sometimes has a certain texture incidental to the felting of the fresh bark with a wooden beater having a grooved face. Basically square or rectangular in shape, the cape has no tailoring. It is simply provided with strings at the top wherewith to fasten it around the neck.

Two items, or rather one item in two ranges of size, are carrying bags of knotless netting—the ubiquitous *bilum* of Neo-Melanesian designation.

While carrying is the principal and explicit purpose of net bags, they are such a regular part of a man's or woman's attire, whether anything is being carried or not, as to be fairly considered costume. The large-size net bag is often worn across the back, from the shoulders to the waist, by men, and is seldom or never filled. Worn across a bare back, with its fairly close mesh, it doubtless helps to conserve body heat, and for men it is probably intended mainly for that purpose. It seems difficult otherwise to account for so large a net bag in use by men who do not traditionally carry large burdens—at least not in net bags. A smaller net bag in which men may carry the few personal possessions they keep with them—betel chewing and smoking material—is sometimes worn in addition to the large one at the back. Men wear the loop of their net bags, laden or not, across the neck, while women wear their net bags with the cord across the forehead as a tumpline. This difference, too, reflects the different weight of burdens normally carried by each sex. A man would be choked if he carried much in his net bag.

The woman's net bag is the real burden-carrying equipment of Northern Tairora. Though comparable in manufacture to the net bags of men, a woman's net bag is used daily in bringing tubers and other food from the garden. Indeed, many women, perhaps most, wear two net bags, using one to carry the poorer sweet potatoes destined for her pigs, the other for the larger tubers that the family will eat. Infants or sometimes piglets may also be transported in the net bag. It is quite common to meet a woman slowly

Wearing a coronet of cassowary feathers and polished nose piece, a man smokes a roll of green tobacco leaves inserted in a bamboo smoking tube.

making her way along a steep or tortuous path, both net bags bulging with their heavy contents, their loops deeply indenting her forehead. Not infrequently she will have a clutch of firewood held atop the bulging bags by her upraised arms, her hands probably also grasping a pandanus mat and a digging stick, spade, or machete. This sight is so common in the region that one may easily forget what effort and grace of body is required and how essential it is to local provisioning.

Thinking about the logistics and the energetics of local provisioning, it is essential to recognize what production entails in the movement of raw materials, over what distances, and over what terrain. Each additional mouth, human or porcine, is a tax on the burden bearers as well as on the gardens of Northern Tairora. Indeed, when humans or pigs are still infants, either or both—not just their food—are often themselves transported the same distances their food must travel. Each additional mile from point of production to point of use is similarly a tax. Thus even without other constraints on the optimum or maximum size of a local group and its usable territory, it seems clear that transportation alone would impose a limit. Surely transportation is a serious constraint on the locational decisions of Northern Tairora—where to make gardens, build houses, station pigs—in fine, where to live and work. As it is, the decisions made often require a heavily laden woman to trudge for distances up to several miles, sometimes over steep terrain, between house or garden and pig station. It seems realistic to propose that the logistical problem in Northern Tairora is a constant stressor of human beings and not rarely an acute one. Nor is it too much to suggest that this stress underlies or reinforces some of the ceaseless locating and relocating of the members of local society as well as of the sites of their operations, even now after the effects of warfare can no longer be considered an active and primary cause. When warfare contributed to accelerate spatial mobility, it is useful to recognize, it was not the sole factor to do so.

NORTHERN TAIRORA USE OF RESOURCES: AN OVERVIEW

In an overview of their use of resources, it is probably clear that the largest investment of Northern Tairora peoples is in the residential site, the men's house and its precinct, and the women's dwellings; the living area, cleared of vegetation and scraped down to the bright tan subsoil; the fences, paths, foot stiles, and the palisade; the tilled garden plots and their heavy, pigproof enclosures; the menstrual huts and pig shelters; the planted trees and crops; and the pig herds which must be slowly built up over time against many demands and risks. These commissary items—the site and its improvements—practically exhaust the nonportable parts of Northern Tairora artifacts. It is a rather substantial property if costed out in hours or hands against the total available effort.

It seems relevant to note that there is little or nothing among the foregoing to compare to the carved posts or masks, the gravesite memorials, the large and elaborate ceremonial paraphernalia, or the ornate men's houses known elsewhere in New Guinea. (One does not, of course, find canoes of any kind, let alone ones with elaborate embellishment.) Abiera has a single, tabular stone, perhaps three feet high, whose probably natural markings are taken by some, as is the stone itself, to be associated with their ancestors, albeit rather indefinably. This stone was moved to its site in the present settlement from a previous settlement. The lack of large investment in religious and ceremonial objects or in art, or the lack of comparable embellishment of utilitarian works, undeniably gives Northern Tairora cultures and others like them their pronouncedly plain and utilitarian face.

Northern Tairora society supports no conscious artists who work as experts to produce for other individuals or for the community. (Expert roles exist, however, in the sorcerers who exercise their magic both privately and against a common enemy.) The most notable creativity in Northern Tairora life is the sometimes fanciful costuming of dancers. Here inspiration (attained in dreams) is expended on the creator's own costume or those of his collaborators, if other dancers are involved in an ensemble, somewhat in the manner of a costume ball. Again, as in the latter case, the creations are a short-term, ephemeral form of art. Since this form of art is, notwithstanding, the nearest to an exception to the "plain and utilitarian" character of Northern Tairora culture, let me pursue the description far enough that there be no doubt about the characterization.

These largest artistic creations of Northern Tairora are frames and structures—like an airplane fuselage—worn in certain kinds of dancing. Not strictly masks for the face or even limited to headgear, they are carried on the head or shoulders of a dancer, or sometimes more than one dancer. (A two-man "rainbow" comes to mind, with a dancer supporting each end of the arc, though this was built by a neighboring Agarabi group and was not in my experience duplicated in elaborateness in anything I saw in Northern Tairora.) That these occasionally large and impressive structures—frames supporting painted bark panels—are thrown away rather than made for keeping after the performance seems again to fit a militantly portable, plain, and utilitarian scheme of life.

Some suggest that the Northern Tairora and their neighbors are impoverished by comparison with other peoples of New Guinea. Yet "poverty" does not seem to strike quite the right note, for it is not so much a lack of wealth as how the people use what wealth they have. Returning to our initial overview, it seems fair to suggest that their wealth is considerable. Certain other parts of New Guinea may be more richly endowed with natural resources than the Northern Tairora area, and there are richer cultures. Yet it is not likely that cultural richness will be found to be the simple reflex of rich local resources.

Has the essential plainness and utility of Northern Tairora life and material culture any plausible explanation? I think so. I suggest that one can logically start by considering that the peoples of this area need and consequently stress a rather high degree of productivity, considering their natural, social, and technological circumstances. This need has been unfavorable to any cultural elaboration or enrichment not directly serving the ends of a production, intensively used in competition and exchange.

A high level of production is required for several reasons. Among them is the cool climate, necessitating well-made, insulated housing and a continuous and substantial supply of firewood or other fuel. Both construction material for houses and fuel to heat them, for many Northern Tairora peoples, furthermore, must be obtained from an increasingly distant forest source. (The same obviously applies to fencing material, the importance of which is discussed below.)

Probably the greatest need for high productivity, however, is prompted by the level and number of exchanges of food and other goods, including fighting services, that have to be sustained by any group that is to remain successful and independent. This need is related in part to such background conditions as the (probably growing) density of population in Northern Tairora; the large number of small-size local units; and the absence of large or effective confederacies or stable networks of alliance. The resulting instability of interdistrict relations is costly and inefficient, leading to forlorn investments of wealth, limited successes, and the recurrent and onerous need to inaugurate new exchange partnerships or revive old ones. Here I am suggesting an inefficiency or a tax on productivity—perhaps waste is not inappropriate—that is endemic to the politicodemographic field of Northern Tairora local groups.

As a multiplier to the above costs we have the use of pigs as the paramount good of local production and an absolutely essential symbol and component of exchange. There is no reason to believe that garden production invested in pigs is as efficient in sustaining human beings, for the labor it costs, as the same food directly consumed by people. To the costs of intensive pig husbandry must be added, surely, the large amount of stout garden fencing required by such intensive husbandry, the cooking and transporting of fodder from its source to the pigs, the building of pig stations and stables for the animals, and the care and management of the herd. A dramatic if less expensive item, finally, is the depredations of pigs on gardens and their attacks on people. The time-consuming and wasteful ritual of slaughtering domestic pigs, by "hunting" them, needs at least to be noted, though it might seem to suggest that peoples of this area can easily afford the waste.

Multiplying and adding to the foregoing costs of production in labor and resources is the prevalence of warfare and its inevitable drain on time and energy. For a community an essential part of remaining viable is a defensible site and frequently its fortification in the form of a fence or heavier palisade. The construction of the latter obviously takes labor and timber. Perhaps this form of "public architecture" could be taken as the substitute—surely in energy terms—for the impressive *haus tambaran* (literally "house of ancestors"—men's house) and other public art of certain other parts of New Guinea. The optimum location of settlement sites for defense tends to place them sometimes a great distance from the nearest source of essentials such as water, fuel, forest material, and garden land. Fighting itself exacts a heavy cost in the making of weapons, magical undertakings, political maneuvering, the loss of people from death, and the loss of time and health from wounds. These costs are all in addition to the direct cost of fighting forays and ambushes, which are carried out not only on behalf of one's own group but not infrequently at the behest of allied groups. One could even add that the need to watch and guard over women working in gardens, as well as the need for them to proceed in groups to their work sites for maximum safety, ties up potential masculine labor as well as preventing the deployment of women to places where they might more profitably work.

Enemy depredations against capital, however difficult to calculate historically, are undoubtedly substantial. In destroyed gardens, burned houses, broken fences (with the consequent encroachment of pigs), or in stolen pigs, the cost of hostilities in goods or disrupted production can mount rapidly. When a group is forced by the tide of politics and killing to abandon its territory altogether, the loss is great indeed. It includes nearly all of the group's assets—the site and its improvements—apart from the human capital the survivors themselves represent.

Comparing this area to the richer cultures of the coast, there is a need to account for the lack of greater development. It is an area of fairly dense and industrious population, yet short of symbolic embellishment in physical form. Basically I am arguing that a preoccupation with urgent production and exchange tends to be preclusive of other concerns, above all in the Northern Tairora context of bellicosity, insecurity, and instability. The conditions lead to costs and inefficiencies—or waste—that then require greater or more laborious productivity.

The habitat of the Northern Tairora may be poorer than those of some coastal and riverine areas, but one may doubt that this alone accounts for the "utilitarian" emphasis in the use of energy and the development of resources. Nor is the utilitarian emphasis a simple function of the intensity of warfare—the more warfare the more utilitarian— a simple "Sparta" model, so to speak. I am quite prepared to believe, on the contrary, that there may be other areas of New Guinea in which fighting is as intensive as in Northern Tairora but with art more richly present and prominently woven into the fabric of life. My argument is only that fighting and other forms of rivalrous exchange in Northern Tairora, a profound and inescapable concern of the people, can be sustained under the conditions in which they live only by a high but costly productivity, above all costly of their time, energy, and ingenuity, and costly alike, if you will, in its emphasis on the materials and activities of defense and production for exchange, as opposed to the symbolic and aesthetic elaboration of life. Perhaps we are also speaking here of the materialistic strain of Central Highlands of New Guinea cultue that has been noted by recent ethnographers.

Pig raising is surely a prime case in point, for, just as visible art forms are more salient in certain other parts of New Guinea, the keeping of pigs is markedly more intensive in the Central Highlands (Brookfield 1962). Like their neighbors and, more important, *because* of them, the Northern Tairora are caught up in this expensive business from which there is no escape (Watson 1965b). Pigs in numbers to match neighborhood demand are an essential part of corporate survival—as much as is the exchange system in which pigs are so vital a part. Yet pigs must be raised at sites often ill-suited to production and husbandry but required for defensive reasons. If the intergroup conditions for corporate survival require this extravagance, they do not, by contrast, require architecture more impressive than men's houses with proud center poles or art more lavish or lasting than the rigs devised for night dances. A given group's public display runs to this standard because parity in local exchange systems is defined much more by individual competence in provisioning and strength in fighting than by visible artistry in the statement of the corporate competence or its ancestral auspices. More pigs as a trade-off for less public art is simplistic, even as saying, "The Tairora do it because their neighbors do it" seems only to beg the question of why the neighbors do it. It will at least be clear that the explanation does not presuppose some gross discrepancy in the mobilization of productive energies between high art and low art. The issue is what energies are mobilized for. There is certainly no lack of the material resources needed for making art. Ultimately, I am persuaded, it *is* a question of what the neighbors do. Why they came to do it or not to do it, however, is beyond the scope of this particular study; but it might be better to start with why Central Highlands neighbors do so much with pigs than with why peoples of some other parts of New Guinea do so much with art.

4. The Social Statistics of Two Local Groups

RATIONALE FOR AN ENTIRE CHAPTER ON CENSUS MATERIAL

In this chapter I present statistical profiles of Abiera and Batainabura, mainly based on a separate census of each local group. It is common in ethnography to conduct a census when the object or locale of study is a social unit with boundaries that are definable as of a given time. Though seldom a perfect isolate, a living community is typically such a unit. The census itself can also throw light on the problem of boundaries, demonstrating in what terms and to what degree one may justly speak of discreteness or definition in a particular group of people.

Ethnographers do not habitually make maximum use of their census data. Population pyramids showing the age and sex composition of small-scale societies, for example, are much less common than they need be. In presenting profiles of Abiera and Batainabura, I wish to include not only total population but a breakdown by age and sex, by residence or household composition, by marital status, and by declared lineage or sib ("name group") membership. I will then consider lineage membership, in turn, in relation to sex, age, residence, marriage, and birthplace of individual members.

That ethnographies often lack a statistical profile of the community studied is presumably because many ethnographers are in fact more concerned with describing a culture, tradition, system, or structure than with describing a community. The community is thus an intermediate rather than an ultimate object of study. One hopes the community is representative of the ultimate abstracted object; one generally takes it as such.

There are advantages and disadvantages in a community profile restricted to census data. A concentrated exposition of statistical material representing a single period of time may seem rather static or lifeless. Probably for this reason census data are often sprinkled about sparingly and usually intermixed with other information relevant to particular questions that arise. Questions will arise from census data, to be sure, that census data alone can-

75

not resolve. These particularly include questions of process and development.

My problem is not solely the present make-up of Northern Tairora communities. I am interested at least as much in laying bare what Northern
Tairora—or representative segments of it—meant before contact. Thirty
years of contact may seem almost negligible in the perspective of an American Indian group. Though in a remote area and without large-scale alien immigration, thirty years in the case of Northern Tairora is surely not negligible. My study is not purposely one of acculturation, but it must inevitably be
one in some sense unless I disregard either the past or the present. I see
little merit in that. I think the deliberate omission of either would impover-
ish the other.

My ultimate interests are in the historical processes that characterize this
small segment of humanity in the situation in which its members live. I seriously doubt that any study could do justice to the question by focusing on a
single moment in time or a single point in space. Why, then, should we have
statistical profiles that represent par excellence a time- and space-limited
focus? The flexibility of social systems in many parts of the Central Highlands of New Guinea has been variously described (Salisbury 1956; Pouwer
1960; Brown 1962; Barnes 1962). One current view stresses systems of rules
that apply contingently or, better, weigh in a particular outcome according
to the immediate givens. Individual options are allegedly made in the face of
conditions that are as unstable in the short run or the given locality as they
may be recurrent in the long run or at large. In attempting to cope with a
question of waivable rules or a pliable organization, it is easy to exaggerate in
the direction either of contingency and anarchy or of overtight, regular
structures. One can ill afford to cut loose, in the face of such vaunted flexibility, from the moorings of detail and degree. I see a detailed description or
profile of at least the situation(s) of a given moment as a desirable control.
For this reason, statistical profiles based on a datable census of a definable
group seem desirable. The profile will reflect at least the momentary expression of condition and contingency.

A further justification of a chapter such as the present one arises from the
nature of the larger project of which the Northern Tairora study is a part. In
order to provide a picture of Northern Tairora communities comparable to
those of Awa, Auyana, and Gadsup, which are being produced by my collaborators in the Micro-evolution Project, I must say as much as possible that is
quantified or quantifiable. Our several groups are not certain to be so different that gross generalizations will suffice.

Among the Northern Tairora I know there is obvious variability among
communities of what would traditionally have been regarded by ethnolo-
gists, probably, as the "same" culture. Flexibility in time has as its counterpart variability in space. For simple taxonomic purposes and for other broad
purposes it is probably sufficient to treat variability as is often done. Many
"cultures" are presented by taking only a single community—or a compos-

ite—as exemplar. Yet Northern Tairora is surely not the first ethnolinguistic series within which substantial local variation has been noted. Differences have long been recognized among the Hopi of First, Second, and
Third Mesa, for example, and indeed among some villages on a single mesa.
This does not invalidate every attempt to characterize a Hopi way of life or
frustrate the effort to distinguish it from the ways of other Pueblo peoples. It
does, however, underline the need to be clear about what is being described
and for what purposes it may fairly be used.

In what sense, then, is it valid to speak of a Northern Tairora culture? One
can surely speak of a Tairora language, even recognizing it as a congeries of
several major dialects within which further, though lesser, local variations
occur (McKaughan 1964). The linguistic analogy is not likely to prove
treacherous, at least for broad purposes like ethnic taxonomy. The problem
then becomes the empirical one of determining what is singularly Northern
Tairora in kind or degree, as distinct from what is singularly Gadsup, Agarabi, Kamano, or Auyana.

For the purpose of describing and understanding Northern Tairora culture as process, the variability from one local group to another can provide
essential data. Consider the position of the analyst who bends his best efforts
to account for a prevalence of adoption in Northern Tairora, basing his study
on a group in which adoption is fairly frequent. Suppose that he is unaware
that adoption is rare or absent in another group, one that closely resembles
the first—a group with the "same culture," so to speak. If the analysis is
good enough, of course, the factors regarded as important in adoption will
prove to be absent from the second community—or to be "mitigated" in
some way. The error in that case will perhaps consist mainly of labeling: the
ethnographer may have identified a "Northern Tairora" characteristic, a certain rate of adoption that in fact varies appreciably from locality to locality. It
is possibly, therefore, a condition that varies from time to time in the locality
first studied. In other respects his work will have been quite good. There is,
however, a good chance of making a mistake more serious than labeling. This
is in failing to recognize or assess correctly the essential concomitants of
adoption. If adoption is a variable consequence of fluctuating conditions
within a series of largely similar local traditions that we may usefully call
"Northern Tairora," the mere discovery of variation may be worthwhile. It is
at least a caution. It invites comparison and measurement. It is the necessary
starting point in the search for explanations. And it can only improve any
description of a "Northern Tairora" system.

I have already noted several qualitative variations between Abiera and Batainabura. These are enough, certainly, to make it reasonable to expect others. In social organization, perhaps, we may not expect such frank contrasts
as that between the occurrence of active and visible ghosts (Abiera) and their
absence (Batainabura). We would probably not expect to find in one community, for example, a segmentary system based on patrivirilocal residence and
something altogether different in the other. Differences are likely to be

subtler ones of degree. Some such differences are just the sort to be caught or reflected in census enumerations. It therefore seems expedient to set the two groups considered in this monograph side by side by means of statistical profiles in order to measure some of their demographic and sociographic variations. I believe that the price of producing for the moment a somewhat static picture and of postponing certain questions will thus be justified.

There are drawbacks in working exclusively from census data, even when the exclusiveness, so to speak, is temporary. A main drawback is that one may pick up inferences in the statistics which other evidence would indicate are not warranted. If one were considering only the other evidence, however, the reverse might be equally true. Ideally, this would argue for an intimate intermingling of relevant data of all kinds rather than between the "narrative" and the "numerical," or the "quantitative" and the "qualitative." Talking or writing is a linear medium, however, and it is a practical fact of exposition that one thing has to be discussed before another can be. The clincher in the present study is the need to present and compare data from *two* local groups, which happen to be variants of each other—or variants of some larger or idealized entity we are calling "Northern Tairora." In the face of this need, shifting freely back and forth from statistical to narrative data, as well as from group A (Abiera) to group B (Batainabura), seems hazardous to clear reading.

ABIERA AND BATAINABURA COMPARED

I will speak of proximity, relationships, environment, demographic composition, and history. Abiera and Batainabura are much alike in some ways, such as population size, but they differ appreciably in other respects. A comparison of the two communities gives an indication of the demographic, social, and cultural diversity of local groups within this single ethnolinguistic area. By considering the differences between Abiera and Batainabura in light of their respective histories and development, furthermore, it should be possible to see some of the processes by which local groups of similar cultural heritage are diversely shaped or specialized.

Abiera and Batainabura are two of perhaps forty-nine Tairora-speaking communities. Pataki-Schweizer (1980) has referred to these as "bounded complexes." For the time being it will suffice to describe each of them as "the largest aggregate of people with a sense of identity recognizing common access to a continuous territory" (Watson 1966:5). Although differing measurably in speech, their difference is small compared with the maximum divergence that can be found among Tairora dialects. McKaughan (1964:99-100) found a lexical similarity of from 97.8 to 99 percent between Abiera and Batainabura, depending on whether a shorter or a longer word list was used:

Abiqera and Batainabura of the Tairora are very closely linked linguistically. In this case, the villages are farther apart geographically than [Gadsup] Akuna and

Tompena. There are also a number of villages in the areas of Abiqera and Batainabura which have little linguistic divergence from each other. In fact, there are
more villages speaking what we may term a "Tairora Valley" dialect of Tairora
than there are villages speaking any one dialect of any of the other languages. In
conjunction with this, we note that there is little geographically to hinder communication in the Tairora Valley area. [1964:108]

By the same measure, the degree of lexical similarity among other Tairora
dialects drops at least as low as 78.7 percent, and a wider survey of Tairora
dialects might reveal even greater differences (McKaughan 1964:99-100).
The phonological similarity between Abiera and Batainabura is also high
compared with other Tairora dialects (McKaughan 1964:105).

The linguistic similarity of Abiera and Batainabura is not surprising, since
the two communities are no more than seven or eight miles apart and are
located in the same northern salient of the Tairora area. Distances up to
thirty miles separate some Tairora communities. Moreover, the predecessors of the present people in each case, according to local tradition, have
occupied much their same vicinities for generations. In the case of Batainabura they have "always" lived in their present vicinity, having arisen on the
spot; but the Abiera have a tradition of ancestral founders coming into the
area from the east at some time in the past. A large swamp lies athwart the
most direct route between Abiera and Batainabura, but the two groups are,
and quite likely have long been, aware of each other. As far as present memory extends Batainabura and Abiera have usually enjoyed amicable though
not consistently close relations. They have in common several of the same
enemies and some of the same friends. To judge from the present, marriages
have occasionally linked some members of the two groups, though obligations to affines and matrilineal kin seem to become tenuous after a generation or two. Active fighting alliances between the two groups have occurred
less often than their professed friendship might lead one to expect. It must
also be pointed out that the Batainabura people speak more of this friendship
than do the Abiera. The Tairora phratry, of which Abiera is a part, is a much
larger and more powerful social entity than Batainabura or any social network it can influence. Abiera itself was a powerful military factor on the local
scene just prior to contact. More than the breadth of the swamp between
them, it was probably the intermediate position of villages of the Noraikora
phratry that limited the relations of the Abiera and other Northern Tairora
groups with the Batainabura.

Both 'Abiqera" and "Batainabura" are primarily place names. They refer
respectively to the immediate locality on which all or a part of the settlement
of the residential group stands or, in the case of Abiera, formerly stood.
Abiera is now usually called Quntoqa by the present residents, and that name
is familiar in most of the immediate vicinity. Quntoqa is the name of part of
the present village site. Earlier the group or their predecessors occupied a
piece of ground nearby which included a spot still called Abiqera. At that
time the government officer inscribed the name of this village as "Abiera" in

the census report and entered it on patrol maps, giving them their "village book" or register of residents. The register continued to bear the old name, even after the site was changed, and that name is therefore still commonly recognized, especially in dealing with outsiders such as government officers and other Europeans. (Indeed, a number of former residents who were originally listed in the Abiera register, but now no longer living at either "old" or "new" Abiera, believe they must assemble at the present village when the census is taken by the government or for other "govermental" activities such as voting.) As group names, Abiera, Quntoqa, and Batainabura therefore designate in the first instance the residents of a given place and a given time. Though the name remains attached to the ground, it may cease to refer to the group. When they move to a new site, usually nearby, the new settlement will normally be called by a name that denotes the new site. Since changes of site are fairly frequent, numerous older place names are remembered as the location of former settlements. In an appropriate context, any of these can be used to refer to the people who once lived there, but only a few such place-of-settlement names ever become long attached to a group, outlasting subsequent residential moves. The nature and sociological significance of the use of place names and group names, and the relation of place names to group names, will concern us below.

We have agreed in the monograph series to use such geographical names and spellings as have now become generally established. Accordingly, I refer herein to the settlement and group in question as Abiera, as the place and the people are known to the government.

Both Abiera and Batainabura are located on the flanks of hills that face in a general westerly direction and slope away on three sides to valleys which are swampy or coursed by streams. The slope at Abiera is much gentler and the village site itself broad enough that all the houses could be arranged in a single cluster. Batainabura has steeper and more broken slopes, such as to make difficult a single or continuous settlement cluster. Batainabura houses are more scattered, with some along a ridge, some running down the two spurs of the mountain, and still others on small tables or in pockets on its slope. A look at the site maps for each village will show the location of nearly all residential and other structures and features for each village as they were in 1963-64 (maps 1 and 2). The scattering of Batainabura residences is apparent, as is the more closely clustered pattern of houses at Abiera. The division of Abiera houses into two more or less compact clusters is not primarily a function of terrain. It must be assumed that it has mainly sociological significance. The reasons for the Batainabura's settlement pattern almost certainly include terrain.

Abiera's lands and local resources differ from those of Batainabura. While looking out onto grassland, the Batainabura settlement has immediately at its back an extensive area of forest. Only a few steps from the village will take one into heavy growth where game, wild herbs, construction material, and firewood are locally considered to be ample. The Batainabura, moreover,

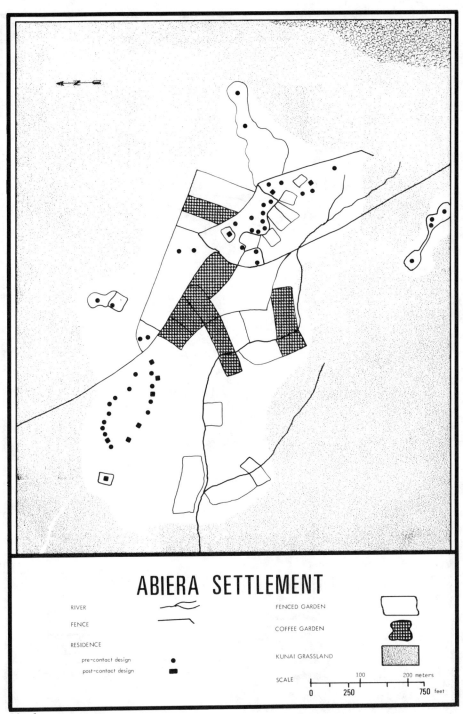

ABIERA SETTLEMENT

RIVER

FENCE

RESIDENCE

  pre-contact design

  post-contact design

FENCED GARDEN

COFFEE GARDEN

KUNAI GRASSLAND

SCALE

100   200 meters

0   250   750 feet

Map 1.

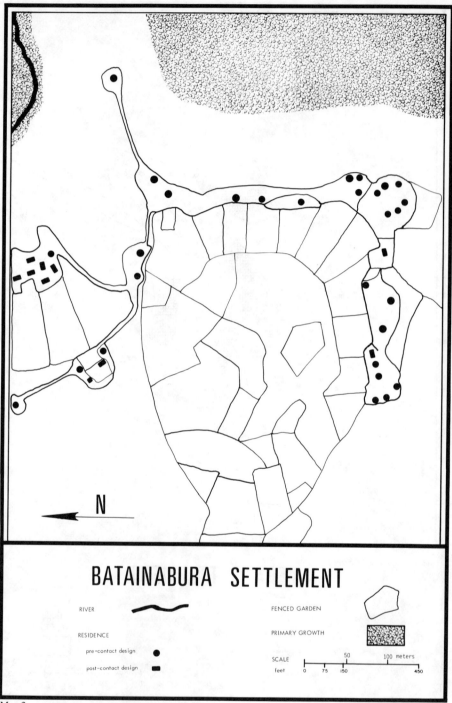

N

BATAINABURA SETTLEMENT

RIVER

RESIDENCE

　　pre-contact design   ●

　　post-contact design   ▬

FENCED GARDEN

PRIMARY GROWTH

SCALE   50   100 meters

feet   0   75   150   450

Map 2.

regard themselves as "bush people" in contrast to people such as the Tairora and Noraikora phratries. These they regard as *"kunai* men" or grasslanders. The Abiera in fact possess a small island of bush crowning the top of the ridge at the back of the village. This dwindling resource is carefully watched and jealously guarded from neighboring villages. One of these villages in particular—traditional enemies—is completely without trees except for bamboos and casuarinas that they themselves plant. The Abiera bush lacks game other than small birds; and the cutting of even a few living trees, especially ones of medium or manageable size for construction, may become an issue in the village. Individual rights to particular sections of the bush are vigorously asserted and sometimes vigorously contested.

The claim of the Batainabura to special knowledge, ability, resources, and ritual skills as "bush people" is generally acknowledged in the immediate vicinity, though it describes certain other Northern Tairora groups as well. Hunting, other than grassland birds and rats, is not unknown at Abiera, but one must go farther to find it—as well as using territory where one's rights are in some sense at the pleasure of others. By and large hunting in the forest is pursued more infrequently and by fewer men than at Batainabura, since it involves a long journey. Bush game and other foods are less often seen in the village than at Batainabura. Game such as snakes, moreover, is not only unfamiliar at Abiera but tends to be frightening or repugnant and unacceptable as food. At Batainabura a large python is a welcome—and of course substantial—addition to the supply of protein and fat. Cassowaries and the eggs of bush fowl are common enough to be well known at Batainabura, in addition to forest marsupials. Edible fungi and other plant material from the bush are readily available there for food, magic, or medicine.

A "bush people's" special knowledge, such as that pertaining to forest spirits, and their familiarity with the bush are in part a protection against its magical dangers. The grasslander's ignorance is said to be a hazard to him if he leaves the main paths or encounters certain of the forest's denizens. Some of the ritual of Batainabura has forest referents or is performed in a forest setting, and much of this apparently has no precise equivalent at Abiera. It is extremely doubtful that the Abiera have any sense of personal or cultural shortcoming as a counterpart to the Batainabura pride in bushmanship and forest lore. Indeed, they find many qualities of the grassland preferable, especially for horticulture. For that matter, a completely sylvan existence would not be easy even for the Batainabura to imagine, since they depend heavily on grassland gardens, although making some gardens in bush. Some of the pride of bush is aesthetic and emotional. Water from the bush tastes better, for example, and Batainabura groups who journey into the forest, perhaps to collect lianas, often return with as many bamboo tubes full of water as they can carry. The preoccupation of the grassland Abiera with the bush is more limited if not more urgent or utilitarian. Above all, they desire the strong vines and timber for framing houses and lashing together fences. Although grassland substitutes are possible, these materials, as well as firewood, come best from the forest. While no pinch is yet keenly felt, the Abiera are as conscious of the limitation of their forest resources as the Batainabura appear to feel theirs inexhaustible. The Batainabura, probably like other people with plentiful bush, tend to be lavish by grassland standards in their use of it.

Gardening and pig keeping supply most of the food for both communities. The greater emphasis on hunting at Batainabura constitutes no exception to the basic importance of horticulture and husbandry. The difference between the two communities in food derived from hunting is, in fact, small enough that detailed dietary statistics would probably be required to assess it properly. Nor is the difference likely to be reflected in a greater overall intake of protein at Batainabura. Pigs and the purchase of tinned meat and fish with money earned from wages or cash crops are a larger factor at Abiera and in dietary terms probably outweigh the lack of game. Practically all of Abiera's gardens are in grassland, and the best land lies in valley bottoms and on both sides of a major stream that flows past the foot of the slope on which the village is located. Here are grown all of the typical crops of the region: sweet potatoes, bananas, taro, yams, winged beans, maize, and several kinds of greens. The Abiera grow tree crops such as nut pandanus and areca palm and since the early fifties have planted increasing amounts of coffee. The latter is entirely a cash crop and today brings more money to the village than any other single source.

Pigs are numerous at Abiera and some 450 were counted in 1963. This figure probably only approximates the actual number. Abiera has built and maintains a segment of an extensive pig fence that runs for several miles through the territories of several Phratry Tairora villages. The fence separates pig range from the valley land where most of the gardens are located. The pigs are allowed to range freely on one side of the fence within an area of open grassland and bush. The fence, erected in recent years, is beyond the scale of any aboriginal structure. It obviates the fencing of individual gardens as long as they are not located in the "pig" zone. As a capital investment—in labor and materials—the long fence certainly reflects the introduction of steel tools for cutting and splitting palings. It also reflects the *pax australiana*, which has produced more stable settlements and overtly tranquil conditions in the area. Thus at least a minimum of cooperation is possible, even among communities that are in other respects hostile. Although the fencing project has drawn heavily for material on Abiera's limited bush resources, it is likely to represent a saving at least of labor. It encloses ample fallow land as well as present gardens and will not soon need to be moved to accommodate shifting gardens.

Some Abiera owners keep their pigs close to the village. They regularly feed them nearby, in some cases just by the fence that separates village from pig range. Pigs appear at their usual feeding points with regularity and most of the time seem to range within calling distance of the place where their owners feed them. Other owners establish pig ranges farther away, and a few keep their herds at a considerable distance, necessitating a walk of an hour or more to carry fodder (mainly undersized sweet potatos) to the animals. Feeding points can be recognized by the presence of well-beaten ground largely bare of vegetation and usually a shelter of some sort. This is typically a conical thatched roof supported by split palings.

Pig houses close to the village tend not to have enclosed walls but merely an open circle of posts supporting the roof, affording shade and shelter from the rain but little protection from the wind or the cold. Pig houses at a greater distance from the village may be more substantial, and some of them duplicate the residential dwellings to be found inside the village. Owners who have far to walk in tending their herds may use such a house as a temporary residence for themselves, overnight or for several days in inclement weather. This saves making a daily trip to the pigs or returning the same day to the village. In one case, an Abiera man keeps his pigs at such a distance as to require two families of his kinsmen to establish their permanent dwelling on his pig range. Like herding specialists, these people, though nominally villagers of Abiera, actually spend most of their time away from it. They do not maintain a full-scale residential base at Abiera, but can readily stay with relatives during visits to the village.

Such isolation would have been unthinkable before the cessation of open hostilities in this area. A well-known story describes the fate of two Abiera men who, before contact, built a house outside the village in order to shelter them while they hunted rats in the *kunai*. Though at no great distance, they were surprised by enemies of Abiera and were attacked. Both were injured and one of them died of his wounds before help could reach them.

At Batainabura more of the gardens occupy crests and hillside slopes than at Abiera. The local terrain differs in some respects, partly accounting for the difference; but an additional factor is fear of a nearby Noraikora group. The presence of this group in the valley below them, the Batainabura say, makes it unsafe to garden in some of the grassland area to which they lay claim. Developing other land involves the labor of clearing gardens in the bush. They do not consider bush soils inferior to grassland, especially for crops such as taro. Indeed, a number of small gardens are in use or old ones in the process of being abandoned in the bush. The initial task of clearing, however, tends to limit the use of bush and its rate of conversion to garden land. Since there is no inclination to abandon grassland gardens that are yielding adequately, and since few people if any consider bush gardens inherently superior, the acreage ratio seems to favor what is now grassland. Present grassland in most cases may have been bush in the past, and in some cases the past is apparently fairly recent.

The major crops of Batainabura are essentially those of the Abiera inventory, but their relative importance is not entirely the same. Yams receive relatively little attention at Batainabura compared with Abiera, which has several sizable yam gardens. Batainabura gardeners say they see no reason to give more attention to yams, though aware that in other areas this crop is important. According to the local tradition, both pigs and the winged bean (*Psophocarpus tetragonolobus*) originated in Batainabura territory. The claim is made that Batainabura bean seed is often eagerly sought by people from elsewhere. Yet there is little evidence in their present gardens to suggest better plants or more emphasis on the cultivation of the winged bean than in other parts of the area. Casuarinas are grown but are not as numerous or systematically propagated as at grassland Abiera. Coffee production is as yet on a smaller scale, and sales are infrequent, since traders have little reason to have their vehicles call regularly for Batainabura coffee. Such visits are now almost a weekly occurrence at Abiera.

The keeping of fowl is common only at Batainabura. Although dogs have the run of the village there as well as at Abiera, only the latter consider that the depredations of dogs make keeping chickens impossible. Batainabura chickens roost about on roofs or in the lower branches of trees. Both sorts of roosts are readily available at Abiera. If it is not the greater opportunities for Batainabura dogs to hunt in the nearby bush, therefore, that accounts for the different attitudes in this matter, one must suspect local differences in the

Sow being deloused and petted by her owners with whom she is much at ease.

training and habits of dogs. Fowl are used mostly for their flesh, the eggs being gathered rather indifferently.

Pigs range more freely within Batainabura territory than at Abiera and have access to much of the village itself. Some pig shelters are located within the residential area and none is found at such a distance as a number of those at Abiera. No single barrier separates pig range from gardens, and each garden or groups of gardens must accordingly be fenced. Though in a few cases two or more gardens are protected by a common fence, the nearest approach to the long fence of Abiera is a sizable enclosure on the hillside immediately below the residential area. Within this are found the gardens of a number of families but probably less than half the garden area of the village. Neither this enclosure nor the next largest one at Batainabura involves intervillage arrangements. Moreover, the fences tend to be built to protect only gardens presently under cultivation, including a small amount of addi-

Woman sewing pandanus leaves together, using a needle of flying fox rib, to make a mat for sleeping or for protection from sun or rain.

tional, fallow land. As gardens are shifted, therefore, new fences have to be constructed to protect them. Sometimes the material can be gotten by dismantling the fences of gardens no longer in use. New lianas will be needed in any case. Thus the Batainabura pattern, although it may permit the individual to be more flexible in locating his gardens and managing his own fencing, is overall more costly than the long fence pattern of Abiera. As far as the cost in bush resources alone is concerned, to be sure, Batainabura is better able to afford such an expense.

Like those of Abiera, most Batainabura gardens are encircled, either singly or in small clusters. Since the pattern of gardens and houses is more broken at Batainabura, it might be more difficult to devise a single barrier to control the pigs. Batainabura more nearly represents the old pattern in this respect than Abiera, however, since it not only lacks the postcontact innovation of the single communal fence, enclosing both gardens and fallow land, but still allows pigs and humans to share almost completely the same living space. In both cases, the aboriginal practice was to house pigs—sows and immature piglets—in the dwelling of the women who tended them, usually the wives of the men who owned or had been lent the pigs.

The number of pigs at Batainabura, like the number for Abiera, is known only approximately. Enumeration is difficult because of the more distant pig ranges, especially at Abiera, and the need ideally to visit each shelter or feeding station at a time when all the animals could be counted. One can also ask the owners, of course, but some of them may give an inaccurate count of their herds, for one reason or another. Batainabura, in any case, appears to have far fewer pigs than Abiera, with perhaps 120, compared with Abiera's 450. For roughly the same number of people this means that Abiera has almost four times as many pigs—a ratio that tends to confirm the view that grassland peoples have larger herds in this area than do bush peoples.

Abiera pig breeders apparently work harder and more systematically to increase their herds, as well as having a better situation in which to do so. The maintenance of herds—and sometimes herders—at considerable remove from the village is consistent with both the pig statistics and with Abiera's greater emphasis on husbandry. By itself the exclusion of pigs from a sizable garden zone at Abiera would not compel breeders to establish their pigs far afield. If their herds were as small as those at Batainabura, that is, the amount of range land immediate to the village would probably be adequate for most of the animals. A number of Abiera pig breeders say that there is too much active magic near the village, however, so that, if kept there, their pigs become sickly or die. Thus they establish ranges farther away, in effect reducing the concentration of pigs in the immediate vicinity of the village, lowering pressure on land, and increasing the supply of forage food the pigs can root up.

The allegation of danger to pigs from magical sources refers to fellow villagers who may be manipulating potent materials, though not necessarily for the purpose of causing harm to pigs. It may also reflect some threshold of overcrowding with a consequent rise in endemic pig disease. Despite the extra effort required, in any case, Abiera husbandmen continue to raise large herds. Batainabura pig breeders, as noted, see no detriment in keeping their pigs at close range—within the village. Batainabura's less intensive husbandry probably does not arise from any failure to appreciate the importance of an expandable range for increasing the size of the herd. It may reflect their easier access to protein from bush sources. It may also reflect their less favorable situation, with the threat of enemies in the path of much of their most logical range land, the bush at their back where pigs can easily go astray or be stolen, or the less productive gardens from which to obtain fodder for pigs. It is possible that these or other limiting factors in some combination frequently coincide in the case of "bush" peoples. In that case, *kunai* peoples would tend to be the more intensive husbandmen. Batainabura's beleaguered situation should not be overlooked, however—unless that too is also typical of bush peoples compared with grassland peoples, under conditions like those in Northern Tairora.

No count of dogs was made. Dogs are numerous in both villages but probably more so at Batainabura. Dogs are used for food from time to time in both Batainabura and Abiera but are rarely bred or acquired primarily for this purpose. The contribution of the dog as a hunting animal is recognized everywhere in the region, but hunting plays little part in the lives of many owners of dogs. It must be inferred, thus, that the dog often serves mainly as a guardian and a companion. Lurking sorcerers and other possible malefactors, human or superhuman, are frequently reported or suspected in Northern Tairora villages. The starveling dogs of New Guinea vociferously announce the visitor, welcome or unwelcome, and their value on this account alone may be sufficient to repay their small keep. Sorcery and ambush, after all, are life-and-death matters.

CENSUS DATA: COMPARISON OF THE POPULATIONS OF ABIERA
AND BATAINABURA

Abiera, with a population of 188, and Batainabura, with 187, seem well matched in size. The numbers vary in either case, depending on when the census is carried out. The two villages were censused roughly six months apart. The present figures thus represent the situation of approximately July–August 1963 at Abiera and approximately February–March 1964 at Batainabura. In both cases the immediate village area with its cluster of dwellings was taken as defining "residents." Abiera's population would be greater if one included a number of connected persons forming two small, named clusters farther up the ridge, a distance of a mile away, and two families (nine persons) living on a pig range several miles distant and on the other side of the ridge. Batainabura had no such outliers and only two isolated dwellings. Both of these were within sight or sound of some of the rest, and the personnel appear in the central points of the village almost daily. As neither could

be considered a residential nucleus in its own right, or be assigned to the
territory or society of any other local group, the occupants are included as
"residents" of Batainabura. With a broader, less spatial sense of "residents"
or attached persons, Abiera's population would exceed Batainabura's by over
a score. Under precontact conditions, prior to today's evident decentraliza-
tion, there would hardly have been such outliers as today, and Abiera would
clearly have been the larger community.

No significant number of persons were absent from either village (e.g., on
labor service) at the time of census. Some persons died or were born during
the field period but after the census was completed. Such changes are not
reflected in the present figures. A long-time resident of Abiera in pique
moved his family to a neighboring group just before the census. These persons are excluded from the figures. Such minor fluctuations are more or less
constant, and in any case it seems expedient to construct a census that describes the actual situation of a given moment.

The age and sex composition of each village can be seen in population
pyramids, figures 1 and 2. Except for children born during the field period,
ages were estimated by inspection and from genealogies. Neither birth dates
nor chronological ages are known for anyone else. Since intervals of ten years
were used for all ages over ten, observer error may not be serious, particularly for internal comparisons. Graphically, these two Northern Tairora communities appear much alike, especially considering that in such small populations even small differences will stand out. Both groups have somewhat
more females of all ages than males (Abiera 54 percent of the total, Batainabura 52 percent). The ages of several individuals were not closely estimated

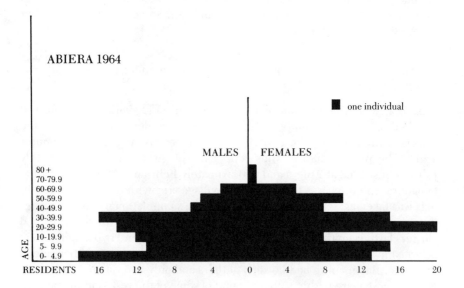

Fig. 1.   Age-sex pyramid, Abiera

at the time of the census, although they can be known within a few years. Nearly all are under twenty. They appear in the population pyramids, however, only when they can be assigned to a specific age category. Adding these persons to the totals gives for Abiera and Batainabura, respectively, almost the same number of males (forty, thirty-nine) and females (thirty-eight, thirty-six) of less than twenty, roughly the age of marriage. Here in both cases males slightly outnumber females, indicating that the excess of females occurs predominantly among the adult population. Naturally when a finer breakdown is made, comparison between the two communities reveals greater differences. Abiera, for instance, has several more male children under five than Batainabura and about twice the number between ten and twenty. In precontact times, such a difference between hostile groups might well have been serious for the one with the smaller male cohorts of fighting age. At the same time, Batainabura has appreciably more children of both sexes between five and ten than Abiera.

The population of both communities tends to drop off appreciably above the age of forty, roughly the limit of childbearing for women, though Batainabura has more persons over this age (fifty to Abiera's forty) and apparently fewer persons in the most active years of adult life, from twenty to forty (Batainabura's fifty-six to Abiera's sixty-four). In both communities there are more females in both cohorts (see table 2).

These demographic differences between the two communities, speaking generally, tend to underscore a well-recognized effect of scale. In small populations, small variations from one period to another in birthrate or sex ratio at birth may not "average out" and thus are magnified. The scale effect is not without social and cultural consequences. Such differences may con-

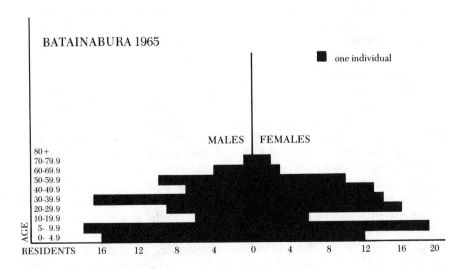

Fig. 2.   Age-sex pyramid, Batainabura

TABLE 2
POPULATION OF ABIERA AND BATAINABURA
BY AGE AND SEX

Age and Sex	Abiera	Batainabura
0-9.9		
Male	32	32
Female	33	31
Total	65	63
10-19.9		
Male	11	5
Female	8	7
Total	19	12
20-39.9		
Male	29	26
Female	35	30
Total	64	56
40 and over		
Male	15	22
Female	25	28
Total	40	50

tribute positively or negatively to the community's viability, or they may limit a community, if it is to remain viable, to certain options. Options of residence, loyalty, aggressiveness, outmarriage, wealth, exchange, adoption, or alliance are likely to be influenced by some judgment of communal prospects. Communal prospects depend on the personnel of a given age and sex available for given significant functions such as childbearing, food producing, or fighting. Moreover, there is evidence that these facts of life are generally recognized among the Northern Tairora. That is, they consciously enter into individual and communal calculations.

A relative deficit of surviving male children for a five- or ten-year period would, under precontact conditions, eventually affect the fighting strength of the group. Diminished fighting strength would adversely affect not only a group's ability to hold its territory and ultimately its pigs and women against other groups, but would tend to lead friends and kinsmen to avoid giving brides to such a weakened group or to avoid cultivating them as allies if alternative, more rewarding alliances were possible. Without a certain inflow of outside brides, a group might then be forced to marry women from within a smaller circle, thus further reducing its claims to the wealth and strength of possible affinal kinsmen or allies. Strength attracts strength, and strong groups readily make allies as well as withstanding enemies. In precontact times probably the principal option for members of a seriously weakened group was to leave their territory and, as refugees, join other local groups with sufficient land but perhaps insufficient manpower. In this way, relatively weak groups might reinforce each other.

Potential host groups apparently did not always exist for a beleaguered group. The chance to kill at little cost must be balanced against the value of recruiting new members. A weak and vulnerable group was a temptation. With reduced fighting power and without strong allies a group could go under for good. If not wholly annihilated before the survivors found refuge, it could at least be destroyed forever as a separate social entity with a name, a territory, and a continuity of its own. It is probably no longer possible to know how many local groups suffered this fate. Such a fate was certainly known, however, because Batainabura men of forty years or more can vividly remember the Oqinata, a neighboring group of Tairora speech. They laughingly refer to these people as "our game," likening the ease and lack of risk in killing them to that of hunting maruspials.

Batainabura has itself been a beleaguered group, spending several periods in refuge within recent memory. Given the precontact ecology of group survival, Batainabura's present prospects would seem quite poor. Besides its historical weakness, it has few males in the range from ten to twenty years and few again in the vital fighting years from twenty to thirty.

How does a small community with Batainabura's population profile now fare in competition with its neighbors? Ecological pressures on local groups change markedly once the *pax australiana* guarantees security against open attack. With little regard for the numbers or influence of the victimized group, the government punishes killings, the theft of pigs, and the seduction or alienation of women. Endogamic choices may now be made with something like impunity, since a major reason for sending brides to other groups has been removed. On the other hand, the Batainabura people may live less well today than the Abiera, being crowded onto less land or land less desirable for pig ranges and gardens. Nor can they now take steps to remedy their plight by allocating their personnel in one way or another. The new politics of parliamentary representation (since 1965) has yet to assume a direct relationship to the perennial pigs-wives-and-gardens issues of village life. Voting strength, unity, and electoral politics may in due course affect the case, but until that time Abiera's or Batainabura's manpower can affect principally the intervillage flow of women, pigs, and other wealth. Land is not yet freely alienable from poor landholders to rich ones, or reassignable from land-rich communities to the land-poor. The possible applications of wealth are therefore confined, more than formerly, to immediate consumption and the prestige of ownership or exchange.

CENSUS DATA: HOUSEHOLD COMPOSITION

Within the settlements as defined, Abiera had forty-three occupied dwellings or separate households while Batainabura, with thirty, had appreciably fewer. The number of occupants per dwelling, accordingly, was much lower

Tairora Culture

for Abiera (4.4) than for Batainabura (6.2). Tables 3 and 4 give the number of occupants in relation to houses for each village. Related differences are numerous and perceptible. For example, a three-person dwelling is by far the most common, or modal, household at Abiera, while at Batainabura a five-person dwelling is by a smaller margin the commonest. Abiera's three persons are in practically all (eleven) cases a wife, a husband, and a child—their own or adopted. At Batainabura there is no such consistency. The largest number of occupants for a single dwelling, seventeen, is found at Batainabura, while Abiera's largest is eleven. The seventeen persons consist of three men, their wives and children, and the aged parents of one of the wives; and the household of eleven is a man with his three wives and their children, one of which, a son, was just married at the time of census. The median occupant at Abiera lives in a household of five, as contrasted with eight at Batainabura. Thus, while half or more of Abiera lives in households of five or fewer, half of Batainabura lives in households of at least eight.

TABLE 3
ABIERA HOUSEHOLD SIZE AND COMPOSITION

Number of Occupants	Number of Houses	Adult Occupants, Male (M) and Female (F)											
		1 M 1 F	1 F	2 M 2 F	2 F	1 M 2 F	2 M 3 F	1 M	2 M 1 F	2 M 4 F	3 M 2 F	1 M 3 F	2 M
1	2		1					1					
2	7	3	2	1									1
3	11	10	1										
4	7	6				1							
5	5	2					2		1				
6	4	3		1									
7	0												
8	4			1			1			1	1		
9	2			1			1						
10	0												
11	1											1	

Neither village has its precontact pattern of residence, and there is perhaps no obvious sense in which, strictly speaking, one can be described as more traditional in this respect than the other. The traditional residence pattern involved the coresidence of the adult or initiated men in large "men's houses" (*baira*), while a married woman, her unmarried daughters, and uninitiated sons lived in separate, small houses. Batainabura's larger households may in one sense be closer to the precontact pattern than the smaller households of Abiera. Moreover, in some cases, several adult Batainabura males and their wives and children shared the same household. One could suppose that this meant bringing in the women and children of these men but without sacrificing the tradition of male coresidence.

TABLE 4

BATAINABURA HOUSEHOLD SIZE AND COMPOSITION

Number of Occupants	Number of Houses	Adult Occupants, Male (M) and Female (F)												
		1M	1M	2M	1M	2M	2M	1M	1M	2M	3M	3M	4M	4M
		1F	2F	3F		1F	2F	1F	3F	4F	4F	2F	2F	4F
1	2				2									
2	2	1					1							
3	3	1	1									1		
4	4	2	2											
5	6	1	1	1			2		1					
6	3	1	1			1								
7	1		1											
8	2			1								1		
9	1		1											
10	2					1							1	
11	0													
12	1		1											
13	2		1							1				
14	0													
15	0													
16	0													
17	1													1

The small household of a single man and his wife and child(ren) is more common at Abiera than at Batainabura. From the standpoint of the large men's house, Abiera's modal three-person dwelling seems radically at odds with the past. Yet here one could argue that instead of moving wife and children into what was a modified "men's house," the man has simply joined them in their own small, separate residence. Accepting that the clustering of men in large, exclusively male households was the key fact of the older pattern, with the men's house a sort of communal nerve center, the separate women's houses of the past could be seen as simply a necessary but adjunct arrangement. The coresidence of adult males would then become the principle that has continued with less change at Batainabura than at Abiera. One effect of the larger average households, however, is also to aggregate married women under fewer roofs than formerly. Thus the contrast with the past is inescapable whatever view is taken.

Without atttempting to weigh every conceivable point, I feel that Abiera has evolved farther than Batainabura from the former pattern. It has at least given expression to a larger proportion of residentially independent nuclear families. It has also abandoned the men's house, as both a physical symbol and a residential fact. A comparable change in a large modern society would be seen at once as having far-reaching psychological, economic, and sociological implications. Because these are remote villages with small populations, however, the apparent magnitude of the change is likely to be underestimated. A recital of the bare facts of "housing" is only superficial.

Apart from the size of households, one important change is almost completely realized in both villages. This is the continuous residential association of cohabiting spouses, in contrast to their residential separation in the past. The change, involving the abandonment of the men's house, was well advanced in most if not all Northern Tairora communities in the 1950s or even earlier. The rapidity of loss of this invariable feature of precontact communities raises some interesting questions about the beliefs and sentiments that had previously supported it, and in particular the relation of residential segregation to ideas of male prowess, female contamination, and the fighting potential of a community. Even here, however, there are lingering expressions apparently related to former practice, and at times certain husbands live with other men or alone in houses separate from their wives. There were two such cases at the time of census in Batainabura. Both were men with two wives. Furthermore, there had been a men's house only a few months prior to census. It caught fire (from arson, it was flatly stated) and partly burned in 1963, but was destined to be rebuilt for further service as an all-male domicile. With the agreement of the owners, I commissioned its repair and rented it for living and working quarters. Except for these accidents of timing, the Batainabura census might have included a larger number of instances of separate residence for married males as well as a residence resembling the men's house of yore.

At Abiera all monogamously married men lived much of the time with their wives at the date of census. Eight of thirty-one—about one man in four—lived in the same household with another man, his wife, and usually their children if any. Two other, monogamously married men each shared a house with a polygynously married man and at least one of his wives. Two men who each had two wives also shared a single household—including one wife of each.

At Batainabura all of thirty monogamously married men resided with their wives, though in one case the wife shifted back and forth between her husband's house and that of her widower father. Here, however, nineteen of thirty, almost two-thirds of these couples, were coresident with others, including one household of three such couples and one of four. A polygynously married man and one of his wives also shared the household of three mentioned above, making it in effect a household of four coresident, married men and wives. In two additional cases, monogamously married couples coresided with a polygynously married man, one with one and one with both of his wives, under the same roof. Two further polygynously married men shared a single house at Batainabura, with the result that of a total of forty-three married men, forty-one of them lived with their wives or, if polygynous, with at least one wife. Roughly three-fifths of these men were coresident with other adult married males. At Abiera all married men lived with their wives or with at least one of them, but only fourteen of thirty-nine such men (36 percent) shared the same domicile with other married men. Thus, although the residential pattern of both communities varies from the past, when it comes to the residence of spouses Abiera's seems to have moved farther in the direction of an independent residence for the nuclear family.

There were no men over twenty who had never been married at Batainabura and only two (age thirty and sixty) at Abiera. Batainabura had one widower (fifty-two) who had long lived as a bachelor. Presumably he was not too old to remarry nor did he lack a potential wife. I shall accordingly consider him one of the three bachelors in these two censuses. Batainabura had one unmarried young man of about eighteen and Abiera three of about twenty. Brides would presumably be found for these men. Abiera had two widowers in their sixties and Batainabura three, indicating that beyond the age of perhaps fifty or fifty-five, remarriage becomes unlikely for a man. There were eight widows at Abiera, all but one in or past their sixties. A single, thirty-nine-year-old widow was in mourning during census and remarried subsequently. Abiera had three divorced women (forty-five, fifty-three, and sixty) and Batainabura one (thirty-five). The hand of the latter woman was actively being sought at the time of census, and she would probably marry again as soon as rival claims to her had been worked out. Neither Abiera nor Batainabura had spinsters in the sense of women never married. Abiera had one divorcée, an albinic woman of about thirty-three, perhaps destined not to remarry.

In fine, a large majority of men of twenty or over were married (thirty-nine of forty-six at Abiera; forty-three of forty-eight at Batainabura). The same is true of women over about eighteen (forty-nine of sixty-two at Abiera; fifty-four of fifty-nine at Batainabura). I conclude that in both groups males beyond twenty are almost certain to be married and are likely to remarry, if widowed or divorced, up to the age of fifty or so. Beyond the age of fifty-five to sixty, they are unlikely to remarry, whether or not single women are available. Women of eighteen are even more likely to marry than men and equally likely as divorcées or widows to remarry up to the age of forty-five to fifty. From the age of perhaps fifty-five or so they are unlikely to remarry, but they usually remain in the community, even if originally from elsewhere, becoming household heads in their own right or joining other such women or living in the households of their married children.

Judging from the small sample of three perennial bachelors in these two villages, bachelors may be men lacking in vigor or forcefulness. They may be undersized by average standards (two cases); but size alone is not a good qualification, obviously, since far more small men are married than are not. Stories are frequently told, moreover, of small men who were redoubtable fighters or forceful in village affairs. Nevertheless the stories seem to imply that they had these qualities *despite* small size. Thus it is reasonable to predict that bachelors may be men outwardly lacking in assertiveness, or somewhat lacking in assertiveness and deficient in physique, or deformed men.

The one widowed or divorced woman of marriageable age in this sample

who seemed unlikely to remarry was the albino previously mentioned.
While not attractive of face, she was not deformed or negatively distinguished in other ways in manner or physique. The conclusion would probably hold that a woman between the ages of eighteen and forty-five is almost
certain to be married in Northern Tairora if not abnormal in physique or
mentality—unless, of course, she was too recently widowed. Albinic women
do not necessarily remain unmaried, and certainly not albinic men, but the
condition seems to have a negative effect on an individual's marriage prospects. Albinos are relatively numerous among the Northern Tairora, though
there was only one in these two local populations.

The residence of unmarried men beyond the age of initiation would not
have been an issue in the days of the men's house. Young, unmarried men
now tend to find residence with their fathers or in the household of a married
elder brother or other male relative. Judging from Batainabura and Abiera,
confirmed bachelors tend to live alone or reside either with other unmarried
men, such as widowers, or with married men living separately from their
wives. One Abiera widower lived with a divorced daughter, an arrangement
similar to that of a Batainabura widower who lived with a married daughter
and her two children, her husband residing in a separate house where she
frequently visited.

The residence of widows and spinsters today may not represent a basic
change from the past, since in the area of these villages there was no common domicile for women, married or unmarried. Abiera widows tend to live
alone if very old (one case), with other widows or divorcées (two cases), with
the adolescent or marriageable daughters of other persons (three widows,
five girls), or with their married sons or nephews (two cases). At Batainabura, on the other hand, three of four widows lived with married sons and
their wives and the fourth with a married daughter, her husband, and their
children, in a household shared with another married couple and their children. The Batainabura tendency toward composite and larger households
thus also includes widows.

In both villages, children of living parents live predominantly, up to the
age of marriage, with one or, if coresident, both parents (sixty-two of
seventy-eight at Abiera; seventy-six of seventy-eight at Batainabura). The
two communities differ appreciably, however, beyond this fact. At Abiera
ten children having at least one living parent—in most cases both—resided
in households other than those of their parent(s). These children were not
formally adopted, however, but were merely being "looked after" in the
households where they resided. Nine of the ten, moreover, were girls, ranging in age from four to eighteen. In seven cases the children resided in
households without children besides themselves or with others like themselves, similarly being looked after. The lone boy was the brother of two girls
who were being looked after. Two fathers contributed half of these ten children—one father two of them, the other father three. Both fathers were
identifiable as polygynists, men with other children, ambitious and impor-

tant men of the community. One was the *luluai*, the government-appointed village headman, the other the *tultul*, his government-appointed lieutenant. A reasonable interpretation is that girls in particular are farmed out by men who have other children of their own. They are usually sent to female guardians who either lack children, female children, or children of this age. The girls when old enough can help the women in the gardens, making a contribution to the households where they reside and in some cases providing companionship for otherwise solitary widows. The relationship so established will presumably also entitle the guardians to a share in the bride wealth when the girls marry. At Batainabura there is no comparable case of guardianship of children having living parents without formal adoption.

The practice of adoption also varies appreciably between the two communities, with six adopted children at Abiera but only two at Batainabura. All six Abiera adoptees were males, moreover, and all were adopted by men with barren wives. In one case the adoptive father's second wife had a daughter. In another the adoptive father had three wives, all childless. All six adoptive children lived in households of modal size—three consisting of themselves and the adopting parents. One is tempted to say of Abiera that only female children are sent to guardians and only male children are given in adoption, being invariably adopted by men with childless wives. The emphasis on a woman's having a child to rear seems a reasonable inference as much as the need of a childless man for a child. The preference of adopting parents for a male child is also strongly indicated. A possible counterargument is that male children may be more readily available for adoption than females. This would be true if the parents have other sons but wish to retain title to *daughters* in order to receive bride wealth. In my judgment, however, it is the wishes of the adoptive parents as much as the willingness of the real parents that determines the preferred sex.

Batainabura had two cases of adoption, one of them a girl. In only one case, moveover, was the adoptive mother childless. Baitainabura had no cases of foster children, whose parents were dead, and there was only one at Abiera, where a brother-in-law had taken the foster child into his household.

For two communities with the same number of children, there is thus an appreciable difference in the proportion of those who are formally alienated from their own parents or who reside for long periods, if not until marriage, in households other than those of their parents. At Baitainabura this is 3 percent of the total number of children, while at Abiera it is 22 percent. It may be relevant, of course, that Abiera has a higher proportion of nuclear households that include only one parental figure or pair of parents.

MONOGAMY, POLYGNY, AND MARITAL RESIDENCE OF WIVES

The majority of censused marriages in both villages are monogamous. Thirty-one of thirty-nine Abiera married men (80 percent) and thirty of forty-three Baitainabura married men (70 percent) had only one wife. At Abiera five men had two wives each and three men had three. No man in either village had more than three wives. At Baitainabura there were twelve men, possibly thirteen, with two wives each but none with more than two. The number of Abiera women with cowives, thus, is nineteen of forty-nine (39 percent) while at Baitainabura it is twenty-six of fifty-six (46 percent).

The "degree" of polygyny of these two villages can be compared in three ways. Baitainabura is more polygynous than Abiera in the percentage of its married women with cowives, as it is also in having more polygynists (thirteen to Abiera's eight). If degree of polygyny were measured by the maximum number of wives married by a single man, however, Abiera would be more polygynous, with its maximum of three.

It is difficult to compare the present directly with the past in any sense but the last. For convenience, I shall refer to this aspect of polygyny as its "intensity." In this respect, at least, (some) men of the past were reportedly far more polygynous. A few of them had many more than three wives. Mátoto, an outstanding big man of Abiera who was killed about 1930, was said to have "at least twenty wives," and names were in fact recalled for a majority of them. Clearly one or more of the relevant conditions formerly favoring polygyny have changed.

A superficial explanation often given by Northern Tairora villagers in accounting for the loss of former practices is that the "mission," or sometimes the "government," has forbidden them. It is agreed by all the villagers that the "mission" and probably also the "government" oppose polygyny. This explanation certainly does not sound out of place in accounting for the decline of plural marriages. Yet it is clear that, despite the wishes of the government or the "mission," polygyny is far from having disappeared in either censused village. Nor are the polygynists all older men. Indeed, polygynous men may not be radically fewer than they were in precontact times, although some informants believe this to be the case. There must therefore be some factors still present that make more than one wife desirable for some men while other factors, which formerly accounted for the large number of wives of at least some men, have been counteracted or eliminated.

It is largely men who are—or in their prime have been—more forceful and ambitious than others who are the notable polygyists. A big man or an aspirant tends to need more than one wife, just as in the past a big man was practically by definition a man with a number of wives. At Abiera two of the men with three wives are forceful and ambitious. The wives of the third, however, are all childless, giving this polygynist a special reason for marrying additional wives. (Subsequently he adopted a son.) He is, in any case, reputed as a forceful and ambitious man. Abiera's polygynists, and especially its most intensive polygynists, are relatively prominent men; and most of the more prominent men are, have been, or are said to wish to become polygynists.

The value of having a number of wives is clear from the value of having one: notably the importance of begetting children (especially male children), possessing large gardens, and owning numerous pigs. All of these assets depend primarily on having wives to produce them. In the economic sense, the desire of an ambitious man for such assets is practically limitless. Within his capacity to manage these assets—or to control his several wives in producing them—he would not soon, in theory, reach satiety. Certainly he would not with two or three wives.

Prominence and power are, to be sure, a two-way street. These attributes have a feedback relation to the means required to achieve them. It takes some promise and some wealth or power—one's kinsmen's if not one's own—to get a first wife, or at least a highly desirable wife, one that is industrious and strong as well as, perhaps, comely. It does not become easier, by and large, to get a second or a third wife in her prime years. (With fighting, the number of young widows was presumably greater and the levirate perhaps more often a benefit to the wifeless brother or ambitious polygynist.) Unless a man has achieved a certain standing that makes him—through his own efforts plus perhaps those of his kinsmen—a likely recipient from their point of view, those with a woman to give will probably not favor him. Today's economy does not provide the same outlets—above all, warfare and the exchanges it occasioned—for a sufficiently forceful and ambitious man to achieve the prominence of the big men of the past. There is little question that women often became wives of such a man in part because their kinsmen wanted it. There could be no doubt of the value of such a marital alliance to the givers of women. Additional women, though probably not unproductive, then became in some degree a mark of affinal esteem and a status symbol. Up to a certain point, the productivity of women was needed to help the ambitious man become a big man. Beyond that point they served more to ratify his status and enlarge his influence. In the early 1960s the management of wives and the wealth they could produce no longer offered a man such scope for aggrandizement. In the same sense it no longer affords the givers of wives comparable advantages, apart from the bride price and subsequent affinal reciprocities.

What of the libidinal aspects of intensive polygny? Perhaps because polygny is so often attributed by Western laymen largely to lechery, anthropologists have countered by emphasizing the economic and social aspects of plural marriage. In any case, Northern Tairora men of today make it clear that many of them regard sexual intercourse as one of the most urgent and unremitting pleasures of life. They expect a man—or some men—to be attracted by and to have sexual relations with various women, limited only by opportunity. Unless Northern Tairora men in the recent past were less lusty, perhaps because of possessing outlets for their energies—notably fighting—no longer available to their heirs, a man could desire additional women because they attracted him sexually as well as for their obvious economic advantages.

It is difficult, however, to argue sexuality as the principal reason for pre-contact polygyny. For one thing, the decline of intensive polygyny since contact would be harder to explain. The increasing ease of adultery—the decreasing likelihood or severity of retaliation—may, to be sure, have lessened slightly the libidinal pressure for polygyny. There is also, by inference, a demographic factor in the decline of intensive polygyny. This is the probable change in the sexual imbalance in adults, with males now more nearly equal in number to females. Women and children enjoyed no precontact immunity to killing from ambush, in the garden, or in the forest. Despite the frequent killing of women, however, men were even more exposed and probably perished more often as a direct or indirect result of enemy attack. If that is true—and the impression from genealogies suggests it, relatively more women may have been available for marriage before open warfare ceased. As noted above, levirate rights may have been invoked more often. The opportunity for polygyny would increase with age and seniority through the operation of the levirate. Hence if male mortality has been decreasing, the proportion of levirate inheritance of women will also decline. An equally intensive polygyny today, therefore, would oblige some men, especially men in smaller and less influential communities, to wait longer or to pay more for brides.

As to residence, cowives—or their husbands—behave differently at Abiera from the way they behave at Batainabura. One can compare only instances of two cowives, however, since Batainabura presented no other form of polygyny at the time of census. Since the dynamics of a triad—three cowives—would probably differ from that of a dyad, moreover, these comments need not be supposed to apply more broadly. At Abiera, all men having two wives coreside with at least one of them, but only one man lives under the same roof with both of his wives. Thus in only one case in five do the cowives live together—in this case with their husband. At Batainabura, with over twice the number of men having two wives, eight, or two-thirds of the total pairs of cowives live together. In six of these cases the husband lives with them. In two cases the cowives live together, the husband in another house. There are three instances of husbands at Batainabura who live apart from both of their wives, though in each case in an adjacent house. When the cowives are separated, it is, in both villages, because only one lives with the husband. In all Batainabura cases the other wife lives somewhat apart, rather than in a house adjacent to the husband's. In one case she lives in another village several hours' walk distant. At Abiera, though the cases are fewer, the tendency is even clearer for two cowives, residentially separated, to live at some distance from each other, though within the same village.

In the three Abiera cases of men with three wives, one finds a variety of residential combinations. No husband lives apart from all three of his wives, nor is there any case of the three cowives each living separately. In one case the husband lives with one wife, and the other two wives live together next door; another husband lives with two wives; and the third man has a large household with all three, their children, and a young man who later brought his new bride to join them. As far as the residence of cowives (but not the husbands) is concerned, there seem to be a precontact precedent for all the combinations represented in either of the present censuses. In the past, strong men with more numerous wives appear to have had some of them living in different hamlets or local groups, a pattern that appears only once in the present population. There are, of course, no instances of men with the large number of wives of the strong men of yore. From very limited data, there is a suggestion that the nearest modern equivalent of the political strong man tends to develop a large household, keeping there two or more of his wives as well as other persons attached to him through involvement in his enterprises.

It is worth emphasizing for subsequent discussion that the coresidence of cowives and their husbands with them is a good deal more frequent at Batainabura than at Abiera. One must exclude Abiera's triads, as noted, since Batainabura has none. Thus two-thirds of Batainabura cowives coreside, but only one of five pairs of Abiera cowives coreside. The husband lives with both wives in six of the eight cases at Batainabura—something that does not occur at all at Abiera. Can one infer that there is less friction between polygynous husbands and their wives, or between cowives, at Batainabura? Are the men and women of that group, as persons, more tolerant and less given to jealousy than Abiera polygynists and cowives? Batainabura's larger household should of course be recalled. Do Batainabura cowives live with each other or live with their husbands more often than not in large households where other families or persons also live? Just the opposite appears to be the case. In five of eight pairs of coresident cowives at Batainabura the household contained no other family. One of these pairs of cowives lived with no one else in a household of two—separate, that is, from their husband. In two additional cases the "other family" was another pair of cowives with their husband and his children—in other words, a household of two polygynous families. In the eighth case the cowives shared a house with a man and his wife, and one other married woman—who did not coreside with her polygynist husband. In four of the six cases where the husband lived with both his wives there was no other family, although the husband's widowed mother lives in one such household. The other two cases are the two coresident polygynous families already referred to, a household of thirteen but including no other family.

It is hard to resist the inference that Batainabura people have less inclination than Abiera people to segregate cowives or their husbands residentially. The large households of Batainabura generally suggest less desire to live apart in small domestic units. The ease of constructing additional houses at Batainabura should not be a factor—or, if one, should have the opposite effect. Batainabura, not Abiera, has the ampler resources in building materials. Were they disposed to live in separate domiciles, therefore, the housing should be no obstacle. Whether personality factors expressed in a tolerance or a positive taste for more numerous coresidence can be credited with the difference between the two communities, or whether the greater use of trade goods—especially trade goods paid for in wages or coffee sales—and the march of modernization largely deserve the credit at Abiera, the two local groups differ appreciably in this respect, one that may not only express differences of socialization but probably affects it. Some Batainabura informants regard the women of Phratry Tairora, among all the women they know, as particularly outspoken and forceful. If the observation is well founded, this is perhaps a trait bearing on the size of households and the coresidence of women, especially cowives.

MEMBERSHIP OF ABIERA NAME GROUPS OR SIBS

The residents of both Abiera and Batainabura recognize a number of named divisions within their respective local groups. Every resident is said to belong to one division or another. They describe these in terms that suggest patrilineal sibs. Their members, for example, are all "kinsmen" or "brothers." They "have the same fathers." Membership in a particular local division appears to be exclusive and thus distinguishes some residents from others. Some local divisons seem to be more closely associated than others, moreover, and together comprise larger or higher-order groupings, which also have names. Other local divisions stand apart from these or belong to different higher-order groupings. Names for both lower- and higher-order divisions either normally occur with the suffix "-xntx" or can take that suffix.

The nature of the divisions and the meaning of their names will certainly not on this basis be obvious to the reader unless he assumes that the findings of other ethnographers for other Central Highlands peoples are fully valid for any Tairora local group. (Even in that case, he will still have to choose among ethnographers and among other Central Highlands peoples in finding his model.) Nor is the nature of the divisions obvious to the Northern Tairora ethnographer in the field when he first begins to consider these distinctions. It will probably not be obvious even if he accepts a local version of the divisions at face value, for local versions are notably incomplete and fragmentary.

A significant part of the question of what these divisions are and mean will necessarily depend on who the members are and where the members of a given division live or whom they marry within the village or beyond. I shall therefore consider first the purely demographic aspects of the membership of divisions. Subsequently I shall discuss these named divisions in light of statements that are made about them by their members, or in light of statements I feel I can make about them. Provisionally I shall call them "sibs"— in preference to calling them "X." It will emerge in due course, I believe, that the divisions *are* a species of sib. Meanwhile, one can be strictly operational in presenting the elementary census data relevant to them. In other words, there is no need to beg questions beyond the implication of the data under consideration.

For immediate purposes I shall simply enumerate the answers received to one or more of the following questions; (1) What is the name of your (or X's) "line"? (2) What is the name of your (or X's) father's "line"? (3) What is the name of your (or X's) mother's "line"? These questions proved to be answerable by a majority of respondents. In answering the first question, however, a person sometimes said "Abierxntx" or "Batainaburxntx". In that case, I explained that this was not what I meant but the next order, local "lines" into which people are divided. For the moment, then, the answers reported here will indicate no more than a willingness of respondents to answer these questions and, by implication, a willingness to identify themselves and others with one "line" name or another.

In proceeding in this manner, I am in effect merely acting on the belief that a certain population divides itself not only into males and females, young and old, married and unmarried, and so forth, but also into another sort of division with names, "A," "B," "C," and so on. I do not have to know the number of sibs or their names beforehand. I do not have to know what the names stand for or, hence, what general sociological designation or category may best describe them as a class. I have indicated that I think the divisions are some kind of segmentary units, probably patrilineal sibs. I need not be right that the divisions are patrilineal, exogamous, or best termed "sibs." I am, therefore, testing the proposition that (1) every resident of Abiera or Batainaura can be self-assigned and assigned by others to some such division, probably without ambituigy, (2) if a given individual belongs to more than one division, they will be of more than one order, (3) divisions will have names that he and others will be able to tell me, and (4) he will be able to tell me the names of the divisions to which a number of other villagers belong. I will expect the statements made in the last two instances about membership of self and others to be largely consistent, but my efforts may not be useless if that does not prove to be so.

It was consistently found that children are ascribed membership in the same sib as their fathers. (The special case of adopted children will be discussed apart.) The figures presented here will therefore be concerned mostly with persons of approximately eighteen years of age or married. In this way one is dealing largely with the active, adult membership of sibs, and their strength in the given village at the time of census. The question of residence is another reason for being mainly concerned with adults. Children usually live with parents, their own or adoptive. Where they *will* live after marriage or after the death of parents, obviously, could not be predicted solely on the basis of their present residence as minors. In discovering residence rules—or their absence—it therefore seems expedient to focus on those whose residence at present gives an indication of current practice and a presumption of continuity.

Of a total of 109 Abiera persons at least eighteen years old, 47 were men. (See table 5.) Among them, these men used five different sib names, as well as "don't know" (DK), in stating their membership—that is, in answering the questions about "line." There were 62 Abiera women, married or of at least eighteen years of age. Collectively these women used all the sib names employed by men and six additional names in answering the same questions. Thus the women used a total of eleven different sib names for their claims of membership, as well as "DK." The five names that accounted for 100 percent of the men accounted for 76 percent of the women. These five sibs were thus the largest as well as the only sibs with both male and female adult membership resident at Abiera. They were also the only sibs with juvenile or minor members.

TABLE 5

SIB NAMES USED AT ABIERA BY MEN AND WOMEN OVER EIGHTEEN
OR MARRIED IN ASCRIBING MEMBERSHIP

Names Used	Male		Female		Totals	
	N	%	N	%	N	%
Poreqórxntx	23	49	18	29	41	37
Komohórxntx	14	30	11	18	25	25
Laqárxntx	4	9	5	8	9	8
Onxmx́ntxqx́	3	6	8	13	11	10
Óndxbúrx	2	4	5	8	7	6
"Kamáno"			4		4	
Tairórx			3		3	
Bárabúna			2		2	
Nóraikóra			1		1	
Pómpiérx			1		1	
Équmáirxntx			1		1	
Don't Know	1		3		4	
Total	47		62		109	

Note: 47 percent of women are Poreqórxntx or Komohórxntx. 76 percent of women are above the line.

The two largest sibs of all, Poreqórxntx and Komohórxntx, together account for almost four out of five (79 percent) of the censused males. They are the only sibs at Abiera, furthermore, in which men outnumber women, even though the female members of these sibs account for the largest number of the censused women—nearly half. Because of their size and relative strength, I will focus attention on these two sibs.

Can one say more at this point of the eleven sibs that are represented at Abiera? Surely that is a large number of named divisions into which to divide 109 persons—if all of them are equally based, for example, on descent, and all equally a part of Abiera. At least it raises the question whether these "sibs" are better considered something else, such as lineages. Some of them, in fact, scarcely exceed in size an extended family. Some are represented at Abiera by only a single member, others by only a handful. What sense does it make, therefore, to call them "sibs" at all? It might make sense, of course, if it could be shown either (1) that the very small divisions are the last remnant of moribund sibs or (2) that they are members or segments of sibs whose membership base is wider than Abiera or lies outside of it. In the latter case the representatives of such sibs at Abiera would be immigrants.

There has been some recent controversy about the nature of social organization and segmentation in the Central Highlands of New Guinea. At least one suggestion has been advanced of a bilaterally organized society, Gadsup, immediately bordering Northern Tairora. There local groups are posited in which no palpable or significant lineal segments occur (du Toit 1962). Another writer has asserted that residence is the key to Central Highlands social organization, among other things, because of considerable moving about (Langness 1964). If we wish to consider the peculiar relevance of residence to the Highlands or to Northern Tairora social organization, however, it will be necessary to deal carefully with any groups whose immediate or apparent basis is not residence. In discussing what sibs or segments occur in Abiera and Batainabura, therefore, I wish to take as little as possible for granted and at every turn to emphasize the elementary facts of self-designation. If with the simple evidence of census data, accordingly, we can reach certain conclusions before turning to other data, or to a consideration of the local view of local sociology, so much the better.

It seems reasonable to suppose that at least some persons at Abiera are native born and as such are included in what may be its working core. Subject to contrary evidence, it further seems reasonable, that the largest sibs must include more of these people than the other named groups. Otherwise, it would follow that Abiera, a local group with a tradition of several generations in its present territory, has a preponderantly alien population or that its largest sibs are preponderantly alien. Though by no means a sociological impossibility, such a state of affairs would at least call for documentation and explanation. The largest sibs at Abiera, as noted, are Poreqórxntx and Komohórxntx. These two are also the only sibs with a preponderance of male over female members, as well as the only ones with juvenile members. Conversely, we note a clear trend for the remaining, smaller sibs, in proportion to their size, to be made up mainly of women and solely of adults. The larger the sib, then, the more masculine its membership; the smaller, the more feminine and the more exclusively adult. The smallest sibs of all are represented exclusively by adult female members. The maximum membership of any of these is four (Kamáno), and three others have only a single representative at Abiera. (Kamáno, by the way, is not a "sib" but a large, ethnolinguistic grouping to the west of Abiera with a population of over ten thousand.) The smaller sibs and the sibs represented solely by females lack juvenile members.

Even without prior knowledge of marriage and residence rules or of rules of descent, one could surmise that the resident, indigenous, or core sibs of Abiera are not the several very small ones or, hence, the sibs represented mainly or only by adult women.

This is further suggested by the name Kamáno already mentioned and by names such as Bárabúna and Nóraikóra—to take only the more obvious examples. Though Tairora-speaking, these are the names of two distinct peoples and territories some distance from Abiera. It follows, conversely, that the indigenous sibs, the core of Abiera residents—whatever else they may or may not be—are those with male and juvenile members, above all those with the largest proportion of male members.

On these grounds one is led to anticipate a predominance of patrivirilocality even if not a marriage rule of local (Abiera) exogamy. As I hope to show, these conclusions gain strength with additional information. Here I am simply concerned to point out that age and sex data alone lead us in that direction. Even with only the information of the census, there is no real possibility, for example, that the Abiera sib segments represented solely by adult females are the native Abiera sibs. To argue that, one would presumably have to suggest that descent at Abiera is matrilineal or at least that residence is predominantly matriuxorilocal. It would be impossible in either case to square such a view with the census facts.

It was an initial working assumption that every adult resident of Abiera of Batainabura would "belong" to a named division, probably to only one, and that he or she would be able to state its name in reply to questions of the sort indicated. So far these assumptions have been borne out for Abiera in a majority of cases but not in all. There were four DK answers, and thirteen other answers were ambiguous. That is, a respondent gave two names instead of one. In table 5 I included ambiguous answers according to the name first mentioned. In table 6 I isolate the ambiguous answers for separate consideration.

Uncertainty and ambiguity, it seems worth noting, occur much more frequently among females than males. Three out of the four DK answers and

TABLE 6
DK AND AMBIGUOUS ANSWERS AS TO MEMBERSHIP: ABIERA

Answer		Male	Female	Totals
DK(Don't Know)		1	3	4
Ambiguous				
Komohórxntx and	Tairórx	0	2	2
	Óndxbúrx	1	2	3
	Onxmx́ntxqx́	0	1	1
	Urala	0	1	1
Poreqórxntx and	Tairórx	1	2	3
	Óndxbúrx	0	0	0
	Onxmx́ntxqx́	0	0	0
	Urala	0	0	0
Óndxbúrx-Laqárxntx		0	2	2
Onxmx́ntxqx́-Tairórx		0	1	1
Total		2	11	13

eleven of thirteen ambiguities were given by female respondents. Such a result could be interpreted as arising from the greater difficulty women had in understanding the questions, but this does not seem to be the case. It seems rather to relate to some other condition in which a woman's "membership" is more uncertain or ambiguous than a man's. In fact, a number of women named their husband's sib in indicating their own membership. These women were further questioned. Otherwise, however, the answers to the questions about "line" were elicited without extra probing, particularly in the case of DK or ambiguity. Further questioning could certainly have reduced or eliminated both types of answers. In my opinion, it would have been undesirable to eliminate the ambiguities. The ambiguities, it turns out, are instructive in their own right. They seem to reflect what is, on independent grounds, the history of local lineage segmentation, and they do so with considerable consistency.

The thirteen ambiguous responses involve seven different two-name combinations. Two of the combinations occurred thrice, two twice, and three once. I make the simple assumption that the more frequent a combination of names, the more likely there is some historical connection or overlap between the divisions or sibs named, and the less frequent a combination, the less connection. Several relatively close connections are thus suggested: Komohórxntx with Óndxbúrx (three); Komohórxntx with Tairórx (two); Poreqórxntx with Tairórx (three); and Laqárxntx with Óndxbúrx (two).

Now, apart from the question of the small size of the sample, the ambiguous responses summarized in table 6 seem to pattern rather well, particularly when viewed in the light of independent evidence of segmentary history at Abiera. Taking the responses only at face value, however, one would conclude that Komohórxntx and Laqárxntx both have some connection with Óndxbúrx. No respondent has equated Komohórxntx with Laqárxntx. The two may therefore be parts of Óndxbúrx—a larger entity of some kind. Thus

Óndxbúrx

Komohórxntx	Laqárxntx	Other(s)?

Similarly one would conclude that Poreqórxntx and Komohórxntx have some connection with Tairórx. Because no respondent has equated these two, however, their connection may be as parts of Tairórx, a larger entity. Thus

Tairórx

Poreqórxntx	Komohórxntx	Other(s)?

We note, however, that Komohórxntx is a "part of" both Óndxbúrx and Tairórx, while Poreqórxntx is a part only of Tairórx. In practical fact, this and other problems largely disappear once the census responses reported here are viewed in light of other information. Ancillary information is obtained from villages and territories neighboring Abiera where some of the same as well as other sib names are in use. In light of the relevant data, a loose and irregular hierarchy of segments and inclusions results which is depicted roughly in figure 3.

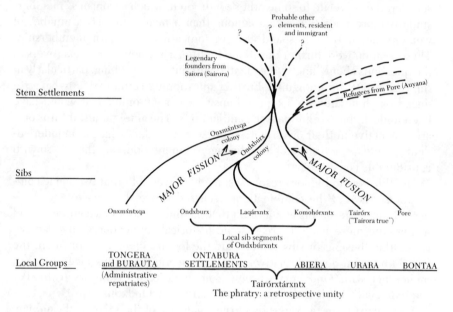

Fig. 3.   Phylogeny of Phratry Tairora

Although it is impossible to derive all of the foregoing conclusions directly from the Abiera census data alone, it is doubtful that those data would support opposite conclusions. The immediate purpose of the scheme, however, is to suggest that even the seeming ambiguities of the local census are reasonable. I will return later to the general question of segmentary history.

Once more taking individual identifications at face value, I would now like to examine residential decisions in relation to sib membership. Abiera in 1963, as map 3 shows, is rather clearly divided into two major residential clusters with an expanse of empty ground between them. One of these, called *quntóqa*, is uphill from the other. The downhill cluster is called *utúbxqáirx*. Do these two clusters correspond in some manner to the membership of the several named sibs? Except for the location of coffee plantations and shelters for coffee seedlings, which have in any case only lately been developed, choice of neighbors seems to be the major reason for individual residential decisions. Most of the gardens, for example, are at the foot of the hill, adjacent to neither residential cluster. Many uphill people, therefore, have to pass through the downhill residential cluster on their way to (some of) their gardens. To the extent that they reflect choice of neighbors, the two residential clusters might correspond significantly to sib membership. But if the clusters themselves do not coincide with sib membership,

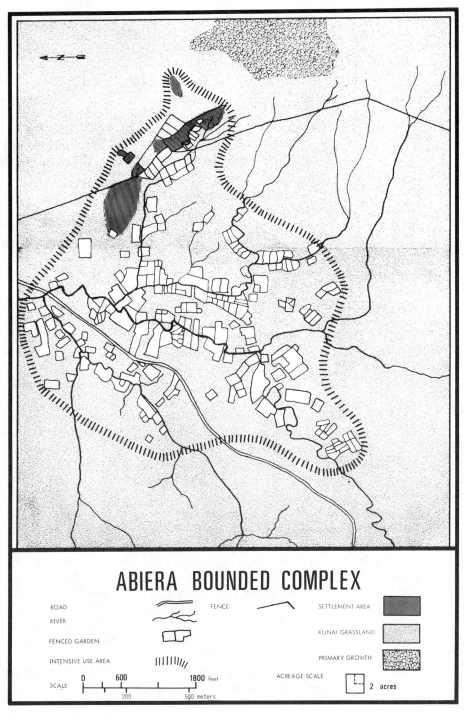

Map 3.

some other line could perhaps be drawn, for analytical purposes, to produce a spatial correlation with the respective personnel of sibs.

Statistically, the fence enclosing the uphill residential cluster makes a significant dividing line. Uphill of this fence live ten of fourteen Komohórxntx men (five of eleven Komohórxntx women), and downhill of the fence live sixteen of twenty-three Poreqórxntx men (seven of eighteen Poreqórxntx women). Three of the four Laqárxntx men also live in the uphill cluster. There was thus well over twice the likelihood (71 percent) that a married Komohórxntx man would live uphill as down and thrice the likelihood that a Laqárxntx man would do so. On the other hand, there was almost thrice the chance (70 percent) that a Poreqórxntx adult male would live downhill as up. In the downhill section of the village, furthermore, Poreqórxntx men outnumber Komohórxntx men four to one.

There seems little reason to doubt a significant residential tendency that coincides with membership in the two leading, named segments of Abiera: Poreqórxntx and Komohórxntx. Indeed, the conclusion seems to gather strength if the individual exceptions are examined in the light of other information. For example, three of the six uphill Poreqórxntx men are married to Onxmẍntxqx women, all seven of whom at Abiera live uphill. Onxmẍntxqẍ is an outside sib many of whose members have been hostile in times past to other Phratry Tairora sibs and in particular to many of the Poreqórxntx sib. A fourth uphill Poreqórxntx man is the son of one of the three just mentioned and shares a house with his father. A fifth was a ward or quasi-adoptive member of the household of a prominent Komohórxntx man, who acted as his sponsor.

I should perhaps not belabor the exceptions. Precise quantitative comparisons with the past are not possible concerning the residence of sib members. Nevertheless, informants old enough to remember precontact times deny that a sib's members were in the past completely segregated from others or all lived together in one settlement. The immediate predecessors of today's "single" village of Abiera, for instance, appear to have been a pair of hamlets. Each of these was occasionally moved, but only for a short distance within the common territory, changing its name according to the site on which it stood. Each hamlet normally had at least one men's house or *baira* at any given time, but the occupants might include more than the men of a single sib. No hamlet is remembered that was exclusively or for long occupied by one sib. One could thus infer that Abiera's 1963 uphill and downhill house clusters in some sense correspond to the aboriginal hamlets. An inference of continuity would be reasonable, moreover, since the village sections of 1963 were spatially at least as discrete—if perhaps not as distant—as the hamlets of yore.

Residential decisions at Abiera, as well as the claims of informants, appear to negate the possibility that the men's house was a crucial factor in the coresidence of sib members. Even now, that is, without a men's house, site coresidence may be as strong a tendency as in the past of this community.

I turn now to the question of marital relations between members of Abiera's sibs. Fourteen Poreqórxntx women were married and resident at Abiera in 1963. Their marriages are as follows: ten to Komohórxntx men, two to Poreqórxntx men, one to a Laqárxntx man, and one to an Onmxntxqx́ man. Thus twelve of these fourteen Poreqórxntx women were married to men of other segments, the great majority to Komohórxntx men. Only two of the fourteen were married to men of the same named sib, and both of these women gave as their birthplaces localities outside of Abiera territory. In other words, they were from other local segments of the Poreqórxntx sib and had come to Abiera as immigrants, perhaps as adoptees.

Of eight Komohórxntx women married and resident at Abiera at 1963, six were married to Poreqórxntx men, one to a "DK" man (whose mother, in any case, says he is Óndxbúrx), and one (describing herself as "DK") to a Komohórxntx man. It is interesting that in these two unions, both perhaps involving partners from within or closely related to the same (Komohórxntx) sib, one partner lists himself as "DK." DK of course represents a very small number within the censused population.

A majority of Komohórxntx men were married to Poreqórxntx women, and a majority of the resident Komohórxntx women were married to Poreqórxntx men. The marriages of resident Poreqórxntx and Komohórxntx women suggest something well short of a closed connubium consisting of these two sibs, however, even overlooking the number of women of each sib who have left Abiera to marry outside. Moreover, although all of the resident, married Komohórxntx women were born within Abiera territory, as many as eight of the fourteen Poreqórxntx women were from other local groups. They appear to have immigrated on account of marriage, and this would again be inconsistent with a local connubium of paired intermarrying sibs.

There is a clear tendency toward sib exogamy at Abiera, though both Poreqórxntx and Komohórxntx show seeming exceptions. Komohórxntx's exceptions, as noted, may have generated intentionally evasive responses to census questions, suggesting embarrassment; but Poreqórxntx's two "exceptions," both of them involving immigrant women, did not. Although the statistical base is very small, there is at least the possibility that among members of the same sib different locality is a qualifying factor.

Of the smaller Abiera sibs or sib segments having both male and female resident members, all the women were exogamously married. Of seven married Onxmxntxqx́ women, four were married to Poreqórxntx men, two to Komohórxntx men, and one to a Laqárxntx man. None, in other words, was married to an Onxmxntxqx́ man. Of four married Laqárxntx women, three were married to Komohórxntx men, one to a Poreqórxntx man. Of four married Óndxbúrx women, two were married to Poreqórxntx men, one to a Komohórxntx, and one to a Laqárxntx.

Six other sibs at Abiera are represented only by women, and in practically all cases the women immigrated to Abiera with marriage, coming as adults from other local groups. This is, in fact, the reason that their sibs are represented at Abiera only by females. Indeed, in a majority of the cases, the "sib" names given are the names of local groups or territories from which the women have come rather than the local counterparts of Poreqórxntx, Komohórxntx, and so on. It is as if a Komohórxntx woman who married into a distant local group were to list her sib in the census of that place as "Abiera." She might even list it as "Tairora," in the sense of the phratry, or perhaps even in the modern, postcontact sense of the ethnolinguistic group. Her disposition would vary with the distance from her community of origin, the farther away she was, the larger the "sib" (grouping) whose name she would need to use in designating herself. Thus four immigrant women at Abiera represented themselves as "Kamáno," the postcontact name of the large ethnolinguistic group bordering the Tairora on the west. I will have subsequent occasion to refer to the use of group and lineal designations under different conditions and its implications for the social order of Abiera and its region.

The evidence at Abiera is clearly against the practice of local exogamy. Fewer marriages than may appear, however, are locally endogamous. To be sure, thirty-eight of forty-eight resident women married at the time of the census listed the names of sibs that are represented at Abiera by both sexes as well as by juvenile members. At least twenty-two of these women, furthermore, were born within Abiera territory. The remaining sixteen, on the other hand, were born in other territories, and most of them came at the time—and presumably because—of their marriage. It is obvious that a married woman's membership in a sib represented at Abiera by both sexes cannot be taken by itself as sufficient evidence of local endogamy. I am disregarding as impractical (though perhaps not insignificant) the question whether the uphill and downhill sections of Abiera could be considered as localities with respect to endogamy or exogamy. Adding the immigrant married women who named sibs represented at Abiera by both sexes to those (ten) immigrant married women who named other "sibs" indicates that over half of the married women at Abiera in 1963 were originally from outside the territory, a majority of them migrating on account of marriage. I will assume that Abiera had approximately the same number of women to send to other communities, or at least that it had as many locally born women of any given age as it had men. On that basis, half or slightly more of the women born at Abiera would have left at marriage. Of women coming to Abiera as brides a majority are members of sibs represented at Abiera by both sexes. A substantial third or more are not only from other localities, however, but from sibs represented at Abiera only by these women.

It can be inferred from table 7 that some Abiera sibs have married relatively more of their women locally than others. That is, they are more endogamous. Komohórxntx, for example, is a smaller sib than Poreqórxntx in total adult membership at Abiera. Yet it has eight locally born women married to Abiera residents compared with six for Poreqórxntx. As many as eight of the married Poreqórxntx women at Abiera, but none of the Komohórxntx

TABLE 7
SIBS REPRESENTED BY BOTH SEXES AT ABIERA

| Sib | Total Adults, Both Sexes | Resident Married Women | |
		Total	Born in Abiera Territory
Poreqórxntx	41	14	6
Komohórxntx	25	8	8
Onxmx̂ntxqx̂	11	7	2
Óndxbúrx	7	5	3
Laqárxntx	9	4	3
Total	93	38	22

women, are from other localities. To some extent, no doubt, quantitative variations like these between groups the size of Abiera sibs must be taken simply as illustrating scale effect. These are very small numbers. It may be relevant, however, that sib Poreqórxntx has a sizable representation in certain of the neighboring villages or territories from which Abiera often gets women, whereas Komohórxntx membership is largely confined to Abiera, except for the women who leave in marriage. In other words, more women of some sibs are available as immigrant brides among the communities from which Abiera brides come. It is not certain how—or even whether—this condition specifically affects the proportion of Abiera women of a given sib who leave their native territory. Nevertheless, it appears generally that the larger the sib, the larger the number of resident adult female members, whether composed of immigrant or of Abiera-born women.

Nothing explicit has so far been said about whether the residence decisions of married couples follow a clear tendency. By itself, of course, the Abiera census might not suffice to support an unqualified generalization. It reflects solely the men and women who are resident there, and it permits only an inference as to the individuals of either sex who have emigrated. The inference, nevertheless, is clearly patrivirilocal.

There is a substantial number of immigrants at Abiera, practically all of them adult females who currently are or have been married to Abiera-born, resident males. The number of immigrant men is negligible. A few Abiera-born men after marriage take up residence in other territories. Sometimes they move to the wife's native territory, but in most cases it is also a place where the husband has kinsmen. In one case an Abiera man went to live at Arogara, another phratry nearby. This was the home of his wife's people, and he had no close kinsmen there himself. His decision was frequently spoken of with derision when the subject came up. It was explained that the man had gotten into trouble at Abiera and thus had been obliged to leave, at some cost to his pride. The point was not principally that he had left Abiera, but that he had gone to a place where he had no kinsmen. The motives of emigrant men seem particular to each case; certainly the decisions do not arise from a common expectation. They tend to be reasons such as an altercation or disagreement, or some other stressful relationship involving given men. Emigrant Abiera men often return at a later time, as did the individual in question—in 1964 after the census was taken. In some cases, male migrants are notably unstable as to residence, shifting back and forth every few years, according to the state of their relations in the respective communities where they can feasibly consider residence.

The pattern of female migration that can in part be inferred from the Abiera census is quite different. Women come to Abiera not because of trouble in their previous communities but because they are sent to marry men resident at Abiera. As noted, a good half of the married women at Abiera in the 1963 census are such immigrants, though only a minority of these are members of sibs not already represented by Abiera-born men and children. The census also permits the inference that an appreciable number of local women have left Abiera to live with husbands native elsewhere. In fact, female out-marriage from Abiera, like female immigration, is common practice, the reason being an expectation of virilocal residence, which is also in the great majority of present cases patrivirilocal. If she is widowed or divorced after many years, an immigrant women is likely to remain in her adopted community, whether or not she remarries.

It is quite likely that patrilocality in postmarital residence is more frequent since Australian administration has stabilized the position of the local group in its territory. Members of a given local group in the past often lived as refugees in other communities, sometimes for long intervals and sometimes without ever returning to the communities from which they had come. This alone suggests a regional rate of patrilocality formerly lower than Abiera's present rates. Indeed, vulnerability to attack and instability of residential location must necessarily have produced or required considerable flexibility with regard to many other social tendencies or expectations as well as postmarital residence.

I earlier raised the question whether one could identify, purely on the basis of census material, which sibs are native and which are outside sibs at Abiera. On the basis of (1) relative size, (2) representation of both sexes, (3) predominance of adult male members over females, and (4) the presence of juvenile members, some of Abiera's eleven sibs differed markedly from others. At least in the sense of their core, some have hence been presumed native, resident, or indigenous to Abiera. Independent testimony bears out the presumption.

I propose now to examine the relation of the sib or sib segment to the birthplaces of its members. In some sense this means where the members of a sib come from or at least where their parents were living at the time of their birth. The residence of an individual or family is not always stable in a given local group, even after marriage, and some persons born elsewhere could have migrated to Abiera as small children or minors if their parents migrated. Not every resident born elsewhere, that is, can be assumed to have come to Abiera only as an adult. But that is by far the predominant tendency, and it is a tendency that has grown with the passage of years since contact.

I will examine here principally the adult members of those sibs or segments considered to be indigenous to Abiera, as previously discussed. The birthplaces of their membership, thus, will constitute a test of the reality of their supposed indigenous status.

A general observation can be made at the outset. The members of Abiera's larger resident sibs list quite a number of different specific birthplaces. Twenty-three Poreqórxntx men and eighteen women give a total of twelve different birthplaces, ten each for men and women, excluding DK. Komohórxntx membership was about equally "dispersed" in the number of its claimed birthplaces, fifteen men and twelve women listing a total of eight different birthplaces at least once. This number consisted of five different birthplaces for Komohórxntx men and seven different birthplaces for the women.

The number of different birthplaces for Abiera's two largest sibs gives a false impression that the membership is highly diverse in local origin. Birthplaces were in fact quite concentrated in space. Seventeen of Poreqórxntx's forty-one members were born at Abiera, whereas no other single birthplace was mentioned by more than four members. Komohórxntx birthplaces (ten of twenty-five) were also concentrated at Abiera. All but three of the other Komohórxntx members, moreover, were born at one of the traditional five places where remembered settlements of this group have been located within the past sixty or seventy years (estimated). That is, the birthplaces of a great majority of Komohórxntx members are within the traditional territory and the past settlements of the present Abiera local group—places, indeed, no more than a mile or so apart at most.

Poreqórxntx membership is slightly more diverse in origin than Komohórxntx, including more members born at places outside the immediate local territory of Abiera. Nevertheless, at least 61 percent (twenty-five of forty-one members) were born within Abiera local territory, compared with 89 percent for Komohórxntx. The specific settlements or hamlets mentioned in these cases are the same as for Komohórxntx. (That members of either sib could be born at the same places is again consistent with the statements of older informants, that residence in a specific settlement did not coincide perfectly or exclusively with sib membership.) The 39 percent of adult Poreqórxntx apparently born outside of Abiera's immediate territory included a majority of women as well as three DK responses. The (nine) women, in other words, were mostly immigrants to Abiera territory, even though they were nominal members of the largest sib at Abiera.

The outside birthplaces listed by Poreqórxntx are all but one in local group territories adjacent to Abiera's and within the boundaries of Phratry Tairora. One man gave his birthplace as Agarabi. This means some local group within the boundaries of a sizable ethnolinguistic group a few miles to the north of Abiera, where his parents were living as refugees when he was born. In the

case of Komohórxntx, the birthplaces that are outside of Abiera's immediate
territory are all localities within adjacent territories, and all are also within
the boundaries of the Phratry Tairora.

   In fine, the membership of the two largest sibs of Abiera is notably restricted and highly local in origin. The majority of members of both sibs—
and the majority of both sexes in the case of Komohórxntx—were born
within historic Abiera territory. Almost all of the remainder were born at
places nearby and in adjacent territories. The birthplaces that are no longer
settlements are easily identified as former sites of settlements. They are not
all contemporary, but all the sites that lie within Abiera territory are within a
short distance of each other. Differences among these latter birthplaces, in
other words, would for many purposes be of little significance. They mainly
reflect the microsociology of the local situation or, as the case may be, the
intimate history of local settlement and the small-scale moves that occur
from time to time for various reasons, some of them magical. This is not to
deny that birth or residence in one as opposed to another of the small settlements of the past had any effect on migratory movement, marriage, or drift
between local groups and territories. It is only to recognize the recruitment
of people from among the small hamlets that stood at some time within its
own territory as distinct from the recruitment of people from outside the
traditional territory. To be sure, the integrity of the "traditional territory"
may not always have been precisely what it is at the moment. Nevertheless,
the tradition is supported by the data on birthplaces and by the present composition of both of the largest—and apparently the most indigenous—sibs of
the moment. In fact, the composition of the smaller indigenous sibs or segments of Abiera is also consistent with this trend.

   Turning to microsociological variants, Komohórxntx seems, by the criterion of its members' birthplaces, a more indigenous sib than Poreqórxntx.
That is, the birthplaces of the members of the latter are less concentrated.
Logically this need mean no more than that (1) the Poreqórxntx sibs or sib
segments in other groups and territories are larger than Komohórxntx segments, or (2) the Poreqórxntx segments are present in more territories from
which Abiera gets women than Komohórxntx segments, or (3) the Poreqórxntx women are more prone to marry or otherwise migrate into Abiera
from outside segments than are Komohórxntx women. Actually, there is
some truth in all three statements. Thus, it is better to say that the Poreqórxntx sib is more widespread and less exclusively concentrated at
Abiera—though at the same time being Abiera's biggest sib—than is Komohórxntx. This statement avoids for the time being the implication that
Abiera's biggest sib is less indigenous than the second largest one. Such a
view is substantiated, but by historical data rather than by the census.

   To take the case a step further, it is evident on grounds other than the
census that the sib Poreqórxntx, despite its growth, has remained undivided
or less divided than sib Komohórxntx. In origin the latter seems, in fact, to
be an Abiera branch of sib Óndxbúrx. That is, Komohórxntx is a localized

segment of Óndxbúrx, orginally undistinguished from it in name but now in process of gaining its own—local—name. Logically one could say, in comparing Komohórxntx with Poreqórxntx, that one is comparing a localized Abiera lineage or branch of a sib with a sib having several large localized but unnamed branches. Since such a statement exceeds the implications of the Abiera census, there is little reason to consider it here—that is, apart from the context of segmentary history and the question of development. To this question I will later turn.

MEMBERSHIP OF BATAINABURA NAME GROUPS OR SIBS

In presenting the lineage and sib data for Batainabura I will follow the same sequence of topics as for Abiera. To simplify direct comparisons, I will, where relevant or interesting, insert Abiera figures in parenthesis, thus (Abiera: nineteen).

TABLE 8
SIB OR PROVENIENCE NAMES USED AT BATAINABURA
BY MEN AND WOMEN OVER EIGHTEEN OR MARRIED

Names Used		Male N	Male %	Female N	Female %	Totals N	Totals %
Hararúnx		20	43.0	16	27.0	36	34.0
Airiná		10	21.0	12	20.0	22	21.0
Táirxqirx		7	15.0	1	1.7	8	7.5
Irérxburx		2	4.0	4	7.0	6	5.6
Baqe-Hararúnx		2	4.0	3	5.0	5	4.7
Taírxqirx and	Hararúnx	1	2.0	2	3.0	3	2.8
	Baqe	1	2.0			1	0.9
	Baqe-Hararúnx	1	2.0	1	1.7	2	1.8
Irérxburx and	Hararúnx			2	3.0	2	
	Airiná			1	1.7	1	
Batainabura		2	4.0			2	
Báqoqx				3	5.0		
Nóraikóra				3	5.0		
Saióra (3)				3	5.0		
Árau (2)				2	3.0		
Andandára (3)				3	5.0		
Baibáto (Andandára?)				1	1.7		
Bobogíra				1	1.7		
Suwáira				1	1.7		
Omaúra		1					
Total		47		59		106	

Many informants style Batainabura as a community made up of only two sibs, but the census indicates a greater complexity. (See table 8.) There are a total of 106 persons at Batainabura at last eighteen or married (Abiera: 109).

Forty-seven are male (Abiera: forty-seven) and among them these men used seven different sib names, singly or in combination), (Abiera: five), as well as "don't know" (DK), in answering census questions about "line" memberships. The remaining fifty-nine females (Abiera: sixty-two) collectively used a total of thirteen different sib names (Abiera: eleven plus DK). Eight names were used by women only (Abiera: six) and one, as well as DK, by a single man (Abiera: none). An additional name used by two men was Batainabura. I do not think Batainabura is a "sib" as distinct from all others of the village nor one represented exclusively by men. A total of fifteen sib names, plus DK, were used singly or in combination at Batainabura (Abiera: eleven plus DK). Seven sib names were used by both men and women (Abiera: five). These seven names accounted for 92 percent of the male responses and 73 percent of the female responses. They were thus the largest sibs as well as the only ones with both adult male and female membership, and they were, with the exception of "Batainabura," the only sibs with juvenile members. In most of the foregoing respects, therefore, Batainabura provides a detailed statistical similarity to Abiera.

Batainabura's two largest sibs, again like Abiera's, account for more than three out of five (65 percent; Abiera: 79 percent) of the censused males. Unlike Abiera, however, males outnumber females in only one of these sibs, Hararúnx. The sex ratio is approximately equal in Airiná, the second largest sib. The female members of these two sibs constitute almost half (47 percent) of all the censused women as opposed to slightly under half at Abiera. The larger of Batainabura's two major sibs, Hararúnx, has a size ratio approaching 2:1 to the second largest, Airiná (Abiera: 3:2). In fact, in the light of equivalences and correspondences, discussed below, the disproportion between the largest and next largest sibs at Batainabura is probably greater still. Almost exactly the same proportion of censused women in both villages (about three-fourths) list membership in sibs having both male and juvenile members.

There are fewer DK and fewer ambiguous answers at Batainabura than at Abiera (see table 9).

TABLE 9
DK AND AMBIGUOUS ANSWERS AS TO MEMBERSHIP: BATAINABURA

Answer	Male	Female	Totals
DK (Don't Know)	1	0	1
Ambiguous			
Táirxqirx and Baqe	1	0	1
Hararúnx	1	2	3
Baqe-Hararúnx	1	1	2
Irérxburx and Airiná	0	1	1
Hararúnx	0	2	2
Total	3	6	9

As previously indicated, the reasons for DK or ambiguous answers (those in which two names were used in describing lineage membership) might be several. A woman sometimes tended to give her husband's sib name in addition to (when not instead of) her own. This was questioned wherever it was suspected. DK answers, it seemed likely, occasionally indicated embarrassment, a respondent whose situation was such that the correct answer was not the one the individual would in some context wish it to be. Although significant, such motives or putative motives are not the immediate reasons for my interest in what I am calling for convenience "ambiguities." Since the ambiguities seem to show a congruence with the segmentary developments of the local group, I feel it is worth a paragraph or two to examine them for possible historical implications. In effect, this implies that what I have called "ambiguities" may be such only in a literal sense. That is, the ambiguities are an accurate reflection of a boundary problem.

There was only one DK answer at Batainabura (Abiera: four). There were nine ambiguous answers (Abiera: thirteen). Ambiguous answers occurred somewhat more frequently with female respondents at Batainabura than with males (6:3), though with no such disproportion as at Abiera (Abiera: 11:2). The nine ambiguous responses involve five seemingly different two-name combinations. Assuming, as at Abiera, that these responses represent no contradictions but the possible overlap or historical connection of sibs, at least two connections are suggested: Táirxqirx with Hararúnx (three cases) and again Táirxqirx with Baqe-Hararúnx (two cases). Lumping Baqe-Hararúnx and Hararúnx, as some informants consistently do, there are six cases (or responses) suggesting a connection between this combination of sibs or sib segments. Were one accordingly to lump the figures of table 9, the membership of the Táirxqirx-Baqe-Hararúnx congeries would be a preponderant 54 percent of the community, or 67 percent of the censused adult males. This can be compared to 21 percent of either the community or censused males for the next largest sib, Airiná. Many informants consistently state that Batainabura consists entirely of Airiná and Baqe-Hararúnx. This view suggests that the lumping operation I have just performed is not entirely artificial. It also indicates that the numerical imbalance among sibs at Batainabura is even greater than it seems in the census (table 8). In other words, there is a much greater imbalance between the numerically dominant sib or sibs at Batainabura than at Abiera, though in both places there is a disproportion.

Can one infer from the ambiguous responses of Batainabura residents any hierarchical relationship such as at Abiera in which some of the named groups may actually be higher-order divisions including others? Whether there is justification on other grounds for such a conclusion, the ambiguous responses of table 9 provide little support. Hararúnx, for example, might seem from the table to be included in Táirxqirx. In fact, the table has been simplified and thus fails to show, for example, that more responses suggest Táirxqirx as a *part* of Hararúnx than vice versa. Yet the latter inference cannot be simply advanced either, since it creates further problems. If there were no other evidence, or if all other evidence equivocally supported it, perhaps it would be worthwhile pursuing the proposition. For the time being, however, it seems better to adopt the more modest conclusion that the census material at Batainabura may refer to groups that are de facto coordinate—or nearly so. They are perhaps linked and confused in the case of some respondents, rather than being clearly inclusive and included groups. I have, at least, no basis in these responses for inferring that the segmentary history of Batainabura's present named groups matches that of Abiera's other than quite generally. This proposition, naturally, deserves and will receive fuller consideration than it can be given solely on the basis of census material. Table 10 provides a compilation of possibly coupled sib names at Batainabura.

TABLE 10
BATAINABURA NAMED GROUPS AND SIBS: COUPLED NAMES

Names	Men	Women
Hararúnx and Irérxburx		2
Andandára		1
Baqe	1	3
Baqe-Hararúnx	1	
Airiná and Táirxqirx	1	2
Árau		1
Irérxburx		1
Baqe-Hararúnx and Táirxqirx	1	1
Hararúnx		
(see above)		
Total	4	11
Táirxqirx and Baqe	1	
Baqe-Hararúnx	1	1
Hararúnx	1	2
Irérxburx and Hararúnx		2
Airiná		1

The Batainabura settlement area in 1964, as map 4 shows, is not divided in a simple way, unlike Abiera's uphill and downhill sections. Batainabura dwellings are strung out in a rough crescent. It is possible to divide the area of settlement loosely into three sections: (1) a section along the spur of the mountain crest at the north of the area, (2) a saddle connecting this north crest of the mountain with another to the south, and (3) the ridge that comprises the south end of the settlement area. These sections may reflect the broken terrain of the settlement area at least as much as they reflect sociological factors, and no section is separated from the others by an appreciable gap. While the residence of sib members does not seem entirely random, census data naturally leave unanswered whether it is related (except statistically) to distinctions as broad as membership in a particular named group. Immediate

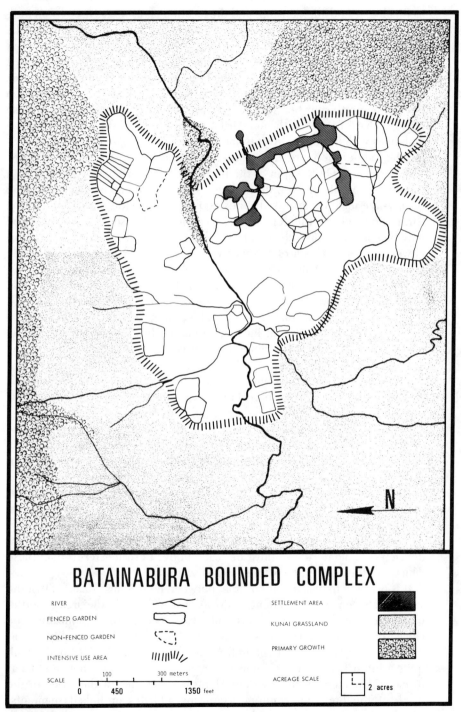

BATAINABURA BOUNDED COMPLEX

RIVER		SETTLEMENT AREA	
FENCED GARDEN		KUNAI GRASSLAND	
NON-FENCED GARDEN		PRIMARY GROWTH	
INTENSIVE USE AREA			

SCALE

100   300 meters

0   450   1350 feet

ACREAGE SCALE   2 acres

Map 4.

factors like friendship, kinship, and the location of resources used by an individual, though not necessarily inconsistent with sib membership, might be of equal or greater moment.

Six (or seven, depending on where one draws the line) of ten Airiná men live on the south ridge or in the saddle between the two mountain crests. Six of these live in three adjacent houses, four in a single house. Two Airiná men live on the north spur but not in adjacent houses, and they, like two of those on top, share houses with non-Airiná adult male coresidents. One Airiná man lives with his family in an isolated house (no. 33). On the ridge (excluding the saddle) there are eight houses in use, having a total of fifteen adult, resident males. On the spur at the north end there are twelve houses, with three more on the path up to the crest. These fifteen houses have a total of twenty-five male occupants. In these terms, one could say that men of the Airiná sib used six of fifteen chances to reside on the south ridge, but used only two of twenty-five chances to reside on the north spur. Hararúnx men, however, used thirteen of twenty-five chances—over half—to live on the spur and only five of fifteen chances to live above it.

As long as one limits the discussion purely to statistics, any tendencies that do not closely approach the absolute will—in so small a universe as the adult male population of Batainabura—be subject to question. It is obvious that the residence of sib mates at Batainabura aproaches the absolute much less closely than at Abiera. The difference between the two local groups, however, need not cause surprise. Although there is a clearer residential tendency of sib members at Abiera for 1963, there is so far no justification for projecting this into a "rule" of residence with efficient normative force or for regarding minority instances as exceptional or aberrant and not equally a part of the scene. Greater or lesser residential commingling may be one measure of relations within or between sibs or the individuals who locally belong in them. Relations of sibs may not be the same from one local group to another. In such terms it is clear that sib membership does not convey as much residential distinction at Batainabura as it does at Abiera, whether or not it conveys distinctions of other kinds. Manifestly, then, this is a variable among Northern Tairora local groups. Unless Abiera and Batainabura happen to be polar extremes, any attempt to speak of "Northern Tairora" tendencies—let alone rules—must be made in even broader terms than those which suit the description of these two local groups.

It is possible to pick a point or line (between houses nos. 19 and 20) in the saddle between the two mountain crests that will divide the area of settlement, for statistical comparisons, into two spaces. Topographically, the choice of this line is reasonable enough, since the saddle roughly distinguishes one crest of the mountain from another, but the line happens to fall quite arbitrarily between two houses that are very close together. Be that as it may, 71 percent of the resident Hararúnx men live in the space to the north of the line, not counting Hararúnx affiliates or linked segments, whereas 70 percent of the resident Airiná men live in the space to the south of the line. Airiná and Hararúnx sibs, moreover, have a remembered traditional ground where each originated. These traditional places are each within a mile or so of the present settlement of Batainabura. For what it may be worth, the respective spaces in which the majority of men of each sib now reside are oriented to each other as are their traditional origin grounds. Thus Airiná men are concentrated on high ground roughly in the southeastern section of the village, nearest traditional Airiná, while Hararúnx men are concentrated on lower ground northwest of them on the way to the traditional Hararúnx site.

The statistical dividing line still leaves about 30 percent of the men of each sib living in the "wrong" space; and no better line could be drawn without producing an absurd gerrymander. Batainabura thus offers no exception to the assertion of informants that sibs were not in the past and are not now residentally segregated. In fact, Batainabura bears out this claim even more than Abiera. Batainabura informants repeatedly stress that members of sibs are residentially intermixed, as if to acknowledge the contrary would imply a lack of sociability among them. One would probably want to consider Batainabura's terrain, as contrasted with Abiera's, before concluding that sociability was the sole variable or was lesser or greater at Batainabura than at Abiera. Abiera's two clearcut village spaces make inevitable a binary residential option, so to speak. On the other hand, it would be possible, with Abiera's terrain, to have one continuous settlement.

In Batainabura's more linear—albeit curved—pattern residential discriminations could at most produce something resembling two portions of a line (my statistical dividing line assumes this condition) in which some members of group A would necessarily live closer to some members of group B than to other A's. Even so, the residence of sib members at Batainabura could be more discrete than it is. It is thus apparent that terrain is not solely involved, whatever part sociability may play.

The lesser sibs at Batainabura, for sheer lack of numbers, could not produce as much scatter as larger ones. Nor would the cluster of their members be so significant, since immediate factors like kinship would more often intervene in a small group. The men of Batainabura's sib Táirxqirx, for example, have an interesting residential pattern. Five of these eight live very close together in one cluster on the northern spur of the mountain and the other three in adjacent houses on the ridge to the south. There is thus no scatter outside of the two clusters. Sibs smaller than Táirxqirx are probably too small to consider in this respect.

I turn now to marriages among members of Batainabura's sibs. Of fourteen married female Hararúnx residents in 1964, five were married to Airiná men, four to Hararúnx men, two to Táirxqirx men, two to Batainabura, and one to a Baqe-Hararúnx men. Of twelve married female Airiná residents in 1964, three were married to Hararúnx men, one to a Táirxqirx-Hararúnx man, one to a Táirxqirx-Baqe man, and one DK. Batainabura figures thus do not support an inference of complete sib exogamy, though at least four out of five of these marriages are exogamous for the sibs of the respective women. The largest number of marriages in each of the two major sibs were with members of the other; but it would probably be an oversimplification to speak of a connubium, let alone one that closely approached closure.

Of six Irérxburx women, two were married to Táirxqirx men, and one each to an Airiná man, a Hararúnx man, a Baqe-Hararúnx man, and an Irérxburx man. Of four Baqe-Hararúnx women, two were married to Airiná men, one to a Hararúnx man, and one DK. Combining Baqe-Hararúnx women with Hararúnx women we find seven of ten Airiná men with wives from these closely connected sibs or sib segments.

Eight other sibs at Batainabura are represented only by women. In practically all cases the women have immigrated to Batainabura with marriage, coming as adults from other local groups. As at Abiera, these women have consistently given their local group names in response to the same questions that elicited from other respondents such sib names as "Airiná," "Hararúnx," and so forth. There were no women at Batainabura (unlike Abiera) from other ethnolinguistic groups such as Kamáno. These fifteen outside women are espoused in approximate proportion to the size of the sibs locally established at Batainabura: nine to Hararúnx men, four to Airiná men, one to a Táirxqirx, and one to a Baqe-Hararúnx man.

The Batainabura census indicates no consistent tendency toward local exogamy or recruitment of women from outside the group. Batainabura data, in fact, reveal a somewhat higher degree of local recruitment or endogamy than is found at Abiera. The finding, moreover, is consistent with the statements of a number of Batainabura informants. Several said, in effect, "We keep our own girls in the village. We don't send them away as brides to outside places." While not literally true, the statement appears to have some foundation. The contrast with Abiera is not apparent, however, if one looks only at the number of married women listing outside sibs. These are the most obvious immigrants, and in both cases they are roughly 25 percent of the women censused. But at Batainabura 64 percent of all the women, regardless of sib, were locally born, whereas at Abiera less than half were. As would be expected, an even greater proportion of Batainabura women who list membership in locally established sibs (81 percent) were locally born (Abiera: 58 percent). (See table 11; cf. table 7.) In fact, there were almost exactly as many locally born Batainabura women in these sibs as men, indicating that Batainabura's population policy has in recent decades been different from Abiera's. (This fact seems consistent with the view subsequently adopted, that Batainabura, having no coequal local groups, may usefully be considered a phratry, unlike Abiera, which is only a part of one.) Such local women as have emigrated (in marriage or by remaining as residents of local groups to which they went as refugees) have apparently either (1) been matched by an equivalent number of emigrant men or (2) constitute the excess of surviving females over males at age eighteen or beyond.

As at Abiera, the Batainabura figures suggest that some sibs have married

TABLE 11
Sibs Locally Established at Batainabura

Sib[a]	Resident Married Women	
	Total	Born in Batainabura Territory
Hararúnx	19	14
Airiná	12	11
Irérxburx	6	4
Baqe-Hararúnx	4	4
Táirxqirx	2	2
Batainabura[b]	0	-
Total	43	35

[a]I have combined some of the sib designations of Table 8, as analysis suggests.
[b]Obviously "local" (if properly a sib) but represented only by men.

relatively more of their women locally than others and are thus, so to speak, more endogamous as sibs. It is not clear, however, whether such variation is the effect of consistent practice or simply a fluctuation that could be expected in groups of small size.

The ages of immigrant women compared with locally born women of locally established sibs could conceivably give some indication of a shifting index of local endogamy-exogamy through time. If immigrant women were on the average older, for example, it could indicate a trend toward greater local endogamy—that is, more outside brides in the past than at present. If younger, it could indicate a trend in the opposite direction. There are initially at least two difficulties in the present case with such an inference. One is the often mentioned small size of the population in which chance fluctuations are impossible to rule out. The other is the possibility that immigrant women married into Batainabura do not behave in the same way as native women. If widowed or divorced, for instance, perhaps they sometimes leave Batainabura for their original communities, thus lowering the average age of immigrant women by removing older women from the group. In any case the figures in table 12 are at least worth considering.

TABLE 12
Average Age of Immigrant Women and Women of Sibs Established at Batainabura

Group	Number of Women	Average Age
Hararúnx	19	42
Airiná	12	41
Irérxburx	6	40
Baqe-Hararúnx	4	33
Táirxqirx	2	42
Immigrants of outside sibs	15	36

Table 12 shows that immigrant women are on the average several years younger than the women of all but one of the locally established sibs. This difference can probably not, for the reasons mentioned above, be taken as clear proof of a recent trend toward greater local exogamy at Batainabura. It tends at least to deny the argument that Batainabura's present high ratio of local endogamy is very recent. The average ages in question do not of course place the average times of betrothal and marriage of these women—inferably about eighteen to nineteen years—in the precontact period. Yet if one were to argue that Batainabura's high index of local endogamy is largely a postcontact phenomenon, he would be forced to see it as having set in almost at once, as soon as the pressure of enemies, and perhaps the need for allies, first began to be neutralized by the *pax australiana*.

This argument fails to recognize that for some years after initial contact, villagers in the Kainantu area were not convinced that the *pax australiana* was necessarily permanent. Their doubts, moreover, were materially increased by the breakdown of civil authority and effective control of the villages for a while during World War II. During this time, intervillage fighting occurred widely and the villages were once more left to their traditional devices. Even in 1955 one could meet villagers in the Kainantu area who were quizzical about the future in light of what had happened after a decade of pacification. Unless some major consideration has been omitted, therefore, it seems more promising to regard Batainabura's local endogamy as a tendency of long standing and one that first developed in response to local rather than exogenous factors. (Again, the suggested view of Batainabura as a phratry is consistent with its higher rate of endogamy.)

The case of Batainabura highlights a problem that, though probably widespread, is exacerbated in a history checkered by periods of flight to other communities. Batainabura people, as noted previously, have lived intermittently as refugees in various other local groups. Batainabura produced more refugees, particularly in the decades just preceding contact, than Abiera did. Under such circumstances, the distinction between "immigrant" and "locally born" women (or men, for that matter) probably becomes tenuous in some cases. An apparent immigrant, that is, could be a returnee or the child of one, and this would arise more often in a group like Batainabura than in one like Abiera, which has enjoyed more or less stable occupancy of its territory for the same span of time. In this light, Batainabura's endogamy may not be sufficiently reflected in the figures of table 11. I have considered 81 percent of the resident adult women of local sibs "native" because they were born within Batainabura territory. The proportion might be increased, in other words, if some less arbitrary distinction than birthplace could be made between immigrant women and others. The attempt to do so, however, besides being extremely tedious, would not necessarily succeed. Each case would have to be studied—the birthplace of the individual, the sibs and birthplaces of the parents, the time and apparent motive of moving to Batainabura—and perhaps additional statements would have to be taken from the individual. It would probably be impossible, even with complete data, to avoid some inferences or arbitrary discriminations. A refugee community is in some sense a floating community. A child born abroad during hostilities may be just as much a part of the group, especially if the parents return, as an infant who chanced to be born days or weeks before the people had abandoned their native territory. Such considerations are sobering when, in schematizing its social organization, one wishes to apply the simple distinction between endogamy and exogamy to a community like Batainabura. Though a statistical profile still appears the best introduction to the rules and system of the community, mere enumeration cannot easily resolve every question, such as when a person is to be considered a frank migrant and when a returning native. The plain sociological fact is nevertheless visible: Batainabura draws some of its nonnative population—principally women—from the immediate descendants of the native born as well as from others less immediately connected with the local group or perhaps peviously unconnected. But Batainabura draws fewer from the latter group than Abiera; and, as noted, it may draw even fewer than the census indicates.

Like the Abiera census, that of Batainabura suggests—as far as the census of one local group can, that a patrivirilocal rule of residence predominates. The village has fifteen resident women listing membership in outside groups or sibs; but only one man is a frank outsider. He is a Gadsup-speaker who lives with his indigenous wife, in his father-in-law's house. His situation is clearly anomalous in the eyes of all concerned. While possibly burdensome, residence with his wife's people quite likely affords him a foothold in the village, one at least more secure than if he had attempted to set up an independent household. His activities are closely geared to those of his father-in-law. Indeed, it is doubtful that he could manage without the active and direct sponsorship of a senior and well-rooted Batainabura man—though that is not to say that a man of exceptional stature could not manage.

Informants recognize that the residence of some locally born men or members of local sibs has been qualified by flight from the native territory. An unknown number of refugees from Batainabura have over the years remained in their villages of refuge. In one remembered case, the hosts are a Kamáno-speaking village twelve to fourteen miles distant from Batainabura. The parents of these persons, or other members of the parental generation, have in a number of instances returned, but some of the now grown children, both male and female, have not. Some of these individuals are remembered by name, though their children and others may not be known when born in a distant host village to which local people rarely journey. Some former residents or their children keep contact through intermediaries or occasionally visit Batainabura. The second generation, if among hosts of another language, is likely to be bilingual, still speaking Tairora with at least minimal adequacy. At Batainabura one still hears talk that the refugees might one day return. It is asserted that there would be sufficient land for them if they did. It is also thought that they may try to claim a share of the money to be received when the government compensates the local group for traditional land it has proposed alienating. The right of the expatriates to a share in the money is not disputed in principle, but when asked to be candid, a number of informants doubted that the money would be shared with them as long as they remain abroad. With equal candor, some informants admit that there is now little likelihood of the repatriation of its long-absent sons and even less of their sons or grandsons. Thus the theme of returning seems to be kept alive more as an ideal than a likelihood.

Since administrative control has stabilized Batainabura's precarious competitive position, it is probably not the fear of being driven out once more that keeps the refugees or their children abroad. Where they have established themselves, the longer they stay the better their chances compared with starting over again in the ancestral territory. The Batainabura case shows the flexibility of residence rules necessitated by the vicissitudes of fighting. Patrivirilocal residence is today, without fighting, a more frequent practice at Batainabura, probably, than it was before contact.

THE BIRTHPLACES OF SIB MEMBERS

The relation of sibs or sib segments and the birthplaces of their members is as much an index of local group recruitment as of sib membership. As in the discussion of the Abiera census, I will consider principally adults, focusing on those sibs or segments that are judged to be locally established. Their membership obviously has more significance for local group composition than the membership of the nine sibs at Batainabura whose very names indicate outside localities or places of origin. The membership of the largest outside sib, moreover, does not exceed three persons. The members of these sibs are women in every case but one; and they are in all cases (with one dubious exception) persons born outside Batainabura territory.

The number of different birthplaces of members is approximately as great in some of Batainabura's locally established sibs as in Abiera's. For example, twenty-one Hararúnx men and nineteen women list a total of nine different birthplaces, six for men and six for women—excluding DK. Among ten Airiná men three birthplaces were listed and three among twelve Airiná women, a total of four different places named in all. The membership of both sibs is in fact more concentrated in origin than the number of birthplaces suggests. The majority of the members of both sibs listed one of two places, Gatarora or Batainabura, as their birthplaces. All but two Airiná (one male, one female) also listed one of these as his birthplace. Half the Hararúnx men and just over two-thirds of Hararúnx women likewise claimed either Batainabura or Gatarora as birthplace. Only one Airiná—a woman—said she was born outside the present Batainabura territory. Excluding DK, no Hararúnx man and only two, possibly three, Hararúnx women listed birthplaces outside Batainabura territory. Thus the membership of Batainabura's two largest sibs is even more homogeneous as to birthplace than Abiera's. Over 95 percent of the Airiná people and over 92 percent of the Hararúnx were born locally—that is, within the local territory claimed by Batainabura (Abiera: 89 and 61 percent). (Note again the "phratric" character of Batainabura.)

I would theorize on this basis that groups who have repeatedly been expelled from their territory might, in returning to it, undergo a process like pruning. That is, quondam members whose parentage, group of orientation, or social prospects make them in any sense marginal might elect not to return when a nucleus of the group reestablishes itself in the traditional territory. Refugees, in choosing a host community among those considered feasible, presumably select one that offers them the best balance of possibilities. If the attachment to the former territory is weaker for some persons than others, a satisfactory existence in the host group would tend to keep them from returning. The returnees would thus tend to include only those with the strongest and least ambiguous commitments to their former territory and its occupants.

It is surely conceivable, on the other hand, that the refugee experience in a series of different host communities at various times might result in the recruitment of a more *diverse* membership, for example, as measured by birthplace. Whether my first suggestion is correct or not, the present one apparently fails to describe the recent recruitment of personnel at Batainabura. In fact, offspring of refugees born abroad during periods of absence from Batainabura territory are seemingly either negligible in number—not likely—or have often failed to return when the local group was reconstituted. Whether this is a condition unique to Batainabura or one that is general among Northern Tairora refugees everywhere, I do not know. At Batainabura, time is quite clearly an important factor in determining whether a substantial number of refugees or their offspring return: the longer the interval, the smaller the number. The census facts strongly suggest a community that, though its people have been much abroad in the remembered past, is nevertheless highly local at present in origin and commitment.

To understand the possible "pruning" effect of alternate phases of refuge and return, it is useful to note some of the factors that impinge on the decision of potential returning migrants. The availability of brides, land, and other resources is an obvious consideration. Here Batainabura's beleaguered military position and the shrinkage of lands considered safely usable for gardening or pig range enter the equation. A weakened group may be caught in a vicious circle as it is less favored in attracting immigrants or allies or obtaining brides. Yet strong local sentiment and the attractions of autonomy in one's own territory may be a potent factor. If coupled sometimes with dissension or uneasiness in the midst of a host group, it is evidently sufficient to overcome otherwise negative prospects. Sentiment in the face of adverse prospects is presumably most decisive for those whose background—ancestry, birthplace, residence, rearing, initiation, and so forth—most strongly draws them to the former territory. A homogeneous nucleus is created, pruned of elements less closely or less long identified with the former homeland who are accordingly deterred from returning by the disadvantages. Warfare is reasonably invoked as a crucial factor in the social organization of Central Highlands peoples (Berndt 1964; Langness 1964). While defeat in warfare may scatter and diversify the personnel of a local group, loosening or disintegrating its sib membership, the subsequent reconstitution of local groups may in turn produce greater social homogeneity.

At least one more factor apparently differentiates Batainabura from Abiera in respect to homogeneity. As previously noted, the established sibs of Abiera are located in the midst of other sibs of the same phratry—sibs of the same name or closely related—established in neighboring communities. Some of Abiera's sibs, in a word, are segments of sibs dispersed among the various local groups of the same phratry. Since Batainabura apparently occupies no such position in relation to neighboring communities, there is no easy entrée, no coming and going of sib mates from other local groups, all of them linked by membership in the larger phratry. There is no larger phratry, in other words; or, to put it differently, Batainabura is itself the phratry as well as the single constituent local group. Batainabura is more of an isolate than Abiera.

The consequences of parochialism and local endogamy are no longer the same, under the *pax australiana*, as they probably were before. The small group and the group with tenuous outside ties may differ from the large group with numerous affines and firm allies; but it is not today a group whose communal integrity may be jeopardized for that reason, as it was in the past.

SIB EXOGAMY AND THE QUESTION OF CHANGE

Table 13 shows the sib or provenience of wives of forty-three adult males. These are the married male members of the six largest named groups or sibs of Batainabura. The largest of these sibs, Hararúnx, constitutes 43 percent of adult Batainabura males—married men or those eighteen or older. By the same definition, the smallest of the foregoing groups, Baqe-Hararúnx and Batainabura, represent 4 percent each of the adult male population censused. There is thus a great range in size among these six sibs, with only two besides Hararúnx having as much as 10 percent of the censused adult males: Airiná (21 percent) and Táirxqirx (15 percent). Sib Hararúnx is thus twice the size of the next largest sib and ten times the size of the two smallest sibs.

As the table shows, at least six of forty-nine, or 12 percent, of the marriages appear to have been contracted between spouses of the same named group or sib. Four of these are Hararúnx-Hararúnx marriages, one is Airiná-Airiná, and one Irérxburx-Irérxburx. Twenty percent of Hararúnx married men, then, are married to women of the same sib or named group.

In fact, the proportion of same-name or intrasib marriages may be larger still if we accept the claims of certain informants, namely that "Baqe-Hararúnx" is simply a part of "Hararúnx." If that is so, then there are two addi-

TABLE 13

BATAINABURA: SIB/PROVENIENCE OF WIVES MARRIED TO MEN
OF THE SIX LARGEST SIBS OR NAMED GROUPS

Husband	N	Wives						
		Hara-rúnx	Airina	Tairxqirx	Irérx-burx	Baqe-Hararúnx	Batain-abura	Total
Hararúnx	(20)	4	4	1	1	1	9	20
Airiná	(10)	4	1	0	1	2	3	11
Táirxqirx	(7)	2	5	0	1	0	2	10
Irérxburx	(2)	0	1	0	1	0	0	2
Baqe-Hararúnx	(2)	2	1	0	0	0	1	4
Batainabura	(2)	2	0	0	0	0	0	2
Total	(43)	14	12	1	4	3	15	49

tional intrasib marriages—that is, a total of eight out of forty-nine, or 16 percent. The frequency of same-name or intrasib marriages involving (Baqe-) Hararúnx spouses would also then rise, becoming six out of twenty-two, or 27 percent. For the present, however, I will accept as valid the name distinctions made by the subjects themselves.

There might be a question, accordingly, whether the largest of the present named groups at Batainabura can fairly be called exogamous. If not exogamous, there is a question whether it may usefully be termed a sib. But if not a sib, then what are these named groups whose members marry those of other sibs at least more often than not? More to the point, perhaps, is what kind of *sibs* are they? I propose to examine the case more closely, focusing primarily on Hararúnx, the largest and obviously the one with the most "intrasib" marriages.

What birthplaces were reported by the spouses in the six apparent cases of intrasib marriage? As shown in table 14, in no case do the spouses list the same birthplace.

TABLE 14

BATAINABURA: BIRTHPLACES AND AGES OF SPOUSES
IN SIX APPARENT "INTRASIB" MARRIAGES

Sib	Husband's Birthplace	Age	Wife's Birthplace	Age
Hararúnx	Near Chanata	47	Irerabura Gatarora	45
	Gatarora	25	Batainabura	25
	Batainabura	32	Gatarora	30
	Batainabura	25	Gatarora	25
Airiná	Gatarora	50	Batainbura	45
Irérxburx	Arau	55	Gatarora Hararuna	40

In one of the other two cases Arau is listed. Arau is a phratry of Northern Tairora within which some elements of present Batainabura or their forebears have in the past taken refuge—and where, in all likelihood, some of their descendants still remain.

Considering different birthplaces is well and good, it may be objected, but surely a sib is either exogamous or it is not. Now the point here is that the present status of sibs may differ from the past. Today Hararúnx, Airiná, or Irérxburx are nominally unified, each a single set of people under a single name; and each may have an exogamous disposition toward future marriages. Their membership, their names, hence the exogamic boundaries at the respective times of birth of the twelve spouses here under consideration, however, cannot be inferred directly from the present standing of the sibs or named groups with which they now identify. The youngest of the twelve spouses is an estimated twenty-five years old, the eldest fifty-five.

What one ideally needs to know, therefore, is the composition and boundaries of each of these three sibs, in effect their corporate histories for the years from 1909 to 1939. What collapsing and merging has occurred? How were the parents of these twelve persons defined? What their own current definition as parents may mean to the marriageability of their respective offspring, from 1964 onwards, may not be the same. The lineal and exogamic status of a member of Hararúnx, Airiná, or Irérxburx named group has almost certainly changed since 1909, including the possible collapse or merging of older named groups. We know, in fact—though only indirectly from the census material—that the exogamic divisions or named groups of modern Batainabura have had quite checkered careers.

Some suggestion of social process and the history of Batainabura sibs is obtained by considering the birthplace provenience of its adult population. I shall focus once more on the six largest sibs at Batainabura. A provenience inventory is admittedly a rough measure. All the sibs are small, but their different sizes mean that, other things being equal, the same diversity will seem greater in a small sib than in a large one. While, in fact, that very situation occurs at Batainabura, there are nevertheless some relationships not attributable to sib size alone. A total of from eleven to thirteen different birthplaces are reported by the eighty-six adult members of the six largest sibs at Batainabura. Two birthplaces are ambiguous, and four censused persons indicated none. (See table 15.)

The larger the number of birthplaces in proportion to the size of its membership, the better the chance that the membership of the sib has been either dispersed or successively relocated in the past. Accordingly, the chance is better that any anomalous marriages apparent in the present census may actually involve spouses who were once defined by different exogamic boundaries. The seeming anomaly, that is, may reflect change. Following the table, Sib Hararúnx, with ten recorded birthplaces among its membership, shows itself to have been either a multilocal personnel or one successively relocated over time, or both. Indeed, this inference is born out by

TABLE 15
BIRTHPLACE PROVENIENCE OF ADULT POPULATION
OF THE SIX LARGEST SIBS AT BATAINABURA

Sib	Censused Population (Adult Male and Female)	Number of Birthplaces (Points of Origin)	Ratio (Average Number of Members per Birthplace)
Hararúnx	35	10	3.5
Airiná	23	4	5.75
Táirxqirx	11	5	2.2
Irérxburx	8	8	1.0
Baqe-Hararúnx	7	3	2.33
Batainabura	2	2	1.0

local history, which suggests that the present Hararúnx personnel are the product of a collapsed local group, if not the remnant of a former phratry, with two or more sibs. One former sib of this local group or phratry is in fact called Baqe. The name still survives, sometimes as "Baqe," sometimes in the compound designation "Baqe-Hararúnx," and, as was earlier noted, sometimes merely as an added comment by or about persons today designated by either name or as "Hararúnx."

Since Hararúnx is the sib with the largest number of seemingly anomalous marriages, it is presumably significant that its membership also has the largest number of points of origin or birthplaces. This suggests, as well as census material can, that the four same-name marriages of Hararúnx may not be anomalous. Rather than increasing the doubt whether the named, siblike personnels of Batainabura observe an exogamic rule, the census material casts lights on the local meaning of exogamy. The census data suggest that circumstances such as separation, merging, and movement mitigate the operation of the exogamic rule, specifically by modifying exogamic boundaries.

Airiná, with only one same-name marriage, contrasts in degree with Hararúnx, and its membership also records only four points of origin. The modern personnel of Airiná again appear to be a group whose forebears may have been scattered at least once in recent generations, and the present members are probably, like Hararúnx's, the scions of a collapsed local group. They are conceivably the descendants of a collapsed phratry, though their smaller numbers, as well as their fewer points of origin, make this less likely, I should say, than in the case of Hararúnx. A further difference between the former status and subsequent careers of Hararúnx and Airiná, respectively, concerns location. The Airiná appear to be living today within or close to the traditional territory of their forebears. It may therefore be that Airiná's spatial dislodgment has been less (if not also less frequent) than Hararúnx's, that the Airiná were not formerly joined with the Hararúnx (or their predecessor elements) in a single local group, and, when the merger occurred, that it was more a case of the Hararúnx moving to Airiná territory than the opposite.

Irérxburx is the third group with a same-name marriage. This single occurrence, like the single one in Sib Airiná, might not by itself warrant the
present extended examination. However, the comparison of these siblike
personnels, in light of the fragmentation, collapse, and subsequent merging
that has apparently produced modern Batainabura and its sibs, can be justified for its broader implications. Irérxburx has eight birthplaces for its eight
adult members—one apiece, obviously the highest diversity possible. This
group, though small, is of sufficient size, perhaps, that the diversity of its
adult members can be considered significant. Apart from those who were
born in recent years in the present territory (that is, at Batainabura or Gatarora), the average age of surviving Irérxburx members is higher than the
average age of the two larger sibs. Taken altogether, these facts suggest that
Irérxburx people may also derive from a collapsed former local group. If so,
it is one that may have collapsed—or one whose forebears at any rate
merged their identity with elements of either former Airiná or former Hararúnx—before those two streams of people themselves merged.

The foregoing suggestions cannot be read as simple history. Nor does this
sketch obviate a full and detailed treatment of local histories, if such can be
developed while there is still time. The sketch will nevertheless have a
cautionary value. It warns against the careless inference that Batainabura's
sibs and other named personnels like them have remained stationary in
space, have followed lineal consistency in recruitment, or have held constant
in designating their own forebears when they merged.

5. The History of Two Phratries

Could one take the "events" of Abiera and Batainabura history at such close range as those of the census, it would make a very long and detailed account. The reader would be inundated with place names; personal names; the names and alternate names of sibs, segments, lineages, and settlements; the content of agreements; the particulars of disputes; the marriages and other exchanges; the killings and counterkillings; the sorcery; the flights and relocations; the host groups; the refugees; and so on. The microcosmic history of such microcosms is eventful. Yet an ample if somewhat less detailed social and cultural history of the peoples of the Northern Tairora area would still be desirable as a basis from which to select cases for analysis and on which to base generalizations about the organization of local society.

A modestly adequate record of the personnel of these two local groups and their forebears is not readily obtained. Establishing the movements of a community in space, the people who joined them, the people who separated and their reasons, the sites and the shifting of settlements, gardens, and pig ranges, the opposing groups, the helping groups, those who gave them women, those who received women from them, and all the rest—such a record requires patience and dogged persistence to assemble and even more to order. Only a part of the difficulty is the sheer multiplicity of events at such small scale. A further part is the lack of both writing and disciplined local chroniclers to help with the task. Even to be able to approximate a connected account of developments is a rare and welcome exception in my experience of informants at Abiera and Batainabura. However much they know, their information tends to be issued in scraps—usually, it appears, something that reflects a high dramatic point or something of particular relevance for the moment, the merest synopsis, or an item of personal involvement in the flow of happenings. Persons or groups enter a story or drop from sight without more than offhand explanation. Their importance tends to be the practical importance they have as contingencies for the group or individual of central concern to the storyteller: how they helped or hindered, were strong or weak, trustworthy or treacherous, generous or niggardly, and so on.

One is sometimes lucky even to get the real actors; a collective, communal "they" or "all of them" is often assigned responsibility for events in which individuals, singly or at most in small number, must have been prime movers. Or a single strong man is spoken of when a larger group must have been involved. All of this, in any case, is likely to be described with little emphasis or concern for the long-run development. It is things-as-they-are, things-at-a-certain-moment, a highly immediate, synoptic, and situational kind of account. It is a truncated, disconnected, episodic history, a quickly shifting welter of events overtly lacking growth, cumulation, or build-up. Gradual changes, the background of events, must usually be inferred. A residential break between two factions of a community, for example, occurs rather precipitately, purportedly at the moment when some of the principals want something in which they are thwarted by members of the other faction. A sense of increasing tension between the two factions is lacking, not to mention any notice of such facts as increasing local population or pressure on resources. There may be no acknowledgement that the factions have been drawing apart for some time before their final split. The trend is summarized or noted only in the culminating incident—if it is not ignored.

A consistent feature of vernacular histories at Batainabura and Abiera is their selective and utilitarian character. The past is used insofar as it is useful to those to whom it belongs—the local people. Their usual orientation is to cases rendered with the partisanship of the participant. The history of segmentation, residence, and land tenure, or the composition of local groups are matters apart. A man may, for example, assert indigenous status for residents whose rights as the descendants of acknowledged immigrants would be less firmly established. This is not a matter of deception, however, but of convention and emphasis. It is a claim of legitimacy more than a historic account. Thus, in addition to the actual ebb and flow of social history is the ebb and flow of conventional emphasis and omission, the selectivity of local traditions.

The case of the Poreqórxntx sib in Phratry Tairora is instructive. Members of this group are found in number at Abiera and in several nearby communities, but their very name suggests an origin outside the Tairora ethnolinguistic pool. Indeed, *Pore* was the traditional name given by Tairora speakers to peoples among whom were those speaking the language today known as Auyana. Though related to Tairora, Auyana is as foreign as German is to Polish. Yet most informants insisted that the Poreqórxntx were indigenous Tairora, their name containing no implication that the founders came from the Auyana country (see map 5) or ever spoke as their native tongue anything but Tairora.

The ethnographer is naturally interested in the uses people make of their history. In Northern Tairora it is a datum of major importance, for the asser-

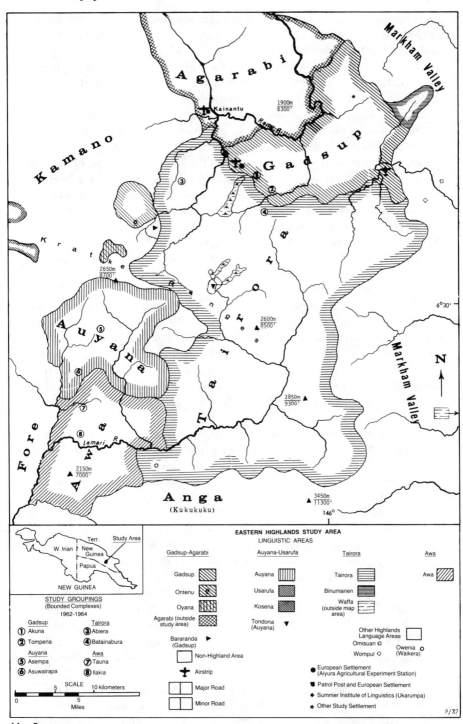

Map 5.

tion of certain kinds of historical connections implies rights, and the absence or denial of such connections implies the opposite. It is one thing if the ancestors of the Poreqórxntx have "always" lived where they are, participating as "Tairora" in the development of that entity from local group to phratry. That would mean the Poreqórxntx forebears did not enter the present groups and territories of Tairora as immigrants within the last one hundred years or so. At least, then, there is no evidence of their admission and assimilation as an alien immigrant group. If, however, the *pore* name is no coincidence, and the forebears of this group are the immigrants they appear to be, the ethnographer may obtain a measure of the historical process, of how radically different an ethnic group may be and yet be absorbed by a Northern Tairora community, and of how soon and how completely they acquire the rights of long-term indigenous residents, erasing the marks of their origin.

The present chapter will not by any means provide a full chronicle of Abiera or Batainabura—not even for the years which memory best serves. Like any history, the chapter will be selective and synthetic. Its selectivity is mainly designed to reveal the strategy of Northern Tairora vernacular histories. By discovering the kinds of events that are omitted or neglected in the purely conventional accounts, as well as the kinds of things that are stressed, one can reveal the pattern of vernacular history and much else about the dynamics of Northern Tairora social structure. For Northern Tairora vernacular histories prove to be in large part an explanation and a justification for Northern Tairora social groupings and alignments. The histories are an explanation from today's retrospect, to be sure, more than an account of the motives and purposes of past actors, though they purport to be such an account.

At least two levels can conveniently be recognized in the history of each local group. One level is the events of the past. To the extent that they can be ascertained, I will attempt to sketch such a history for each group. The other level is the conventional use that local people make of the events of the past. In reporting this level of history, one is stating what is most readily recorded, with the least resort to prompting or probing or to comparison with other accounts. I wish to consider each level of local history in light of the other. The purpose of comparing these two levels of history is to characterize the process of Northern Tairora tradition as an adjunct to Northern Tairora politics and sociology. This purpose need not exclude an interest in the quality of Northern Tairora life for individuals and groups, but that is secondary. The character of life is little stressed by Northern Tairora raconteurs, moreover, for they tacitly assume the same life conditions throughout most of their history. Thus their concern—and therefore mine—is in effect sociology and politics within a constant cultural frame—that is, without culture change.

The chapter will in one more sense take history rather narrowly. It will be almost exclusively concerned with the movements of groups in space-time, that is, with fission, segmentation, merging or fusion, naming, and territoriality. Here again, I follow the emphasis of vernacular history. Generally speaking, I am attempting to provide here as much information as possible to the end of enlightening the census data reported in the previous chapter. In other words, if the two censuses are taken as descriptions of certain aspects of Abiera and Batainabura at a particular juncture in their respective careers, this chapter on history will suggest, if it cannot show in detail, how each community arrived at that juncture.

It can presumably go without elaboration that "reconstruction"is involved in writing such a chapter, for reconstruction is involved in all historiography, even in writing a report of a crime committed last night.

Abiera

Abiera's history as a part of Phratry Tairora is traced directly to a previous community called "Tairora." In a sense, there is more than one account of the founding of Tairora, and these accounts appear to exist in different compartments of the local mind. A mythical pair of siblings, Elder Sister and Younger Brother, allegedly established all the peoples of the world. In their travels, Elder Sister, and her little brother came from a place to the southwest of Abiera. Proceeding to the northeast—toward the Markham Valley— they left behind them along their way the ancestral nuclei of every present-day community and people of the area. Thus was Tairora also, by implication, founded. A song cycle known as *hakóri* (Agarabi: *akóriye*) describes at length the travels and deeds of the two. This mythical account is complete and exhaustive in the eyes of older informants, and in support of their view they point out that even the origin of the white man is included. When they reached the Markham Valley, Elder Sister and Younger Brother went on to the coast, where they founded the race of Europeans, endowing them with all of their distinctive possessions and attributes.

It is not only the mythicoritual character of the *hakóri* song cycle that differs from other accounts of the origin of Abiera and Tairora. The *hakóri* represents the population of Tairora, the ancestral community, as having been established *in situ* and without predecessors, as well as by mythical personages (*báriqa*) from the southwest. *Hakóri* establishes by implication a connection between all present speakers of the Tairora tongue, furthermore, not to mention other peoples of the earth. In other contexts, however, Abiera informants deny such a connection. They consider the people of Phratry Arogara to the south of them, for example, to have nothing to do with Tairora history. The Arogara "have another story." It is even sometimes contended that Arogara speak a different language, though there are to the outsider's ear only differences of dialect. When similarity of languages is not denied, it is simply dismissed as irrelevant to any connection between Arogara and Phratry Tairora people. These neighboring groups are also traditional enemies.

Whether in *hakóri* or other accounts of Tairora's origin, there is at least no

uncertainty about the location of the ancestral community. A site identified
with Tairora is well known to nearly everyone old enough to take an interest
in such matters. It lies approximately two miles to the south of Abiera, on
the way to Bontaqa, another Phratry Tairora village. There is indeed a former habitation site at that place—or more likely a complex of sites. The people themselves point to old cooking pits, some now visible in profile where a
cut was made for the government road; and in their gardening of the area
they often come upon other features. J. D. Cole made an archeological survey of the vicinity and found it literally peppered with former habitation
sites, but the local people feel they know which is Tairora proper (Watson
and Cole 1977).

The Tairora community is the conventional point of origin (*ógxrx*) for all
the members of the the Phratry Tairora today. Its story, hence, is their story
and Abiera's story, though no one lives at Tairora now. Tairora was founded
by a man called Gáiburuxnátx, accompanied, in some versions, by his two
brothers. This founder is not formally mentioned in *hakóri*, to be sure,
though a question on the point may result in an effort to rationalize the two
accounts. The founder and his brothers came from the east and stood on the
ridge above the future site, surveying the country. They came, according to
informants who profess to know, from a place near present Saiora (see map
6). Thus they would have come from beyond Batainabura. Accordingly, I
asked at Batainabura about an individual by the name of Gáiburuxnátx.

A legendary individual called Gáiburuxnátx is indeed known at Batainabura. There, however, this personage is a woman who figures prominently
in a story about *ihálabu*, a renewal ceremony no longer observed though still
remembered by older informants. She carelessly (or wantonly) invites her
husband to copulate with her, failing to inform him that preparations for the
renewal ceremony are under way. (He does not know of the impending ceremony, having been absent on a journey.) He dies as a result of his pollution
by the woman—evidently his wife. This is the reason, it is suggested, that
the people have now abandoned the *ihálabu* ceremony, because of its danger. Batainabura informants are generally unaware of Gáiburuxnátx as the
founder of Tairora.

Abiera informants are ignorant of the female Gáiburuxnátx (Tairora: "ancestor's wife"?) and are surprised to hear of her. They neither deny the
authenticity of Batainabura's version, however, nor doubt their own.[1] The
hint of a female founder who might have been masculinized in subsequent
conventionalization is at least interesting.

Gáiburuxnátx liked the look of the Tairora country and, descending the
ridge, built his house at the site of that name. The area was quite empty of
people at the time, though it is said to have been, then as now, a large ex-

1. There is a general disposition among people of this area to accept as authoritative a local
account of what are obviously local matters. Indeed, the very idea that each group knows best
its own things is pointedly stressed.

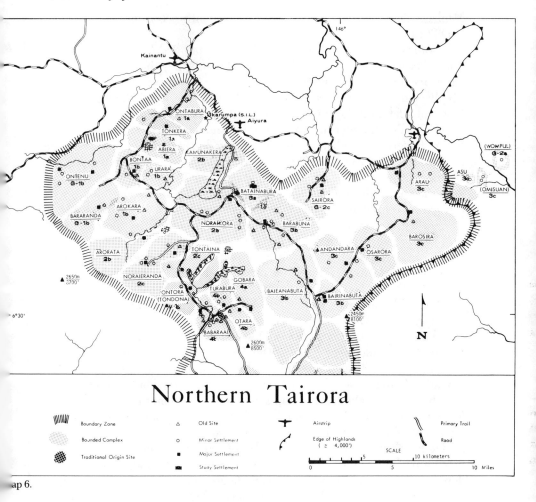

Map 6.

panse of grassland with little remnant bush, suggesting long occupancy. If they paused at all, Gáiburuxnátx's two brothers remained only briefly at Tairora, going off in other directions to found other settlements and lineages. Some say one of the brothers went to Nompia (see map 6) to found that people. While probably a part of the traditional account and not the informant's speculation, this detail resembles certain others in being more tentative than the rest. It may be no less "true" than other details, that is, and it is at least of sufficient interest to be included as a part of the story. But it is not today of primary concern to Abiera chroniclers. Such a connection with Nompia may have been of greater interest in the past, however, indicating the varying emphasis that different events are given, evidently according to their social or political relevance.

Gáiburuxnátx had at least two offspring, sons *PeNkxpeNkx* and *Ai-ai*. These became the "fingers" of his posterity and thus the first native-born ancestors of the present Phratry Tairora. Some informants, moreover, identify the sons of *Gáiburuxnátx* in principle with the sibs of Phratry Tairora. Since their father is the apical ancestor of the present phratry, the vernacular imagery makes the idea at least plausible. Ambiguity arises, however, since these "fingers" immediately follow the founder. To suggest that the sons founded the modern sibs of Phratry Tairora, therefore, would imply that the sibs in question existed from the beginning of the Tairora settlement. This is not in keeping with the conventional account of these specific sibs. Nor is convention consistent on what the *original* sibs of Tairora were or what they were called, nor on their connection with the present sibs. The relation of the founder's offspring to the several sibs of Tairora today thus remains quite hypothetical. A questioner may be referred to some older person, very likely someone now dead, for information on which son was the specific progenitor of which sib. The belief that PeNkxpeNkx or Ai-ai founded the sibs of modern Tairora, in any case, nicely illustrates the telescoping of vernacular history.

From the era of Gáiburuxnátx and his sons to the next remembered events is a period of uncertain length. The founding of Tairora by this man is thought to be the beginning of the entire Phratry Tairora, numbering today around a thousand people. The original Tairora settlement itself reputedly soon became a sizable local group solely from the numerous progeny of its founders. It became large enough, in fact, to furnish personnel for the colonization of several offshoot local groups, some of them continuing in the area today as sibs. Yet the interval is largely empty of names, and those that may be put forward are known only to certain persons and seem to be ordered in no consistent way. Pressed on the question of so few original people generating so many, an informant often acknowledges that there were probably "others" in fact. Their names are unknown to him, but he suggests that they may be known (or, more likely, may have *been* known) to older authorities and guardians of the lore.

It is fair to regard these founders as not only legendary but the names of some of them as stock names. That has already been noted in the case of Gáiburuxnátx, who is known in quite another guise at Batainabura. The names PeNkxpeNkx and Ai-ai, in fact, and perhaps that of their father as well, may be drawn from a repertory of legendary names that reaches beyond Abiera and Batainabura, even crossing linguistic boundaries to include other parts of the Kainantu area. The reduplication of these names, doubtless of mnemonic value, is untypical of contemporary Northern Tairora personal names, but names quite like these crop up in more than one legendary or mythical context and in more than one community of the Kainantu vicinity. Though such names resemble each other, often closely, the personages so designated vary. At Abiera, for instance, PeNkxpeNkx and Ai-ai are founding ancestors of the second order, but at Aiamontina, an Agarabi village perhaps fifteen miles distant, one of them is the man who originally stole the sacred flutes, the drum, and the bull-roarer from a primordial woman, the original owner. In such a role a figure will be styled *bxriqx* or bxriqxbáinti (Agarabi: *mxniq* or *mxniqbanta*), that is, "legendary man"; but this means "ancestor" only in the very general sense of a man who lived in the distant past. The term *bxriqx* is not applied to persons in the ordinary genealogical sense of kinsmen of remembered generations.

The founding of Tairora, then, as Abiera chroniclers in this case represent it, somewhat resembles the founding of Rome. Its reputed founders appear to be quite conventionalized, and its founding occurred in a conventional past, probably one more remote than informants themselves can recognize. That past is not well connected with the present nor with the immediate past. That is, the immediate past, the past for which reliable and consistent individual names or deeds are obtainable, seems to follow a substantial interval during which names are inconsistent or unobtainable. In Tairora vernacular history the effect is to make the time of origin seem more recent than, in other respects, available information suggests it to be. Time is collapsed or telescoped so that Gáiburuxnátx and his offspring would seem to have lived about five to seven generations ago. Intervening generations have largely been forgotten and conventional names from older accounts—probably legends—have been substituted for the actual names of the more recent people, just as the founders have been conventionally reduced to a single man and his two sons.

Naturally I know neither the time of founding nor the duration of settlement of the original Tairora vicinity, though it is possible that excavations in this area will eventually reveal something. Ethnologically it is easier to speculate about events that occurred during or by the end of occupancy. From the number and size of subsequent social divisions, from the conventional account, and from the existence of some present members of Phratry Tairora who trace their lineage directly to the Tairora personnel (that is, not through one of its constituent sibs of a different name), this local group probably produced the offshoots that are today attributed to it more than a century or two before contact. If the time span can be established, it would be of some help in determining rates of population growth and the rapidity of spread of daughter communities. It will also provide a measure for the development of traditional history. One surely cannot overlook that the historic Tairora—the local group so well remembered by the members of the phratry today—was probably not the first settlement in the vicinity, nor perhaps even the first settlement of Tairora-speaking people. Quite possibly it was only the last or best remembered of a sequence of Tairora settlements, but the one immediately preceding, generating, and giving its name collectively to the offshoot communities that now fill the valley and constitute the phratry. In this sense the "Tairora" of the vernacular account would represent the telescoping of a series of earlier settlements into a single, remembered—indeed, more recent—settlement, just as the ancestral names represent a telescoping of several generations of forebears into a single, remembered but, in fact, ancient handful of names. Even the coming of the founder from a "place near Saiora" may indicate an influx of people more recent than the first settlement of Tairora and its vicinity—that is, a group that joined others already resident in the vicinity of Tairora.

The founding ancestors are commemorated only in their names, in the traditional account of their descendants, and in the site of Tairora. Monuments other than the site itself appear to be lacking. The graves and the bones of these men, for instance, are not mentioned, and none of the megaliths that remain in use or are recognized in this vicinity are specifically attributed by Abiera informants to Gáiburuxnátx or his people.

Tradition, as noted, has the founder of Tairora entering empty country. Unless he arrived much earlier than is conventionally assumed, this can hardly have been the case. As mentioned before, numerous archeological sites are evident throughout the vicinity—far more than conventional history recalls. Some of these manifestations differ from modern structures though nonetheless recognized as "theirs" by the modern Tairora. (Large, circular earthen structures are a notable example.) Gáiburuxnátx's predecessors in the Tairora area, if not the people actually displaced by him, may well have included groups of Agarabi, Gadsup, or Oyana speech. (I have no reason to suggest, however, that these people built the circular structures.) These three languages are closely related (McKaughan 1964), and the modern areas of all three adjoin the territory of the Tairora (see maps 5 and 6). The territory of Phratry Tairora is in effect a salient between Gadsup-Agarabi and Oyana. Abiera traditions do not record a displacement of any such peoples from the area of the Tairora, to be sure, and such a tradition may also be lacking among the other peoples.

Oyana (Ontenu) and Gadsup (Aiyura) villagers, at any rate, view this small cluster of Gadsup-Agarabi-related speakers to the west of Tairora as the product of a remembered migration from Gadsup. Such a migration allegedly took place within fairly recent times—certainly since Tairora speakers have been occupying their present position. There is no reason to deny the occurrence of migrations from Gadsup to Oyana, between whom there continues to be active marital exchange. There is little evidence, however, to support the view that a recent migration actually established this small cluster of Oyana speakers. Indeed, estimated lexicostatistical differences between Gadsup and Oyana run from a maximum of 850 years (Wurm 1960, 1961a) to a minimum of 357 years (McKaughan 1964:99). Even the lesser figure is beyond the postulated recency of the Gadsup migration and, no doubt, also beyond the range of traditional local histories in recording events of this sort with modern sib and personal names. Moreover, since Oyana speech resembles Agarabi more closely than Gadsup, there is further cause to doubt that a Gadsup migration founded the Oyana cluster.

My opinion is that the Oyana cluster is an isolated remnant of Gadsup-Agarabi speakers, cut off about three centuries or so before contact by an incursion of Tairora speakers. The general direction of the incursion would be the same, incidentally, as the direction taken by the traditional founder of Tairora. The movement could have been the migration of a refugee group or some other, perhaps more hostile, expansion. It established, in any case, a salient between Oyana and the main block of their Gadsup and Agarabi congeners to the north and east. McKaughan, to whom I originally proposed the idea, considers it sound from the standpoint of language relationships and has adduced further considerations (1964:108). Subsequent migration and marital interchange between Oyana and Gadsup (or Agarabi) would of course be possible, and local traditions that claim it are probably correct.

If substantially true, this reading of traditions, movements, positions, and relationships again reveals the foreshortening of vernacular histories in the Northern Tairora area. It reveals the specific foreshortening of Abiera's view of the founding of her parent community and especially the elimination from the record of any information such as to imply preemption or to becloud a claim to territory. If the time estimated—say 350 years—is approximately correct as a minimum, then, to be sure, continued maintenance of territorial rights against effective challenge would suffice to establish the Tairora claim as firmly as such claims can ever be established under the conditions that prevail in this area. Little could be served in Tairora history by recalling—were it possible to do so—the prior tenure of other, especially alien, peoples. A convention of "empty country" would thus fulfill all needs and have little challenge.

Recognizing that the vernacular history of Tairora is foreshortened also allows more time for the peopling of the Tairora Valley with groups who today regard themselves as part of a single—Tairora—phratry. It is not necessary to suppose that this population, from its presumed start in a single Tairora settlement, was built up wholly by natural increase. Yet it is not likely that a mere handful of immigrants of the Tairora ethnolinguistic group, arriving among a substantial alien population, could alone have succeeded, in a century or less, in "Tairorizing" them all. A minimum of two or three centuries is more reasonable.

The territorial expansion of an ethnolinguistic pool is suggested here. The salient occupied today by members of Phratry Tairora is one border of what may be an expanding Tairora-speaking population and ethnolinguistic pool. It may not be irrelevant to the postulated encroachment on neighboring groups, moreover, that the Tairora ethnolinguistic pool is in fact the largest in the immediate area. The ultimate questions raised by such an expansion—demographic, ecological, psychological, and political—can only be noted for the moment. But such implications presumably justify a fine-toothed combing of local microhistories like Phratry Tairora's. Tairora expansion on this salient has seemingly been at the cost of eliminating other ethnolinguistic codes from the area and their replacement by a Tairora language and largely Tairora culture. The elimination is not complete, however, for there is evidence of unusual Gadsup-Agarabi influence in the Tairora Valley—influence not matched in other parts of the Northern Tairora area, even parts, such as Batainabura, that adjoin the Gadsup. For one thing, people of Abiera refer to their annual renewal ceremonies (no longer observed) as *órxnx*, using this Agarabi word (Gadsup: *órande*) instead of *ihálabu*, an obvious Tairora term, found, for instance, at Batainabura. Indeed, the Abiera literally "fetch *órxnx*" from certain Agarabi villages. The *hakóri* song cycle (Agarabi: *akóriye*), previously mentioned, also appears to have an Agarabi provenience, since the cycle (at least by that name) is little known or unknown in Tairora-speaking groups bordering the Tairora phratry. A third example is the *hampu* (Agarabi: *ámpu*), an elaborate ritual for drawing women to their lovers or would-be husbands in enemy villages. Phratry Tairora people specifically acknowledge *hampu* to be an Agarabi derivation, and it is unknown or unused elsewhere among the Northern Tairora. Certain varieties of sorcery are also known to Phratry Tairora people by Agarabi names.

It is sometimes stated that few if any New Guinea peoples war for territory. Such a statement can be challenged, in my view, if meant to imply that New Guinea peoples do not expand in territory at someone's cost, or contract at their own, or that warfare plays no part in such territorial changes. It may widely be true, however, that warfare is not consciously or systematically practiced for the capture and immediate use of territory. But in the Tairora vicinity local groups withdraw from the threat of repeated attack if they do not feel confident of confronting it. They seek the relative safety of distance or of more defensible positions, if their own territories afford it. Otherwise they seek asylum in the territories of dependable hosts. In either case, formerly occupied areas might be emptied of occupants, sometimes offering an expanding group the opportunity to move in and settle them.

Through fission a colonizing group might find it desirable to use areas of bush, garden land, pig range, and settlement sites separate from those of the parent community. The coming of the Tairora founders to the Tairora Valley may have had the character of such a gradual expansion; or the Tairora speakers—or the founders of phratry—may have come initially as refugees among hosts of Agarabi-Gadsup-Oyana speech, subsequently dominating them; or something may have occurred resembling a frank expulsion of earlier occupants of the valley. In light of the processes visible in the ethnographic present, what occurred probably involved a certain amount of assimilation or absorption, quite likely involving alliance and intermarriage with some segments of the ethnolinguistic groups eventually displaced. A fairly gradual process is indicated, in other words, in which small groups of Tairora language and culture were variously arrayed against small groups of other languages or cultures.

A gradual process of expansion could well generate the present tradition of Tairora military success and bellicosity yet permit the selective enmities of

Phratry Tairora people against individual communities of Oyana, Gadsup, and Agarabi, at the expense of whose ancestors Tairora expansion perhaps developed. A gradual process would not make uncompromising enemies of every group of Tairora against every group of these neighboring languages, nor would it produce a tradition of a conquering Tairora group expelling its predecessors wholesale from the territory it now claims. In fine, such a process would facilitate the empty-country theme of Tairora tradition.

To return for the last time to the conventional theme, had the Tairora Valley actually been found empty and settled by the Tairora founders as pioneers, the implications for the history and ecology of this area would be quite dramatic. Such an event would suggest some spurt in population or an intensification in the movement of peoples in recent centuries with large, unoccupied areas being rather rapidly peopled. While proof of such a development would give great weight to the hypothesis of a population explosion in the Central Highlands in recent centuries (Brass 1941: Raulet, unpub.; Oomen et al. 1961; Watson 1965a, 1965b; Howlett 1967:9), it is not necessary to go so far in support of the case. A slower expansion of Tairora speakers and its displacement of other groups would seem quite enough— even to satisfy the requirements of the population explosion–sweet potato hypothesis.

At some time within the span of tradition known to certain older Abiera residents, and certainly before the abandonment of the last settlement of Tairora, one or more groups of Auyana-speaking people were present or were entering Tairora territory. Older Abiera informants believe that they came as refugees driven by enemies from their own country, substantially the same territory as that today occupied by people by Auyana speech (see map 5). It is conceivable that Auyana speakers were already present in the area when the Tairora founders came—that is, as prior residents. The argument here would be essentially the same as that advanced in connection with the "empty country" theme. Moreover, present Auyana territory is not so far away as to make this inconceivable, though, unlike the Oyana, Auyana territory is not adjacent to Tairora on this part of its ethnolinguistic boundary. Not only Abiera traditions, however, but traditions of the present Auyana themselves (S. Robbins, pers. comm.), unequivocally support a recent refugee origin of these people in Phratry Tairora. Two conclusions follow: (1) if there were Auyana-speaking occupants in the present area of the Phratry prior to the settlement of Tairora speakers, their ranks have been subsequently augmented by more recent Auyana refugees; (2) some if not all of the refugees probably came within the last seventy-five years or so. Otherwise the tradition of a refugee origin would be weaker than it is. The tradition is already moribund, at any rate, at least among the Phratry Tairora descendants of the refugees, though it may be better known among the modern Auyana.

Descendants of the Auyana group are today called Poreqórxntx, that is, the "*pore* or Auyana people." More generally the term *pore* is used in this

area by Tairora speakers (as well as Agarabi and probably other ethnolinguistic groups) to refer to the people or peoples to the south of them.[2] The Poreqórxntx are sociologically a sib, comparable to others in Phratry Tairora. A
local segment of Poreqórxntx is in fact the largest sib group in Abiera. Except
for the probing of the ethnographer and the candor—or, better, knowledge—of the older informant, Poreqórxntx members stress that they are
full-fledged phratric Tairora, their fathers and grandfathers having "always"
lived at Tairora as members of the local group. Younger men tend to insist,
therefore, that the name *pore* means nothing but the designation of their sib.
Its similarity to the vernacular name of the Auyana enthnolinguistic group,
say these informants, is pure coincidence.

A few Poreqo individuals assert that they are "strictly Tairora." The claim
may not lack technical foundation, but historically it is at least ambiguous.
Without special qualification, "Tairora" (literally Tairórxtárxntx) refers to the
membership of the phratry so called. A small number of individuals, however, are sometimes designated "Tairora" in the logical sense of a sib. These
are otherwise unaffiliated persons (or their descendants) who were among
the last to live in the Tairora settlement before the local group remembered
by that name ceased to be. The last residents of this local group, in all likelihood, included some persons of *pore* descent, as well as descendants whose
predecessors were, so far as tradition acknowledges, Tairora speakers. Individuals of either kind might in the sense indicated claim to be "strictly
Tairora." That is, they—or their fathers—continued to reside in the parent
local group or territory for some time after offshoot groups had moved out to
settle elsewhere, in at least two cases founding the present-day sibs of the
phratry. When the parent local group itself ceased to exist at Tairora, its
surviving residents, including those known as Poreqórxntx, dispersed to take
up residence among the other local groups that had by then developed
within the phratry. In speaking of themselves in the context of other phratry
members, therefore, these former residents of Tairora, or their descendants,
sometimes refer to being "strictly [or "true"] Tairora." They simply mean
that they, if anyone, have the right to be identified with the parent group,
since they or their fathers lived there more recently, if not for longer, than
any other members of the phratry that derives its name from the community. Carried to its logical extreme, however, this line of argument becomes
hard to sustain. It would make some members of Sib Pore more "Tairora"
than some descendants of the phratry's indigenous forebears, because the
latter broke away from the parent local group before settlement there
ended. The ambiguity nonetheless nicely highlights the principles on which
membership in Northern Tairora descent groups is based: paternity or filia-
tion is stressed in the short run; but in the longer view what is important is
descent from progenitors coresident in a conventional ancestral group,
which gives its name to the sib or phratry in question.

2. The term *pore* is probably widespread in the region, and it may in fact be the origin of the
modern name of the ethnolinguistic group today known as Fore.

Older Poreqo informants with whom I spoke do not quibble. They readily acknowledge that their forefathers were immigrant refugees whose native tongue—when they came, it was called *pore*—is the language now called Auyana. They further point out that the refugees had not only been hard pressed before they left their native territories in Auyana country but continued to have a hard time of it among their new neighbors. By no means, they insisted, were the Poreqo soon able to find relief in exile, for the kinsmen of their hosts, if not the hosts themselves, kept them constantly off balance. The original refugees, in fact, underwent further dispersion through flight. Mátoto, a strong man who died about 1930, finally consolidated the position of the remnant Poreqo group in the area, thereby apparently making them his clients and willing cohorts (Watson 1967a). He gave them his personal assurance that they would be able to live at ease with his group as their hosts, and his power was evidently sufficient to make the guarantee effective. Indeed, with the addition to Abiera's ranks of the Poreqo men, Abiera became, from perhaps 1910 or 1915 until contact, a military power to reckon with in the Northern Tairora area. Until Mátoto, according to one elder informant, the Poreqo had lived precariously, some of them even being driven into farther refuge areas such as Agarabi. Europeans assumed political control of the area in the early 1930s, soon after Mátoto's death. The general effect was to stabilize local politics and guarantee the status quo. No serious question has since arisen concerning the future of the Poreqo sib in Phratry Tairora.

Although a military crisis originally forced the Poreqo ancestors from their native territories and seems to explain their presence as a sib in the Phratry Tairora, one elder Poreqo man also described their origin as a descent group in the conventional terms of a founding figure. In this case, the principle founder was an ancestress, and the informant feels that her people, the first wave of the native-born (Tairora) Poreqórxntx, took their lineage from her. According to the informant, the woman was held in highest regard by the Tairora. Many of them, recognizing her qualities, wanted to marry her, but she always refused her suitors. The implication is that she was a widow at some point, but this was not explicit. The reference to a woman at least suggests a female link of some kind with Tairora. The key is possibly that the original refugees followed common practice in choosing for asylum a place where they already had affinal connections through intermarriage. Such a detail could not be confirmed with my informant, however, and it must remain merely a logical possibility that the Poreqo "ancestress" was a Tairora-speaking bride (or one of several) originally married into the Auyana group, either while they still lived in their native territories or after they reached their refuge in Tairora phratric territory. Affinal ties through marital exchange are generally assumed, either as the basis on which a decision to seek asylum is made, or subsequently as a means of establishing or cementing relations between refugees and hosts. The story of the Poreqo ancestress, however, was known only to a few elder specialists.

Today the Poreqórxntx, with whatever accretions or losses have occured in the meanwhile, are the largest sib at Abiera and are strongly represented also at Hapárira and at nearby Bontaqa, a local group which, partly for this reason, is closely linked with Abiera. There are Poreqo representatives in other Tairora local groups as well. It may be of some significance that the Poreqórxntx, though now a large group, have shown little tendency to subdivide or develop a distinct name or local identification for any of their local branches. The Poreqórxntx of Abiera may be contrasted in this respect with the Komohórxntx. The latter are equally a local segment of a large sib (Óndxbúrx) but now designate themselves in this special local sense, Komohórxntx, presumably as a prelude to further segmentation within Sib Óndxbúrx. It is possible that the original designation of Poreqórxntx as an alien group has produced through opposition a solidarity in their ranks that may not be matched in the ranks of every Northern Tairora sib.

The name Poreqórxntx is not intrinsically different from most sib or lineal names in this vicinity. To be sure, it is not the name of a particular local group, but is it nevertheless a territorial designation indicating the conventionally accepted provenience of the group and their putative founders. Non-Tairora-speaking women married into Abiera, for instance, are known by similar inclusive ethnic designations, like "Kamáno", rather than by the name of their own specific local group. In the case of this sib, the name carries an alien connotation only because the term *pore* refers to the people of that (Auyana) country (or to the country of that people) and because it is a country that is ethnically alien. One has to learn another language, for one thing, to speak to native-born *pore* people. Quite as important as their name in the identification of the Poreqórxntx sib is that the country of the *pore* and the people of the *pore* country continue to exist. Indeed, since contact, the Tairora of Abiera can come and go in visiting friends and trading partners in Auyana more freely than before. In this contact, however, the members of Sib Poreqo have no special advantage and, indeed, seem less important than members of Sib Kómoho.

It would probably be a mistake to emphasize the name as a name more than this. It is but a reminder that the Poreqórxntx arose from an immigration of outsiders still remembered, while the other sibs with origin place names, as far as is remembered, arose from conventional division within the ancestral community—its conventional "fingers." The Poreqo name and its connection with an alien group of the present day thus only serve as a trace element for someone, such as an ethnographer, concerned with the history of local migrations. Neither an immigration of this sort nor subsequent phratric affiliation is unique in the social processes of this area, and the passage of time has nearly erased it from memory.

What concrete effects can be ascribed to the sense of the alien about the Poreqórxntx? At Abiera they are, as noted, the largest sib (see table 5), and their women furnish the largest number of brides for the men of the second-largest—traditionally indigenous—sib. It would be socially disadvantageous, if not destructive, to widen the distinction and the distance between Poreqórxntx and Komohórxntx. Despite the cessation of open fighting, Abiera people are still by no means indifferent to their numbers compared to rival groups. During a period when several deaths occurred in short succession and were attributed to enemy sorcery, men commented to the following effect: "They are killing us all [or "killing us like insects"] because we cannot fight them now (under the laws enforced by the Administration). But our women are having lots of children; and as fast as they kill our people, new ones are being born."

The origin of the Poreqórxntx may occasionally be brought up in disputes or altercations within the Abiera community. In this context, it seems to have little if any more weight or meaning than other convenient epithets that might be flung at a disputant. Were it the intent to deny the rights of a Poreqo sib member to land, for example, there would be small basis indeed for acting on the charge. Poreqo people have been a part of the Abiera community for nearly as long as the community has existed—certainly since before the present settlement was founded. Poreqo men own trees—having planted them—and the gardens of Poreqo (in fact, more than Poreqo dwellings within the village) are intermixed with the gardens of others. Children of Komohórxntx parents have been given in adoption as well as wardship to Poreqórxntx. It is easy, thus, to face down any such challenge. The slander—if one could even call it that—is too weak to be intimidating.

Most disputes begin by involving only individuals; and to make an epithet of a group designation tends at once to give allies to a Poreqo adversary. To complicate the matter, many Poreqo are already one's affinal kin, with whom certain behavior—cooperative or circumspect—is enjoined by custom.

Although far from occupying a separate part of the Abiera settlement, the Poreqórxntx are relatively discrete compared with the residential intermixture of the sibs of Batainabura. While substantially smaller in numbers than the Poreqórxntx, however, the Komohórxntx tend to act as spokesmen and to dominate the political life of the community. Both the *luluai* and the *tultul*, for example, are Komohórxntx men. It is true that these men are appointed to office by the government. Such appointments, however, are not usually made at random; they tend to reflect local politics. In the communities of this area it is common for a residential section of a village, a faction, or a sib segment to request the government to include one of its men among the village officials. Now that offices exist, group spokesmen are considered more effective where they hold such an office than without it.[3] That both village officials are from the same sib also means at Abiera that both come from the upper part of the village. Thus neither the Poreqórxntx segment nor the lower residential half of Abiera, where they predominate, has a man in office.

My own evaluation, for what an impression may be worth, is that the Ko-

3. Appointed village officials no longer exist—since 1967—in the Northern Tairora area.

mohórxntx sib contains more of the forceful, energetic, and assertive men of the local group. Indeed, the Poreqórxntx have by contrast a large number of quiet or passive men. This could be chance variation, given the small size of the two groups. It may, however, reflect the recency of the Poroqo recruitment that the voices of their men are so uniformly soft in the conduct of communal business.

One last point is surely the very defensiveness of some Poreqo individuals in stressing their strictly indigenous character and disclaiming all alien implications. One or two men made a practice for a while of correcting me when I used the name "Poreqo": they carefully substituted "Tairora." It is not that their very name is prejudicial or a secret among themselves that they are trying to suppress. It is rather that the outsiders with whom they are familiar do not usually distinguish so finely between the local peoples, something my questioning had led me to do and to do with an emphasis that evidently aroused their concern. I apparently provoked anxieties when I first brought up the question of a possible connection between the Poreqórxntx sib and the Auyana. To the representatives of the government and to most other Europeans, the term *pore* would mean nothing, even if it were known; but my questions were probably deprived of such innocence by my recognizing its meaning. The anxiety about these questions of mine, incidentally, tends to confirm the local view of sibs and sib history as relating closely to rights and loyalties; and any challenge to title, as it were, is a possible challenge to privilege and immunity. In my experience, the spontaneous acknowledgement of the Poreqórxntx sib as a politically distinct and potentially agonistic part of Abiera was limited to such expressions as the reproach of an old man of the lower section of the village. He chided me for being too considerate of people of the village's upper section and asked that I take note of the people who had helped me most with my work, giving me food and other favors. These—so he claimed—were not the people from above but those from the lower section of the village, where I happened to have my house. The old man was a Poreqo, and the Poreqórxntx are of course concentrated in the lower part of the village; but he chose to speak of sections of the village rather than of sibs.

It was not possible to learn either when the Poreqo refugees first came to Phratry Tairora territory or whether their migration was a single movement or one with subsequent accretions of other Auyana. As noted, it is practically certain the the main block of Auyana refugees were present before Tairora ceased to exist as a local group. It is all but certain that the earliest Auyana to arrive did not come before one or more offshoot segments had been detached from the Tairora parent community, establishing themselves as independent local groups with their own local names and territories. In at least two cases the offshoot local groups from the Tairora community formed the nucleus of the eventual sibs which mainly constitute the present Tairora phratry. These sibs are known now as Onxmx́ntxqx́ and Óndxbúrx, but it is not clear how far either group had progressed toward becoming a sib at the advent of the refugees appearance from Auyana. The coming of the refugees itself quite likely hastened the process, notably in the case of the Onxmx́ntxqx́.

The claim of Poreqórxntx informants that their founders are legitimate "Tairora" no less than the founders of the Onxmx́ntxqx́ or Óndxbúrx, is at least consistent with other evidence. Obviously Auyana refugees came to some part of the present territory of Phratry Tairora. That is where their descendants live today and where a substantial number of them have un-questionably lived for at least two or three generations. (To my knowledge, there are no surviving Poreqórxntx whose native language is Auyana—other than recent recruits, where such exist, from Auyana.)

The Tairora local group, whether its time span was short or long, would obviously include members of sibs beside the Auyana refugees. It would be unusual if Tairora did not in fact include representatives of several older sibs. Names now disused are sometimes enumerated by elderly informants. With sufficient diligence, possibly, one could hope to identify, even today, some of the sibs named in such lists. Some of the names doubtless refer to person-nels that were relatively prominent at Tairora, but others may be the names of rather minor elements whose main membership lived elsewhere. Some of the groups named may have flourished as separate entities for a certain time, subsequently merging into others or in some other fashion disappearing as named sib entities, much of this possibly even while Tairora still existed as a local group.

The lists given by older informants sometimes include up to a dozen or more names. Such names clearly mean something as part of the larger tradi-tion of the Tairora settlement and the phratry. Collectively they betoken a claim to antiquity, to priority, to linkage and hence to legitimacy. The very knowledge of such names, moreover, lends to the possessor an authoritative air. For particular purposes a given name may be relevant, or may be thought to be, and it may therefore be cited in what is agreed to be a proper context. To disentangle all the names and discover the size of the group re-ferred to, the period during which it flourished in Tairora, its provenience (assuming it is not now regarded as "indigenous" to Tairora), and its histori-cal relationship to the other sibs or sib segments of that local group would nonetheless be thankless—and perhaps endless—labor. Beyond the task of simply recognizing what the names meant for some specified time at Tairora there is the question of their posterity: which of the sibs that constituted the Tairora local group at various times—or parts of which sibs—contributed personnel to the founding of the settlements that later split from Tairora? It is not impossible to obtain partly overlapping lists of sib or lineage names from different informants in answer to such a question, but one could proba-bly not resolve the discrepancies completely nor go beyond a certain point in establishing the sociological identity or provenience of the sibs named.

It is surely possible to disclaim the question altogether, but doing so, in my opinion, is tantamount to admitting that one has failed to grasp much of the Northern Tairora social process. Another approach is to assume that the processes of fusion and fission just beyond the immediate reach of reliable detail basically resemble those that are closer to the present. The process of vernacular history and the process of splitting, migration, and merging are then reasonably well illustrated for the past by parts of the tradition still open to inspection. It would thus be the local group Tairora, and not some particular sib once represented there, that went by the name "Tairora." In that sense the Auyana refugees were "Tairora," too. That is, as residents of Tairora they were called Tairora—or eventually came to be.

By the same token, one must assume that the sib presently called Poreqórxntx could not have been so called in its home territory. The name is an alien (Tairora) one, to be sure, but even the Auyana translation of "Poreqórxntx" would not in their home territory properly distinguish the forebears of this group from any others of their language, since it signifies the entire ethnolinguistic group—over four thousand people, scattered in separate and sometimes hostile local groups. Indeed, as previously mentioned, there is no need to believe that the original refugee group or groups, prior to coming, possessed *any* common sib name. That is, it is not likely that they were all members of a single sib. Their collective name, Poreqórxntx, in any case, superseded whatever previous sib designation(s) they possessed. *The new name expressed their historical conjunction with the new local group or its sibs*—and in due course their part in what became the phratry. It also expressed the sociological equivalence of their members—that is, their common position in relation to their hosts and affinal counterparts. Being all alike expelled from their own territories and seeking a common asylum were attributes, to be sure, that largely defined the common position they held in their new situation, whatever their prior diversity.

In almost precisely the same way the local personnels of Onxmx́ntxqx́ and Óndxbúrx became sibs and their erstwhile local, origin place names became sib names. Beginning first as the names of local groups formed with personnel from parent Tairora, they became sib names when, because of changing circumstances, the local personnel increasingly came to share (1) a common position in relation to the other groups most significant to them and (2) a position distinct from that of the parent community. In other words, just as with the Tairora local group, and probably the Poreqórxntx forebears, one or several earlier sib designations represented in their ranks were absorbed in the new, collective names, Onxmx́ntxqx́ and Óndxbúrx. This process recurs, apparently, in each case when a more diverse local personnel comes to constitute a sufficient sociological unity in their own eyes and those of partner groups—in other words, when they have a common political, territorial, and especially marital position with respect to the other personnels most relevant to them.

Three major sibs, Poreqórxntx, Onxmx́ntxqx́, and Óndxbúrx, and increasingly autonomous local sib segments such as Komohórxntx (a segment of Óndxbúrx) at Abiera, today constitute the major membership of Phratry

Tairora. Several groups of small membership are known by name at Abiera (see table 5) and in other local groups of the phratry. Presumably the remnants of sibs or of local sib segments, they were separate enough at some point in their respective histories to justify a claim to sib status, even if their subsequent lack of reproductive success now makes their separate future unlikely. Such small groups are obviously quite sensitive to the effect of scale; and a short-run difference of two or three births, migrants, returnees, or deaths in a given cohort can easily seal their fate as continuing entities.

There have almost certainly been immigrant blocs in Phratry Tairora besides the Poreqo, but ones less visible than the latter for any of several reasons. Their arrival is not as recent and their present merging thus is more complete; their alien provenience is less clear; or their numbers are small. Indeed, some such personnels probably exist no longer as social entities separately named within Phratry Tairora. To put it another way, the case of Poreqo is representative of a common process of refugee recruitment. It may be less representative, however, in the impressive size of the group that presently constitutes the sib-ified descendants of the refugees.[4] These facts and considerations remind one, in any case, that it is an oversimplification to see Tairora as a three-sib phratry.

As with the sib name Poreqórxntx, so with Onxmx́ntxqx́ and Óndxbúrx: these could hardly have been sibs or sib-segment designations for Tairora local group personnel prior to their migration. Each is a place name, and the precise place of that name is, in both cases, familiar to most people. In the vernacular history of the Tairora phratry, it was on the site so named that the forebears of the present sibs, respectively, settled upon leaving Tairora. Thus the origin of each group is conventionally attributed to (1) the detachment of a part of the resident personnel of the Tairora parent community; (2) their migration, initially or eventually, to a separate, locally autonomous territory; and (3) their settlement on the site whose name becomes both the name of the community and sib. And at some future time, pending developments in which they come to behave as a single sib, the name becomes attached to them as a sib designation. Local groups, then as now, shifted their settlement sites from time to time, probably tending, as now, to change the collective name of the resident group according to the name of the site currently occupied.

It is not at once obvious, therefore, how the name of one particular site and settlement comes to be the name of a sib. I would suggest that the length of time during which the resident group is identified with a particular site name has something to do with the matter. The group will usually have

4. Poreqo is large in part possibly as the result of incorporating in a single sib, multiply dispersed, a larger number of different refugee elements—all ethnolinguistically *pore*—than in the usual case. A refugee bloc less distinct ethnolinguistically from the host group would perhaps be less likely to grow by the continuing accretion of further socially distinct refugees. A kind of "ghetto" effect, in other words, may have been present among these village horticulturists.

been spoken of more by one site name, or more encompassingly, than by another. That name will likely become its sib designation—when circumstances favor the development of a sib from among the local personnel. The other suggestion is that the name of the site, settlement, and local group *last* identified collectively with the personnel in question, before they assume sib status, in relation to other sib groups, has some likelihood of becoming their sib designation.

In the vernacular history, the members of the present Onxmx́ntxqx́ sib are descendants of a group that left Tairora to settle at the locality still known as Onxmantxqa. They have since moved from there. The members of the present Óndxbúrx are likewise descendants of a group that left Tairora to settle at the locality still known as Óndabura—quite near a present settlement which the Administration today designates as Ontabura. The two migrations occurred at different times, that of the Onxmantxqa group apparently first and probably prior to the arrival of at least the earliest Poreqórxntx founders. It seems clear—as well as consistent with the conventional account—that neither migration ended the local group at Tairora. Both the major sibs of Abiera, in fact, claim a more recent connection with Tairora than they feel other sibs and local groups of the present-day phratry can fairly claim. In other words, they claim that among the original colonizers of Abiera were some of the last to leave Tairora. In partial support of the claim is the fact that Abiera territory includes some of the territory of former Tairora. Some Abiera gardens are on the alleged Tairora site, and, as mentioned, the gardeners occasionally cut into a cooking pit or other feature identified with the phratry founders' community.

Abiera's claim to a more direct or longer continued relationship with the parent community of the phratry obviously does not invalidate claims of Tairora-Onxmantxqa and Tairora-Óndabura continuity. That would be tantamount to denying the phratric connection among these groups, which is universally recognized by friends and foes, even at considerable distance. The principal difference between Abiera's two major sibs and other sibs of Phratry Tairora is in the sequence and recency of detachment from the parent community.

CONTINUITY, LITERAL AND RELATIVE

Continuity is relative. If other things are equal, the more recent tie is the stronger link; the longer two personnels are parted, on the other hand, the weaker their connection. Continuity is also subject to selective emphasis. The names used in designating groups in the vernacular histories of Northern Tairora show the use that is made of continuity. The designations of some groups reach back to earlier junctures and origin points than those of groups more recently formed. A given designation continues to adhere to a personnel even while the developments are occurring that will modify the grouping and give occasion for new designations, in effect new continuities.

The retrospect of conventional history is a key part of the process. Telescoping and simplifying events, convention obscures less urgent continuities in favor of linkages more current or more viable. The record of much development is omitted in the statement of this actuality. Once established, group designations tend to be pushed backward in time, confusing or obliterating the emergence of the groups so designated. The name is a synopsis of a group's linkage and thus, pragmatically, its origin.

Against an unclouded statement of support and obligation the recapitulation of a personnel's slow development from a welter of conflicts and options has no immediate value. Thus in the vernacular version, it would appear that the sib today known as Onxmx̂ntxqx̂—and the name itself as a sib name—came into being at the very moment when the forebears of these people left Tairora. In fact, they were probably first a colony, not even a separate local group. They could not possibly have been a sib of that name after all, if they came from Tairora. If a new sib could spring into being at the moment of migration, it would imply not only the sudden creation of entire new sibs or descent groups but the overnight obliteration of prior alignments. The rise of an Onxmx̂ntxqx̂ sib hinged on a cumulation of events subsequent—probably by a generation or more—to the migration of certain Tairora personnel to the new locality. They obviously had to live there for a while in order to become known by its name. Convention here is thus anachronistic: it projects a modern sib name to a point farther back in time than, in its present connotation, such a personnel or name could have existed.

One effect of vernacular history on Tairora group identities is to widen the gap between offshoots of the same parent group. In the short run, the development of a sib is held to the rate at which a sense of autonomy can actually grow and the membership increase. The vernacular view, after the fact, foreshortens this differentiation, however, making it fully retroactive to the beginning of its development.

Simplification in Tairora vernacular history is a process of tidying up. In the Onxmx̂ntxqx̂ case, the accretions of other people, the factors that caused older descent group names and loyalties to be submerged and discarded—even the names themselves forgotten by many informants—these accretions are lacking in the conventional account. A preceding "Tairora" with the collective forefathers of the phratry, a segmentation and a migration of people to Onxmantxqa to become the sib of that name—the stream of actual events emerges through the vernacular with almost this simplicity. Simplification thus abets telescoping by eliminating from the record the knowledge that might qualify it—but which might also reflect loyalties more diffuse than those that purportedly prevail.

The Onxmantxqa Colony. What does conventional history have to say about the motives for segmentation? Because the colonization is recent enough, probing the development of Onxmantxqx̂ turns up reasons. For the colonization of parental Tairora one can elicit only guesses. There is no known parent colony for Tairora either, to be sure, and nothing but a general direction which the colonizers are supposed to have taken and their general provenience, "near Saiora"—whose similar name, in fact, suggests a possible folk etymology.

Interestingly enough, the reasons given for the Onxmantxqa colony tend to recur when explanation is sought for the founding of other colonies: the desire for good land. The impression is strong today at Abiera that those who initiated the Onxmantxqa colony purposely sought new ground. It is not uncommon for an informant to say that the colonists were drawn to their new territory because they "liked the ground" or "liked the water." He may make this observation, moreover, as if there could be no other reason of equal weight for the decision to stay in the new territory—as if that were always the reason for colonization. (This stereotyped motive for migrants is interesting to consider in light of the claim that peoples like those of the Central Highlands of New Guinea did not fight for land.) But apparently the discovery of the good new ground and their first use of it came about through the prior establishment there of a pig range. The future colonists thus appear at first as Tairora residents who began by keeping their pigs near the place called Onxmantxqa. Subsequently they learned that gardens would do well in the vicinity, and they made gardens there. Thus a base already existed, it would seem, should ever a reason arise to leave Tairora. Quarrels and animosities conventionally appear to have arisen between the colony and the parent group only *after* the emigration, however, rather than as a principal cause of it. The initial withdrawal was purportedly unmarred by ill-feeling. Here there is likely some simplification in the conventional version, but at least the emphasis does not seem misplaced. It is hardly conceivable, for example, that people would strike off with no idea whatever of where they might go or with nothing awaiting them at their destination. Nor could they prudently permit a serious rupture to develop with their immediate group while yet lacking some feasible alternative to continued coresidence. In view of the necessity of gardens and pigs, a dissident segment of the local group could establish in a new locality with the good prospect of producing gardens in that area and probably some expectation as well of access to their remaining gardens in the parent territory. In a word, the ground literally had to be prepared for a new colony before emigration was feasible. The sole exception would be flight on account of a sudden, grave, or irremediable breach. Even then the migrants could leave only by seeking asylum in an established community where help was available to them from their hosts while they were establishing themselves. Given the choice, a group might well prefer founding a colony to finding asylum. In this light, the Onxmantxqa segmentation, perhaps like most, was apparently not unanticipated.

In the vernacular history, the several colonizations from Tairora appear to be at close range. There seems no reason to quarrel with this point. The very names now given to the migratory groups, for one thing, locate their moves in space. From the site of Tairora to Onxmantxqa is less than two miles.

Óndabura is perhaps twice that distance, but by the time it was established, the new Óndabura colony could enjoy some security from that earlier founded at Onxmantxqa, lying between Óndabura and Tairora. In moving, the colonists were limited by the distance men and women could conveniently and safely cover, first, in traveling from the parent settlement to an outlying pig range they had begun to use, then to the new gardens and houses they made there, and subsequently—though probably only briefly—in traveling from the new settlement to the gardens they still for a time kept in the parent territory. The aspect of a planned and partly deliberate move seems further confirmed by the relatively short distances between Tairora and its colonies.

If a phratry is to grow from the successive colonizations of a local group, it is likely that the territories of member groups must be contiguous. The short-range colonizing moves of the daughter groups of Tairora fit the pattern of a continuous phratry territory. In forming a phratry, the need for defense and security is not the only factor that tends to limit colonies to short distances. Indeed, longer-range moves may occur no less commonly than short ones; but these, in contrast to colonies close at hand, occur for different reasons and have a different result. Long-range moves are typically precipitated by emergency and result in the asylum of refugees in the territory of a host group. If the refugees do not return to their native territories in due course, the effect of a move to the territory of another group is eventually to alienate them from their erstwhile lineage mates. Their ultimate alienation comes about as the refugees are naturalized into the descent system of their new coresidents. Thus they join a phratry, or help to found a new one, rather than extending one of their own. This was of course the case with the Poreqórxntx in joining Phratry Tairora; and it was similary the case of the Baqe group, discussed below, in leaving Tairora and joining another phratry.[5]

5. Since it stands apart from a discussion of the vernacular history, I shall only mention here the question whether Tairora-speaking peoples, as an ethnic group—or in particular the progenitors of Phratry Tairora—have a greater tendency to split off colonies, in effect a lower threshold of segmentation, than neighboring peoples living under similar circumstances. I suspect that such differences may exist, involving broad psychological characteristics such as the intolerance of crowding together in large numbers, and the relation of the individual to his fellows—trust or suspicion, feelings of dependence or independence, security factors, taste for warfare, and so on. One could probably not expect to find conclusive evidence bearing on a question of this kind in the history of Northern Tairora groups alone, though the factors noted, quite as much as the carrying capacity of land under a given mode of use (pig breeding, for instance), are pertinent to segmentation and colonization. That distant ancestors of the Tairora-speaking groups broke from a parent group much earlier than the ancestors of the several remaining language groups of the Kainantu family diverged from each other (Wurm 1964, McKaughan 1973) is at least logically consistent with the suggestion I have made, though it may not help the case much to say so. The local groups and phratries speaking Tairora dialects occupy a disproportionate amount of all the territory occupied by speakers of Kainantu languages (cf. Pataki Schweizer 1980). This again is consistent with a highly segmentary career as an ethnic group; but it is admittedly a fact too large of compass and complexity to be offered here as more than a suggestive note, and so I leave it.

Following the colonization of Onxmantxqa and Óndabura, these linked groups of the nascent Phratry Tairora were strung out in a rough, south-to-north line, some five or six miles long, the axis matching what is today called the Tairora Valley. This stretch of country is substantially the core of the phratric territory at present. Subsequent territorial expansion has come from colonies of the original colonizing settlements, retaining the earlier south-north axis. That the direction of colonization from Tairora was predominantly northward is not noted in the vernacular histories, but it may nonetheless be significant. The perennial enmity of the Tairora-speaking Arogara and of the Ontenu, to the south and southwest respectively, is still alive in Tairora politics, and it seems to represent a relationship of long standing. Phratry Tairora's two enemies, moreover, are perceived as perennial allies of each other. Quite likely these groups constituted a block to any marked expansion to the south as well as, perhaps, exerting pressure on the Tairora community in the opposite direction. Indeed, such pressure was apparently involved in the eventual abandonment of the settlement at Tairora and the move of the remaining residents to Abiera and Urara (see map 6). The founding of the local group that has continued as Abiera (and the one at Urara), in other words may have been a retreat from combined Arogara-Ontenu attacks.

The Abiera group were obliged to abandon their settlement once more, in fact, again under attack from Ontenu and Arogara. This time, the main group took refuge farther to the north in or near the territory of the present Óndabura people. The close connection acknowledged today between the Sib Óndxbúrx and the Komohórxntx sib at Abiera apparently reflects this asylum as well as the traditional connections that initially made asylum feasible. The elements that fused in the present Sib Óndxbúrx, that is, overlapped with one or more that are now fused in Komohórxntx—in addition to their comon phratric link. Thus today there is, on the one hand, an acknowledgment by some Abiera informants that the Komohórxntx "are the same as Óndxbúrx" (in effect a local segment of that sib), and, on the other, a disposition to call them by their own distinct name.

"Kómoho" is a personal name and hence an apparent exception to the general Northern Tairora rule of naming sibs for the local provenience of their personnel. The use of a personal name in this case, however, can be explained in such a way as to throw light on the practice of sib nomenclature in Northern Tairora culture. Since the Óndxbúrx-Komohórxntx evolved their siblike size and local (especially marital) autonomy entirely within the same territory, they have no provenience, other than "Óndxbúrx," to distinguish them from other exogamous personnel coresident there. No migration, in other words, has marked them as "the people from X" or as "those who went to Y." It would be confusing at present to call them "the people of Abiera," for that name is already in use with a meaning that includes nearly the entire local population, of which the Komohórxntx are not even the majority. This reasoning does not, of course, account for the selection of a particular personal name, nor in doing so will I go further than to suggest that, as the founder of a principal lineage of the Abiera sib segment of Óndxbúrx, the name of Kómoho (whose grandson is only forty-five) probably had the necessary salience.

WHY SIBS ARE NAMED FOR PLACES

A broader question is why so few sibs of Northern Tairora—certainly of Abiera or Batainabura—are designated by any other than place names. Surely other local sib segments have evolved, as have the Komohórxntx, a size and degree of autonomy sufficient, for example, to revise exogamic boundaries. That is, they have reconstituted themselves as personnels for whom marriage with members of the same-name sib *elsewhere* will stand as outmarriage.

I suggest that three factors operating jointly could give sib nomenclature in Northern Tairora its strongly locative tendency. The first is a cultural conviction, that peoples indeed possess some essence that is theirs by virtue of the land in which they or their forebears have lived. (This view in Northern Tairora culture is discussed at length in chapter 7.) Second, there is a significant frequency of movement or migration such that nearly all sibs will sooner or later *have* a provenience that is pragmatically distinctive of their personnel. Northern Tairora society seems amply fluid to afford this condition. In such circumstances cohesiveness is implicit in a locative nomenclature. While other names surely distinguish one personnel well enough from another, it is hard to think of any sort of nomenclature superior to a set of names in which personnels are literally mapped to a topographic (and magical) grid. Such names will be remembered when a named founder no longer is remembered as a person. Setting each grouping or sib off from the others perfectly, such names have little ambiguity. Migration gives a special edge to such designations when one personnel are to another, from the day of their arrival, "the people of X," and thus to themselves, from that day onward, can behave in a unique and solidary manner. The prevalence of locative designation in immigrant societies such as those of the new nations of the Americas stands as a parallel.

How long the Abiera forebears spent in asylum with the Óndxbúrx is hard to judge, although the exile itself seems to have occurred around 1900 or perhaps a bit later. From the accounts of informants one gets the impression of a fairly short period. This may well be the case, for the longer a refugee group spends away from native territory, the less likely they are to return to it. In any event, the nucleus of the present Abiera group eventually returned to their former territory and successfully reestablished themselves. Their ability to do so is seen as having hinged on possessing the strength to ward off attacks from enemies—Ontenu, in particular.

At this time or shortly thereafter the history of Abiera—indeed of much of the immediate vicinity—began to be dominated by the career of a well-remembered strong man, Mátoto, who lived until about 1930. A reconstruction of his career has appeared elsewhere (Watson 1967a), and it may suffice for immediate purposes to note that his career closely coincides with a radical shift in the politicomilitary fortunes of Abiera.[6]

According to the vernacular accounts, at least three major developments occurred during the height of Mátoto's career. Each involved the recruitment or alienation of personnel within Abiera or Phratry Tairora, and Mátoto is traditionally credited with having the principal hand in all three changes. One was the consolidation of the position of the Poreqórxntx refugees, already noted—in effect their final recruitment as a part of the Abiera local group. The present claim of these people to membership in Phratry Tairora depends, however, as we have seen, not on understandings with Mátoto but on the earlier residence of the Poreqórxntx in the territory of the local group at Tairora. Mátoto, that is, did not make them a sib of Phratry Tairora any more than he made them the Poreqórxntx sib; but he did—or is so credited—prevent their alienation from Tairora and their consequent recruitment as a refugee sib of some other phratry.

In a second case, Phratry Tairora—the Abiera community in particular—lost a group of people through alienation. This development perhaps began in the classical manner of a Tairora colony when some of the residents of Abiera began to keep their pigs on the eastern or far side of the ridge, down toward the stream today called Tairora Creek. The later descendants and adherents of this group—or some of them—are now known as Baqe. The name is that of the lineage or phratry these emigrants eventually joined—both the cause and expression of their alienation from Tairora. Earlier, however, they were simply identified as "Hurútx" after the site of a settlement they erected as, following their pigs, they gradually moved out of Abiera. Like the Onxmantxqa and the Óndabura groups, they made gardens and eventually built houses at Hurútx in order to live closer to where they ranged their swine. At this time, in other words, Hurútx was simply another colony, having sib segments that interlocked particularly with those of Abiera, the parent community. In an altercation that subsequently arose—so say the modern Abiera—a Hurútx villager killed a man from Abiera. This calamity became a *casus belli* between Mátoto and his men and the villagers of Hurútx. Fighting continued and the Hurútx were overpowered and obliged to flee as a result, taking refuge among groups of another Tairora-speaking phratry to the east. Here they affiliated as part of the Baqe sib or phratry.

6. It is technically an anachronism to speak of "Abiera," although simpler to do so. Other sites have been occupied at different times during the history of this group; hence they have been known by a succession of other site names. Indeed, *Quntoqa*, a name superseding "Abiera," is now current because it is the site of their present settlement, which has shifted since they lived at Abiera. As used here, therefore, "Abiera" stands for the recognized continuity of a local group and its territory. It is not meant to imply that the group lived continuously on the Abiera site itself, the literal meaning of this usage.

The alienation of the Hurútx-Baqe from Tairora is not the end of the story as far as the present chapter is concerned, because, interestingly enough, the episode indirectly links the histories of the two phratries that are the subject of the chapter. Fighting continued between Tairora groups and Baqe groups even after the expulsion of the Hurútx colony from Tairora territory. Quite likely there were antecedent and continuing motives for hostilities between the Tairora and the Baqe to which the asylum and eventual affiliation of Hurútx people with Baqe only added strength. In any event, the Tairora, particularly those of Abiera, continued to press the Baqe, eventually driving them—or some of them—into refuge with an allied local group at Hararuna. Some of the Baqe people merged with some of their Hararuna hosts, moreover, remaining at Hararuna and later forming a sib today referred to as Baqe-Hararúnx. Since the people of Hararuna themselves subsequently merged with a local group at Airina to constitute the two major sibs of present Batainabura, the tangled web of colonization and exile, alienation and affiliation comes full circle. The movements just sketched touch three phratries, two of which include the communities of Abiera and Batainabura, the focus of this study, as principal representatives.

The third major realignment of personnel within Phratry Tairora during Mátoto's day is in some respects the most interesting. It involves mainly the Onxmx́ntxqx́, who, from the conventional version, appear to have been the first or oldest extant colony of Tairora. (It is quite certain at least that they were the first among those commemorated today as sibs within Phratry Tairora.) Fighting broke out at some point between the Onxmx́ntxqx́ and other sections of the phratry. From all available testimony the initiative was taken principally by Mátoto and the Abiera people. If so, these events would have occurred around 1915 or 1920, probably at the height of the strong man's career. Màtoto succeeded in driving the Onxmx́ntxqx́ from their portion of the phratric territory and into one or more asylums, including one with nearby Kamáno-speaking groups. Another part of them allegedly sought refuge with Agarabi-speaking groups.

Since Mátoto is credited by both friend and foe with having the major hand in expelling the Onxmx́ntxqx́, it is difficult to question the prominence of his role. The reasons for animosity between the Onxmx́ntxqx́ and their adversaries within the phratry are not equally explicit, however, since only the conventional allegations—the stealing of pigs, women, and crops—are generally made. These allegations quite likely have a basis, but of course such acts themselves constitute an aggression that must have its own motive, quite as much as furnishing the motive for further aggression. The underlying causes of hostility thus remain obscure: The ambition of a powerful Mátoto? A suspected weakness and vulnerability of Abiera because of its alienation of the Hurútx people to Baqe? Or the consequence of Abiera's recruiting and espousing (literally!) the Poreqórxntx? The latter, as a former prey of their neighbors, quite likely now had to be defended, or to be joined in common cause, against their oppressors. The oppressors seem from pres-

ent evidence to have included the Onxmx́ntxqx́. There is still considerable
feeling, indeed, between members of these two sibs.

There is equal reason, by the way, to indicate that the recruitment of the
Poreqórxntx was related to the alienation of the Hurútx colony, though
whether as a cause or a consequence cannot readily be answered from the
information of local informants. As a cause, the coming of Poreqórxntx into
Abiera could easily shift internal allegiances and the balance of power, opening the way for the altercation and killing that led to hostilities between
Abiera and the Hurútx colony. Considered as a consequence, the weakening
of Abiera by the loss of Hurutx kinsmen may have made the ultimate recruitment of Poreqórxntx personnel the more urgent for the parent group. Such
contingencies of local history surely affected the calculations of Abiera's leadership—whether that of a singular Mátoto or of a more diffuse directorate.
Local accounts, however, while recognizing the relevance and the political
cogency of such moves, concentrate more on the fact of intergroup enmity or
amity, and emphasize its expression in fighting or friendly exchange.

It is evident in the history of the Tairora-speaking peoples of this area that
a community, with a name that normally shifts as the site of its settlement
shifts, becomes under certain circumstances a sib with a relatively fixed
name—one that merges and supplants the names of the sibs and sib segments previously constituting the community. The attack on and expulsion
of the Onxmx́ntxqx́ suggest the sort of circumstances under which this may
occur. Even if the Onxmantxqa colony had originally consisted of and continued as a single sib, which is not typical of Northern Tairora local groups at
present nor for any visible reason is likely at Onxmantxqa, the fact remains
that that sib at some point ceased to be what it had been and became the
Onxmx́ntxqx́ sib. There was thus at least a breaking away from the sib(s) in
which Onxmantxqa people had membership in common with people of the
parent group—and probably of other Tairora colonies. There was very likely
in addition a coalescence of the members of two or more original sites of the
Onxmantxqa colony into a single sib with the present name. Social nomenclature as practiced by the Northern Tairora suggests that a local group's
name is seldom a sib name while still primarily the name of the local group. I
do not imply any fastidiousness here, like a reluctance of local people to risk
ambiguity, but only that the developments that coalesce a local group into a
new sib must commonly if not always include a move in space. Thus the
name of a sib usually proves to be the name of a site on which the claimed
forebears of the sib have *in the past* lived.

There are evidently at least two reasons for this condition. One is that
coalescence, or even a simple change of names, requires a development
drastic enough to alienate a group of people from others with whom they
have till then shared a common sib membership. It must be a development
away from the common allegiances and common oppositions of the past, giving to the sib segment in question new and disparate allegiances and opposi-

tions. This, in the Northern Tairora scheme of things, is typically if not always a development involving a change of location of the affected group. Beyond increasing the distance of a progressively alienated group from its erstwhile congeners, the move both produces and is a product of a changed set of relationships. The move thus expresses and instigates relationships that are not congruent with—that do not neatly overlap—the allegiances and oppostions of the past. War by other Phratry Tairora groups against the residents of Onxmantxqa not only intensified the common allegiances and oppositions of the residents themselves but sharply distinguished them in this respect from their former sib mates who now warred against them. In addition, as exiles from their native territory, the people from Onxmantxqa had a common refugee status implying a relationship with their common hosts, one of mutual opposition against their former fellows.

Quite apart from the felt animosities and the alienation from their respective former sib mates, moreover, the sib(s) to which the Onxmantxqa people had belonged could probably not survive the removal of the people (in one or more locations) with its attendant new set of relationships. It would be pointless for the hosts of the Onxmantxqa people, for example, to know the various prior allegiances of members of the refugee group. The group status of the refugee membership is undivided, as far as the hosts are concerned, just as it has lately been singular in the eyes of the enemies who expelled them from their own ground. The local name by which they have collectively been known at once recognizes their separateness, distinguishing them from enemies once their kinsmen and sib mates. Northern Tairora politics, like others, may sometimes make strange bedfellows, but the Northern Tairora system of social nomenclature tends to reduce the estrangement apace. Like a layered plant after developing its own roots, the stem to the parent is clipped, the scion now nourished in other soil.

I indicated a second reason why the name of a *former* site, and not that of the present settlement, is typical of Northern Tairora sibs. In Northern Tairora genealogies a former site is as a rule the point to which all the so-called sib members can most logically be traced. They are the descendants of forebears who lived together in that community and who, even more in retrospect, were "brothers." As the descendants of "brothers," therefore, the people presently designated by the name of the former community are logically each other's sib mates. Their several former sib designations are submerged, along with the loyalties that once connected them uniquely to others of such designation, the names eventually being lost to tradition. The shallowness of Northern Tairora genealogies expresses as much as it facilitates the process. In the immediate case of the expelled Tairora sib or proto-sib, the group is, to be sure, the "people of Onxmantxqa," as the emerging sib name itself will commemorate. But, more than that, the common link of these displaced refugees is where they (or their fraternal forebears) formerly lived together, not where they live now. If they divide and flee to several asylums but remain mutually identified and later reassemble, even more will the common link be the place where they or their forebears once lived.

If a further point is needed to explain the derivation of Northern Tairora sib names from those of *past* settlements, perhaps it is sufficient to recall that Northern Tairora settlements frequently move and just as often change names—even, it appears, with relatively minor relocations. There is thus, so to speak, no lack of previous settlements from which to select a name that will suitably encode the group's particular allegiances and oppositions as well as the "common descent from brothers" that distinguishes them. This point is of course a very general one indicating more the ease of the practice than its essential purpose.

ONXMANTXQA REPATRIATION

In all likelihood, the alienation of the Onxmantxqa group from its fellow sibs would have been as final as that of Baqe except for a new condition which was completely exogenous and unprecedented in Northern Tairora social organization. This was the impact in the area, shortly after 1930, of Australian government patrols. The Upper Ramu Post was established at what is now Kainantu, almost within sight of some of the exiled Onxmantxqa group. Within the next few years, government officers attempted to communicate to the local people the nature of the peace it was their primary mission to impose. In a number of cases they endeavored to discover groups displaced from their former ground by fighting and to adjudicate the validity of each claim. Numerous instances of displacement existed in the area, to say the least, and some can no doubt be identified today with little difficulty. In certain cases these people may have remained unknown to the government; or their claims were old and difficult to evaluate; or the people were attached to the communities where they now lived and where an increasing number of them in fact were born. Such reasons could well outweigh for those concerned the attraction of returning to old territories or attempting to reconstitute a local group that could never duplicate the one disbanded by their flight.

Occasionally a nucleus of exiles were restored to their original lands, receiving from the government its guarantee of their tenure. Perhaps rarely if ever was such a group restored in its entirety. Often the members and their offspring were scattered in more than one refuge. Furthermore, some former members, married into the present community or otherwise well situated there, or without strong enough ties to the returnees, opted to remain. These were not always single individuals, moreover, but quite often a sufficient number to make a viable, localized sib in the midst of those who had harbored them. What might be called here the openness of local society, its well-founded practice in reordering loyalties and affiliations, is nowhere better revealed than in the mixed response of displaced Northern Tairora to the Australian amnesty.

Land claims and indemnities later became important as the government acquired Northern Tairora lands for Australian settlers, with money payment. This must be considered apart. The right to receive payment for title to land that one could not or did not wish to validate by personal use—occupying the land and defending it with one's own strength—was not part of the aboriginal system; and the vigorous response of Northern Tairora litigants to this innovation of Australian custom since World War II is therefore irrelevant to the present issue.

That the Onxmantxqa people were among those restored to their former ground and were successfully reconstituted there as a separate local community (now two) is apparently the result of at least four factors. First, Onxmantxqa exile, if I have correctly placed it around 1915-20, was recent. The chance for repatriation came soon enough that a sufficient number of people still wanted to return. The passage of time, as well it might, erases old attachments and normally assures that new ones develop. Second, Tairora-speaking refugees would have little difficulty in establishing the credibility of their case to the government officers. Surely an asylum among people of alien, Kamáno and Agarabi speech had meant persecution by a victor through means now no longer allowed. In addition, as noted, a large bloc of Onxmantxqa exiles, fortuitously, had taken shelter in the shadow of what would become the government station. They would thus sooner learn of government ways and discover the new options of the *pax australiana*, including repatriation. And they themselves would sooner be discovered inside the small perimeter of what the government considered "controlled." Finally, in decreeing the return to Onxmantxqa and the founding of a local group at Tongera (see map 6) just prior to World War II, the government would find no need to dislodge numerous other people from the reclaimed lands. Mátoto and the Abiera had not preempted the ground, nor had enough time elapsed for other groups to colonize any large portion of it.

That the people of the Onxmantxqa were exiled among people of alien speech should not be construed as by itself a major cause of their repatriation. Speaking Tairora among Kamáno and Agarabi hosts may have helped them somewhat in retaining their self-identity, even as speaking Auyana may have given the Poreqo a salience greater than that of refugees who shared the speech of their hosts. It would, as noted, help make them more obvious to the government as candidates for removal. With the passage of sufficient time or a change in one or two circumstances, however, there is little reason to think the Onxmantxqa exiles were bound to return, either by their own effort or with Austrailian sponsorship. As previously noted, the permanent recruitment of refugees by their hosts is common in this area, regardless of language or ethnic differences. Indeed, I will subsequently discuss a group of Batainabura refugees whose history in this respect matches Onxmantxqa's. Equally alien among Kamáno-speaking hosts, however, they voluntarily remain in exile today, many of their younger members, born there, now increasingly unknown to their collateral kinsmen at Batainabura.

The pathos of "exile" seems to have little place in this social order. It is a practical business concerned with security, making a living, and finding mates. There is loss but not despair.

There are numerous instances in the Kainantu area of refugees who return to their original ground (for example, both Abiera and Batainabura), as well as of those who remain with their hosts. An aboriginal precedent for the Onxmantxqa exiles' return, however, is doubtful. Since their exile resulted from hostilities principally involving elements of their own phratry, their permanent alienation from the phratry under aboriginal conditions would probably have been inevitable. That is, they would have joined their hosts in one form or another. The history of Batainabura affords just such a case of an unhealed breach within a phratry, and the irreparable alienation of the Hurútx from Abiera may be cited in Tairora history. The people of Hurútx, as noted, ended by becoming Baqe.

The government-sponsored return of the Onxmantxqa exiles, furthermore, has created a situation that seems for the time being quite anomalous. Burauta, one of the two principal settlements where Onxmantxqa returnees are today concentrated, is literally within shouting distance of Abiera. Village altercations and raised voices, for instance, can readily be overheard (and are attended with relish) at Abiera. While there are a number of persons—notably younger men and boys—who freely come and go between the two places, there are many who do not and whose anxieties about hostile people there are considerable. Sorcery is commonly suspected by members of the one group against those of the other, and a death at Tongera or Burauta tends to evoke immediate concern and a scrupulous display of innocence by Abiera men. If it were not for the changes brought about by Australian control, it is doubtful that a situation like the present one would remain tenable for long within the same phratry. Now, to be sure, the enforcement of peace allows a generation to arise for whom the animosities of the past, however exciting, seem less relevant if not yet wholly unreal. These people, as time passes, will find it difficult to recognize the novelty of their position within Tairora territory or the miraculous reestablishment of their forefathers within the ranks of the phratry.

It is necessary to bear in mind that the history of Phratry Tairora, outside of myth or highly stylized legend, probably falls within the last 250 to 300 years or less—the span of memory. In fact, I doubt that one is touching many events much earlier than 1800, although the root causes and conditions may sometimes precede that date. During this period, the phratry has grown as a separate entity. We do not know with much clarity, however, from what it separated, nor whether it did so *in situ* or with an initial movement of people, nor with what stimulus of further departures and arrivals. This is not to question that the departures and arrivals visible today tell the main story of the phratry as it survives. As far as we can see, the phratry has developed through a process of budding off of daughter groups, each establishing itself first as a local group, and in some—ostensibly all—cases later becoming the core of a named sib. In one instance, the phratry underwent major growth through the recruitment of a large refugee group which likewise founded one of its major sibs, Sib Poreqórxntx. The phratry has also lost people, notably through their alienation and fusion with local groups of other phratries. At least one remembered group, Hurútx, was alienated, and the Onxmantxqa people would in all likelihood have been a second but for the Australian intervention. It is hardly necessary to comment on the eventful, indeed turbulent character of the situation revealed by Phratry Tairora's history.

Today the Tairora phratry consists of perhaps a thousand people strung out in six to eight local groups lying along the drainage of the Tairora Valley. Colonization has continued. Indeed the process has apparently quickened in the postcontact period, and separate settlements are now established that are too small or too distant from the parent village, probably, to have been safe in the precontact days of open fighting. For every local group whose name figures in the precontact history of Tairora there are now from one to several derivative local groups, some of them already as large as the parent. Even the people of Onxmantxqa who resettled at Tongera just before World War II contributed, in the late 1950s, to the birth of a second community, Burauta—incidentally heightening Abiera anxieties.

WHY COMMUNITIES REMAIN SMALL

The continued colonizing of communities seems to call for reflection on the tendencies that promote segmentation. What has prevented the buildup of ever larger settlements in the Northern Tairora, of villages of 400-plus, for example, such as are now found among some of their ethnolinguistic neighbors? The Australian government has worked, on the one hand, to guarantee the traditional access of individuals and groups to land and other resources. In so doing it has possibly increased the expectation of permanence in established local groups, although there is no suggestion from the histories of Phratry Tairora and surrounding areas that the expectation is new for groups that remained strong. In occasionally restoring to displaced groups their previous land, the principle of permanent ownership with alienation-only-by-legal-consent has at any rate been developed by government. Yet while the expulsion of groups from their territories has now come to a halt with the outlawing of warfare, the segmentation of groups has not; and it may even have increased through more favorable postcontact conditions. It is therefore warranted to suggest that precontact tendencies toward segmentation were not solely a consequence of fighting but were partly independent of it. It is conceivable, of course, that new conditions have produced new reasons for segmentation and colonization, distinct from those of precontact life but at least as favorable.

The need of more land for cash crops and to feed more people and pigs is undeniable. While this must be admitted, I am loathe to believe that the cessation of open fighting and the giving of Australian guarantees changed *all* basic conditions affecting the life of the local group. It is interesting to note, furthermore, that the modern reasons given for the founding of colonies, and even the standard sequence involved, such as following better pig ranges farther afield, appear to resemble the motives of the past. I am therefore inclined to see a continuity in the factors that tend to hold the Northern Tairora local group to a certain upper size at which or beyond which its population is reduced by segmentation and the founding of colonies. I believe the essential point is that these conditions—or some of them—were not contingent, or not principally so, on the prevalence of open fighting. The threat of attack, indeed, may have provided a certain brake on segmentation, a limit to the founding of colonies. The suggestion receives support, at least, in the numerous colonies founded within Phratry Tairora since the threat has been eliminated. If warfare was a brake, it would tend to confirm the tradition that only a small number of colonies were founded from the "original" Tairora local group. This basic few, in effect the seeds of today's sibs, may not be wholly out of line with fact. The contrast between pre- and postcontact Tairora in this respect is as real, in other words, as it is apparent.

BATAINABURA

The multiplicity and the confusion of some of the names that follow is not untypical of what the ethnographer encounters in pursuing the historical movements of people among the Northern Tairora and neighboring language groups. To schematize such information tends to eliminate many of the details. It may be one way of reducing the confusion, and there is an attempt elsewhere in these pages to arrive at a comprehensive scheme. Much of sociological import, in my opinion, attaches to the group and segmentary names that are used by peoples like the Northern Tairora for their local personnels. Both the continuity and the change and proliferation of names in this area are a crucial part of social and political identification and of larger sociological processes. The names are in effect tracers by means of which not only the people themselves but the ethnographer, if he observes the necessary cautions, is best able to follow the elements so identified through the currents in which they move, splitting, merging, disappearing, or coming into being. Having suffered through the business of trying to order what at first seemed chaotic and nearly hopeless, I am doubtless human enough not to want to toss aside the results. At the same time, I cannot imagine a more vivid or graphic method of conveying to a reader the intricate currents and eddies of family, community, and territory in this part of the world. The need to identify general principles sufficient to account for the events is clear, but I am convinced that to state general principles without some depiction of what they generalize would, in this case at least, be to omit a significant part of reality. Were the reality in fact like the Brownian movement, to be sure, the attempt to generalize it would have to be as broad as the

effort to sketch it in total detail is futile. At times I think we may be somewhat better off.

Among the sibs at Batainabura there seem to be no migration accounts in
which the founding ancestors enter the country from outside. The absence of
such legends and the purely mythical character of Airina and Hararuna origin accounts thus stand in sharp contrast to the origin traditions of Phratry
Tairora collected at Abiera. Since Batainabura myths root the people intimately to the same area as their ancestors, moreover, it seems warranted to
assume that the core groups or traditions have been longer in their traditional vicinity than the Tairora people have been in theirs. Other than that,
one could only guess that historical disruptions differently affecting the two
areas will account for the difference in emphasis.

The specific account of the founding of the Tairora community seems essentially historical, despite its obvious conventionalization. It is not concerned with the origin of men in the world but only with the arrival of the
first men of a particular lineage in the particular country they now claim. We
are thus left with contrasting traditions—Batainabura's, which begins in obviously fantastic events, and Tairora's, which commences in an essentially
realistic and credible migration. The Hararuna myth describes the origin of
man *in situ*, the Tairora account the immediate arrival of a given group at a
given place and time without reference to its ultimate origin. So distinct a
difference is presumably not without meaning. I suggest that the Hararuna
myth indicates a longer occupancy of the vicinity with which the myth deals
by the people who regard it as their own myth. The occupation of the Tairora
vicinity by the present people and their forebears, on the other hand, seems
more recent.

The Airiná sib, their name, and their ancestors are associated with a widespread folktale of the region, complicating the interpretation of their origin
story. This association presumably masks some less remarkable—and perhaps more "original"—origin. The Two Brothers Story surely predates the
Airiná group, and the tale is far more general than the Airiná people now
associated with it. The association of the Airiná sib with the Two Brothers
Story and the mythical ground whereon the action unfolded thus has a different character from the Hararuna origins. "Airiná" was the younger of the
mythical brothers (McKaughan 1973:638-51).

Whatever one's conviction about the implications of antiquity and continuity, it is clear that these particular origin traditions have at least one thing
in common: a preoccupation with tying a present group, as descendants of
the first and only inhabitants, to its claimed and traditional territory. This is
typically the present territory, a part of it, or one nearby.

In the mythical traditions of Batainabura sibs an obvious lacuna exists between the time of origin and the rather concrete and credible account of
subsequent divisions, fusions, and movements. In neither sib is it possible to
construct a convincing lineage from present persons to putative founders.
One leading man of the Airiná sib, for example, listed four persons, repre-

senting four generations, from the first owner of the land to himself. Aigyaqe was the first to take charge of the local territory, he said, giving it to his son, Hararunata ("wife of Hararuna"?). The latter gave it in turn to his son, Gohaqi, who gave it in turn to his son, Maho. Maho gave the land to the speaker, who is accordingly linked to the "source of the ground" (*bxtxógxrx*) and is in charge of it (*bxtxbéhx*). One might infer from this account that Airiná people have been in their present territory no longer than three or four generations—from mythical founder to present. But it is more likely that they simply work from short genealogies such as are common among Central Highlands peoples.

The present composite community of Batainabura—not merely the settlement—is quite recent. That is, Airiná and Hararúnx, the two major sibs whose association forms the community, were not associated as coresident groups until perhaps early in this century. Before that the forebears of present Sib Hararúnx were a part of another social and territorial entity, a local group or a phratry known as Barabuna. Barabuna territory is nearby and is visible from the present settlement. It lies in the grassland at the foot of the mountain to the northeast. This vicinity is still called Barabuna. It includes the site of Hararuna and the spot on which the mythical casuarina stood as well as the tree still growing on the spot. The Hararuna forebears were not the sole occupants of Barabuna territory but shared it with the forebears of another group known today as the Báqoqx. The Báqoqx are now a part—probably a sib—of a community whose territory lies over a steep ridge to the southeast of their former territory and of Batainabura. This community, its settlement, and its territory are collectively known today by the government as Barabuna. The latter name is explained by Batainabura informants in two ways. It is of course a name proper to the Báqoqx people, in view of their former residence in Barabuna territory, but on this basis the name is equally proper to themselves. They feel that the name has received its present exclusive association largely through governmental practice. In any case, ancestral Barabuna was not included in the territory of the community presently known by that name, whereas it still lies in part within Batainabura territory.

Batainabura informants speak of former Barabuna as consisting of three parts, Baqoqa, Hararuna, and Airina. I have used the term phratry for such a grouping of local groups or sibs who assert common descent, who possess a tradition of common origin, and who occupy an unbroken stretch of territory. Despite a history of recent fighting between them, informants say their closest ties with neighboring groups are with the Báqoqx people. There is sufficient coming and going, changing of residence from one territory to the other, reclaiming of old land, and other activities to bear out the report of a former territorial group that has only lately been dissolved and of relationships that are still well remembered.

Other peoples of the area support the claim that Barabuna was such a group, not the modern community of that name. Certain former refugees now living in villages of the north end of the Tairora Valley always refer to their ancestors accordingly as "Barabuna." They themselves are referred to by local Tairora as of "Barabuna" provenience. In visiting the kinsmen of their fathers or mothers, these one-time Barabuna refugees often visit persons at Batainabura.

The purported relation of Airiná as a sib of long standing within the Barabuna phratry is possibly anachronistic. There are at any rate some confusing facts to suggest that this claim illustrates the conventional telescoping of a more tangled history. The recent Airiná do not seem to have shared the Barabuna territory with the forebears of the other two personnels who lived there. They derive rather from a territory that has been autonomous since the other personnels were joined. Whatever connection the ancestral Airiná may still earlier have had with the people at Barabuna, it is their *present* conjunction with Sib Hararúnx—now that the Báqoqx are gone—that mainly supports the claim of a more inclusive phratric sentiment. Forest traditions are emphasized by the Airiná, while the Barabuna personnels were apparently grassland people. References are made to past fighting between them and Airiná and to intermarriage that suggests separate local groups if not a different phratry. Independent historical movements are still remembered, and I shall summarize them below. All this evidence points to an autonomy of considerable standing between ancestral Airiná and former Barabuna. Indeed, almost the only fact to indicate a possible earlier connection—apart from the present claim of one—is the proximity of Airiná's traditional territory to that of former Barabuna. Since Barabuna in the sense of a phratry is as recent as the time of its segmentation—still well remembered—any previous phratric connection that included both Airiná peoples and former Barabuna coresidents is not likely to have been the one now conventionally projected.

The present inclusion of Airiná in a phratric sense in Barabuna in no way confronts us with an unfamiliar situation. There is a close parallel in the case of the inclusion of the Poreqórxntx sib at Abiera (and elsewhere) in the Tairora phratry. In other words, just as the Poreqórxntx claim to be Tairora in the phratric sense, basically because of their coresidence and association with the ancestral Tairora group, there has developed a feeling that the Airiná, along with the Hararúnx, were a part of Barabuna phratry. The basis of the fusion, in both cases, is the (later) historical conjunction of the groups in a common territory, their continued coresidence, and the consequent development of common traditions.

There are several differences of detail between the two instances of fusion. One is that it was not the Airina, strictly speaking, who joined the phratry, for the modern Hararúnx have joined *them* in what was once largely Airiná territory. Another difference between the two phratries is that Barabuna is not only a smaller and newer phratry but apparently a looser one. The reason for looseness is that the linking elements of the Barabuna phratry, the former residents of Barabuna territory, the Báqoqx and Hararúnx, in each case have joined with different, formerly independent groups. The Báqoqx, in establishing the modern "Barabuna" community of government maps, have joined with one, possibly two groups—now sibs—whose origins lie outside the immediate framework and tradition of the parent phratry. The Hararúnx have likewise joined with the Airiná, as we already know, and with another outside group, as we shall shortly see. Instead of having to incorporate a single outside group—or what in tradition has become one group (Poreqórxntx) in Abiera—Barabuna has been stretched in its phratric sense to include several outside groups, now sibs, differently combined in different localities with the linked and linking groups. Not only has the social cement of a common Barabuna tradition had much less time to harden, therefore, but it will apparently be called on to produce adhesion among more numerous and diverse elements if, as seems doubtful, Barabuna is to become a phratry like Tairora.

I suspect that one further factor may prove crucial as between Phratry Tairora and the tenuous Barabuna. This is that the outside groups, not only more numerous, cannot be traced back to the original, founding territory whose segmentation gave rise to all segments of the phratry. The Poreqórxntx—whether originally a single group or elements of several—were at some point before its abandonment coresidents in the territory of the ancestral Tairora community. Even if this did not occur before the colonizing of Óndabura or Onxmantxqa, it occurred while the parent community still existed. And the parent community, including Poreqo people, directly or in a colonizing chain, gave rise to several unmistakable Tairora local groups, notably Abiera. Thus the Poreqórxntx—and their coresidents with them—have all but buried any tradition of an origin separate from that of the Tairora parent. They are now at least once removed from their earlier origins as refugees and immigrants, the tradition of which would presumably have been much clearer during the life of the original Tairora group. On the other hand, the distinctness of Airiná origins from Hararúnx—and hence from Barabuna—is fairly salient, and presumably the same applies to the outside groups with which the Báqoqx have joined in establishing the government's "Barabuna."

In these two cases (Tairora and Barabuna) we see both centripetal and centrifugal sociopolitical forces at work. Segmentation, with its remembered links, produces a larger if less intensive unity over areas of expanding size— a unity whose intensity diminishes with expansion. Expansion in space differentiates the linked groups, despite their common tradition and origins. Local opportunities and necessities of fusing with other elements of separate tradition lead each of them sometimes to form composite communities. These rapidly intensify their own unity by developing common local traditions. Thus are larger sociopolitical entities, originally founded on common tradition and supported by a phratric truce and connubium, eroded at their margins by the openness and incorporating capacity of their constituent groups. Above all, they are eroded by the local group's need to be open and to be able to incorporate or, sometimes, to be incorporated. Ability to incorporate means the ability to develop new, common or incorporating traditions. And these are *ipso facto* traditions that differentiate the erstwhile links of the network from each other and weaken their linking traditions. All that is possible beyond the local level, therefore, is a fluctuating concatenation of sociopolitical entities, larger or smaller, waxing or waning, but entities never able to exceed a certain limit in either duration or spatial range. This ultimately means that they cannot maintain a sufficient commonality of tradition.

Since the local group and above all the territory remains more continuous than the phratric tradition, the connubial network, and the peace-keeping alliance, it bears out the common claim of New Guinea ethnographers that this is the largest effective unity. It would be as accurate to say that it was the most continuous unity, thus changing the referent from space to time. And the territory is markedly more continuous than the personnel, not only in the obvious sense that the individual dies while the land remains but in the sense that territorial names, boundaries, and their cores change more slowly on the whole than the genealogical (and traditional) composition of the occupants from one time to another.[7]

Yet territorial boundaries change, too, and in fine we face a situation whose fluidity challenges formulation. The greatest continuities at last are probably those of language and culture. This is suggested not only in the general sense, that the structure and content of language or culture are ordinarily less labile than group membership, but also in the immediate regional sense, that, as pioneer students of the Central Highlands have recognized, the location of particular languages or speech communities shows a continuity in time (Wurm 1960, 1961a, 1961b; 1962; 1964). The price of this continuity, incidentally, is the very fluidity and incorporativeness of the social groups who are the language and culture bearers. Thus Auyana speakers who move into an area of majority Tairora speech become Tairora speakers, and Tairora speakers who settle permanently as refugees among Kamáno or Agarabi eventually speak Kamáno or Agarabi.

At least once in the past, prior to the segmentation of Barabuna, some informants recall, the ancestral Airiná were driven as refugees to seek asylum with Barabuna. Their adversaries on this occasion were Gadsup speakers. I have failed to identify them as to local group, but the possibilities are numerous, since traditional Airiná territory bordered that of the Gadsup ethnolinguistic group just as Batainabura territory borders it today. Numerous local groups of Gadsup, moreoever, are regarded as traditional enemies of long standing. Indeed, the stereotype of "enemy" (*nábuta*) is extended in-

---

7. Small wonder, perhaps, that people carry territorial designations abroad when referred to or when referring to themselves. What other designation would serve as well? There are situations, moreover, in which "the people of Y locality" carries more force than "the peoples whose fathers were of X locality."

discriminately to nearly all Gadsup groups by many of the present people of Batainabura, although some qualifications are obviously needed. Gadsup groups are remembered as having made incursions in the past well into the area occupied by Tairora speakers. Older informants also cite the Oqinata, a Tairora-speaking group whose territory lay in the grassland to the west of Barabuna. This group was allegedly wiped out entirely by its enemies, including Gadsup. Informants insist, by the way, that the Oqinata failed even to have survivors who could seek refuge among other groups, though it is doubtful that, even if true, this included the women.

The Airiná later returned to their own territory from Barabuna, but their asylum makes it clear that even if there had been no previous approximation between Airiná and Barabuna, the basis for approximation now existed. There is, of course, some reason to believe that the two communities already enjoyed amicable intercourse involving, for example, the exchange of goods between Airiná with bush resources and Barabuna with the specializations of the grassland. One Airiná informant remembers that an ancestor of his obtained a bride from Barabuna, although it is not clear whether this was before or after the Airiná asylum among them. A typical result of asylum is the development or multiplication of affinal links, and it is probable that the remembered bride was not the sole link between the two groups while they were territorially still autonomous.

The event that is conventionally said to have split the Barabuna group, ultimately bringing into being in sharply separate localities the modern Báqoqx and Hararúnx sibs, was irresistible pressure from an outside group known as the Tuntuqirx. This explanation is apparently slanted and oversimplified, however, for a number of informants recall internal dissension within the Barabuna group that seems, at least in part, independent of, if not prior to, the pressure of the Tuntuqirx. One informant, who speaks with some authority on the traditions of the groups at Batainabura, describes a more or less classical segmentation by colonization. Gánamo, a "younger brother," had planted gardens in an area near the territory of modern Barabuna—that is, in the far southeastern part of traditional Barabuna territory and in any case well away from the then Barabuna settlement. Since his crops came up well, Gánamo decided he wanted to settle nearby. He took his women and children and moved. Presumably he took others with him as well. An elder brother of his, Biakopo, became incensed at the move, not wanting to leave the parent settlement himself nor willing to have his sibling do so. Ill feelings and apparently fighting erupted over this or some corollary issue. A rift was created between the two future personnels which the subsequent attacks and territorial encroachment of the Tuntuqirx have only confirmed. The incursion of Tuntuqirx groups into the area, that is, drove Gánamo and his group, the future Báqoqx, farther to the southeast, probably causing them to seek asylum on the other side of a steep ridge where they joined with some of the extraphratric elements with whom they helped found the present community known as "Barabuna."

The encroaching Tuntuqirx themselves are said to be a group driven out of Arogara territory (see map 6), their trouble arising from a disagreement over the ownership of some cassowary chicks. Moving eastward, they joined with other elements to form what is today an extensive complex of sibs and local groups in the phratric territory known as Noraikora (see map 6). The occupants of Noraikora territory include more than the Tuntuqirx. It is the Tuntuqirx on whom Batainabura enmity is focused, however, even though Noraikora at large is regarded with hostility.

There seems little question that the eastward movement of the Tuntuqirx involved the preemption of land claimed by Barabuna—in other words, the capture of territory. Not only was ground allegedly preempted but also the use of adjacent territory not yet actively claimed or exploited by the preemptors. The nearby settlements of strong enemies ultimately forced the Hararúnx to abandon the active use of land nominally still theirs. Thus it may be the withdrawal of a resident group, to re-station their pigs and settle at a safer distance, that typically shrinks their perimeter of effective use. Eventually the claims of the former occupants to a part of their traditional territory become reduced to talking points. This is what has largely occurred for Hararúnx in the face of the Tuntuqirx threat. Space is security, and more space was needed between enemy settlements than simply enough to provide for gardens or pig range.

It is probably true that expulsion by a more powerful enemy does not always result in the preemption of the abandoned territory or even deny the original owners the use of a part of it. The refugees may return from asylum and reclaim their traditional lands entirely. The victors in the meantime may have made no more use of the territory than to despoil the gardens and destroy the fences and dwellings. Unless one is to suppose a static population as well as one committed to the peaceful accommodation of independent groups in space, it does not seem possible, even on general grounds, to argue against the occurrence of land conquest and territorial displacement.

The Oqinata, already mentioned, may be another case generally pertinent to the question of territorial conquest. Indeed, the elimination of the Oqinata is conceivably a part of the same eastward movement of the Tuntuqirx, for their territory apparently lay in the main path of the Tuntuqirx expansion or migration.[8]

---

8. Batainabura men today laughingly report that they used the unfortunate Oqinata for "hunting," picking them off "like opossums." The implication is not only that the beleaguered community was too weak to keep attackers at bay but that they were somehow bereft of effective friends to help them in their plight. This is at least consistent with the claim that the Oqinata had nowhere to flee and hence were killed on their own ground to the last individual. The literal truth of this claim may be doubted, since it is widely conventional among peoples of the Kainantu area to speak grandly of "finishing off" an adversary, even when many of the people are still alive and a flourishing contemporary group. It is nonetheless evident that the Oqinata were never reconstituted as a territorial group. Their former territory was effectively incorporated into others, including, probably, that of the Noraikora (Tuntuqirx). This is thus another form that territorial conquest can apparently take in the area under discussion.

The initial adjustment of the resident Barabuna group—the future Hararúnx—was apparently to relocate their settlement, but still within traditional territory. The Harúrunx site itself was probably settled or resettled at this time as a result of one or more such shifts. Meanwhile, open hostilities developed to the northwest between Tairora groups, including Abiera, and a group called Baqe. As previously noted, Baqe was itself originally a part of Tairora. The Baqe had killed a man from a Tairora community, and fighting ensued which dislodged them from their territory, adjacent to or within the present Kamunakera territory (see map 6). They (or some of them) sought asylum among the Barabuna (Hararúnx) group. There is no explicit indication of what prior relationship existed between the hosts and the refugees, although present Batainabura informants profess to regard it as axiomatic that hosts can expect to receive brides from refugees in exchange for granting them asylum and coresidence. This is obviously a sensible arrangement, as well as a reasonable exchange for the food, help, and security, since it makes affinal kinsmen and intermarrying sibs of host and guest. Indeed, the food and mutual assistance are exactly what should characterize relations between the receivers and the givers of brides. In addition, there can be little doubt that the continued pressure of the Tuntuqirx, plus the departure of the Báqoqx segments, would be a factor predisposing the Hararúnx to any feasible reinforcement of their ranks.

The present people of Batainabura maintain that they have long been friends of Phratry Tairora. Is friendship consistent with their befriending and harboring a group of refugees who were outcasts of the Tairora phratry? I do not know the answer in this specific case. One general observation, however, is that rarely if ever in Northern Tairora politics can a matched array of mutual enmities and amities be created by any given move toward alliance or opposition. Politics, indeed, makes strange bedfellows, as seemingly it must. Nearly any decision, in other words, must be a calculated chance. By the time of the Baqe recruitment the Hararúnx had evidently become dedicated enemies of the Nóraikóra, particularly of the Tuntuqirx; and the Nóraikóra were traditional enemies of Phratry Tairora. The mutual enmity for the Nóraikóra could thus serve as a counterbalance for giving aid and comfort to the fugitive Baqe. It is also likely that a beleaguered community like the Hararúnx—themselves, probably, just a few years from having to abandon their settlement to flee or merge with Airiná—may not have felt able to afford the luxury of a nicer matching of friends and enemies. Presented with the opportunity to obtain women and, at least temporarily, additional fighting strength, they may have regarded other considerations as quite secondary. A further possibility is that the community was not in fact united on this matter and that the decision of the majority or the more forceful members to aid the Baqe weakened communal bonds and alienated some elements.

In exploring issues such as these with informants, I found them fascinated with the plausibility of my questions. It was almost as if we were sitting by the fireside in the men's house helping to plan vital strategy. When the question was a nice one, however, the comments usually turned out to be the suppositions of the informants, not direct reports of the known reasons the men of the time had for their actions. Hindsight doubtless adds a further measure of distortion. What I intend by my foregoing paragraph, therefore, is not a valid representation of the specific reasoning followed by Hararúnx men in deciding to offer asylum to the Baqe or the decision of the Baqe to join them. It is rather an assessment of the situation they confronted at the time, insofar as I could grasp its dimensions. I believe this is of some value in discovering what course the political behavior of these groups followed, before the appearance of the *pax australiana*, and how that course is best described in general terms.

Whether or not prolonged, and whether or not the receiving of brides was a prearranged part of it, the Baqe asylum with the Hararúnx was quite productive from the latter's point of view. A number of Baqe women married men of the host group and, naturally, remained behind with their husbands and children after the majority of Baqe subsequently returned to their own territory. It is further apparent from the testimony of some informants that some of the Baqe men also remained behind, failing to return to their former territory, now called Kamunakera. There is certainly ample precedent for the decision of some to remain with their erstwhile hosts, even when the main group returns to its territory. Indeed, it is from all accounts quite common. As to the rationale, I see no reason to differentiate this choice from the decision of one man or a few to depart their native community while the majority remain. Either the advantages of continued residence with the hosts are relatively greater for those choosing to remain or the disadvantages of returning to the former territory are greater for them than for others— perhaps, in the latter case, because of their more immediate involvement in the altercation that originally provoked their flight. Conceivably in some cases, it might disembarrass the remainder of the returning group to omit certain of their former fellows, for example, if those omitted were considered by the adversary group as the main authors of the trouble. This might prove face-saving, moreover, in the case of two adversary groups, once it could be alleged by the host group that only the good people were still among them.

Be that as it may, a sufficient number of Baqe people joined the Hararúnx on this occasion, through marriage or for other reasons, that the name Baqe-Hararúnx is used today practically as often as Hararúnx alone. The compound name is known either as a synonym for Hararúnx, in designating the entire sib, or as a special designation for a part of the sib, if a speaker is pointedly distinguishing persons with this particular ancestry. I have used the compound term in the latter sense in reporting Batainabura census data for sib membership, but I seriously doubt that the usage is perfectly consistent among Batainabura speakers or can be made so today without more effort than local people would regard as reasonable. The number of Baqe men and women who remained among the Batainabura, however, may not have exceeded even ten adults. Such a number, indeed, would be quite sufficient to loom large in the lineage of a group the size of the Hararúnx.

The merging of a number of Baqe refugees with the host Hararúnx group is, in one sense, but an example of fusion. This recurrent process among the local groups of the area involves above all a bloc of refugees and their hosts. The use of the compound name, Baqe-Hararúnx, however, though somewhat variable, raises the question how such a name evolves. I recorded no other compound name in my field research in Northern Tairora. Indeed, the place-of-origin principle of Northern Tairora would seem to favor the use of single names for descent groups. Though it is only a guess on my part, I suggest that two circumstances have contributed to the special usage in this case: (1) The merging of Baqe and Hararúnx is quite recent and it began, moreover, rather soon after the Baqe first joined the Hararúnx as coresidents. It is therefore not yet complete. (2) There still exists a Baqe sib elsewhere—but in another phratry—with members of which some Baqe-Hararúnx still have active relations.

While each personnel occupied the settlement where the Baqe first joined the Hararúnx as a bloc of refugees, there was probably no fusion in a single sib. Each was maritally a sib to the other. The fusion of elements of Baqe and Hararúnx arises thus from the subsequent common fate of the Baqe remnant and the native Hararúnx; but the Baqe were too newly arrived, as it were, to be *from* Hararúnx. They were still "from Baqe." Time will doubtless erase both the "newness" and the unique provenience.

A group of Kamáno-speaking refugees from the village of Yabungka or JabuNka (called Gábuba by Tairora speakers) briefly found asylum in Hararúnx territory. The home territory of these refugees is (depending on the map used) some ten to twelve miles from Hararúnx. Despite the obvious recency of this move (the site of JabuNka dwellings is readily pointed out), men with whom I spoke at Batainabura did not know what might have prompted the choice of Hararúnx as a refuge by this group of Kamáno speakers. These informants were ignorant of previous intermarriage and did not recall refugees from their own immediate area ever having sought asylum in JabuNka territory. The case illustrates the spatial range and ethnic diversity of the contacts that arise in this area through warfare and asylum. JabuNka is probably three or more ethnopolitical steps from Hararúnx. The JabuNka asylum, incidentally, helps account for the subsequent flight of a group of largely Hararúnx refugees to JabuNka.) The reasons for the original contact between the two groups—if it was original—remain obscure to me. Possibly there were trading partnerships that linked the two groups. Or possibly the enmities and amities of the JabuNka refugees were such that they simply had to find a refuge at a greater distance than sometimes is the case, and find it among an alien group without prior reasons for refusing them. It is evident in other cases that the initial base for seeking asylum need not be broad—perhaps no more than one or two men, if they are influential, and if the refugees are initially handicapped by no serious local enmities. One also recalls that the

Hararúnx were being pressed by the Tuntuqirx at the time and could doubt-less benefit from the added manpower.

The stay of the JabuNka in Hararúnx territory was evidently brief and, if women were exchanged, some informants are unaware of it. Indeed, I could obtain no sense of immediate reciprocity on the part of the Kamáno speak-ers, although, as noted, they later reciprocated in receiving a group of Har-arúnx refugees. It is probably significant that the Kamáno refugees remained residentially distinct throughout their brief stay and also that a dispute over women is said to have precipitated their withdrawal.

It is quite likely that the Hararúnx had counted on the JabuNka refugees to strengthen them in their struggle with the Tuntuqirx and to make it possi-ble for them to remain within their native territory. If so, the departure of the JabuNka may have had something to do with the Hararúnx's failure to hold their remaining territory. In any event, the Hararúnx finally decided they could hold it no longer, and arrangements were made with their former refugees, the Baqe, to occupy land and build a settlement within Kamu-nakera territory to the north. It must have been a fairly obvious decision where to seek asylum, since by now the Hararúnx had close affinal ties with the Baqe, some of whom were coresidents, and through them ties with the larger Kamunakera group of which Baqe at large was a part. Land was given, and they built a settlement in Kamunakera territory, just behind what later became the Highlands Agricultural Experiment Station at Aiyura. In this case removal apparently did not occur without forewarning, and advance preparations may have been made by their hosts to receive them, perhaps even by some of the Hararúnx to prepare the site.

It is not inconsequential for a local group to receive a sudden increment of one to several score of persons. Housing is surely one of the least of the problems, for until new houses can be built refugee men can double up in the men's house and women and children can scatter among the several women's houses. In fact, the suggestion is clear that there was often little need for even such transitory crowding, because temporary shelter of some kind was used by the newcomers while they built more substantial dwellings for themselves. The refugees, moreover, typically settled on a separate site. Food was a more urgent problem than housing, simply because the supply of garden food cannot so rapidly be increased. Under ideal conditions, a local group would have food resources sufficient for short-run hospitality for a siz-able number of guests, as in the case of a sing-sing; but the continued needs of long-term guests presumably required an urgent expansion of local gar-dens by the hosts and the rapid establishment of gardens by the refugees.

The Hararuna asylum among the Baqe-Kamunakera seems to differ from others at greater remove. The old gardens in Hararuna territory could be visited with caution and supplementary food brought from there, since it was only a few miles distant. Indeed, a secluded route through dense woods lay along a ridge running from near Hararuna to the site of their refuge in Kamu-nakera territory; and this route is specifically mentioned in connection with

Hararúnx movements during the period of their asylum. It gave them concealment in salvaging remnant crops and hence some protection from their Tuntuqirx-Nóraikóra enemies in the valley below the ridge.

With larger groups of refugees or relatively small host groups, or with more distant asylums, the case would differ. The refugees could contribute less food from their own herds and former gardens, assuming these were not completely pillaged; and the resoures of a small host group would be relatively less adequate to cope with the needs of the additional personnel. In part for this reason, it seems likely refugees did not always go in a single group to a single asylum. Indeed, they were probably often split and dispersed among two or more host groups. For other reasons as well, different hosts were preferred by different refugees. Some might have closer ties in one community; others, including fellow sib mates and coresidents, would have them elsewhere. Since hosts were often affinal or matrilineal kin, obviously there would be a different pull on different persons, whose mothers or wives came from different places, or whose sisters had married into different outside groups. Both logistics and sociology must have weighed in the final outcome. That refugees frequently went to different groups and places naturally complicates the social history of Northern Tairora.

The duration of Hararúnx exile with the Baqe in Kamunakera territory was apparently not long. Some informants, at least, believe that no marriages were contracted during this period between men of the host group and Hararúnx women. In the view of some, the reason for returning was principally the wish of the Hararúnx to reestablish themselves in or near their former territory. Others allude indirectly to the weakness of the hosts as defenders and allies, suggesting that this afforded the Hararúnx only an insecure refuge. There is a further suggestion that some enemies of the Hararúnx were not the enemies of all sections of the host community, making the refugees anxious about their safety. Any or all of these reasons are quite credible, and each of them probably played some part. Moreover, each of these factors is reported in other cases. There is nothing unusual about the pull of a refugee group to return to its own territory. Any factor unfavorable to remaining in exile obviously may favor returning. The territory was not distant, moreover, and the path not perilous. In all likelihood their territory was visited and revisited by the refugees, keeping it constantly in their minds. It is further asserted that the Airiná, possibly feeling pressure from the Tuntuqirx or other enemies, invited the Hararúnx to return to their vicinity, promising them assistance in reestablishing themselves on a nearby site. This is represented by most Airiná informants as the determining factor. Following the hidden path along the forested ridge, the Hararúnx returned and built a settlement, selecting a grassland site as far as possible from the settlement of their Tuntuqirx foe.

The increasing approximation of the Hararúnx—or Baqe-Hararúnx—and the Airiná is apparent. It is not clear that the two local groups had yet become a single composite community. Living in separate settlements, though apparently closer to each other than previously, they were faced with a common and feared adversary, the Tuntuqirx. They appear to have reached some mutual understandings. The Hararúnx, however, could not be considered refugees at this point nor the Airiná strictly their hosts, despite the probable importance of Airiná promises of support. The groups were each in fact living on territory partly claimed by the other. The arrangement was thus nearly symmetrical.

Tuntuqirx pressure continued, and now not only the Hararúnx but also the Airiná were driven to abandon their settlements. A contingent of the refugees at this time went west to live among the JabuNka (Gábuba), a Kamáno-speaking group. Few of these people have apparently returned to Batainabura. Of those refugees who did later return the majority seem to have fled to a site in or near Arau (see map 6) territory, to the east. The JabuNka contingent, to judge from the men still remembered at Batainabura, consisted largely of Hararúnx, with only one or two Airiná men, at most, in a group of twelve. The alignment of refugees in this episode again illustrates the tendency to divide in seeking asylum. The fairly sharp division as between Airiná and Hararúnx tends to confirm that the two erstwhile autonomous personnels were still quite distinct from each other at the time of expulsion. It was in Hararúnx territory, to be sure, that the JabuNka themselves had earlier found brief asylum, presumably establishing the link that led some of the Hararúnx now to seek refuge in turn among these same people, their former guests. This appears to be relatively distant asylum. The assimilation of the group that went to JabuNka, or their alienation from their former group, was such, moreover, that the majority of them have elected to remain among their hosts and few if any have ever returned to join their former sib mates and coresidents. They remain at JabuNka today, many of the older refugees still remembered; but they are not now expected back except for the brief visits of individuals.

The main Airiná and Hararúnx group appears to have gone to a site near Árau, as noted, and no further refuge is mentioned. It is quite possible that an odd individual or two found asylum elsewhere, either later rejoining the main group or being forgotten by all but certain persons whom I did not happen to interview on that point.

In due course, their new refuge in or near Árau proved unsatisfactory to the Hararúnx-Airiná when the group was attacked by men from the Báqoqx (now the government's "Barabuna"). The Árau people did not come to their assistance, but allegedly remained neutral witnesses to the fighting. It is not clear how much responsibility Árau people had actually assumed for the Hararúnx-Airiná refugees or whether the refugee settlement was actually in the immediate jurisdiction of Árau. There is a large area of no man's land where the site may actually have been (see map 6). In any case, the Báqoqx were not the enemies of Árau, even if they were at the time enemies of the Hararúnx-Airiná. Although this therefore appears to be a familiar instance of enmities and amities that do not match sufficiently as between hosts and refugees, Batainabura informants today imply that the Árau people betrayed them or at least were disloyal or cowardly not to have helped them. It did not, however, make them enemies of Árau, for later on elements of the Batainabura groups were once more to seek refuge in Árau territory.

Beyond this point it is increasingly difficult to disentangle the web of movements, suggesting how much more complex earlier movements may have been than current report makes them seem. The complexity of recent movements, that is, may arise largely from the fact that the people who took part in them are either alive or nearly all remembered, while the report of earlier movements is probably simplified because of the tendency to drop persons whose descendants no longer affect the lives of the reporters. Hence one hears only of certain refugee segments and of certain asylums. Traditional history, in depicting the mainstream from the point of view of one group or locality no doubt delivers the ethnographer from much labor, but at the cost of an incomplete view of events.

On the other hand, there are certain peculiarities that do perhaps complicate the recent history of Batainabura to a degree not everywhere matched. Successive expulsions from the home territory are inevitably disruptive, making the record more difficult to trace than that of an undisturbed group. The present people of Batainabura and their immediate predecessors have seen repeated exile. Batainabura's own founding is very recent, moreover, and until then one is in fact speaking of other peoples, as no "Batainabura" yet exists. Although once put to flight, Abiera has been more continuous, and before its founding there was the parent Tairora. For Batainabura, however, one must deal with at least two heretofore independent local groups— quite likely different phratries—still living in separate though adjacent territories up to perhaps the turn of the century or later. It is hard to credit that previously these prime movers could ever have been members of the same phratry, but if they ever were, separate subsequent careers and distinct allegiances had developed to differentiate them appreciably from each other. From then on, a common fate at the hands of common enemies, notably the relentless Tuntuqirx, progressively drew together the two local groups. Through a series of simultaneous or overlapping expulsions and through occupying some of the same asylums, these two major groups, now as sibs known by their earlier place names, gradually approached the jointness of the present local group. This was given lasting confirmation about 1930 by government guarantee in repatriating the main sibs as a composite group to a composite estate made out of their respective former territories.

Compositeness, as we have seen, is not peculiar in the make-up of local groups of the Northern Tairora area, and Batainabura is therefore not in this respect unique. It is like Abiera, for example. The compositeness of Batainabura, moreover, if not born solely of political and military urgency, at least receives much impetus from it. Again this seems not untypical. That the aboriginal territories of the major component groups are adjacent, with parts of each incorporated in the territory of the present local group, differs from the

Abiera situation, to be sure, where neither main sib is able, even if it cared to, to trace itself to any separate, immediately prior ground. But more significant than the ability of each main Batainabura sib to indicate its once separate native soil are the individual loyalties and oppositions of these sibs, in a word their distinct—and quite *recently* distinct—histories. Crossed by several periods in exile, not always together, by a series of different asylums among which the refugees, even from one sib, appear to have been divided, and by the division of returnees from nonreturnees, as well as earlier and later returnees, the case is such that to trace the present personnel through the vagaries of all their comings and goings would ideally require detailed family histories. I do not have such data. What follows is at best an approximation, therefore, emphasizing what seem to be the principal developments.

The attacks of the Báqoqx on the Hararúnx-Airiná refugees apparently dislodged some or all of them from their Árau asylum. Some of the refugees appear to have drifted back to their traditional territory. One or two men at Batainabura today claim, in fact, that they never left it, maintaining there solitary homesteads! They imply that their obstinacy stems from superior valor and courage in the face of enemy threat, but it is obvious that if they did in fact remain, it could scarcely have been solely on the basis of *sangfroid* in confronting impossible odds. Interstitial individuals exist who are, for reasons of personal connection, such as marriage, relatively immune to the hostilities involving the majority of their own and certain enemy groups. There is one such man (only one!) today among the Tuntuqirx—a prominent man, in fact, who freely visits Batainabura and is welcome. Those who assert that they remained in traditional Batainabura territory through the exile of their fellows do so with a sense of prior claim now in rights to land and community authority. They imply a status somewhat resembling that of a strong man, although it is not possible now to play this role in other respects. Nor does their claim put them in the position of making allocations of land.

This doughty few were presently joined by returnees from Árau, but it appears that some did not return directly and others not at all. An unknown number moved from Árau to Andandára territory (see map 6), apparently without an interlude in home territory. Asylum in Andandára matched their needs for security, at least against the Báqoqx, for, unlike the Árau, the Andandára are enemies of the Báqoqx. I do not know if there were prior marital links between Airiná or Hararúnx and Andandára. (Nor do I know if there were any with Árau.) There are links, now, of course, as the census shows.

As Airiná and Hararúnx refugees returned to their native territory, it is all but certain that they were on their way to becoming, if they had not in fact become, a composite group. Whatever the prior composition of each local group while still autonomous, moreover, Airiná and Baqe-Hararúnx had by now largely attained the sense of unified sibs as well as sibs linked to each other. In one sense, of course, Batainabura is not as complete or solidary a composite today as Abiera. There is still Hararúnx territory and the old site of its settlement; and there is still Airiná territory and the old Airiná site of the legend. There is nothing that quite corresponds to this situation at Abiera—no distinct Komohórxntx site or territory, no traditional Poreqórxntx sector. The remembered former settlements of Abiera people such as Tairora, were themselves composite—or at least are so remembered. They are thus claimed equally—whether or not with equal validity— by both the major sibs of Abiera.

Whatever further forging of a common fate and a common tradition the personnel of Batainabura might require, they were not long without help from the outside. The pressure of both Báqoqx and Tuntuqirx remained strong, especially that of the latter. Two specific instances are recalled by one informant when the Báqoqx routed Batainabura, though apparently neither defeat resulted in the flight of people from the territory. That the Báqoqx once attacked them in the forest near the old Airiná site where they were burying a corpse suggests that, to the Báqoqx, Hararúnx and Airiná were becoming a single political entity. At least once more the Tuntuqirx drove the Batainabura people into refuge.

Again this time some of the refugees settled in the vicinity of the no man's land near Árau. Other refugees apparently found their way again to Andandára. Still others—either on this or some prior occasion—went to the Gadsup-speaking village of Tompena, where a nucleus of Airiná is still recognizable today as an established personnel—perhaps a sib—within that neighboring community. Their alien origin is not notorious, however, nor is it treated as a subject to be suppressed. But it is rather difficult, as proved to be the case with the Poreqórxntx at Abiera, to obtain information about the provenience of the "Airináranta" at Tompena. Like most people, they are more concerned with asserting traditional claims in the community where they live and expect to continue to live. Under the circumstances, there is much less—if anything—to be gained from stressing one's origin elsewhere. A keen interest in lineage is not matched by a wish for exotic identity.

It was apparently during this period, when the nucleus of the future Batainabura group was located near Árau, that the first goverment patrols arrived in the vicinity. In fact, Batainabura informants report that their settlement was on one occasion, during their last Árau exile, mistakenly attacked by a government patrol. A man was killed. The constabulary thought that the refugees were a part of Árau proper, so it is said, against whom the government's reprisal was actually intended. To compensate them for the mistaken killing, it is believed, the government gave the refugees gifts of axes, knives, and other trade goods that at the time were superlatively valuable.

The government later made an even more significant gesture in convincing the refugees that if they returned to their native ground, their rights there would be guaranteed and enforced, if necessary by arms, against their enemies. This assurance, at once so unprecedented and so full of possibilities, convinced the leaders that these few powerful men were their great and particular friends. Subsequent events apparently did not disappoint them. They have only the kindest recollections of their early contact with Australian administration. Little bitterness is felt, in fact, over the mistaken killing of their fellow refugee. They do not question that it was an error and one of a kind they can comprehend. When the government forces took reprisals against Tuntuqirx settlements, the delighted repatriates concluded at once the depredations were on their behalf. Indeed, to a people for whom Phratry Noraikora were hated enemies, the early years of government tutelage— roughly from 1932 to 1945—must have often been filled with joy at the adversary's suffering. The "Noreikora" (or "Nory-kory," as early Europeans of the vicinity then commonly called them) figure often in the Kainantu patrol reports of this period. Warning after warning, arrest after arrest, reprisal after reprisal were directed at one or more of the "Noreikora villages." In the eyes of the patrol officers at Kainantu, it seems, the Noraikora people, even more than the "Taiora" at large, whom they frankly considered the most recalcitrant of the local peoples, were only to be reached by severe methods. The actual severity, in fact, far exceeded anything reported officially, with public beatings administered by the police to individual men (and women?) of Noraikora, stripped naked, the "roasting" of at least one, probably several men over live coals, and, in one notable case, the murder of a Noraikora man by a noncommissioned officer of the constabulary, who split his head open with an ax while other constables pinioned the victim's arms. Since the insolence and disobedience of the "bighead" Noraikora did not cease, allegedly, with the first serious reprisal, it appears that the peoples of this phratry continued for some time to be subject to administrative punishment. Some of it was obviously outside the law and perhaps also outside the knowledge of the assistant district officer in charge at Kainantu. To the people of Batainabura, however, the harshness of the constables was altogether reassuring of their good fortune in having so powerful—and so discriminating–an ally. They felt they were at this time nothing less than the "*kiap*'s favorites." Their enthusiasm for the Australian *kiap* (government patrol officer) of that day, even with the passage of time, is very great.

In guaranteeing the refugees their old—now composite—territories, however, the government did not expel the Tuntuqirx, no matter how much they may have cowed them. What the Airiná and the Hararúnx got for territory, therefore, is but a poor toehold in a part of what they formerly claimed. As previously noted, a good piece of the rest—particularly the territory of the Hararúnx—is still nominally theirs. In the local view, it is not usable, however, because to make gardens or to keep pigs there, so near the Tuntuqirx, would be dangerous and foolish. The claims of Batainabura people to lands preempted by the Tuntuqirx, in this case land on the far side of the Tuntuqirx village from them, did receive token acknowledgment in a postwar payment for land alienated to D. McBeath, a European settler. Some 35 to 40 (Australian) pounds from the government, as it is recalled, were distributed among certain of the villagers. To be sure, the Tuntuqirx were not excluded from this settlement by the government, apparently receiving a larger amount.

The elation and the sense of special friendship of the early contact period did not last beyond the war. The personal justice and direct action of some of the first government officers in the area, above all the reprisals and gratifying atrocities of the constabulary against Noraikora, finally came to an end. They were replaced by bureaucratic formality compared to which some of the freewheeling government behavior of the past would have been considered scandalous and unconscionable. Sadly, some of the older men of Batainabura now feel, history has passed them by. They are today only one among a great many faceless communities with which the government has more or less concern, largely depending on whether "trouble" brings them to the attention of the government officers. They are not recognized by the present government personnel as having any particular claim or distinction, nor are they remembered as the earliest and closest allies of the administration the way the people saw themselves. That is the unmistakable impression the older men have of the past. They have joined a multitude of uniform color. While to other Northern Tairora of the vicinity the existence of Batainabura is clearly the government's deed, the episode is either buried in government reports or lost with the records destroyed during World War II at Salamaua.

In fact, the Batainabura are even more obscure today than many other peoples, since they live off the beaten path. Inconvenient to reach, they are seldom visited. In order to vote or be censused, they must troop down from their own settlement to one of the hated Tuntuqirx. A new vehicular road reaches the Tuntuqirx, though both road and people are on ground the Batainabura regard as theirs. One old man claims that an early *kiap* made him a paramount *luluai*—the first in the area. The badge of his office was to be given to him as soon as it came. Perhaps it is true, but the government is unaware of it. To this special friend of "Noti" (Mr. Nurton), one of the first patrol officers to contact the Batainabura, the message is clear: "The government's road from the Markham came directly through us. We were the door for them. But now they have moved the road and our road is no longer theirs."

Over the course of their merging histories, the beleaguered Batainabura sibs lost a great deal of what they say is theirs. There is no evidence, however, that it is only land shortage or fear of the Tuntuqirx that presently unifies Batainabura, nor that their existence is or was wholly the artifact of pioneer patrol officers. Their composite unity, in fact, though much more recent than that of Abiera, and surely with no comparable record of successes, may well be greater. If the Hararúnx could comfortably regain access to the bulk of their claimed land, the separate and distinct traditions of the two major sibs could conceivably furnish foci for a segmentary recrudescence. At present the traditions seem rather to be sources of mutual pride. The myths of the individual sibs are becoming myths of Batainabura. The traditional lands separately claimed are becoming lands jointly claimed. Residentially the members of the sibs are more randomly intermixed at Batainabura than at Abiera. Such factional sentiments as occur are organized more along an uphill-downhill axis than a sib axis, although, as was pointed out, there is some coincidence. My strong impression, furthermore, is that feelings of distinctness are not as near the surface in Batainabura as they are in Abiera. In fact, they are ordinarily imperceptible. The habit of common action is apparently well rooted even if its fullest expression has been in sharing formidable foes and a series of common setbacks. Pruned by different phases during which it was a haven for refugees or was itself in exile (each period of exile subdivided by the number of different asylums to which the refugees went), stripped by who can tell how many more forgotten experiences of all but the people with the clearest loyalties, Batainabura, considering that it emerged at all, might well be sociologically homogeneous. A marked local endogamy links the major sibs as intermarrying personnels. Perfect harmony among men is surely not to be sought in the Central Highlands of New Guinea. Batainabura offers at least equal homogeneity and perhaps more harmony than Abiera, to judge from my six months' observation of each community. The basis for it was developed perhaps in less time but evidently by a more drastic unification: continued failure against enemies versus consistent success. In both Batainabura and Abiera, however, the needs and outcomes of fighting have been prominent in shaping the present community. In both cases bedfellows of political convenience more than genealogical orthodoxy have become coresidents and kinsmen.

To emphasize variable political and military factors in the shaping of the two communities is not to minimize the importance of the basic social processes that justify calling them open societies. Here the point is not that the extremity of their peculiar situation compelled the proto-Batainabura groups, in merging, to repudiate or violate the normal tendencies of their social system. Rather it compelled them—if that is the word—to use certain of the provisions of their system more intensively or more exclusively than they might otherwise have done. Had either the Airiná or the Hararúnx-Bárabúnx been equal to the challenge of their adversaries, they would presumably have held their territory. They would probably not have sought supplement, that is, in ever more intimate alliance with outsiders, intermarriage, increasing coterritoriality, and ultimate residential unity. These developments, however, are not in any sense abnormal to the experience or the perceptions of Northern Tairora peoples. Quite as much as colonizing, refugeeism, recruitment, and fusion belong to the system. Following the detachment of the Báqoqx to form part of the government's "Bárabúna," to be sure, neither the Hararúnx nor the Airiná local group was in a position to colonize.

The recent history of Batainabura may make fusion and fission appear mutually exclusive alternatives. Be that as it may, except for the short run or the particular case, both processes taken together best characterize the capacities of the local system. The history of Phratry Tairora and Abiera indicates that both colonizing and the incorporation of aliens proceeded in close succession if not side by side. Indeed, there is an apparent complementarity between this pair of processes: new members for the community must be recruited, in part, evidently, because colonizing sometimes dangerously reduces the membership and defense force of either the old or new group, or perhaps both at once; but, equally, bringing in members from the outside may involve a restructuring of loyalties and oppositions within a community, contributing to the detachment of disaffected members into separate colonies or increasing the chances of alienation of colonies already established.

If there is in this counterpoint of splitting and joining a semblance of cyclic regularity in given local groups, or if in the field at large there are factors making for such regularity, it is not at present obvious. The possibility should be noted, because such regularities have been posited elsewhere in the Central Highlands (Meggitt 1962, 1967). Several observations are possible concerning the matter of cyclic regularity in societies of small scale. First, apart from the social or cultural reflexes or biorhythms or the periodicities of earth and climate, there may be no more reason in small-scale groups to seek for simple cycles readily observed by an ethnographer in a short span of field research than there is to seek them in large-scale groups. Indeed, there may be _less_ such regularity in small-scale units for the very fact of their smallness—the scale effect. Fluctuations abound. If nothing else, this chapter and the entire monograph is witness to the extent and depth of such fluctuations, seen either as local differences—that is, seen statically—or seen as differences of phase within a generalized process. To suppose or to discover in any or all of these fluctuations a periodic pattern _locally discernible_ is the issue, or the task. How sharp a pattern? How much is it to be defined as a sequence of successive conditions that can be seen at the immediate local level? Northern Tairora local groups and Northern Tairora phratries both normally consist of quite small populations, say 100 to 300 or so for local groups, and perhaps 200 to 600 maximum for phratries. (Phratry Tairora, as noted, exceeds this maximum, but for reasons that may have no precontact parallel.) Periodic patterns—beyond those deriving from the biological and the climatic—may perhaps be better sought in the larger social field than in the local unit. Northern Tairora local units are very much affected by their field of interaction, and the field is far less directly determined by the circumstances of any one local unit than the latter is by the field. Finding periodic patterns in the larger field may in the long run prove to be the better chance.

The net impression, though in the short run hardly one of a steady procession, is that of a long-term flow of personnel both into and out of the sampled communities. Communities so characterized can in some sense be termed unstable. This quality requires more than mention, to be sure, but is no less a fact for not being at once explainable. Short of fairly extensive analysis one could only suggest some of the factors producing—or permitting—instability. In broadest terms, the Northern Tairora situation allows for considerable opportunism which must, of course, be nourished by the existence of opportunities for movement as well as constrained by risks that may somewhat control it. If the local community, within certain limits, is open to entry and departure, so likewise must be its neighbors. A given community, that is, can be open because other communities within reach of it also are.

Several of the factors involved in Northern Tairora society may either brake or stimulate movement, depending on the circumstances. One limit to free movement is the pressure of the field, above all warfare: the need for a community to remain strong in order to remain at all. For the individual this means the need to keep or find a place in a viably strong group. However, the individual also needs to find and stay within a group in which he has positive relations as well as adequate access to resources and women. This is sometimes a limit on movement and sometimes a motive for it. The local group is collectively pushed to gain or to retain personnel, up to a certain minimum; and the individual actor is sometimes under pressure to restrain his ambitions or his complaints—in effect, his movements. If he does not really do so in the interest of an abstract common good, then at least he does so in the interest of his own.

On the side of fission is the relative lack of social control. Apart from intermittent strong leadership there is practically no superordinate control to which an aggrieved party may appeal. Sodalities are absent. Kinship and locality furnish the sole unifying sentiments through the process of vernacular history or convention. From an individual's standpoint his residence, his marriage, and his descent (which, as is evident throughout this chapter, become readily joined and revised when the occasion requires) afford him a network of personal linkages from which he may contingently expect help in defending his interests. But against a member of his own group these mechanisms are socially divisive if pushed very far. The cement of fraternity workhardens under repeated blows, growing too brittle with time.

Individual ambition and the personal grievances it may produce tend to divide a community. Familism and personal loyalties sometimes make leadership itself divisive, for the community at large if not for the immediate cohorts of a particular leader. There is no intention here to suggest that Tairora speakers are peculiarly subject to division or uniquely lacking in cohesive processes or mechanisms compared with their neighbors of the wider Kainantu area. They may be more or less prone to divide than these, depending on what a detailed comparison might reveal. The present point, however, is only to suggest representative features of the Northern Tairora situation—features that plausibly account for the fluidity of membership of Northern Tairora social units, and which therefore, along with ecological pressures, underlie segmentation, with or without open strife.

The title of this chapter refers to "two phratries." The sense of *phratry* is not beclouded, at least, in the case of the Tairora group to which Abiera belongs. Tairora is clearly a continuous territory occupied by local groups, like Abiera, that are interrelated and contiguous. The great majority of the membership of these groups belong to—or are married to persons who belong to—several nonlocalized sibs, all tracing themselves to a common source, on which basis they make uncontested claims to phratric identity. Equally important, this territory and its major occupants are identified in substantially the same way and with the same name by outsiders who know them and by those who claim membership. Beyond reasonably well-defined Tairora boundaries, moreover, lie other territories and other personnels. These are distinguished by name from Tairora, both by the Tairora and by themselves, although not necessarily lacking connection with members of Phratry Tairora. In a word, the social nomenclature in the case of Phratry Tairora is followed with consistency and appears to be in agreement with local principles.

PHRATRY BATAINABURA

But what of Batainabura? In what sense may one speak of Batainabura as —or as part of—a phratry? Batainabura itself is of course, like Abiera, a local group. To what phratry does Batainabura belong? An unqualified answer is not useful. In simplest terms, Batainabura is a territorial unit that cuts across a series of sibs, each of which is connected to one other sib but in only one of two ways: it is connected either by coresidence or by a tradition of common descent. That is, no two sibs of the series are connected to each other both by residence and descent. Thus Sib Báqoqx, residents of what the government designates as Barabuna,[9] is connected with Sib Hararúnx of Batainabura by remembered descent (or former coresidence); but these two sibs are not, of course, coresident. They are separated not only by residence, moreover, but by the fact that each resides with a distinct and unrelated set of people. Sib Hararúnx resides with Sib Airiná at Batainabura, and Sib Báqoqx at Barabuna resides with a sib called "Toqukena" by the Batainabura people. One could follow the chain further and in several compass directions, but in asking whether Batainabura is a phratry, and in considering what an answer means, it will suffice to focus on the present facts.

Peoples at a distance (the Tairora, for example) sometimes speak of the residents of both the Batainabura and Barabuna local groups as "Barabuna," implying in some sense a phratric unit. Members of Sib Hararúnx tend to confirm this in speaking of Sib Báqoqx as being their own people. Dr. Larry Grossman, who has studied at Barabuna, says that the Báqoqx (who may not be so known in their own locality) reciprocate this sentiment so far as being connected to the Hararúnx (pers. comm.). Is there not, then, a Barabuna

9. The reader may recall that "Barabuna" was originally—and is still—the name of a site within present Batainabura territory, where lived the common forebears of the now apparently moribund phratry.

phratry constituted by the residents of these two adjacent communities? If there is, then Batainabura is one part of a phratry consisting of two local groups.

The problem is that of the two sibs that would constitute the core of such a phratry—by sharing a common descent—each is coresident with a second sib that does not share common descent with any of the rest. Moreover, while at Batainabura the Airiná and Hararúnx appear to be developing inter-marriages and common traditions, which will possibly eventuate in a genea-logical as well as residential common identity, this identity will probably not be susceptible of extension to Sib Báqoqx, who have in fact been enemies of Sib Airiná. For their part, the Hararúnx (as well as the Airiná) consider the Toqukena people to be frank outsiders if not enemies.

Thus does the complex and independent movement and merging of re-lated migrants with unrelated hosts or cofounders lead to ties that partly war-rant, partly defeat the claim and prospects of phratry. In this case the gov-ernment's hand in restoring the Batainabura peoples as a residential group perhaps need not be blamed for creating an anomaly. At least it is not one that might not otherwise have occurred. The anomaly, if any, would be the restoration of former territory to people who might not on their own have been able to make good their claim to it.

From present evidence I doubt that Phratry Barabuna will emerge from the process that seems to be unfolding. The time for phratries may of course be passing—or at least the time for the formation of *new* phratries. The sup-pression of warfare probably affects the case. That being so, the chance of consolidating a Barabuna phratry, quite apart from the problem of internal structure and lack of cohesiveness, would not be favorable. I have not weighed the changing future prospects for phratries at large, however, but only the immediate problem of Batainabura-Barabuna. It is worth noting that the sentiments that have traditionally contributed to the development of phratries are still being expressed, even if, in the claim of a phratric "Bara-buna," perhaps for a lost cause.

If Phratry Barabuna is wistful retrospect, a hope forlorn, then what is Ba-tainabura? It is at least a local group. It is evidently a local group more iso-lated from any others than it would be as part of a phratric cluster. It shares with no principal other(s) a territory, a special peace, or an intensive con-nubium. Its claims of common descent poorly justify or rationalize any clear-cut larger social utility. I suggest, however, that it is useful and meaningful to consider Batainabura itself a phratry—a phratry composed of one local group. What reasons can be advanced for this position? Surely not the need for taxonomic tidiness in the table of organization of Northern Tairora soci-ety, a plan within which all local groups must belong to phratries because many or most of them do. One could, of course, accept the surface fact and say merely than many or most Northern Tairora local groups are found clus-tered in larger entities, which it seems well to call phratries, but that there are also unclustered local groups, like Batainabura, which it seems better not to consider as phratries. To do that is to add the criterion of a plurality of subunits to the other criteria of "phratry." To what end? In order to recognize local groups both within and local groups without phratries? Such a purpose is at least as vulnerable in the opposite direction, begging the question of whether one of a cluster of local groups is the same as a solitary local group.

It seems probable that a single local group in Northern Tairora society is not the same as one of a phratric cluster. The difference between them, moreover, may be largely what would be expected if single local groups must serve phratric purposes—that is, "operate" as phratries. The main characteristics of phratries, as noted, are name, common descent of the membership, common territory, collaboration for peace-keeping, and an endogamous network. None of these features is distinctive of phratries versus local groups. Common territory and peace-keeping are as characteristic of the latter as the former; but a different degree of endogamy, if it occurs between single and clustered local groups, might suggest a justification for considering the isolated single group functionally phratric. The single group, in other words, would more nearly approximate connubium than one of a cluster of local groups.

My evidence on this point is limited to the case of Batainabura. As far as it goes, however, the evidence is affirmative. Batainabura is substantially more endogamous than Abiera. Endogamous values were also avowed by Batainabura on more than one occason. The intermarriage of members of local sibs at Batainabura runs at 81 percent, compared with Abiera's 58 percent; and brides of resident Batainabura men list birthplaces within local territory by a rate of 64 percent against Abiera's rate of less than 50 percent (see Chapter 4). Closer scrutiny—or better data—could possibly increase these differences, for example, by eliminating some brides at Abiera whose sibs are represented locally but who themselves are from other segments of the sib located elsewhere in the phratric territory.

Still another point may be made about the case of Batainabura. Considering development and process, we might on several grounds argue that Batainabura is a *nascent* phratry. It is, so to speak, just commencing to behave phratrically, but the local personnel there, as presently constituted, are very new and cannot be expected at once to realize a fully phratric profile. Their numerical indicators will reflect the past—for example, marriages contracted when Batainabura in the present sense did not yet exist—even if their sentiments and current behavior reflect their present circumstances and their phratric future. But, in fact, the sentiments also lag, as we have seen, for some are still wistful about a different alignment of personnel, which they call "Barabuna."

The people of Batainabura and their neighbors, to be sure, do not yet speak of Batainabura in the context of phratry. They deny it by implication, furthermore, in referring to another relationship—Barabuna—in such a context. In the perspective of history, however, this should not stop us. Local pracitce can easily be accounted for by pointing out that people do not know of "X" phratry until such a phratry emerges sufficiently to command their attention. Meanwhile, if they speak of any phratry, they will speak of an *existing* alignment, even a previous and waning alignment. Presumably they will refer to one which, like Barabuna, possesses some—even if not all—of the attributes they consider indicative, rather than to a nascent or potential unit in which the "wrong" attributes occur, or the "correct" attributes still do not. The limitation of Batainabura to a single local group may conceivably be a "wrong" attribute in local eyes, though I have no evidence of that. Common descent, validated in the previous coresidence of the Barabuna forebears, is clearly a correct attribute and one of sufficient pertinence, it would seem, to override several discrepancies. This must therefore be a major principle of Northern Tairora organization.

Future developments may submerge Barabuna (not the government's "Barabuna") as a named social unit, even for occasional reference; or they may reduce the discrepancies that make it tenuous at present, giving it a fuller lease on life as a phratry. Pending the outcome, neither in the occasional local usage nor in any other sense is Barabuna as a phratry fully consistent with local principles or fully comparable to a phratry like Tairora. The realities of the Northern Tairora social system are revealed by this difference. Batainabura history and Northern Tairora social processes are both highlighted. Only in the sense of "becoming" (and let us emphasize its logical corollary, the sense of "having been") can full resolution be found as between local principle and local practice.

As between "phratry" at Abiera and "phratry" at Batainabura, we see an example of the fairly successful resolution of local principles of residence and of kinship in an expanding group, and, on the other hand, an example of the stress between these principles. History, including the history of Australian local administration, traces a different course at Batainabura, casting up a static or shrinking group whose existence is nevertheless somehow maintained. The pull between locality and fraternity in the case of Batainabura-Barabuna, from one point of view, is not simply that connected people have failed to remain coresident; it is rather that separation, although essential to expansion, may—and in this case does—carry even short-run implications inimical to an expanding social unit. In the Batainabura-Barabuna separation it produced incongruous coresidents who obstruct the simultaneous and unequivocal application of local conventions of fraternity and locality. People who live together are brothers. People whose forebears lived together are therefore descendants of brothers, hence are themselves even more surely brothers. But brothers of others cannot be brothers of ours—especially if they attack us—because the others are our enemies. Brothers do not fight each other, and those who fight each other are not brothers. These several principles seem to define the process fairly well. Quite likely an efficient definition is also possible from the standpoint of territory. That is, if one distinguishes the territory of aliens and the territory of congeners, the act or fact of residence can then be used to produce a serviceable definition of Northern Tairora social process in those aspects that have been examined here. To that issue chapter 6 is directed.

6. Social Process in an Open Society

To look at Northern Tairora in synchronic, cross-sectional terms, one would probably say the people make a sedentary use of space. They also appear predominantly patrivirilocal in residential choice. Their imagery of grouping is rather consistently one of fraternity and common ancestry, with patrilineal emphasis.

Local groups are distributed among territories with fairly definite boundaries, each with from one to several settlements or hamlets. Physically, the individual settlements are more or less distinct, though closely related ones are often closely connected. Each settlement is generally named for the site it occupies, though occasionally for a previous site. The local group takes its collective name from the sole settlement, the principal settlement, or a settlement previously occupied by some significant portion of the membership or their forebears, who are claimed as founders. The local territory and the entire local group, irrespective of settlement, bear this name as well as the name of their particular sector if different. Broadly speaking, then, Northern Tairora local groups are known to each other by names reflecting their residential history or that of their founders. Hence the name of a stem settlement is commonly used.

The Northern Tairora array themselves in patrilineally oriented sibs. These are named personnels claiming common descent, largely through male links, from some of the same ancestors. The ancestors are usually named. Sibs are further grouped into patrilineally oriented phratries of from two to several sibs—named personnels whose component sibs claim a similar connection by common descent with each other. Northern Tairora phratries vary greatly in size. As measured by the number of their constituent local groups, they may be as small as a single local group in a single territory (Phratry Batainabura), or as large as a half dozen local groups or more (Phra-

199

try Tairora). The size of the phratry personnel is approximately proportional to the number of constituent local groups. When the phratry comprises more than a single local group or territory, the members of its sibs may be and often are residentially dispersed among its local groups and territories.

Sibs and phratry names, like local group names, also reflect significant points in the residential history of their personnels. There are apparently no generic terms with which to distinguish them as indigenous categories, but the relative size and inclusiveness of my "sibs" and "phratries" are nonetheless explicit in conventional metaphor. Sibs are seen, for instance, as the "fingers" of a phratric "hand." Or they are styled as the vines or branches of a common phratric stem. Sibs, especially the local segments of a dispersed sib, tend to be exogamous, and members of different sibs within a local group often intermarry. While neither a settlement nor a local group is endogamous, the personnel of a larger phratry appear to approach being a connubium. Yet endogamy is neither their unequivocal ideal nor exclusive practice. Local groups may not only arrange marriages with peoples outside the phratry but may sometimes recruit them en bloc to membership.

The personnels I call here "local sib segments" are quite variable. They may be separately named or not, or their names not widely known. At a minimum they consist of those members of a dispersed sib who live in a given local group. To use hierarchical language, they are less than a sib but frequently more than a lineage. With increasing size and continued residential separation, the local sib segment also normally increases its social distinctness. The members may, for example, commence to intermarry with members of their own sib who reside in another local group—that is, with members of another local segment. Some distinct local name attaching to them gradually becomes more common as a term of reference for this personnel, in time perhaps, rivaling or exceeding the sib name in currency. In this light a local sib segment may be considered transitional: it is a potential sib, or protosib. In a phratry of one local group, however, since sib membership cannot be dispersed among different local groups, the term "local sib segment" is irrelevant.

Local Units Compared with Lineal Units

We have already noted that there is little indigenous development in Northern Tairora culture of what might be called the systematics of social groupings. Every personnel is known to various outsiders by its particular name as well as by its location or territorial range. Whether a unit is defined by kinship alone, by residence, or by both, or whether it includes, is included within, or overlaps other units, are facts also certainly known to a given individual insofar as the personnels have relevance to him. There is at any time, in other words, a specific map on which a normal adult Northern Tairora could project many individuals and a number of personnels with varying degrees of precision. There is no explicit table of organization with

(*Left*) Plantains and sugar cane for a feast are exposed for viewing on a platform built for their display.

(*Below*) Before a feast, food is collected and displayed in large piles. Men sit in the midst to converse and share betel nut and tobacco, greeting guests as they arrive.

Costumed dancers from nearby Bontaa in daylight display of solidarity.

The all-night sing-sing: young male dancer wears his distinctive headdress created for the occasion and quite likely dream-inspired. (flash photo)

While the food is cooking in earth ovens, men and children (mostly boys) sit together and watch.

Exhausted from dancing all night, and chilly at dawn, a woman wearing her dancing bustle and other regalia kindles a fire.

A tired all-night dancer rolls herself a smoke to meet the day.

Young boys play with cast-off dancing paraphernalia that has been stripped of its valuable plumes.

which to interpret the map or to use in comparing the part known to one individual with that known to another.

If we make two columns, one for the recognizable *local* units of a Northern Tairora phratry, from smallest to largest, and the other for the recognized *lineal* units, it may help establish such a table of organization. "Local unit" means here the set of people—the personnel—who persist as coresidents or common occupants of a given physical structure or site. "Lineal unit" means the personnel to whom a given genealogical status is conventionally ascribed, whether or not genealogical status is the sole ascription.

Local	Lineal
women's houses	families
men's houses	lineages
hamlets or settlements	local sib segments
local groups	sibs
phratry qua maximal	phratry qua maximal
territorial group	descent group

Of all these units the phratry is the only personnel in which both locality and lineage recurrently coincide. Sibs are commonly dispersed except when a local group is also a phratry. Although by designation localized, local sib segments are not necessarily coterminous with the membership of any residential group. When close at all, however, they most nearly coincide with the residents of a particular settlement. The men of a lineage tend to share the same men's house in more cases than not; but in more cases than not they probably also share the men's house with other men. The occupants of a women's house are regularly the female and juvenile members of a single family. They do not usually include the initiated males; nor, in the case of a polygynous man, do they include his other wives and their children as often as exclude them.

In the foregoing I am speaking not primarily of statistical discrepancies but of normative differences. Were one to be concerned simply with discrepancies, as opposed to different identities, he would have to say that at no level in the entire Northern Tairora social system does any residential set coincide precisely with any set of persons to whom a common genealogical status is assigned. Although it is a central trend of Northern Tairora society that kinsmen live together and that those living together are presumptive kinsmen, the characteristic ebb and flow of personnel in this society, for one thing, is too great for any precise match. But I am referring to more than a lack of match where a match is expected. Normatively, the members of a sib are not invariably expected to be coresidents of the same local territory; nor are the members of a local sib segment expected to be the exclusive occupants of a given settlement. The members of a phratry, on the other hand, are normatively said to be those men and their offspring who are both genealogically related to each other by common descent and occupy a continuous stretch of territory which is identified with them.

As the only unit in which locality at least normatively matches lineage, the phratry will be a convenient starting point for discussing Northern Tairora social structure. In this discussion I will draw instances primarily from Phratry Tairora (see map 6), today a group of roughly a thousand people, not counting in-married women and other residents not native to the territory. Abiera, one of the two main study groups on which this monograph is based, is a local group of Phratry Tairora.

In size modern Phratry Tairora is quite likely large by aboriginal standards. Two of its present six or so local groups, Tongera and Burauta, are descended from groups driven out prior to first government contact. Those wishing to return were later restored by administrative fiat to lands within the phratry—creating, incidentally, a most unphratric sense of fear and suspicion in certain other elements of the phratry. It is likely, in other words, that some or all of these emigrants would not normally have returned to the midst of their erstwhile oppressors. In that case, modern Phratry Tairora would perhaps consist of fewer local groups and would comprise fewer inhabitants—possibly five hundred to six hundred or so. The phratry would still at that size be larger, however, than some of its neighbors by a factor of two to three.

Core members of Phratry Tairora, in a sense familiar to ethnography, style themselves as one people fraternally linked. They usually claim that they and their ancestors have lived together as long as anyone can remember—though not necessarily always on the same site or even in the same territory. If they moved, however, they moved as a body—as indeed members of Phratry Tairora report their forebears having done. These notions, of course, fit with a claim of common ancestry as well as with one of a continuous co-residence of the intervening generations. The phratric name "Tairora," like the names of most of the larger, more lasting units of this society, is indeed the name of a place, a known site, in fact archeologically recognizable, where those common ancestors are said to have first settled after their legendary move. The name of the phratry thus symbolizes a common origin point for all those claiming descent from the inhabitants of Tairora; and though only a handful of individual ancestral names are known today to members of the phratry, and these probably not to all members, the legendary settlers are accepted as the phratric ancestors.

Northern Tairora society has no personnel larger than the phratry, or at least none with more than a shadowy existence. The wider use of the same language is of course obvious to all. The existence of foreign languages is also a familiar fact, several being within easy social range of Phratry Tairora. Even so, the boundary of their own language to the south is quite vague. Because of increasing dialect difference and the prevalent multilingualism, and ultimately because of distance, it is in doubt who can and who cannot be counted as speaking the same tongue as themselves. With no basis in common action, moreover, nor any basis in common forbearance, such as the prohibition of open hostilities, a personnel defined only by common speech would thus be ill-defined. That there exists an aboriginal term for an ethnolinguistic congeries loosely corresponding to a part of today's recognized "Tairora" language cannot therefore be taken to imply the existence of a larger personnel as a social or political reality of the same order or kind as a phratry.

A phratry, then, is the largest Northern Tairora genealogical entity known having land boundaries, a specific name and history, and a fairly clear social expression in common action, including near-connubium and common residence. In this fact surely lies the explanation for the relatively close normative match between lineage and residence at the level of phratry, in contrast to the lack of match at lesser genealogical or residential levels. It is simply that, in the absence of any greater geneaological or residential entity, one is either in the same phratry with given others—who are hence presumptively brothers of his—or he is in a different phratry and hence is in principle no kinsman. He is not, in the latter case, the presumptive or actual brother, nor could he have the same ancestors as the people of the first phratry. The same is not true, however, of sibs or lesser genealogical sets, for although one may be a member of sib A, he is still the phratric kinsman of members of other sibs of the same phratry, sharing their principal claims to common ancestry. He may move anywhere within the phratric territory without changing his—or his progeny's—descent group identity. If he permanently leaves the phratric territory, however, his children or theirs will presumably no longer be members of either the original phratry or, hence, of sib A.

Pragmatic outsiders in Northern Tairora society (not just ethnographers) may find it expedient to view or treat as kinsmen those who live together. All things considered, this is probably the safest assumption to make, especially of any enemy group, or in the absence of more specific knowledge. Whether or not the residents of a local group or phratry all have an equal right by pedigree to claim to be each other's kin is a point too fine for many immediate concerns. What cannot be overlooked, however, is that anyone who lives permanently in a territory or settlement with others and is accepted by them for some purposes can only be considered a member of that group. Since groups tend to be spoken of with a fraternal or patrilineal rhetoric, the same rhetoric is apt to be used of all the members in one context or another.

Things are not so simple, however, to the insider. Indeed, a resident may quite deliberately choose not to live as close as possible to his nearest coresident kin. Brothers sometimes act this way, and, as we know, Northern Tairora sibs are frequently dispersed. One's sib brethren thus sometimes live closer to their counterparts in another sib than to their congeners. A set of kinsmen who keep too strictly to themselves, furthermore, may in time or under certain circumstances become a matter of concern to their coresidents. The issue involves their commitment or loyalty to the rest of the group. The point is stated quite explicitly by some informants, who evidently recognize that although kinship unites persons, it divides personnels. Residential segregation is most characteristic, it would appear, of the recently arrived immigrant bloc, on the one hand, or, on the other, of a set of protoemigrants approaching the rift of their departure. The conventional wisdom about too discrete and clannish a group is thus not unfounded.

The history of Phratry Tairora and the processes of which I am speaking here refer of necessity to the ethnographic present, above all to the time of active fighting. The membership of Northern Tairora personnels was then markedly more fluid at all levels than it is today. The cessation of warfare and with it of dislodged peoples seeking asylum, together with the government practice of inscribing villagers at birth in local registers, have each played a part in damping the movement of population in this social field. Now, indeed, the correlation of kinship and residence may be intensified.

THE POLITICAL TURBULENCE OF WAR

Warfare in the Nothern Tairora area was fierce and perennial, at least within the short span of the recent past that one can now penetrate. Warfare in this region cannot be characterized adequately as sport, nor is it some sort of sociological ballet—a counterpoint of reciprocities with nicely balanced, hence stable, opponents keeping each other trimmed and pruned in geometric equilibrium. On the contrary, it was unbalanced as often and as much as a momentarily ascendant adversary or alliance could manage to make it; and that was enough at least to result in the growth of some communites and alliances and the dislocation or disappearance of others. Any stability of which warfare could be claimed as cause or outcome must be at some higher systemic level than that of the local group or phratry. (In the scale of Northern Tairora phratric activity and perception, incidentally, such a higher level would be comparable to a planetary level for modern superstates!) The contention that warfare may have functioned to distribute people in the landscape (Vayda 1961, 1971) may mean that the warfare waged was compatible with the continued existence of some of the warring communities. That is, it did not lead to emptying the countryside in which they lived, nor did it cause them to become jammed into pockets too small for the continued existence of those that continued to exist.

To argue as some have that warfare was not waged for territorial aggrandizement (Berndt 1964) is perhaps true in a sense but is also misleading. In a sense it is only to state the plausible, for with neither plantations nor colonies, nor a system of warlords and frontier marches, people like the Northern Tairora could not expect to make immediate and direct exploitative use of lands from which they might succeed in expelling enemy groups. Much less could they make use of a conquered living population. Even so, it is misleading to suggest that warfare did not contribute to the rearrangement or reallocation of particular peoples in space. Groups were certainly dislodged and were thus obliged to move elsewhere, joining other groups or founding new settlements if open space made this option more attractive. (Sorenson [1972] has offered evidence of the large-scale pioneer settlement of virgin land in recent times among the nearby Fore.) Such moves might be

210 *Tairora Culture*

temporary or permanent. The nonaggrandizement thesis is usually based on too short a view—too thin a slice of history. The occupation of "conquered" territory could hardly follow rapidly upon the expulsion of former occupants, since the rate could not exceed the rate of population growth or the recruitment of outsiders by the ascendant group. It would further depend, no doubt, on the budding off of new communites to fill up the adjacent empty space, a slower and longer-range process than is apparently considered by those who see no "conquest." Present Phratry Tairora itself appears almost certainly the result—or, perhaps better, the by-product—of such territorial expansion or aggrandizement.

Even the creation of no man's lands—empty buffer zones which may once have been occupied—implies important population displacements and relocations. In further testimony to the relocation of people, the grassy hills of the Northern Tairora area are dotted with former habitation sites, their slopes striated with disused garden trenches, visible at a distance to the naked eye, especially in the sun's slanting light.

Warring, finally, is an activity for which the lives and cultures of the Northern Tairora and their neighbors are profoundly adjusted. The masculinity rituals, the quest for individual status through fighting prowess, the exchange competition—all illustrate the point. To argue in the absence of other suggested life purposes that fighting had little or nothing to do with resources, including security and space, is to make of this major cultural emphasis of local society an anomaly of major proportions, at least for certain current theories of cultural ecology and adaptation. Consciously purposeful or not, warfare nevertheless continually reordered the ethnic landscape, keeping it in flux. The rise and fall of local groups, sibs, and phratries measured the fluidity.

Sufficient case histories of phratries in the Northern Tairora area are lacking wherewith to assess the average rate of growth or collapse of local and lineal units or to detail other aspects of a standard career from inception to dissolution. Yet we know something about these matters. The history of some phratries, for example, is distinctly "cataclysmic," as Barnes (1962) has suggested may be true for the Central Highlands generally. An entire group—sib or protosib—may be severed from the phratric body; or, with initially alien personnel, a whole new sib may be introduced into a phratry. Though cataclysmic, neither sort of event is wholly without warning. Each is almost certainly the sequel to prior developments of one kind or another. Detailing such histories as are known can give at least a sense of the kinds of events that may impinge on Northern Tairora personnels. It indicates some of the options and the consequences, from the individual to the largest social group that answers to a common name or retains any sense of common loyalty.

Certain general principles, more or less continually operative through the various situations faced by Northern Tairora groups, are expressed at every stage of recent history. They are in essence the guidelines, explicit or not, followed by Northern Tairora personnels in dealing with the problems of their social existence. These are the decisions that affect the size and character, the membership and dispersion, and the defining rights and obligations of personnels or social divisions. Such "stable configuration" (Eggan 1950: 323) as Northern Tairora society displays is in theory the result, on the one hand, of the application of these principles and, on other other, of the recurrent conditions and circumstances of Northern Tairora life. Even our shallow histories give us some idea of these recurrent conditions and circumstances, which are listed and discussed below.

1. People within reach are friendly or hostile to any given person or group. Even apparently neutral parties are potentially friendly or hostile, for the appearance of neutrality may consist only in a passing uncertainty on one side or both. I am not speaking here of a neutrality based on the mutual disutility of being involved at all, as when the parties are simply too distant. Another neutrality, actually a stalemate, arises when the neutral personnel are about equally disposed (as friends or as enemies) towards the parties in question. Such conflicts and ambiguities are a typical consequence of having a membership of mixed origin.

2. Amity and enmity are relative expectations, shading into each other. One is surer, on the one hand, of the amity or enmity of some parties than of others, and accordingly also expects a stronger or weaker demonstration of the state of the relationship.

3. Enmity and amity are circumstantial—expectation being governed not only by a continuing or anticipated social relationship but by usage and occasion. The appropriateness of given tokens of amity or enmity is similarly governed. There is a time and a place as well as a form for demonstrating amity or enmity.

4. Enmity or amity are not static but conditional, changing slowly or rapidly, depending both on previous action and on immediate advantage. Indeed, the possibility of change is great and is the point of much of the maneuvering within the Northern Tairora area.

5. The history of a relationship is highly relevant to amity-enmity—that is, whether it is an unbroken record of hostility, mild or severe, or a mixed record. The longer and more consistent the history, the more stable will be the further relationship, and the surer one's future expectations of it. It is harder, in other words, to reverse or modify the net value of a long and unbroken record. Parties with such a record in the Northern Tairora area are considered each other's true or traditional enemies or friends. Stability of this relationship in such cases almost seems to be self-regenerative. It is at least much proclaimed.

6. It is easier in Northern Tairora to reverse or modify a record of amity than one of enmity. In other words, centrifugal social forces, in the short or long run, exceed centripetal ones. This would be inevitable unless population growth were zero, or unless individual communities at all levels were capable of exceeding the limits of size that appear to obtain in this area.

These limits are ultimately govered by factors of distance, transport, crowding, defense, and perhaps disease, including swine diseases. Unconditional amity (or absolute friendship) is therefore scarce if not unattainable. People must accordingly strive to keep their communities at or above some minimum safe size and to keep as friends groups strategically important to them.

The phratry itself is an expression of security, in principle of unconditional mutual support. In my limited observation true friendship is most often found between a given group and at most one or two others. There are usually other friends, to be sure, but somewhat more tentative or more recently committed ones. A continuous and long-standing record of mutual support and necessarily also a substantial overlap of shared friendships and enmities are a part of the basis of such a relationship. Along with marriage, exchange, and military alliance they are sufficient, in theory, perhaps, without any claim of close kinship, but close affinal kinship is apt to be a concomitant of the relationship.

7. The friends of your friends ideally should be your own friends as well, their enemies your enemies, though it is almost inconceivable that this could ever wholly be true. The enemies of your enemies, thus, might well be potentially your friends. It is sometimes necessary to make enemies in keeping or making friends. And so forth. It is rarely practical, in any case, to value one's relationship with a party for itself alone—that is, without some attention to the amities and enmities that prevail in one's own case and in theirs. In other words, whatever one does for or against a second party is apt to be of some potential interest to one or more third parties, and Northern Tairora culture has ample etiquette for demonstrating such deeds ceremoniously to the third parties concerned. Presenting bloody arrows from a slain mutual enemy is an example especially appropriate when the third party is known to have a fresh and still unrequited death at the hands of the enemy in question. The arrows can be placed on the grave of the victim to quiet his ghost. The presentation of arrows of course makes his kinsmen and late coresidents beholden to the presenters.

8. Friendship and enmity have both a collective or group face and a serial or individual one, the strength of the former depending significantly on the uniformity of the latter. The relations between individual members of a group and relevant other personnels match each other closely only in some cases. The degree of uniformity varies, apparently, with distance and the length of time the personnels have been in intimate contact. Individual in-group members are apt to be most uniform in their relations with distant out-groups (where of course their relations are also probably slight) or with out-groups not long in close contact. In other words, with the out-groups they have long and intimately known, the members of the in-group are more likely to vary in their relations to individual members. True friends and true enemy groups, previously discussed, are evidently out-groups with which, despite closeness and intimacy, the quality of individual relations is relatively uniform.

It is immigration and the intergroup exchange of women that mainly promote diversity among in-group individuals in their relations with out-groups and individual out-group members. One man has a mother or a wife from a certain out-group, while his coresident's wife or mother is from a different out-group. Perhaps the two out-groups are enemies, or one or both of them are currently hostile to the majority of the first group. The possible combinations are intricate. They sometimes seem infinite.

It would require a simpler social field or a social strategy foreign to some of their express aims for Northern Tairora deliberately to marry their enemies. They do not, at least, make a shibboleth of the possibility. To seek out the implacably hostile group with whom to contract a marriage would in the first place be difficult. In the second place, there would be little point in doing so, since none of the continuous affinal reciprocities could safely ensue—or could ensue at all. The marriage would be largely a loss to the bride's group.

That any group into which one may marry will for a lifetime be friendly is, on the other hand, uncertain. And so it happens that men may find themselves the sons or husbands of women, hence often the sister's sons or brothers-in-law of men, from once friendly but now hostile groups—but not because it was planned. The idea of getting a bride from a group that will from the outset be unable to insist on affinal payments is obviously a coup. It can happen but it is also considered remarkable.[1]

Here it is worthwhile to recall that Northern Tairora is a social field of small political units. Enemy groups stand cheek by jowl with friendly ones, since communities are closely spaced and numerous. Each, in many respects a separate polity with its own external relations, is left to its own devices for internal control. Organized largely on the basis of consensus, not delegated authority, Northern Tairora groups frequently find the diversity of sentiments and crosscutting loyalties of their members a severe limitation on decisive and prolonged collective activity, or on consistent and sustained relations with given out-groups.

Within these limits there is a law of exemption such that a party whose amity is bespoken by one friend against another, the enemy of the first, can sometimes, conditionally, abstain. Such an exemption appears to affect mainly the closer relations of an individual so that, for example, he may not

---

1. A rather elaborate ritual known as *hampu* (Agarabi: *ámpu*) was formerly practiced by older personnels of Phratry Tairora. (Some Batainabura informants say they have heard of the ritual but none believe it is known in sufficient detail ever to have been practiced there.) A lengthy and complicated ritual, *hampu* constitutes a collective effort by several of the young men of a group, using magical means, to draw women—married or not—from another community to become brides for one or more of the participants. Often if not usually directed toward enemy groups, this means of acquiring brides, when successful, is tantamount to seduction and elopement or kidnapping. It ostensibly offers a way around affinal reciprocities, since the women are said to leave secretly and without the consent of their male kinsmen. The existence of *hampu* indirectly suggests that arranged marriages with one's enemies are not normally contemplated by Northern Tairora peoples.

be expected to give offense to his brothers-in-law or other men of his wife's group, even though they belong to a group with whom his own group is currently engaged in hostilities.

Beyond a fairly narrow circle, the conditional character of the law of exemption becomes more marked. This is to say that the probable course of action of a given party is more ambiguous. The decision is contingent, in effect negotiable, and a friend may be suborned to betray normal expectations on behalf of another party, also his friends or would-be friends. Against this possibility the only assurance lies in having sufficiently strong and numerous friends—parties with a longer, more intense, or more consistent history of amity toward oneself than toward any of one's enemies. Such friends by definition will not be indifferent. Under any probable circumstances their relations will be positive. They are likely to share a majority of their most significant amities and enmities with oneself, which further limits the chance of subornation.

The problem of ambiguous friendship appears to be basically inescapable, however, in an open field where, as noted, there are numerous actual or potential contending groups among whom size and strength varies at any given moment and from time to time and degrees of amity and enmity are within limits modifiable at will by suitable action, such as exchanges of goods and women or making common cause against a third party.

Although not stated as one of the rules of Northern Tairora life, it is surely a background condition—a cultural given—that the actors prize a capacity for violence and value a readiness for predatory and aggressive action. Not surprisingly they attribute the same values to some of those with whom they interact. The general effect is a prevalent wariness and suspicion in the conduct of much of life. Nor is this aggressiveness attributable simply to a need for flamboyant self-dramatization, though that is clear enough. It is often considered simple prudence, for example, to shoot a stranger whose presence in one's territory is unexplained. This means that only the soundest and least suspect relations, if any, can be free from the possibility of sometimes abrupt reversals of polarity. Suspicion evokes suspicion as predation evokes predation and violence violence. Under the circumstances it is relatively easy to suppose that parties who were friendly yesterday, particularly if some straw in the wind or a conceivable advantage of theirs now suggests it, may perhaps no longer be so today. One knows, of course, that they know this, too, as well as knowing that the party who anticipates or takes the initiative in shifting from amity to enmity has the advantage of surprise over the party who counts too heavily on stability, or the one who is for any other reason loath to take the first step toward change.

Friendship, alas, seems harder than its opposite to promote or maintain. In addition to the need for friendly efforts to be continuous and often costly, they must also be essentially public and explicit. In Northern Tairora culture such efforts consist of hospitality and feasting; the giving of gifts, children, or brides; or the lending of help against adversaries. The quality of friendship is overt and assertive. Even fairly slight tokens of amity, accordingly, may be handled by Northern Tairora in an explicit, ceremonious, often flamboyant way. The style is so marked as sometimes to seem to outsiders either offensively boastful and ostentatious or grossly mercenary in its detailing of even the smallest consideration or favor, something to be counted like a debt, as it were, against one's vaunted friends.

Countergifts are typically required as a part of this same strenuous concern with public demonstration and acknowledgment. Much is clearly at stake. In this context, secret plots or preparations for friendship—a surprise party? the beau geste? an anonymous gift?—hardly make sense. As far as the party whose friendship is being sought is concerned, invisibility is a contradiction. In the absence of sustained acts of amity, and sometimes even in their presence, the actor is free to worry and to suppose what he will.

Secrecy, on the other hand, is often an essential part of a hostile strategy. Above all, when hostility is not expected from the given quarter, this is its very advantage. Much of sorcery or magical attack, moreover, is of its very nature covert. To perform sorcery in public is to invite an attack on its magical efficacy—sometimes simply by wetting down the essential materials with water. When sorcery is practiced in the name of one group against another, mere word of it is sufficient—in fact, usually superfluous. Private sorcery between unacknowledged enemies would almost certainly be secret, quite apart from any technical reasons. The theft of pigs and crops, as well as adultery, are likewise stealthy for at least as long as stealth assures the possibility of repetition with impunity.

I know of no covert magic for friendship. Love magic to give a man control of a woman for sexual purposes is of course directed against the kinsmen who would nominally control her. The same is true of the *hampu* ritual for enticing brides without negotiation. (Incidentally, regarded as hostile magic, *hampu* is perhaps an exception to the rule of covertness. It is deliberately visible, and the magical smoke that is produced as a part of the performance is meant to be smelled by the target women.)

In evoking the old saw, "Better safe than sorry," the foregoing discussion suggests the narrow limits of safety. Under Northern Tairora conditions, suspicion is the better part of prudence, and a quick response is apt to be less costly than hesitation. Anyone who has ever been in a settlement at night when word of an intruder was passed can only have been impressed by the speed of the murmured report that flies from house to house and the almost instantaneous mobilization of armed men who only moments before were asleep. To be sure, an intruder is a present danger not to be compared directly with suspicion or allegations of possible treachery by purported friends. Yet the deadly climate of life is suggested, I think, by such an observation—the contingency, the uncertainty, the need to be able to change quickly from one mood to the opposite in confronting possible harm.

Even the rapid escalation of disputes among kinsmen or coresidents, many of which abate without bloodshed or bruises, seems not unrelated to the wariness and quickness of response to a challenge. Someone has described the temperament of Central Highlands of New Guinea peoples as "mercurial." The term would also apply to Northern Tairora—though for what it is worth my impression of some of their neighbors is of shriller pitch by comparison with which some Northern Tairora seem distinctly taciturn. The social and cultural context of the regional temperament is in any case strongly suggested by their politics.

Up to this point I have given principally rules and observations that would predict or account for the fluidity of the social field in which the Northern Tairora live, which in turn helps to make understandable (1) the general character of their social relations, (2) the numerous and pervasive sources of anxiety about relations, and (3) some of the factors that limit security. In this, there is nothing that would specifically predict a sib or phratries of the Northern Tairora sort. Indeed, I have so far simply—though only very generally—assumed such units as necessary to a discussion of the character of social life. On the whole, I believe the foregoing premises of Northern Tairora social life are as elementary and radical as I can conveniently make them. In fact, some of the premises are surely generic to the human condition, though their applicability in the immediate case may be more marked than in the general run of social fields.

THE RELATIVE COSTS OF KINSHIP AND FRIENDSHIP

The risks and costs of amity would make kinship necessary for the Northern Tairora if nothing else did, for kinship is on balance probably more economical than friendship. It is a "better buy," so to speak. I have already emphasized and will allude further to the risks of Northern Tairora kinship and its fragility. My argument notwithstanding, kinship is no curse of which the Northern Tairora would rid themselves if possible. The rapidity and urgency with which they make affinal and phratric kin of erstwhile strangers should cancel that impression.

I do not propose here to argue some novel justification for kinship, adding to the well-known "functions" already and repeatedly traced in the anthropological literature, but only to state that, under Northern Tairora conditions, by contrast with the costs of even the fastest of friends, kinsmen provide more security more of the time for less cost. Kinship, while reversible and even fragile, is less easily, or at least less quickly, reversed than all but the highest degree of friendship. The certainty can be greater that stealth or sudden treachery are not in prospect with coresident kinsmen than with personnels at a distance.

Forbearance pays a larger part of the cost of kinship than it does of friendship, and forbearance requires a less strenuous outlay of wealth in prestations and hospitality. The opportunity for forbearance (as well as the practical need of it) is naturally greater, too, among coresidents than between peoples separated by open country. Much of the reward of kinship, further-more, is in mutually beneficial collaboration—production, education of chil-dren, defense—activities essential to the conduct of life in local terms.

If under Northern Tairora conditions the kinship circle has ineluctable limits in size of membership and size of territory (limits which neither local logistics nor local means for creating and maintaining *esprit de corps* can defeat), and if kinship ties are ultimately fragile and frequently disrupted, with a recurrent alienation of sib and phratric mates, there is nevertheless— indeed all the more—a need to keep a kinship circle manned, a local terri-tory held in sufficient force for local personnels to remain viable in this par-ticular, competitive field. Friends are deeply needed, too—even at the high price and with the uncertainties of friendship. They are reserve manpower, marriage and trading partners, outliers, gatherers of intelligence. But friends are not enough. They cannot be at hand on short notice for defense or to help with children. Indeed, without sufficient kinsmen there are not apt to be sufficient friends, for friends are valuable to each other's security only as groups of them have mass and power enough to be of value. It is not, thus, a question of kinsmen or friends, but rather of each because of the other.

In the following discussion, I will attempt to indicate how the Northern Tairora perceive their shifting prospects for security and how in particular they continually recodify the probability of "mandatory friendship"—kin-ship. The ways in which they do so, I will suggest, preclude at least some kinds of social groupings among Northern Tairora, whether or not the man-ner of perceiving and codifying people narrows the remaining possibilities to precisely the forms of grouping that are evident in this society. I am no lon-ger concerned with their general anticipations of the behavior of men at large but with the principles by which, de facto, the Northern Tairora pro-gressively subdivide men at large into subsets or social divisions according to their different anticipations of behavior. The subsets and the way in which they are symbolized correspond to different classes of expected relations. Usage as well as symbol confers on each class a sense of charter for behaving. I will describe the ways in which these subsets of people and of anticipations are recognizable to the outside observer and are rationalized by the North-ern Tairora. I will above all attempt to suggest the manner of their formation and the continual flow and revision of their membership.

To the outside observer the Northern Tairora world of "people of primary relevance" seems conveniently divisible into two fairly commonplace con-tinua some of whose local implications have already been noted: "friendship" and "kinship." The two continua crosscut each other, and if one were to di-chotomize their polarities as fixed values, a four-cell matrix would result.

There is some reason to believe that the foregoing distinction also approxi-mates Northern Tairora notions. The people pragmatically recognize de-grees of friendship, of course, and pragmatically recognize degrees of kin-ship—as when they disapprove of kinsmen who fail to act in an expected manner or commend those who do so. More important for understanding sets like Phratry Tairora is that people recognize not only nonkinsmen who are close friends but kinsmen who are less close than some friends, who may in fact withhold support, or who may conceivably support an enemy against them. While the Northern Tairora conception of "kinship" naturally implies a negation of "enmity," local ethnohistory supplies ample acknowledgment of unfriendly or hostile kinsmen. Thus all four cells of the matrix are populated, though by no means with equal density. There is unquestionably a strong association—cell 1—between kinship and friendship. Kinship could be likened to a kind of mandatory friendship at close hand. Disregarding the contradiction, the point is that kinsmen do for each other the positive

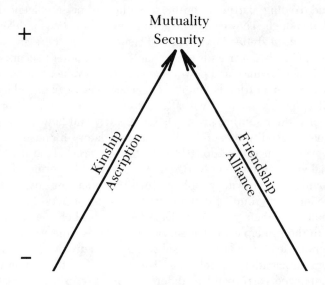

Fig. 4.   The Convergence of Friendship and Kinship

sorts of things that friends also do, though kinsmen do more different kinds of things, perform their kinship more often than friends perform friendship, and, in principle at least, have less choice about it, in theory none. The polarity is the same even if the intensity, the frequency, or the variety of the performance differs. Nonkinship is far from isomorphic with enmity, certainly, and nonkin may not infrequently, as noted, be more friendly than some kin. Around this point, in essense, turns the basic play of Northern Tairora politics—perhaps the dynamic of any society which, despite overt claims of a genealogical grouping, possesses relatively open groups.

We previously considered the continuum of friendship and enmity. Here I shall attempt to deal with kinship and nonkinship. In recognizing certain continuities of that domain, I will hope to identify what one might call the formation of kinship, or kinship process.

Nonkinsmen are a variety of parties, individuals, and groups of various sizes and degrees of inclusiveness with whom one has friendly or hostile relations on a decisional or discretionary basis—not, that is, because one claims a fixed, status-based relationship with them as "kinsmen." These parties are near enough in space, numerous enough, and potentially if not actively important enough to one's own life, however, that—kinsmen or not—they cannot be ignored. In the case of some parties, fairly stable and enduring relations develop—stable amity or stable enmity. In addition to stability, frequency and intensity of relations also vary. Under Northern Tairora conditions, amity, especially prolonged amity, can lead to a relationship more closely resembling the security of ideal kinship and one that, in fact, under certain conditions becomes that of kinship. With the accretion of tradition, in other words, a friendly relationship becomes in time less decisional and discretionary. As relations become more binding, negotiation is increasingly replaced by obligation—here again a resemblance to kinship relations. Concretely, children or brides may be exchanged between such friendly parties, with attendant gifts and hospitality, making the parties exchange partners and affines. Nonbelligerency follows from friendship, and alliance tends to follow nonbelligerency, with mutual aid in confronting mutual enemies. Should adversity favor and bring into being their protracted coresidence at any point, two groups of friends may fairly rapidly become de facto kinsmen and in a generation or two jural kinsmen through a growing convention of common ancestry.

In a society in which centrifugal forces outweigh centripetal ones, certainly, one could hardly suggest that every allied or affinally related party is marked for ultimate kinship. In local groups that do not exceed a certain size, moreover, this would not be possible unless the population were shrinking. The only conceivable exception would be if in every group the core of kinsmen were intermittently reduced, through fission or the founding of colonies, at an incredibly high rate. While no such rate is evident, there is indeed clear evidence of this kind of circulation of personnel in the history of Phratry Tairora and in that of at least the one other phratry for which I have the best data.

I am at present convinced that under precontact conditions this circulation is a general part of the regional system. Present or recent kinsmen are by various means gradually or precipitately disaffected and become, as it were, disaffiliated. They are usually replaced—if the remnant group remains viable—by recruiting other personnel. Their replacement—either before or after the fact of disaffiliation—is often by immigrants with whom there may be little or no initial claim of kinship or common descent. Typically such immigrants are not enemies, of course; but for various reasons they may not be one's most active or closest friends. One's closest friends may have no wish or need to surrender their own autonomy at the precise time the host group is ripe for recruiting new members. The closest friends of the migrants, on the other hand, may not be recruiting when the migrants are obliged to abandon their own territory. Sometimes the replacement of emigrant kinsmen is by population growth. This may, in fact (that is, through crowding) be a factor in their emigration.

Why should kinsmen emigrate, however, if their very departure makes replacement necessary? The question must certainly be recognized, and dealing with it is probably fundamental to any understanding of Northern Tairora society. Why should replacements, when not from internal growth, be from nonkinsmen rather than nonresident kinsmen? This is a related issue that must also be dealt with. The answers seem both interesting and attainable.

Kinsmen are (1) persons whom one can address or refer to by kin terms (largely Iroquois terminology; see Murdock 1949) in Northern Tairora, or (2) persons with whom one claims descent from common ancestors as indicated by a collective name shared with such persons and symbolizing their common ancestry, or (3) both. If the analyst adopts a larger genealogical perspective than the Northern Tairora do, he may note that kinship in the sense of common descent is, after a certain passage of time, very often a matter mainly of the consensus of the living—that the parties in question are or are not kinsmen.

The connecting links of descent are usually said to be, and in the majority of cases appear to be, from males through males. To my knowledge there is no instance of consistently female linkage, generation after generation, although occasional female ancestors are recognized as such and are known by name. It is less that the legitimacy of female links is denied in principle than that it is less frequently asserted in practice than male linkage. The assertion of descent is thus patrilineal or patrilateral in emphasis in so far as it matches genealogy at all. It is male kinsmen who are mainly counted. The names of women deceased a generation or two ago are lost from genealogies sooner and much more often than the names of their male contemporaries; though the latter, except for men of some renown are forgotten soon enough. Great grandfathers only infrequently are known correctly by name; great grandmothers even more infrequently. The Northern Tairora sphere of relevant antecedents thus is skewed toward males as the reference points. To the extent that the strong local tendency toward patrivirilocality prevails, the undispersed core of coresident kinsmen will largely be adult males, of course, with a much lower representation of adult females.

The Northern Tairora expect at least close male kinsmen normally to reside together. They tend to treat coresident males (and females) as close kinsmen, whether they are kinsmen in a genealogical sense or not. The Northern Tairora marriage rule, resembling the ethnographer's patrilocality, anticipates that men after marriage will reside in the same community with those whom they call their close male kinsmen or brothers. "Fratrilocality" would perhaps be nearer to the Northern Tairora sense of things, as well as to the actuality of Northern Tairora life.

As a corollary to treating coresidents as kinsmen, the Northern Tairora tend to treat nonresidents as nonkinsmen, particularly across a phratric boundary. One could arrange the population in a two-by-two matrix of resident and nonresident, kin and nonkin. So doing (see figure 5), he would find

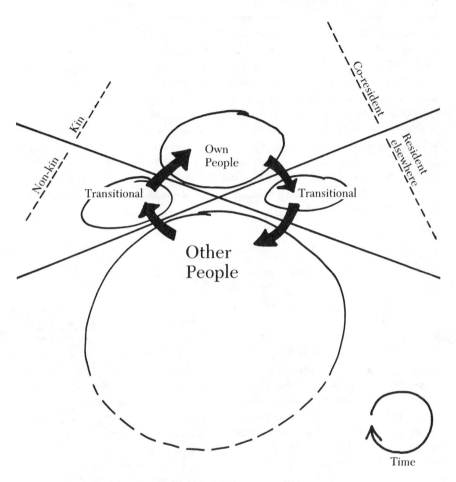

Fig. 5. The Making and Unmaking of Kinsmen

at most points in Northern Tairora history that the largest blocks of men fall into resident kin and nonresident nonkin. The skeptic may note that this proves nothing more than that kinsmen live together, nonkinsmen apart, surely a universal and an inevitable tendency of mankind. That Northern Tairora society is thus representative (if hardly preceptive) surely need not dismay us. Of greater interest here, is that movements of personnel between the two largest categories of men take place such that resident nonkin occur almost constantly in the Northern Tairora system or social field, as well as nonresident kin. The descendants of nonresident male kin do not remain kin for many generations, however, nor do the descendants of resident males long remain nonkin.

Northern Tairora residence groups rather characteristically contain a significant proportion of various sorts of "protokinsmen," as it were. As a complement, the areas surrounding and outlying Phratry Tairora—and those likewise of Batainabura—contain significant numbers of erstwhile kinsmen, lineages whose progenitors are or were kinsmen but who are not now so regarded, or whose descendants will not be. They are or will be nonkin, that is, by being or by becoming kinsmen of their *present* coresidents, thereby disaffiliated from the phratric mates of their forebears. Northern Tairora chroniclers can readily cite examples of both kinds of transitional personnels, even though local ideology in certain respects—as might any genealogical version of membership—seems hard put to accommodate them. With such persons Northern Tairora society also at times has its difficulties—in the main ambiguous loyalties and conflicts of status. The difficulties suggest among other things that the causes of disaffiliation must outweigh the penalties of being disaffiliated.

THE KEY ROLE OF THE LOCAL GROUP

In considering the subsets of Northern Tairora kin and the continuity of their personnel, it is practical for several reasons to begin with the local group. These are the occupants of a named settlement and the principal users of its territory. For one thing, the local group, as Linton (1936:209-30) long since pointed out, is in some sense a generic human phenomenon, though its form and the processes by which it is shaped and maintained may vary appreciably. It seems clear, in other words, that Bontaqa, Abiera, Óndabura, Tongera, Burauta, Hapárira, and so on, the territorial groups of Phratry Tairora, are local forms of Linton's archetypal "local group." Second, as was noted, local residential groups and their territories are named, facilitating their use as the reference points of much of Northern Tairora social discourse as well as apportioning the phratric territory for proprietary purposes, not to mention directional reference. Third, the local group, despite not being uppermost for size or inclusiveness in the hierarchy of Northern Tairora society, is in many respects the most autonomous unit of the system.

I would suggest, in fine, that the Northern Tairora local group is pivotal in the processes here under consideration. It is the locus of the centrifugal-centripetal movements of local society. It is the point of entry into the phratry of immigrant nonmembers as well as of those who become members by birth. In other words, it is the locus or focus of recruitment, for phratries as such do not recruit. They are, so to speak, recruited *for* by their constituent local groups. The local group is also the starting point for fission. It is some part of the original local group that founds a new settlement, perhaps first as a colony within its own territory, but when the splinter group is made up of refugees from a hostile parent group, sometimes as a protosib within the local-group territory of another phratry. Finally, the local group is the unit that will be dislodged—and typically dissolved—if its territory becomes no longer tenable. Other local groups of the phratry may not be simultaneously dislodged, however, nor follow soon afterward. In fact, the surviving local groups seem generally to continue in their respective territories, presumably a further measure of the autonomy of local groups—from each other and thus from the phratry.

If these several qualifications appear to the reader to make the local group the central territorial unit of Northern Tairora society and to suggest that the larger phratry is something of an epiphenomenon, I can only say that I share that opinion. To emphasize the point we may recall the existence of Batainabura and perhaps other phratries of but a single local territory, suggesting how basically the local group is the starting point and origin of the phratry.

In the perspective of history—a short enough perspective in the Eastern Highlands—the local group seems a sort of tube, enlarged at both ends, receiving through one end, over time, influxes of people from various sources. Immigration can be divided into two main types: (1) the small-scale dribble of returning kinsmen, collateral kin, and occasional individual nonkin, and (2) the large-scale movement of refugee blocs of potential sib size into the local territory. Small-scale immigration typically consists of widows, divorcées, orphans, and the disgruntled husbands or children of male or female members of a local kin or descent group. These come individually or in family groups, and, both because of their small size and because they usually have some initial claim to local kinship, they readily become a part, if they remain, of the respective sib or local sib segment to which they are linked. In due course, probably seldom more than two or three generations, they are completely absorbed and no suggestion of erratic lineage would arise but for an ethnographer's inquiry. Occasional nonkin may also immigrate—an individual man, perhaps married to a woman from the local group and for some reason disaffected from his own community of previous residence. These individuals may remain to some extent isolates throughout their lives, though they may not be seriously disadvantaged thereby. In nearly every sense their children or children's children will probably be unquestioned members of a local sib or sib segment. Even the inquisitive genealogist will fail to ferret them out unless he finds unusually expert local informants to help him.

The general point is not that people are careless with their system—whatever such a charge might mean. Indeed, they are doubtless as careful as life allows or requires them to be; but the defining character of this system is its openness, not genealogical closure or exclusiveness. There seems therefore little warrant for the use of such phrases as "genealogical amnesia" in describing the use of genealogy by societies like Northern Tairora, as if some defect or duplicity were implied. The qualification of membership is more significantly related to performance and demonstrated loyalty than to sheer lineage. Manpower is recurrently in short supply and immigrants are likely to be welcomed by their kin if they have any, and by their friends or sponsors if they do not. Paradoxically, recruitment may in the long run exceed the group's ability to consolidate or retain it. That is, the need for manpower in units at the local level tends to be greater than the available means to forge durable, long-term loyalties, capable of surviving internal as well as external stresses.

The second kind of immigration is that of blocs of people, dislodged from their own territory by warfare and often without prior or direct kinship connection with the local group—or with only affinal connections. These, in other words, are likely to be—if indeed they are not invariably—people from outside the phratry. Arriving en bloc, they are not apt to be incorporated into local descent groups in the manner of individuals or families. Outsiders as nonkin or affines are a potential intermarrying group, a source of brides. This advantage is apt to figure early in the relations between an immigrant bloc and older resident personnel. The possibility of intermarriages thus defines the two personnels as sibs in relation to each other rather than making of the newcomers potential recruits for an older sib. Blocs of alien or affinal immigrants are therefore primary prospects, if they remain, to become a new sib within the ranks of their host community.

The precise former status of the migrants *inter se* cannot be inferred simply from the fact of their arrival en bloc in a given host group. While they are usually former residents of a single local territory, or are closely identified with it, it does not follow that the migrants were previously all members there of a single sib or residents of a single settlement. Nor do they necessarily include the entire membership of any former personnel—local group, sib, or settlement—represented among them. Local groups may divide when dislodged and seeking asylum, even as they divide (in fission) when a part of the personnel leaves the rest behind to found a colony nearby, in the home territory. Northern Tairora sibs, unless very newly arisen, are usually found dispersed among the local groups of a phratry. Thus all of a sib's members may not be living in a single local group at the moment of its flight. Nor is there any reason or great likelihood that sib members from elsewhere will all join the refugees in flight.

In their new position, as guests of a host group and residents of its territory, the immigrant personnel face various possibilities, some of which increase with the length of their stay and with the slowly vanishing likelihood of a return to their own former territory. The immigrants, for one thing, will be treated by their hosts as a collectivity, in effect as a sib, and in the same manner will be given a collective name. Usually if not invariably this will reflect their provenience—the name of the country or territory from which they came, or some other with which they are collectively identified. If that territory is near enough to be commonly known by its specific local name, that name may be used. If the immigrants are from afar, some broader—such as a phratric or even ethnolinguistic—designation may be given them by their hosts and their new neighbors. Phratry Tairora thus has a Pore sib, *pore* being the aboriginal name for one of several ethnolinguistic congeries to the southwest of them, whence came as refugees the forebears of Sib Pore. The designation chosen quite likely will not be a prior descent group name, or at least one that distinguished the present personnel. Some of the reasons have already been indicated. In many cases a former sib name would be less meaningful than a new designation, one which indeed reflects the pertinent history and identity of the personnel in question. The identity of the new personnel with any former one may also contradict the use of a previously current name. As former members of the given phratry, they are now living outside its social and territorial boundaries, and neither its name nor others current there may therefore reflect their present membership or status.

Having emigrated, our subject group is possibly on its way out of its former phratry as well as on its way into that of its hosts. Moreover, the members of this group will participate most intensively in the local group and phratric connubia where they now reside, even though ties, including marital ties, with members of the old phratry and connubium may not be wholly severed. They will exchange with the new people. They will also tend to adjust their amities and enmities to those of their host—now increasingly their own—local group. And if their hosts should be enemies of some elements of the former phratry, or friends of its enemies, the severing of remaining ties will quite possibly be accomplished sooner rather than later.

To summarize, the immigrants are, or are to become, members of (1) a single sib, (2) a sib new in both name and membership, and (3) a sib no longer part of the phratry whence came its immediate personnel, but (4) a part of the phratry of which the host group are members. A common name and a new one thus reflect their real status. Their new identity makes their undeniable provenience a simple and obvious way to refer to them. The reference, furthermore, is consistent with Northern Tairora convention: coresidents, as presumptive members of a descent group, are common descendants of a group of coresident forebears, who themselves, because of coresidence, were descendants of a single set of ancestors, typically brothers. If only because of the prevalent movement of Northern Tairora society (but probably in addition to other reasons), the ancestors will usually have been coresident at a previous location, a local group residing on a previous site whose name some of their descendants may still bear—unless it has been lost in the refugee process just described.

Sib Pore comprises descendants of forebears who were given asylum perhaps three generations or so go. Today they have practically unassailable credentials despite originally being not only from outside Phratry Tairora but also from outside the ethnolinguistic group. Nor is Sib Pore the only refugee group of alien linguistic origin in Phratry Tairora, for at least two other blocs are identified, respectively, as Agarabi and Kamáno. Nor apparently is Sib

Pore the most recent one. Indeed, in contrast to the two just mentioned, their foreign origin is more nearly forgotten. Their very name is now commonly said to be but a coincidence rather than indicating alien origin.

The recruitment process obviously does not stop with the arrival in the midst of a host group of a large enough bloc of alien outsiders to constitute a sib. The emergence of a new sib is certain also to realign indigenous elements of a local group. The asylum of Sib Pore seems to have been, or become, a part of local strong-man politics. Their arrival clearly strengthened the hand of Mátoto, an outstanding leader of that time (Watson 1967a). It is strongly suggested that such a reason—the political maneuvering of ambitious and forceful individuals—is often at work in the recruitment of outsiders—*above all* of outsiders. I will return to this theme later in this chapter.

In proportion to the usual size of Northern Tairora local groups, the recruitment of a bloc of refugees is an event of great importance. There can have been few events in the careers of local groups—or local group leaders—more significant for the collective success or failure of the community. The presence of a new sib in the making may help to consolidate older elements of the local group. Loosely linked local lineages may be realigned in a single sib, perhaps with a stable new name. Sib Baqe-Hararúnx at Batainabura exemplifies this outcome, for the two major components indicated by its name were once unconnected personnels deriving from different phratries. (The Baqe left Phratry Tairora about the time the forebears of Sib Pore immigrated.) Various names are usually available. The probable question is: which name evokes the widest loyalties? Which covers the largest number or the most influential portion of the membership of the realigning indigenous group?

Even with no revision of membership, a group that has recruited refugees is apt to change its relationship to other parts of its own phratry or other segments of its own sib. A main factor is the radically revised connubium, one that increasingly includes the members of the immigrant group as major affines. The sibs or local sib segments of a host group begin to build a large new part of their network, one they scarcely share with other sibs or local sib segments of the phratry. Connubial and other realignments may finally reach the point of estranging the recruiting group from the rest of the phratry. Animosities once controllable may erupt, leading to a fatal rift, perhaps a failure of its phratric mates to help the estranged group should they become beleaguered.

Rifts and departures can, of course, be salutary if they leave the now separate parties pruned of ambiguous loyalties. Emigration permits dissident elements to found their own colony, while the parent local group coalesces around the immigrants and their sponsors. Eventually the colony may become an autonomous local group in its own right, and if it later joins or is joined by another group, an entirely new sib may result. The founding of an additional local group and perhaps later a new sib further revises relations among the local groups of the phratry. In the course of these changes, relations may in fact become precarious and open hostilities develop among local groups. The phratry itself will probably be pruned in the process and perhaps reduced in size if a sufficient number of immigrant recruits do not replace the departing indigenes. In any of this the machinations of leading figues, vying for personal advantage, are often evident.

It is clear that the centripetal-centrifugal balance is delicate in Northern Tairora local groups. The threshold of residential separation and subsequent lineal fission is low. At the same time the limits of viable number for a local group are narrow, and the load limits of social networks small. This is the dilemma, and it is surely one way of viewing the instability of Northern Tairora social life: the need for coresidents one can treat as kinsmen; the difficulty of holding them within the constraints that kinship imposes. The recruitment of a bloc of outsiders by one local group of a phratry is likely to be not only the first step in the formation of a new sib comprising the immigrants. As a sudden event of relatively great magnitude in the Northern Tairora scale of things, compared with the overall size of local groups and descent groups, it may also produce major ripples on their waters. This influx of alien people, now coresidents, is likely to be followed by the erosion of some of the previous kin structure, with a better than even chance that the relocations will now and then result in estrangement and what can be called disaffiliation.

Relations within a phratry are more vulnerable to the changes, more readily disrupted, because they are in principle kinship (status) relations. They lack the flexibility and tactical discretion of negotiations with refugees and potential affines. Notwithstanding the trouble it may cause, a local group or its leaders can recruit whomever they like to join them as coresidents. While the recruited refugees will likely prove acceptable to some, there is no guarantee that all elements of the phratry will approve of the newcomers. Yet the sponsors need not in advance of the decision win approval from those who may be affected by it. Thus, in short, while the sponsors of refugees are exercising an option that is theirs to exercise, they may in doing so change some of the prior status commitments they have to their local and phratric kinsmen. By their decision, for example, the sponsors may create a third sib in a previous two-sib organization, or a fourth sib in an organization of three. And they, as the sponsors, will have recruited a sib that is closer to them than it is to others, especially to any who opposed the invitation or who find too great a cost or too little in common with the newcomers to support them. To generalize: the more powerful and the more variable life's contingencies, the more precarious are relations founded on fixed, ascriptive rights and duties, such as kinship. The Northern Tairora solution is to retain kinship while making recurrent revisions.

Resettlement can be summarized fairly succinctly: if a person resettles among people of another phratry, the association with them will tend to make his descendants members of that phratry. If one is joined in his own phratry, however, his association with the immigrants will tend to make

them members of his phratry. Hence the territorial metaphor of Northern
Tairora makes a nice match with the formal linkage of people. No mystical
association with territory need be invoked at this point in the exposition—
although local imagery suggests such an association. Nor need any mystical
association with remote or shared ancestry be invoked, although this, too, is
strongly abetted by local imagery.

Refugees come as a group of people who collectively shared a former territory, possibly even a single settlement; who collectively shared the depriva-
tions of defeat, expulsion, and asylum; who collectively feel vengeful toward
common enemies; and who collectively enjoy the security and hospitality of
the same hosts, of whom they are in common the beneficiaries and clients.
They are now also a group of people who increasingly give their daughters or
sisters to their hosts and marry their hosts' daughters or sisters. Collectively
they are therefore affinals of their hosts. They are identical for all of these
compelling reasons, and their identity is as a kinship unit. Hence they are
functionally a sib or descent group. Indeed, their identity as such is possibly
greater at this point in the cycle than it may ever be again. With the passage
of time, and especially if their membership grows and is gradually dispersed
among other local groups of the phratry, the erstwhile new sib will come to
be accepted as one of those springing from the same soil and ancestry as the
remaining sibs of the phratry to which their forebears brought them. This is
a relatively easy matter in Northern Tairora social process.

Nor should it be thought that the history of Sib Pore in Phratry Tairora is
necessarily an exception because of its alien ethnolinguistic origin. One need
not argue that the change of language occasioned by the change of phratry is
without importance, for language is surely some additional index of simili-
arity or difference. However, there are cases of immigrant groups of the same
language as their hosts whose subsequent history—from protosib to sib—is
essentially parallel to that of Sib Pore. The asylum of Sib Pore at Abiera,
involving a group that is ethnolinguistically foreign, is helpful to the present
case in underlining the truly nonindigenous character of recruited groups—
that is, in allaying any suspicion that kinship does somehow provide the initial path to recruitment rather than—as I insist—paving it after the fact. Nor
is Sib Pore the only such instance of foreign immigrants that could be cited.
Even from an admittedly small complement of phratry histories, I know another half dozen such cases. There are at least two more personnels in Phratry Tairora of foreign ethnolinguistic derivation—one Kamáno, one Agarabi.
Until the administration restored them to their former territory, a large bloc
of Phratry Tairora were refugees among Kamáno speakers. Tiny Phratry Batainabura reckons a former linkage to an immigrant group now a part of the
Gadsup-speaking district of Tompena, and another in JabuNka, a Kamáno-
language group. In the remembered past they themselves gave temporary
asylum to a Kamáno group that, as things turned out, did not remain to join
them as a part of local society. And so forth. Students of New Guinea will be

able, no doubt, to recall the frequency with which the Neo-Melanesian term *hapkas* (mixed people) is used in characterizing certain local groups. At least in the Eastern Highlands it is very common.

REJECTED KINSMEN, ALIEN RECRUITS

I suggested earlier that the Northern Tairora local group could be viewed as a double-ended tube. The ends are open, even flared. At one end immigrant personnel enter, passing into the local group. The length of the tube—to project the analogy—would represent the length of time a given personnel and their descendants remain a part of the given group. We have now seen in a simplified model the flow of personnel from outside into the local group and the creation and recreation of sibs as a part of the process. We have also seen a model of the fission of local group personnel such as may, inter alia, be set in train by the recruitment of outsiders.

As elsewhere, the budding off of kinsmen is a process that can occur without the recruitment of outsiders to catalyze it. Population growth in groups of fixed size naturally produces recurrent emigration. No external stimulus is needed. The recruitment of new blocs of alien people is so common in Northern Tairora, however, that it may be impractical to determine in precisely what cases fission has occurred without the catalysis of alien recruitment, or without being soon followed by alien recruitment. When population growth is alone enough to people local groups and found new colonies, however, why should there be a frequent recruitment from outside the phratric perimeter? It is perhaps time to return to the questions posed earlier: why replace insiders with outsiders? Why slough off kinsmen if their places are to be taken and must be taken by nonkinsmen? What can outsiders bring to the remaining core of the local group that is more acceptable, or of greater value, or less cost, than what the emigrant kinsmen contributed?

A number of factors recurrently dispose Northern Tairora local society to an erosion of kinship—factors that amount to prevalent conditions. Most of these have already been suggested, in fact, in the previous pages. They are discussed below.

1. *Fission.* Various mechanisms operate to impose a fairly low limit on the size of groups. Some of these were noted in chapter 3, such as distance, transportation costs, and pressure on resources. Personal irritations and grievances and the accumulation of unresolved or ill-resolved offenses (namely, dealing with the perennial triad of pigs, women, gardens) are also clear in these small, acephalous communities. These mechanisms appear to be perennial. It is worth noting, incidentally, that local group size in Northern Tairora is smaller on the average than among their neighbors north, east, and probably west of them (Pataki-Schweizer 1980: 54-75). Fission through population increase is a likely and basic given, for I know of no one who has suggested population decline in this part of New Guinea; and most who have

considered the matter suggest population expansion, even dramatic expansion (see, for example, Sorenson 1972 for a recent argument along these lines).

2. *Warfare and Refugees.* A second basic and prevalent condition is the intensive warfare of this region, already noted, and surveyed by Berndt (1964), as well as others. Robbins (unpub.) has given a detailed and valuable reconstruction of some twenty-five years of fighting in the history of a single Auyana district. As near neighbors of Phratry Tairora—and the ancestral source, incidentally, of Sib Pore—the Auyana can presumably be taken as fairly representing the local experience of warfare. Beyond a doubt, fighting, and the sudden and ever-shifting alliances between local groups that fighting incurred, frequently dislodged local groups from their territories, sometimes permanently and sometimes with the result that they were relocated as residents of a host at considerable remove from their former territory. Sib Pore at Abiera, previously noted, is just one example. Outsiders in some number, therefore, are frequently available for recruitment. For their own part, they may be in desperate need of asylum. They come as petitioners needing a haven, whether or not also as personnel locally and temporarily in demand. They are not everywhere welcomed or, even if initially welcome, may not become permanently ensconced.

3. *Disgruntled Émigrés.* The fission of local groups from internal pressure may sometimes, like warfare, create personnels in need of asylum. Unlike the dislodgment of whole local groups, however, fission produces groups of a size smaller than the average local group. More often than in warfare such migrants, as noted, may found semi-independent colonies at short remove, within or adjacent to their parent territory. But the outcome varies, and if their departure was precipitate or violent, or if their subsequent relations incur deep and irreparable wounds, a small daughter group will be precariously situated and perhaps in time obliged to leave the site of their new-founded settlement, becoming refugees. Although the founding of a colony within parent territory is normally foreseen, the daughter group may later find good reason to seek asylum among distant or unrelated hosts. For a group of refugees, the urgency of their situation is much the same whether they were originally dislodged by the action of external enemies or by that of kinsmen.

Though simplified to provide the basic illustrations intended, the phratric histories of chapter 5 will surely strike a reader as tortuous. The instability of these personnels may even appear unreal, especially when it is recalled that no great depth of time is involved. In my collection of ethnohistorical material, however, these events are quite typical of the convoluted and intertwined careers (or personnels) of Northern Tairora sibs, phratries, and local groups. Conceivably one might, better than words, devise a flow chart to display a century or two of the history of several representative Northern Tairora phratries (if one had the full data, and the patience, to do it). This would presumably result in an intricate tangle of merging and splitting lines, such as perhaps to boggle the viewer's—if not the writer's—mind. It is, in any case, because of this character of local history that I find an image of a fluid or moving field more accurate and more suggestive than the better-known table of organization or structural chart of ethnography. Beyond the sheer need for depiction, however, I consider these episodes of the social field essential background for the analysis of its structural forms and for recognizing the principles that they express. It is all too easy, otherwise, to mistake what are in fact the *norms* of local process for "discrepancies" of local structure.

Four further propositions suggest why the resident local group, for its part, might (1) wish to recruit at all and (2) might prefer to recruit outsiders en bloc—prefer it, that is, to retaining or securing the return of a bloc of disaffected kinsmen. Kinsmen, of course, individually and in family groups, can and do return—in what I hve previously referred to as "dribbles." This is a matter apart from the present issue of larger bodies of migrants.

4. *The Need to Maintain Manpower.* Local groups frequently need more manpower than they may have to remain in viable competition with each other. They compete in warfare, for the acquisition of brides, trade, and exchange, and ultimately in trying to hold not only the territories they exploit but sufficient buffer zones between themselves and their enemies to give tolerable security to their lives and their livelihood—wives, pigs, gardens, and access to their resources. They particularly need more manpower after the loss of men through fighting or from other causes, above all after the departure of some of their number through the fission of a local group.

In small local groups (in precontact times seldom exceeding 175 to 200 persons of both sexes and all ages), the significance of fluctuating membership is, so to speak, amplified. Given this effect of scale, Northern Tairora local groups are caught between the need for a sufficient fighting and working force and the psychological and sociological need to maintain a reasonable curb on domestic friction, or to retain the loyalty of a given personnel. Over time, Northern Tairora local groups may gyrate between an intolerable reduction in number and a rapid build-up through outside recruitment.

In the short run the budding-off of a daughter group, especially when not acrimonious, need not be catastrophic. The colony may be near enough—frequently within earshot—and also on sufficiently good terms to present a common front with the parent group against common enemies. Each may constitute no more than a settlement within a joint territorial tenancy.

5. *The Momentum of Separation and the Souring of Kin.* A distancing process is a commonplace sequel to initial fission. Disaffection or estrangement is in some degree inevitable in the selection of the personnel who depart and those who remain. Once separate, two settlements, as a rule, become gradually more autonomous. The more important disadvantages or inequities to individuals that result from this process are adjusted by their movement from one community to the other, as single persons or families (dribbles). The result is that each residential group comes in time to repre-

sent a community of interests that are, on the one hand, progressively more fully shared among its own members and, on the other, progressively more distinctive of them. Status relations are probably maintained in general but their content shrinks apace. The day will come—is, in fact, conventionally foreseen—when, acting on its own interest, one community will make a commitment adverse and intolerable to the interests of the other. This is likely to be both a cause and an assertion of widened independence. And so the process unfolds.

The problem of adequate numbers will thus arise through the increasing autonomy of parent and daughter settlements. It arises suddenly if there is a dramatic rupture between the two groups. This is seemingly a familiar event in Northern Tairora life, and in the long run it is perhaps all but inevitable. Short-handed in consequence, Northern Tairora local groups are therefore intermittently receptive to the possibility of recruiting new personnel.

6. *The Advantage of Newness and the Corruption of Prolonged Coresidence.* New people previously unconnected or but slightly connected (perhaps as allies, trading partners, members of a strong man's network, or affinal kin) offer several advantages besides the sheer addition of their number to the ranks of a depleted and recruitment-minded community. As nonmembers of any of the local sibs or descent groups, they are a potential source of brides for the men of the residential group as well as of women to help form marital alliances and to command bride wealth from other local group in a network. Affinal linkage of the new recruits to the indigenous group quickly establishes or confirms their membership, and presently their kinship, in the local group of their erstwhile hosts. They become only an additional intermarrying sib or sib segment within the community.

A second advantage of outside recruitment is that new people come with a clean slate. They bear no burden or bear a lesser one of grievances. They have not as yet been accused of fornicating with local women, stealing local pigs, defaulting on obligations, or quarreling over matters of exchange or wealth distribution. Nor are they suspect of pilfering the gardens, areca palms, or pandanus groves of fellow villagers. Their sorcery is not as yet indicted for damaging the health or welfare of local persons. Finally, new people, above all refugees, come at first as clients, not as equals. Transitory though this condition may be, it is surely of some initial importance, since it tends to remove them as potential rivals.

The disadvantages of existing residents and kinsmen are basically the reverse of the foregoing advantages of new personnel. Since they are already present in the phratric territory, the established residents can hardly augment the local group's manpower resources. As to what they already contribute, furthermore, there is perhaps some grumbling. The interests of such coresidents are apt to be parallel and competitive, moreover, especially in regard to the perennial scarcities: women, wealth, and power. (It is these, not land, that are seen as scarce.) The ambition of rivalrous local strong men is the extreme instance of competition, because preeminence is indivisible.

As a result in part of their competitive interests, old residents will already have been brought into conflict with each other, their differences perhaps given focus in the rivalry of two or more ambitious men, or expressed in the fissive situation described in section 5 above.

7. *The Politics of Clientage.* Finally, the importance of new people in the schemes of ambitious men, alluded to several times above, must be added to the list. It is a factor of considerable force in favoring the recruitment of outsiders. Indeed, this force for recruitment is perhaps no more episodic than others. Strong men, it is true, rise and fall, and the strong men of one day may not be the equal of others. There may or may not thus be, in a given local group at a given time, a strong man to offer convincing sponsorship to a refugee bloc. Yet the strong-man factor is not the only one that fluctuates, for local groups themselves wax and wane in their interest in recruitment.

In polities like those of the Northern Tairora, the strong man's authority depends on his own personal attributes and efforts, for he has no prescribed following, no legitimacy in the sense of formal office (Watson 1967a; Sahlins 1963). His leverage with his fellow kinsmen and coresidents quite clearly comes from a large personal network, which he himself builds and which typically includes more outsiders, and outsiders at greater distances, than do the networks of his lesser fellows. This "distance factor," as it were, has been noted more than once in connection with strong men of the Central Highlands (e.g., Salisbury 1964; Watson 1967a; Lowman 1968), and in the present context it is worth emphasizing. The sheer size of his network is almost certainly one aspect of the strong man's power—his partners, potential clients, sources of information, debtors, creditors, those who are hoping for favors or security. To increase the network it is necessary for him to go outside the local group, usually beyond the phratry. A man of influence will eventually be in contact with groups outside his own phratry, that is, with nonkinsmen. Indeed, one need not aspire to preeminent influence to find it useful to have contacts abroad, and trading partners are by no means the exclusive prerogative of leadership. In dealing with outside groups, the strong men, however, is likely to be more than the ordinary trading partner or affinal kinsman. He is the main spokesman for his group. He may well, in fact, seem to speak with greater authority abroad than he can at home—where he is at least among *pares* even though aspiring to be *primus*.

The relations of phratry members to each other—as affinals or as lineals—are relations of status. Kinship is—more than friendship, at least—ascriptive and involuntary. Phratric relations, such as they are, are therefore less decisional and discretionary—in other words, more committed—than relations one may achieve contractually, so to speak, with outsiders and nonkinsmen. For the strong man this fact may give a distinct advantage to dealings with outsiders. He has more latitude and more leverage with nonkinsmen than with his existing coresidents. He can conceivably even enlist their help against members of his own phratry or their friends, something not so easily arranged with other members of the phratry.

THE DYNAMICS OF STRONG-MAN POLITICS

It was probably characteristic of the strong man, given the opportunity, to reach out for contact—in effect for contract—with relatively distant, hence relatively uncommitted, peoples. And we may understand in this light the stereotype of the strong man who "walks unharmed up and down the whole valley" (Salisbury 1964). We can comprehend his otherwise puzzling willingness to expose himself to the risks of distant, sometimes solitary journeys across hostile territories. While his doing so, flagrantly and boastfully, doubtless had the desired effect in dramatizing his singular power and invulnerability, it does not seem likely that such hazardous travels would be undertaken out of sheer bravado—literally empty of all other purpose. We can also understand how a strong man sometimes used his influence and command over local manpower to aid in fighting much farther from home than could be justified by the purely defensive and immediate interests of his own group (Watson 1967a). More than bravado or bellicosity, more than a pretense of important and secret business took him abroad, beyond the range of his fellows. The strong man's distant contacts, far from incidental to his station or merely emblematic, were probably in fact a major part of his standing with his own people. Whether or not a threat for him to hold over their heads, distant contacts could give him a measure of independence: the power of enlisting allies, if need be, in a cause of his choosing—if not also one of theirs These allies were too distant for the ordinary man to know or too little beholden for him to sway. For the strong man, they were allies with whom one could contemplate decisions—such as the possible alienation of some of one's own coresidents—that would otherwise be self-defeating. Under the circumstances, it is hardly surprising that the strong man is a principal beneficiary in the recruitment of nonkinsmen, sometimes from a surprising distance. Indeed, he is also the recruits' first point of contact with the host community, even prior to their need for refuge; and he is their strongest source of legitimation within the community, if asylum is needed and granted.

The strong man's private strategy must partly match the collective interest of a local group. He must serve some need of theirs in serving his own. In this likely convergence of interests, the strong man himself, up to a point, can be seen as the instrument of the local group, meeting problems of recruitment, politics, defense, and marriage through the pattern of enlisting foreigners to help in fighting and occasionally to join the ranks of his own group as residents. There is no question, in the latter instance, that he benefits personally in his ambition to possess the loyalty of a group of people who, at least for a time, are not apt to challenge his sway over the members of their adoptive local group.

As previously discussed, outside recruitment may hasten the disaffection of some faction within the community, perhaps promoting their withdrawal to colonize a new residential site. It may even precipitate their wholesale

alienation and open hostility. From the point of view of the strong man, however, the outsiders in such a case will at least replace dubious or obstinate
coresidents; and, while they are less well known, they are favorably known
and are presumably well disposed to their local sponsors. Their disposition,
moreover, is nourished by no mere convention of loyalty such as a jejune
kinship or a pale claim to common descent. Their support is fed by practical
need and hearty self-interest, and usually by a growing number of affinal
bonds—bonds both strong and current.

One might be tempted to say that the strong man has a centripetal effect
to counter the fissive and centrifugal trends of Northern Tairora society, but
the claim would be one-sided. To be sure, the focal role of the strong man in
drawing outside personnel into a local group is centripetal enough; but it
seems inescapable that his role in their recruitment is typically also predicated on the weakening of the local group by fission and dissent in which he
himself is hardly neutral. From actual or impending losses of manpower
arises the very need for new blood. Sometimes this need may arise with the
conscious acquiescence of the strong man; and possibly sometimes it arises
from his deliberate design to divide the group. Making fission more certain,
his means are the very encouragement of immigrant outsiders who are loyal
to him but not to a rival strong man or to an opposite faction. Thus the strong
man may be as much a part of centrifugal as of centripetal movements of
personnel.

Truer to the case would be to locate the strong man at the heart of a continuing dialectical movement whose strophes are initiated at the level of the
local group, their effects ramifying throughout the phratry and the alliance
network of the social field. This dialectic can be styled as one of loyalty and
disaffection; or of coresidence and exile; of trust and suspicion; of recruitment and expulsion; of naturalization—rhetorically styled as kinship and
common descent—and alienation; of restraint and violence. Though perhaps
suggesting a tidiness and regularity not found in actuality, these antinomies
at least do not portray the strong man as the direct and simple function of the
social structure, a response to its need, as has been suggested for the strong
men of the Mae Enga (Meggitt 1967). Indeed, the strong man could be said
to work both for and against the rest of the community and they for and
against him. It is thus no paradox that a Northern Tairora strong man seems
often (perhaps always) to be known as "bad," nor that he himself is likely to
proclaim the reputation, pointing it out to the questioner lest it be overlooked. Consistent with this argument, the reputation for antagonism appears to be a part of his pride and a conscious element of his style. It is the
proof of his potency.

One of the essential facts of Northern Tairora society is surely its medley
of intersecting but typically noncoterminous sets of persons, each described
by a slightly different array of conventional loyalties, in effect a distinct social
identity: first, there are residential groupings, which are local groups with
their assignment of common defense and common ownership of resources;

those are crosscut by descent-based groupings, which I term sibs and local sib segments, assigning the reciprocal exchange of women, bride wealth, birth, initiation, and death dues, as well as hospitality. All of these in theory are met and ultimately completed in the phratry, normally a connubium and peace-keeping area which combines both the principle of common descent and the fact and meaning of a common territory.

It would be conventional to suggest that there is strength and cohesiveness in the interlocking and overlapping of Northern Tairora society, strength arising from its very medley of intersecting social arrangements. To make such a claim, I think, would be to argue a checks-and-balances theory of strength and cohesiveness. True enough, the Northern Tairora social process produces no cleanly carpentered societal edifice, but one full of culs-de-sac and crude angles, with odd posts and studs, and beams of many different sizes, reflecting a liberal and pragmatic use of rules and rights rather than any rigid or simple adherence—that least of all—to asserted principle.

Such a system can hardly be said to call forth its leadership with any simple summons, whether leaders respond steadily or, as Meggitt has suggested for Enga (1967), they answer in a clockwork alternation in which, as needed, the role is now powerful, now weakly realized. Seemingly no such group would ever be caught short for leadership: if it needed the strong leader, it would have him. One may still, obviously, believe that the Northern Tairora strong-man leader needs the group, and they him, even as they succeed intermittently in producing able and credible aspirants for the role he plays. But one need not—and in Northern Tairora one cannot—argue either that the strong man is precisely what the group requires to enhance its security or that the group invariably offers him precisely the following he needs to achieve what he must if, in the terms recognized by the society itself, his name is to be memorable.

Far from finding the situation ideal, the strong man may find that expediency obliges him to revise it. In doing so, however, he may violate some of the claims that society asserts as uncompromising. He may, for example, fail to defend or even contribute to rejecting some of his own kinsmen, thus permitting or forcing them to leave the local group, thereby estranging them rather than supporting established kin ties and erstwhile loyalties. By his actions, he may contribute to the further complication of local society in which former insiders, alienated, now progressively become outsiders, just as people once outsiders now progressively become insiders. He may help to perpetuate if not increase the very medley of crosscutting groups and subdivided loyalties. He may minimize the development of any lasting and univocal personnel other than his own particular following, newly selected and pruned of dissidents, and enduring for only as long as his own vigor and drive endure or exceed that of any rival. This following, like other personnels, is also transitory. Were they not, their existence might obviate the strong man's maneuvering, or might prevent it. This would presumably curb his self-serving while he is, as it were, in their service.

A cohesiveness based on intersection, overlap, contingency, and compromise is all very well perhaps for a society like Northern Tairora. One can adduce several persuasive (and sticky Panglossian) reasons why this is just the right society for people in their situation. But it is also a society that both invites and frustrates the efforts of a would-be leader to organize a clean, unfettered following with uncompromising loyalty to him or to his enterprises.

A notable weakness or, at any rate, a characteristic of Northern Tairora society is its precarious social control. Such a defect appears intrinsic to the very contingency of the loyalties that abound in the system. This defect is seemingly compatible with the emphasis on individual strength and assertiveness—the ability to defend one's private interests, or to help defend those of others to whom one owes the strongest and least ambivalent support. In this sense we could say, for analytical purposes, that the system "calls for" the strong man as leader. He both approximates the group's personality ideal of strength and possesses a real competence, however arbitrary or despotic, as a warrior outside and a peace-keeper within. The leader is likely thus to find the group receptive to some of his ambitions, while perhaps resentful (but often ineffectual) in resisting those of his acts that further aggrandize him—at the cost of intimidating or humiliating others. But there are two closely related conditions that constitute exceptions to this apparent fit between leader and led. The aspirant strong man may not be alone in his aspiration: he may have rivals. His putative followers, therefore, may have other options for leadership, loyalty, and even residence. So a situation that may be said to beckon the strong man to fulfill himself, in another sense makes it likely that his response will sometimes be to reject a part of his presumed following, hence rejecting some of the conventional loyalties of the system. For the cleanest and least compromised following may be one that includes a substantial leavening of new people. Moreover, the more amply he fulfills his role, the more the strong man is apt to flout some of the values of the community, earning the epithet "bad man" as well as the awe or envy that are evidently linked to such a name, albeit pridefully linked.

It is in the foregoing sense that I am reluctant to credit any suggestion of the optimal fit of strong-man leadership with the balance of the Northern Tairora social system. The relationship hardly seems unequivocal, short of gross compromise. There is obviously no question that strong men, the local group, weak social control, and other features, such as intensive warfare and a refugee system, are all attributes or parts of a single social order called Northern Tairora society. There is thus, of course, no question that each "fits" the other in various discernible ways; for either we are discussing a viable social order, one in which the interacting parts are at least minimally compatible, or we are discussing a pathology or an impossibility. It is against seeing wholeness as wholesomeness in an irreducible compatibility or perfection (proof of which is claimed in whatever degree compatibility may be present), it is against flawlessness that I balk. For in claiming some ultimate harmony or synchronism of social forms and relationships, in my opinion, one incurs several hazards. Violence is done to the description of a social order, certainly one like Northern Tairora—and perhaps most others. And thereby an image is projected of functional completeness and immobile regularity—a tableau that must be changeless but for the intervention of exogenous factors. Neither the timeless fixity of a particular structural state nor a slightly modified version of it—tidy chronic regularity, seems characteristic of Northern Tairora social process, above all at the local level.

THE MULTIPLICATION AND EXTINCTION OF SIBS:
THE GROWTH AND FISSIONING OF PHRATRIES

We are now in a position to bring the present argument to bear on the question of how the social units—the several sorts of personnels—of Northern Tairora society recurrently arise and disappear. Specifically we wish to indicate the relation of local group recruitment and fission to the formation of sibs, and its relation to the expansion and realignment of phratries. In bringing the present argument to such a close, it will be necessary, as always in such discussions, to indicate variable circumstances and different possible outcomes. Ideally, the discussion should also take us to the point where we can undertake to recognize underlying values or principles of Northern Tairora culture implicit in and expressed by these social processes.

The argument up to now has detailed the dynamics of local group recruitment of outside personnel; the politics of strong-man leadership; and the social means by which growing—and increasingly strife-ridden—local groups are fissioned, their personnel redeployed and redistributed among other groups. In developing the argument, I have used such general terms as the "flow" of people, the social field, the disaffiliation or alienation of kinsmen. I have characterized the local group as a funnel in relation to the social field. I have proposed that the local group is the fundamental unit of Northern Tairora society because it is the basic staging area in the formation and revision of the other personnels of this social field.[2]

We are, then, conceiving of the Northern Tairora social field as one of fluid manpower movably deployed and locally concentrated for various essential activities, including the reproduction and education of children to re-

2. In probably a majority of studies of traditional New Guinea societies the local group is considered the fundamental social unit. As commonly viewed, the local group is virtually autonomous, unconstrained by any other alignment of personnel or power equally stable or continuous. Hogbin and Wedgwood (1953-54) express this view in their well-known proposal of a taxonomy of New Guinea personnels. The present argument is concerned with instability and change, but there is no inherent conflict between the claim of autonomy and the view of Northern Tairora local groups as fundamental in forming and reforming sib and phratry personnels. Indeed, the near-autonomy of the local group is presupposed in their ability to pursue their own recruitment and fissioning policies, making such decisions without effective brake or intervention by other bodies.

place themselves or—intended or not—to be redeployed. Having established that a considerable flow of persons exists, our purpose is to conceptualize how this flow is continually molded and remolded, regulated, or channeled recurrently into social units of the type one finds in Northern Tairora. If a rapid dissolution of existing personnels accompanies the relocation of their members, we must see how equivalent personnels—local groups, sibs, phratries—are formed from the membership of the relocated and dissolved personnels. That question, I suggest, translates handily into one concerning the multiplication and extinction of sibs and, again, one concerning the growth and fissioning of phratries. Taken broadly, this issue is not confined to local society but is a generic question of social organization. The question may be given in a particularly acute form in Northern Tairora, however, because of the characteristic openness of personnels to the admission of outsiders and the attendant discontinuities of membership.

Wherever there is both a growth of population and a relatively fixed size limit of its organized personnels, there must be some means of reducing or breaking up units grown overlarge into units not exceeding the maximum viable size. How much the process results in an absolute increase of the number of personnel units at any given level, as opposed to the recurrent collapse and reshuffling of existing personnels, appears to vary. It seems to be normal in some systems, for example segmentary systems, that each newly created unit tends to be an addition to the existing number. Each tends to "nest" inside a parent body, moreover, to produce a pyramid when the social field is represented as a hierarchy of size and inclusiveness.

In Northern Tairora, as we have seen, the largest units—phratries—fall short of being inclusive enough to organize any substantial portion of the social field. They are, in other words, relatively small and therefore relatively numerous. Since phratries are territorially discrete, the result is to organize the social field as a series of peoples and countries each with a certain degree of distinction—that is, an ethnic character of its own.

A more fundamental difference between Northern Tairora and a pyramidal-segmentary organization is that the reduction and breaking down of units does not occur only, or even mainly, because they have simply grown overlarge. Sometimes, in fact, the exodus of a portion of the membership is followed in short order by the advent of others. Units that have become too small, in other words, are built up by recruiting persons from other units. The breaking point at which the fissioning of a personnel takes place may fairly often produce units below the viable size of a personnel in this social field. These may in turn become recruits for some new merger for the exit of a bloc of persons from a given personnel does not invariably lead to their establishment as a separate personnel within the original parent body. In joining, rather, an alien personnel, they become estranged from the onetime parent body. If the formation and reformation of social groupings is taken in its generic sense, we are thus examining here a particular variety of the general phenomenon.

As the staging area for the formation of personnels and the expansion and revision of phratries, as the source or agency for creating and modifying these personnels through the reorganization of manpower of the social field, the role of the local group could be schematized as shown in figure 6.

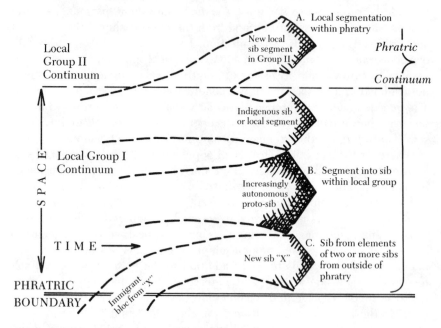

Fig. 6.   The Role of the Local Group in Multiplication of Sibs

Like all schema a simplification, this one suggests that a phratry grows directly and simply by the multiplication of its sibs. But in fact it grows by the multiplication of local groups, whether or not sibs are also increased in number. Moreover, the local group may be a staging area for additional sibs in *other* phratries than the one of which the given local group is part. Why not, then, chart the process as shown in figure 7?

Figure 7 also suggests in the local group a recurrent course of events leading to the growth of a phratry. It fails, however, to show the relation of phratric growth to the addition of a new, migrant sib within an established local group, a development that may occur (in the short run) with or without any simultaneous increase in the number of colonists or local groups. Actually, phratric growth tends to be expressed in an increase of either or both sibs and colonies, as well as in population. At the very least, then, we must admit it is artificial, even if necessary, to discuss the growth of phratries exclusively in terms of additional sibs or of additional colonies and local groups.

It may be useful here to review the several type sequences in which local groups play a part in the multiplication of sibs. A local group is involved in the formation of a new sib (1) when through fission it gives rise, first, to a new colony which then in time becomes autonomous, increasing the chance that its local sib segments will begin to act as sibs, (2) when through fission it gives rise to an emigrant group whose flight takes it to asylum in another phratry, where, as noted, it will become—or be reorganized as—a sib, (3) when the local group is forced, in one or more refugee contingents, to abandon its territory, (4) when the local group recruits migrant refugees from outside the phratry, and (5) when, through growth and other causes, local sib segments become increasingly independent of the parent sib—in reality, become increasingly independent of the other local sib segments heretofore acknowledging the same sib name and marital status. The change can be signaled, for example, by members of the two personnels commencing to intermarry.

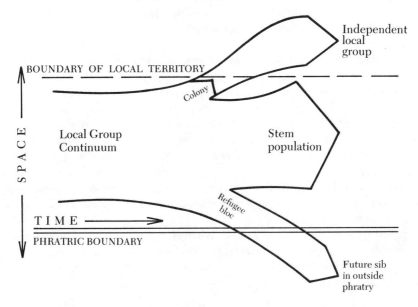

Fig. 7.   Multiplication of Local Groups

The immediate local implications of each of these five type sequences have been discussed or can readily be inferred from previous discussion and that which follows. In all five cases the formation of new sibs depends ultimately on one or both of two sources of persons: (1) population growth, or natural increase of the local group, and (2) population movement, or migration into the local group (immigration) or out of the local group (emigration).

To be sure, these are the elemental causes of changing membership in any personnel or population. If there is any special circumstance of local society, it is possibly in the rate of population growth or the small size of the maximal personnel in relation to the social field; but more surely it is in the scale of migration and especially in the frequency with which migrations are accompanied by or are the concomitant of the fission and alienation of personnels purportedly founded on a genealogical principle. It is of course the changing alignment of personnels, each with its multiple ramifications, as effected by growth and migration, that we are considering here as Northern Tairora social process.

In the social field at large, growth and migration presumably do not operate independently of each other, though migration, being the more dramatic, short-term, and large-scale phenomenon, may often appear the sole factor, at the local level, in realignments of Northern Tairora personnels. Population growth is likely to play some part in the rise of new sibs in type sequences 1, 2, and 5—that is, in the budding off of colonies within the local territory, in the separation of emigrant groups that lodge in other phratric territories, and in the trend toward independence of local sib segments. This last sequence is presumably a response in part to a sufficient membership—that is, to natural increase—whether or not the recruitment of migrants plays a part.

The role of migration in the rise of new sibs is most obvious in type sequences 2, 3, and 4—that is, when segments of a local group emigrate, when local groups are forced to abandon the local territory as refugees seeking asylum, or when a local group recruits a refugee bloc from outside the phratry.

The present typology is not solely concerned with the rise of new sibs within a given local group or a given phratry. Instead, the larger social field is taken as the stage in order to recognize also the new sib of extraneous origin. Type sequences 2, 3, and 4 involve new sibs whose membership is extraneous to the larger personnels in whose midst they are formed. Type sequences 1 and 5 involve new sibs whose personnel are indigenous to the phratry in which they take form.

It is not surprising to find a close match between migration and new sibs whose personnel are extraneous to the local group or phratry, and to find a match, on the other hand, between growth and new sibs whose members are largely indigenous to the phratry of which the sib is a component.

The Growth and Dissolution of Phratries

The growth of a phratry, as we have seen, can be taken in three senses: the number of its component local groups, the number of its component sibs (or local sib segments, if one takes the longer view), and the size of the phratric population. These three measures are interrelated, to be sure, though the number of component local groups is probably more closely reflected in the gross population of a phratry than is the number of its sibs.

The foundation of a new phratry naturally presupposes the fissioning of one or two previous phratries. I can conceive of new phratries coming into being in Northern Tairora society from the splitting of a single previous phratry—without the necessary involvement of any extraneous personnel.

This might happen most readily in the instance of an emigrant group founding a colony in heretofore untenanted country at a great distance or in a location physically separated from the parent personnel by intervening territories. Such a description suggests an open frontier and the pioneer settlement of unoccupied country. Sorenson (1972) has suggested that the southern Fore area was recently pioneered by groups that planted sweet potato gardens and settled in virgin forest. There may be a parallel case of pioneering in other areas such as Southern Tairora. In any case, Sorenson does not consider the implications of Fore pioneering for the proliferation of sibs or phratries. I can cite no case from my own data illustrating such a development. This is not surprising, since Northern Tairora has no open frontiers and has not been pioneered in recent centuries. The possibility of a new phratry from the simple fission of an old one must thus remain for now hypothetical.

In heavily settled country like Northern Tairora, the opportunity to stake out a pristine patrimony does not ordinarily exist. The formation of a new phratry must accordingly take a different course. Since it is enacted in landscape already largely claimed and occupied, the new phratry takes form in a part of an existing phratric territory, necessarily that of some members of the founding group.

The founders are often a local group that has been increasingly alienated from their phratric congeners. Their growing alienation typically turns on the recruitment of extraneous migrants, either by themselves or by other local groups of the phratry—in some cases, perhaps, by both. Such unilateral recruitment, as would be expected, is accompanied by the development of new friendships and alliances—indeed, by new *kinship* as well. New relationships are developing, in fine, which are distinct from and incompatible with the relations that formerly defined a phratric bond among these local groups. Estrangement proceeds to the point where the founders-to-be of the future new phratry commence to act with an autonomy befitting their autonomous destiny more than their nominal present status. They already have residential autonomy, since every local group has its own local territory. To this they need only add a measure of connubial independence and perhaps unilateral military or political decisions before the split is irreversible. Relationships, to be sure, are inevitably revised when distinct, new, and eventually incompatible elements are added to a field. Such an outcome is likely to be recurrent with the relatively free and uncoordinated recruitment of foreign personnels by individual local groups acting unilaterally—without a consensus of the wider phratry.

In the formation of a new phratry, marital and other exchange lines are redrawn to the effect that the founding local group takes on the endogamic character of a phratry. The difficulty or unease of the extraneous recruits—now of course a sib—in finding marital partners among the remaining local personnels of the phratry is a typical symptom. It may also be a cause of the shift of the endogamic boundary to mark off one portion of the phratric membership from the rest.

The case of Batainabura, previously noted, appears to illustrate the developmental phase during which a phratry constitutes a single local group. Batainabura, as observed, consists of two main sibs, each from a different former phratry—indeed, phratries that were once enemies. One sib, Hararúnx (or Baqe-Hararúnx), is the remnant of its former phratry, thanks to the emigration of a substantial bloc of erstwhile phratric brethren. Weakened thereby, the Hararúnx bloc was obliged to join or be joined by others to bring the membership up to sufficient strength to hold some portion of the remaining territory. Since the ancestors of Sib Airiná appear themselves to have been facing a similar plight, the present merger with the Hararúnx resulted. The merged personnel were certainly not without traditional ties—or, perhaps better, *a tradition of ties*—with other phratric personnels. Yet they were distinct enough in joint interests and relationships to constitute a phratry. They were, by the same token, too distinct in these respects—in effect, too distinct in their collective inheritance or history—to be a part of any existing phratry.

The distancing of two parties is, of course, normally a mutual process. It is unrealistic to conceive of a new phratry arising through the purely unilateral disaffiliation of one group while the erstwhile congeners continue purely and solidly to represent the position of yore. What Bateson (1958) termed "schismogenesis" applies fully to the case: it is a bilateral or mutual process in which two parties (in this case both of the extraneous sibs) move away from each other. As a rule, we are thus speaking of a minimum of four parties: at least two sibs, which, combined, are becoming a distinct new phratry; and the parent phratry of each sib.

As the reader may readily suppose, this formulation is once again quite simplified. It presupposes, for example, a simultaneous distancing of each of the constituent sibs from its respective phratry; in fact the distancing of one sib may precede the other by a substantial interval. Nor do the remnant elements of the parent phratry continue unchanged except for the departure of the given disaffiliated bloc. The balance of the original phratry may be rent in other ways as well; or it may on its own be subject to modification by the recruitment of other, extraneous personnel. Other sets of conditions are conceivable.

The Growth of an Existing Phratry

In the case of a single founding local group (if there are any other initial forms of new phratries), the growth of the phratry, naturally, is from the growth of the founding group—its expansion through colonies which may in time become new local groups, or its recruitment of an extraneous personnel which becomes a new sib within the phratric fold. This is the local group in its guise as "funnel" or staging area for the formation of personnels. As long as all phratric elements have been formed in the single funnel or staging area, the cohesiveness of the phratry is presumably at its highest.

Once a phratry consists of two or more local groups, however, the implications of growth are more complex. While there are no additional *kinds* of new personnels that can arise, the fact that new personnels may arise from different staging areas—different local groups—implies an eventual dilution or weakening of phratric bonds. Local group A, for example, may recruit an extraneous personnel with whom, as coresidents, they develop close intersib relations (notably marriage), while local group B may not feel close to the new sib taking form in local group A. If local group B meanwhile recruits a group of refugees into their ranks as coresidents, the situation in relation to local group A is apt to parallel that which has developed with *its* new sib. With additional new personnels, locally rather than phratrically formed, the complication of relations advances at more than a simple arithmetical rate. Thus while new sibs especially may represent sudden spurts of growth and new colonies and local groups a substantial if slower source of growth, the price of this growth is apt to be a palpable decline in the cohesiveness and *esprit de corps* of the phratric membership at large. It appears to be, both logically and in historical fact, the recruitment of extraneous personnels that most of all contributes to a loosening of the tenuous bonds of the multilocal phratry. The recruitment of outsiders may strengthen its ranks but only by shortening its life span and keeping the phratry from being the stable, enduring form of membership one might suppose it to be from the fact of its relative size, its genealogical ideology, and the encompassing connubial role it tends to play. The consequences of such stability—if it existed—might be phratries much larger in membership and much wider in territorial extent than those of Northern Tairora.

In fine, the phratry is a grouping that arises with the establishment of one or more local groups each with a membership that is collectively separate in social identification, marital behavior, and territory from any other single phratry. The phratry increases with the expansion of its local groups, is diversified with the multiplication of sibs commencing within its local groups, and adds local components as its constituent local groups establish colonies, each tending to grow more autonomous with time. The composition of the phratry, as well as the size of its membership and its disposition in local territories, is thus but the collective and cumulative product of events and decisions of any or all of its constituent units, local or lineal. The fluidity of any of these is multiplied for the phratry by the fluidity of the rest. The centrifugal tendencies of local personnels are thus translated into centrifugal tendencies of the larger phratric body. Struggles of strong men for preference will be centrifugal or centripetal in phratric effect, depending on whether the strong man finds advantage and succeeds in developing a phratry-wide base or public, or whether his interests lead to more divisive alignments.

Normally the phratry is a peace-keeping unit—whether or not a war-making one; it is a near-endogamous connubium; and it is in theory a territory within which individual members may move freely from one local group to another, even taking up residence in local territories other than their own without incurring for themselves or their descendants a short-term personal risk or a long-term change of descent-group identification. The practice of any or all of these options by the membership may be called centripetal or cohesive; and surely when all of them are put into regular and frequent practice one can speak confidently of the phratry as a relatively cohesive body held together by its sense of kinship. This type of formulation all too easily makes of kinship a kind of force capable of insuring a certain outcome or capable of insuring against other conceivable outcomes—such as internecine warfare. Since they claim kinship, are in principle a peace-keeping group, and, at least in the best of times, do not attack each other, the members of a phratry are easily characterized as demonstrating the efficacy of kinship, the strength of sentiment as force or cause. Such facts thus conceal rather than showing kinship as effect or even as epiphenomenon.

In analyzing the Northern Tairora phratry and indeed Northern Tairora society in general, it seems worthwhile to recognize kinship as having a dual character, one in which it is an expression of hope or intention and not a simple imperative or prime mover. Kinship is both acknowledgment or assertion and compliance with a behavioral rule or etiquette. In a Northern Tairora local group, sib, or phratry, if not in every other such group on earth, membership is as membership does. To venture further into the co-option of familiar phrases: the personnel of such groupings ultimately vote their membership or kinship—quite literally—"with their feet." To stay is to belong—when staying also includes keeping peace, intermarrying and exchanging with certain partners, and so forth. To leave is not immediately to break off kinship, for one may return and revive it—soon or even after a long interval. But to marry otherwise, to exchange with different partners, or above all to break the peace—these are declarations of lapsing intention, in effect of lapsing kinship.

Breaking the peace is surely the most precipitate declaration of lapse—if one wishes to compare the several forms of negative declaration. Perhaps breaking the peace is so precipitate because it is inherently the most flagrant and the most irreversible act. Even moving away, as noted, is reversible: one can move back. Nonintermarriage is slow and cumulative, and because of multiple contingencies, a single, exceptional default is subject to various possible rationalizations. Internecine fighting, in the Northern Tairora scheme of values, is less conclusive per se than the infliction of injury or death. In practice, all declarations of position are ultimately negotiable, but a flare-up of anger, even flying arrows, is one thing to reverse, while a casualty or a killing is more indelible. Even here, however, one would seldom confront an isolated act, completely opposite in value to all other acts or assertions of a given actor or personnel. A fight resulting in an injury or a death would far more often be the culmination of a mounting series, or an escalation of acts of estrangement, than it would be a pure accident. The pure accident could be dealt with, probably, in less drastic terms.

The consideration of "culminating acts" has still another side, for in Northern Tairora the "last straw" seems often to be a veritable *straw*. Speaking of their bitterest enemy, the Tuntuqirx, Batainabura informants say it was a disagreement over cassowary chicks that prompted the outbreak of fighting leading to the flight of these migrants from Phratry Arogara. (Now settled in territory claimed by Batainabura, they are considered to be encroachers.) The Batainabura report this alleged cause without comment, as if there is no need to question it. Evidently it is not too trivial. But surely Northern Tairora phratries, despite the instability I have emphasized, are not apt to break up simply over the ownership of a few cassowary chicks. Whatever the full details of this case, the reported cause must have been just the ultimate declaration of a rift that had been widening faster than could be counteracted.

In seeing such a report in its fuller context, it may be helpful also to recall the earlier discussion of the need in Northern Tairora for well-advertised demonstrations and boastful protestations of positive sentiment in maintaining amicable partnerships. In their absence, and especially in the presence of negative demonstrations, even "trivial" events can have a disproportionate effect.

That the "last straw" metaphor proves useful in speaking of Northern Tairora social histories is not by itself remarkable. The commonness of straws in the history of these personnels, however, indicates how frequent are the rifts the straws complete and how prevalent therefore are the escalations that precede them and prepare the way. It is necessary to recognize the role of straws in considering the sense of kinship in Northern Tairora society.

THE SENSE OF NORTHERN TAIRORA KINSHIP

The previous discussion, if nothing else, begs the question: what does kinship mean in Northern Tairora culture? It will be possible to give a fuller answer, I believe, in the next chapter; but two observations at least can be made here. There is evidently a need, in the first place, for Northern Tairora to use a genealogical rhetoric in speaking of the persons and personnels who behave toward each other in certain ways. It is evidently difficult if not unthinkable to deny for long to any substantial portion of one's coresidents in good standing the status of kinsmen. I was unable to observe any personnel of which the adult members were all first-generation recruits of extraneous origin. After more than thirty years of suppression of warfare and the systematic registration of persons in their "proper" settlements or domiciles, there were no refugee groups of more recent arrival to be found. I do not know firsthand, therefore, how early, in what terms, or with what etiquette such outsiders begin to be treated by their hosts as kinsmen. The initial marital exchange—which may, to be sure, predate coresidence—makes it possible to give an affinal treatment *per extenso* to the immigrant personnel as a whole. Coresidence must surely help the case, since it clearly constitutes kinship behavior. Together with peace-keeping and especially with engaging in a joint effort in defense or making war, the essential conditions or causes of kinship are present. To refuse to call such coresidents kinsmen may be an act as negative and potentially disruptive as if they refused to act like kinsmen, which is to say, like coresidents.

This brings me to the second observation, a point that has previously arisen: kinsmen are as kinsmen do. The activities just enumerated give to a Northern Tairora the overt sense of kinship. They are characteristic, that is, of the relationship among kinsmen. It does not seem too much to say that in Northern Tairora society the observation of such a relationship must to a degree warrant the use of kinship reference or rhetoric with respect to the given parties. The behavior, in other words, sanctions the claim of kinship quite as much as—to make a more familiar statement—kinship sanctions the activities.

In the actual course of events, to be sure, both senses of sanction—behavioral and ideological—tend to develop apace. Yet given the recurrent merging of wholly extraneous personnels, it is simply not realistic to posit the existence of a kinship sentiment prior to the opportunity of either party to interact. Certainly there is no initial connection by birth to provide such a claim which could then conceivably be realized in interaction. It therefore seems more convincing to suggest that, in numerous and by no means abnormal cases, behavior has priority, conferring upon Northern Tairora persons or personnels the semblance of kinship, following which the conventional assertion of kinship takes form and becomes in due course unchallenged and unassailable.

It is hard in this light to resist the view that the intention of kinship and the will to behave as kinsmen—commencing, no doubt, with coresidence, marital exchange, and the mutual support of each other's security—are a sufficient condition of emergent kinship. It would follow equally that compliance and regularity are a necessary condition of remaining kinsmen. Negatively, it would follow from these terms that the failure to behave as kinsmen is a sufficient condition of terminating kinship.

In all of this, to be sure, the merging emphasis of an Iroquois terminological system (Murdock 1949) must smooth the way and hasten the lexical semblance of kinship. Collaterals of ego's (zero) generation are siblings except for a mother's brother's children. In the first descending generation all collateral kinsmen, except sister's son and sister's daughter, are terminologically equivalent to a male ego's own children.

The regular use of collective, group-wide terms in speaking, for example, of marriage and other exchanges, is similarly an aid to the merging of extraneous personnels in a common pool of kinsmen. Thus, no matter what the degree of their consanguinity with the bride, members of her sib or local sib segment normally speak of having jointly presented her to her husband's people, the other intermarrying sib or sib segment. If she is married into another local group, the same normally applies, *mutatis mutandis*, to all members of her own local group "We" and "they" are liberally bestowed and often invoked.

Affinity is an easy step, especially given the collectivized rhetoric of exchanges—giving *our* women to them, or marrying *their* women, and so forth. The passage to "consanguinity" (or more accurately the passage to its Northern Tairora analogue) is less rapid, though probably no less certain, unless coresidence and the other prescriptions are interrupted. Iroquois-type kinship terms are scarcely a profound basis for this passage—though certainly no impediment to it. It is the deeper reasons for a belief in the "consanguinity" of coresidents with which I shall be concerned in the following chapter.

I can shed no special, uniquely local light on why the preferred idiom of personnel unity in Northern Tairora culture is a genealogical one. As an example of a nigh universal phenomenon, the Northern Tairora use of a kinship model presumably involves much the same major reasons as are recognized or premised elsewhere. Under local conditions the assertion of genealogical claims could perhaps be thought unpromising. Certainly the rapid making and unmaking of kinsmen and descent-group members, and the contingent character of kin relations, defy the more stable view of "kinship" conventional among us. The generational continuity of a kinship of bone or blood, penis, semen, or womb is scarcely compatible with the terminability of those Northern Tairora alignments that are overtly predicated on a kinship model. The Northern Tairora use of the model in the face of such generational discontinuities as mark their society argues for the power or appeal of the model. It also raises the question of the actual way in which the Northern Tairora figure brotherhood, parentage, and descent—the ultimate images and premises of their kinship. With that question we shall now deal.

7. The Dogma of Descent: The Fraternal Bond

"They have eaten our food so they understand us."
—Aukwa of Batainabura

The social processes by which Northern Tairora personnels are formed, dissolved, and reformed are described in the previous chapter. In the Northern Tairora view of personnels the members are fraternally linked. Their fraternity is partly defined by a common, largely masculine connection to the same ancestors. Implicit in this view are certain beliefs about the nature of the linkage between successive generations. I shall term these the Northern Tairora dogma of descent.

Even a limited sample of the histories of Northern Tairora local personnels shows a record of the recurrent fission of avowed kinsmen and descendants in common. In small numbers or larger blocs, they are repeatedly transformed into ever more distant kinsmen, not infrequently into nonkin and even enemies. Put more positively, the record shows the regular transformation of kinsmen into other people's kin. This is accompanied by a fairly prompt, supporting shift of claimed ancestry in common. History and the use of genealogy, in a word, appear to challenge or contradict descent in its simplest, most familiar sense.

Contradiction, like the dogma itself, is a matter for demonstration. Despite the patent discontinuity of local personnels, images of social continuity are used by the Northern Tairora. This is not in itself remarkable, for continuity in some terms is no doubt predicated in every human ideology. The ethnographic question is: in what terms is continuity predicated and in the face of what circumstances?

The Northern Tairora ideology of fraternity, kinship and social grouping may be well suited to their circumstances. Whether it is, however, is not for *a priori* judgment but for discovery. We are interested in seeing "how good" is the Northern Tairora ideology and in recognizing what constitutes its goodness or shortcomings. Is it the degree of fit between what is said and what is done? The use of suggestiveness where explicitness is not needed? Diffuse metaphor where precision must always be contradicted, either by the direct opposition of social fact or by society's refusal to follow any invariable or easily summarized path? Is genealogical metaphor and a familistic idiom serviceable where a sociologistic or associational one could not evoke sufficient sentiment or effective loyalties?

The ethnographic task turns first on this: if in speaking of their personnels the Northern Tairora continually assert "descent in common" or "kinship," what does "descent" or "kinship" mean to them? Here is the purely logical or semantic question. The question of performance ensues, namely, what prediction or presumption of behavior, what choices or decisions does their assertion permit or imply; and how close a match is there between implication and fact? These are two of the questions on which the present chapter will focus in describing the Northern Tairora dogma of kinship and common descent as it applies to local personnels.

There is still a third question. Call the first one for convenience the *semantic* question: what is it, really, that they say? The second question, performance, raises the issue of statistical verification, so to speak: how well do they do what they say they do? This issue has a presumed bearing on the credibility of assertions and ideals, which leads us to the third question, *efficacy*. How appropriate and hence how successful is the Northern Tairora ideology and its underlying dogma in accomplishing what ideology is presumably intended to accomplish? It should provide a basis for common sentiments and loyalties among those who need such unity for certain ends. It should do so to the extent of their need for it. In other words, how much can they believe what they say; and how does believing help them do what they do?

Concerning the relation between a dogma of genealogical continuity and the actual performance of those claiming it, two opposite views are possible. In one view, already noted, there is obvious slippage; in fact, there is contradiction. A set of prescriptions about solidary personnels has their members descendants in common of the same ancestors, hence brothers, hence destined to behave fraternally, and so forth. Such prescriptions, to say the least, seem imperfectly adhered to, for groups are again and again joined by people whose previous claims of ancestry are distinct from their own. This observation presupposes, however, that "descent in common of the same ancestors" implies an intergenerational continuity between any given person and the stated ancestors comparable to, analogous with, or based on a continuity of procreators and progeny. Let us style this first view the premise of *biology*.

In the second view, the slippage between Northern Tairora descent dogma and the performance of personnels may not be what it seems. The intergenerational linkage may not be restricted to physical progenitors in a literal somatic progression. As a corollary, the critical linking information transmitted from one generation to the next is not confined to physical progeny. Whatever the information, whatever the means of intergenerational transmission, it does not demand a strict continuity as of seed or somatic substance, spirit or inherited style. Its linkage is not solely that of a series of particular begetters and their own begotten. Nor is there between the begotten and some influence or agency, perhaps external to the begetters, a linkage that is nevertheless uniquely and infallibly identified with the begetters in their procreative capacity. We may tag this the premise of environment or *nurture*.

Intergenerational linkage is thus the essential issue of Northern Tairora descent dogma. In no culture, probably, is intergenerational linkage wholly a question of procreation; and only in some cultures is procreation the primary issue. Nor is the linkage inevitably one of a prenatal transmission of information, nor yet one of information that is encoded in a substantial form, such as blood, bone, flesh, semen, or genes. To be sure, if information distinctive of his progenitor(s) is transmitted to an individual as a part of his procreation, there is little question that this links one generation and the next. The question is: how significant is this distinctive (procreative) inheritance as a part of the whole individual? The prenatal transmission of key information need not imply that the progenitor is the transmitter nor that the information is in his likeness. It simply allows the possibility—the strong possibility, no doubt—that such may be the case. The extent to which the inherent distinctness of an individual is encoded in a substantial or somatic form, again, by itself does not imply that it be in an ancestral likeness; but if some body substance is received from a progenitor (prenatally, procreationally), that makes an indelible tie, whether or not a distinctive one, whether or not one of great significance, and whether or not in the likeness of the progenitor.

Images of descent, ancestry, and parentage—hence, of siblingship—are not inevitably biological or procreational in emphasis. They do not necessarily emphasize prenatal influences. They may, for example, emphasize the nurturant role of parents, or the disciplinary one. Conceivably they may stress the industry or domesticity of the parental provider, the strength of the protector or guardian, the tutorial role, perhaps, or the sanctity of the individual of superior wisdom, the renown, or the greater rapport of a senior or parent with the power of the world. The notion of intergenerational continuity can be seen as some form of transmission involving the growth, education, or rearing of offspring by parents, or the continuity of a tradition from generation to generation. Here the parental or ancestral stamp would consist in the excellence, knowledge, strength, or gift of life that was passed on by previous generations to the offspring. In fine, various images could conceivably underlie a dogma of intergenerational linkage, procreation in any sense being only one, and not in all cultures the most significant one. Who is linked to whom could vary, depending on what is transmitted—what aspect of the role or roles of forebears is emphasized in the imagery of descent. According to this emphasis, the degree of consistency or fit between dogma and practice might be great or small, not simply as practice varies but as dogma, too, varies.

Turning from general and preliminary considerations to the empirical question of Northern Tairora dogma, we might ask, first, what assertions spokesmen actually make concerning their named personnels. The following are among the more common claims in which the dogma of descent is invoked:

"We [members of Personnel X] are all brothers."
"We had the same fathers/grandfathers/forebears."
"Our common [male] forebears were brothers."
"We came from the same place (hence are brothers)."
"We are descended from [male] forebears who lived together and were brothers, and such thus are we."
"We are all from this [present] place (hence are brothers)."
"Our name is the name of the place we (or our forebears) came from (hence the fraternal name of this group)."

At least one other claim, albeit gestural, deserves mention. In a territory with which one is unfamiliar, one sometimes asks a local person who he is or what is his group. Repeatedly the answer is a mute but eloquent patting of the ground. What is the meaning of this kinesic convention? That the respondent is of this group, or more specifically, of this territory? In the context of other lococentric claims this ground-patting response seems suggestive of a tie between person and not just a place where he is associated with certain other individuals, but possibly between him and the land itself.

To the Northern Tairora, common location, even more so common provenience, affords palpable evidence of a connection between the members of a group. If true of contemporaries, it seems even truer of their forebears. The strong presumption of siblingship in coresident forebears is consistent with the usual inference that men who live together are probably brothers; but beyond that, contrary evidence is more apt to be vague or forgotten concerning forebears than contemporaries. Far more than the former the latter may include immigrants whose outside provenience is undeniable. Oblivion, it is easily argued, erases the discrepancies of the forebears, helping thus to preserve the dogma.

As a description of a central process of society, this recalls the notions of "shallow genealogy" and "genealogical amnesia," sometimes ascribed to Central Highland New Guinea peoples. These concepts imply that these people may manage to assert unambiguous descent by forgetting ambiguities. A willingness to dismiss contrary knowledge aided by the passage of time, this suppression of the awkward would not only make the dogma of descent a gross fiction but possibly a conspiracy. The argument raises the question why a fiction that repeatedly requires *de facto* contradiction should ever arise, trammeling a people who, if they need dogma, would be better off with something credible, even a dogma without descent if descent is absolutely unconformable with practice. Supposing that one could somehow account for this custom within the group itself, moreover, how does one explain the concurrence of out-groups, including enemies, in papering over tattered pedigrees? There is always, of course, the idea of a culture lag, the claim that the players are reading from a tired old script, when in fact the cast, the stage, and the action have changed. Before turning to unsupported speculation, however, it is worth noting that the amnesia argument makes an *a priori* judgment of the local meaning of descent. Is it in fact the fiction implied?

The Northern Tairora connection of territory with lineage, I believe, transcends a purely sociological or residential tie. Behavior appropriate to kinship or common descent, admittedly, tends to characterize coresidents. In the present case, however, the difference is in the behavior and in an intrinsic and positive relation that is assumed to develop between person or personnel and land.

I do not dismiss all other factors of community in favor of these. Nor do I say that without them other factors would be insufficient. Conceivably affinition, convenience, or pragmatism might by themselves suffice for the recruitment and affiliation of foreigners. The ethnographic task is still to explore Northern Tairora ideology, in what may be its redundancy as well as in its lacunae. Thus, if the Northern Tairora have a sense of intergenerational continuity that involves a nurturant tie or one that involves the land, that must be looked into as well.

An array of Northern Tairora ideas concern the intergenerational linkage of persons. It will be well to look especially at parental-filial linkages, as these must surely bear most directly on a dogma of descent, with its lineal or parento-ancestral model. It will be appropriate, therefore, to ask what is the link—the kinds of linkage—between parents, or fathers, and offspring. I will continue to speak of that as the intergenerational link or continuity.

A major Northern Tairora concern is with the health and capabilities of their children, with promoting their growth into adults who will be strong and thus bring strength to the community. The people speak about it constantly, about having children who will grow large and strong, and about the "hard work" it takes and the cautions that must be observed if the hard work is not to be lost. Northern Tairora concern is focused on both physical and magical factors that influence the individual's capacity and mode of response to life, and his consequent contribution to his parents' and the community's welfare. The judgment, vigor, and valor of a man, or a woman's capacity to garden, raise pigs, and bear children are the practical terms in which one holds his own in the life of this society. Coping or succeeding are the proof of competence or strength.

With no gross differences of inherited wealth, or restrictions of access to important resources, knowledge, tools, or skills, competence becomes largely a question of what an individual innately is or what he can be brought to become. Where certain kinds of competence are matters of group as well as individual survival, and where individuals are regularly pitted against the rival competence of outside and hostile groups in a high-stakes competition, there is little cause for surprise that the concern with instilling competence is intense or that it is communal. Nor is there surprise at a competence in which strength is key. Strength and growth seem highly precarious, requiring prudence and constant nurture. Throughout life, but especially in infancy and childhood, the individual is vulnerable to adverse influences.

The Northern Tairora know—indeed they dwell on the fact—that mature individuals differ greatly in energy and ability and consequently in "name," social influence, or renown. The best are the exemplars of "hard work"; the least suggest neglect or failure. Clearly the people take such differences into account in assessing the prospects of communities as well as those of individuals. A strong man, even one who may be characterized as "bad," may be a community asset; and the attempt to produce a generation of men who are strong is conscious and purposeful. Indeed, it makes heavy demands on communal energies—again the theme of "hard work." Individual and communal success and the recounting of successes are perennially absorbing, a recitation in which the retiring can identify with the most forceful and prestigious, since to a degree each is the product of all. "Materialism," loosely attributed to many New Guinea peoples, perhaps finds here one of its principal expressions in the lives of the Northern Tairora, because gardens, pigs, productive wives, numerous children, and deeds bespeaking competence and power are the material evidence of the capability and mastery that are at such cost instilled into growing humans.

How does the concern with an individual's capability and mastery, his strength, have a bearing on Northern Tairora notions of descent? The Northern Tairora frequently speak as if people distinctively are, know, or do according to what their particular kinsmen and forebears instill in them. Depending on the sense in which they mean it, the formation of the individual may thus, as an inheritance, have a bearing on the Northern Tairora theory of descent.

We are speaking of a culture in which the membership and participation of males is emphasized, in which their masculinity is an undeniable preoccupation of the community at large—indeed, one of its major resources—and one where the community itself is in some sense patrilineally organized. In Northern Tairora culture semen is considered a kind of body stuff for the making of the human individual. There is thus the possibility previously noted that this body stuff is seen as a basic connection in the individual's kinship or his descent. Logically, such a connection would imply that the particular semen or body stuff that goes into a given individual is peculiar to *his* parentage or ancestry, that it is distinct as to some attributes of temperament, physique, spirit, or other inheritance from the semen or body stuff of any individual of other parentage or lineage. Procreative facts might in this case be of some moment in the individuation of the Northern Tairora, hence in the dogma of descent. On the other hand, even as a paternal substance, the significance of semen might be quite general. It may be confined, for instance, to emphasizing paternity, the essential patrilaterality of begetting. Hence, as far as descent is concerned, the meaning of semen may be used to rationalize the maleness of linkages or the potential maleness of male infants.

If semen is seen as symbolizing a distinctive and unbreakable tie between an individual and his male progenitor, as a fact endowing him socially, perhaps, with rights and duties that are his only in virtue of his particular, biological paternity, giving him a social as well as a physical identity which would be different had he a different progenitor, if the paternal substance is considered as central as this to the inheritance of a person, the further implications might well serve logically to found and to organize, in the most full-blooded, "consanguineal" terms indeed, the genealogical figures used in styling society and in rationalizing descent-based personnels.

The warrant for any of the foregoing conclusions, however, must be found in the local notion of "semen," or, if it exists, in the notion of some other recognized paternal substance. And that notion must be understood in conjunction and on balance with any other elements which, in the local view, enter into, or influence, the formation of human beings. Once Northern Tairora views of the formation of the individual, including procreation, are understood, they may throw further light on indigenous ideas of descent. What, then, are the views of the Northern Tairora concerning the procreation and formation of human beings?

The major elements, or, in our present terms, the major kinds of information, that appear to form and influence the maturing individual, as the Northern Tairora view the process, consist of (1) progenitor's semen, (2) blood of the progenetrix, (3) woman's milk, (4) various foods, (5) waters, (6) beneficial (positive) magical power, such as the growth-promoting ritual, (7) detrimental (negative) magic, such as sorcery of various kinds, (8) intervention of supernaturals (ghosts, *wera*, etc.), and (9) child-rearing practices, or—in terms nearer to Northern Tairora thinking, precept and example—education.

The foregoing list appears to exhaust the main categories of substance or influence that make, promote, and inform the development of the human being. Some of this information may inform all individuals uniformly—that is, constituting them humans—while other parts of the information inform individuals distinctively. Among the latter, some information is distributed according to class or category (attributes shared with some but not other persons), such as male or female; or categories of ancestry or descent; place of birth; residence; and so forth. And some of the information, finally, is distributed idiosyncratically—attributes unique to particular individuals.

In the case of uniformly distributed information, differences of parentage or ancestry logically do not matter. In the case of those kinds of information that make individuals distinctive, they may follow from parentage or ancestry, or they may spring from some other source. If such information follows from parentage, it may follow from the progenitor, from the progenetrix, or from some combination of both. Or the inheritance may be proportioned as between progenitor and progenetrix, some following from the male, some from the female, and so forth.

PRENATAL INFLUENCES

Of the types of information recognized by the Northern Tairora as critical in the formation of the individual, semen and blood, along with precautionary and positive pregnancy magic, reach the individual prenatally. Hence the information contained in semen or in blood must include any distinctive inheritance received by an individual uniquely from his progenitors. Such lineal or ancestral information as is tied to the procreative process must likewise reach the individual by paternal semen or maternal blood. While the impregnation of women by totemic spirits illustrates a different possibility, as in Australia, I found no clear evidence of this process in Northern Tairora.

The remaining several elements of the list need not be tied to procreation. They can enter into the formation of the individual postnatally. Moreover, they are not intrinsically dependent on a progenitor as the source or agency of transmission, as might conceivably be the case if society insisted, for example, that only a known progenitor might administer magic or instruction to his progeny.

Semen is listed first above because it is first in the process of making a human being as well as an element receiving considerable emphasis in Northern Tairora imagery. The major point for present consideration is whether in North Tairora theory the semen of one progenitor is different from that of another; and if it is always or sometimes different, whether any such differences depend on or coincide with the descent of the progenitor.

To a Northern Tairora, so far as I can judge, semen is a uniform substance. There is no explicit belief that might be comparable to the notion of genes or chromosomes. There is likewise apparently no idea of procreation according to which each progenitor, though different as an individual, must differ as a progenitor, and his progeny therefore differ as progeny, in some way that could reflect descent. Even idiosyncratic differences, distributed randomly as to descent, would be of interest in this regard; but while there seems to be a tacit acceptance that no two individuals are alike, the idea remains undeveloped that the differences among progeny are a precise or primary consequence in some sense resembling a biological inheritance.

The Northern Tairora do not view semen, in other words, as a variable composite of elements. As a simple stuff, it lends itself poorly to a belief that traces differentiation among offspring to a paternal source. Semen seems to resemble food as a material essential to making humans—necessary, that is, to form and build bodies. But there the resemblance ends. Once built and grown to maturity, through various forces, both favorable and unfavorable, the bodies will naturally display different degrees of vigor and capacity. Here the distinction between food and semen arises, for the Northern

Tairora seem to attribute differences in individual temperament not to semen but to feeding or other postnatal causes. Food, at least, is a category of
numerous and various components, differing appreciably from area to area.
It is thus quite plausible that the Northern Tairora view food as a source of
differentiation among peoples.

That semen is not a vehicle for carrying individual information to individual progeny, and that it does not vary in any way that consistently reflects
the variability of individual progenitors, is probably not remarkable, even in
a culture in which considerable emphasis is given to the procreative (and
indeed the magical) role of semen. I can cite no comparative statistics but
doubt that Northern Tairora culture is either unique or unusual in failing to
make such a procreative assignment of this body fluid. Nor is there here, any
obvious contradiction in the general importance assigned by Northern
Tairora to semen. As a key stuff in the creation of a human being, semen
contributes, obviously, to Northern Tairora views regarding males as the primary if not unique progenitors of their offspring, while the female procreative role is stereotyped as secondary, even ambivalent, above all in connection with male offspring. As a key substance and symbol of masculinity,
semen can despite that be undifferentiated or only vaguely differentiated
from male to male. The very crucial masculinity and potency of this substance is seen, incidentally, in the danger to the male of exuvial sorcery practiced on his semen. Of all exuviae, the most dangerous to a man to let fall
into hostile hands is semen. Though not taken lightly, other exuviae such as
hair, fingernail parings, food leavings, bits of clothing, and especially feces
are dangerous to men and women alike, but for a man the risk of their hostile
manipulation ranks well below that of semen.

Perhaps, if asked, a Northern Tairora might agree that the semen of a
strong man is "strong" compared with the semen of other men. Any such
admission, I suspect, would reflect no well-developed conviction about the
variability of semen but only the *ad hoc* disposition to consider a strong man
strong in a variety of ways. A strong man's semen is not as such exempt from
the risk of exuvial sorcery, for example, but his great strength as a man may
place *him* beyond the sorcerer's reach in instances where that would be
lethal to an ordinary man. That is rather a question of his *máraqúra* (see
chapter 8), his spirit or power. An informant would probably make no generic claim that the semen of strong men endows his children with the same
qualities as his own. No surprise was ever evinced, for example, that the
children of the strong man, Mátoto, were not potential Mátotos.

What of other qualities of semen more specific than its basic value as body-
building stuff? What qualities might vary as between the progenitors of different descent categories? There is nothing specific, as far as I know, in
Northern Tairora thought. I never heard the prominence of a group, or some
particular capacity or skill of theirs—though these are attributes in which
groups are assumed to vary—directly attributed to the seed of their fathers.
It is fairly commonplace in Northern Tairora rhetoric to refer to the fathers

or forebears of a given personnel in their capacity as progenitors. The mention of semen in such pronouncements, however, is a quite generalized figure, not a suggestion that the semen—as distinct from the visible prowess and example of the fathers themselves—was instrumental in making proud, exemplary heirs. In my opinion it would be disproportionate with the Northern Tairora view of individuality to find any large part of it contained in a mere fluid, semen or not. For what a person is is to them his style and his capacity, epitomized as the case may be in such terms as strength or heat and cold. And style is taught or learned through the direct influence of one's mentors and their magic.

The sense of intergroup differences appears to be deeply intrinsic, practically indelible, as it were; but the root of such differences seems closer to magic or to an ethnic mystique, a tradition, than to a substantive, somatic—in a word, racial—distinctness. In the Northern Tairora scale of things, I expect, the latter would seem shallow or trivial by contrast to the more valid and prideful roots implicit in their theory of group character. It is the experience of every Northern Tairora that every personnel has its nearly anonymous members, men of no renown in their own time, "rubbish men" soon to be forgotten afterwards. One is told sometimes, perhaps as a whispered denigration, that so-and-so "has no name." This means that he will not be remembered—his name will die with him. It does not mean that his father or progenitor also lacked name, nor does it necessarily imply that any son of his must be obscure. In part the lack of name may be the very fact that the man has no sons; but he is obscure in any case because his energies and ability are not sufficient in any prestigious activity to command respect. In addition to the "rubbish man," personnels all have their prominent members. There are, moreover, outstanding local groups as well as those that seem almost to shun prominence, to be withdrawn. Some descent-based personnels in the past are said to have been eliminated to the last (probably the last *male*) member—the ultimate obscurity! With semen an established synecdoche, it seems telling that it does not figure prominently in explanations of the strength or weakness, success or failure of either individuals or personnels.

Blood of the progenetrix is accepted as an inevitable component of procreation but, especially in male children, is regarded with ambivalence by the Northern Tairora. Maternal blood is considered deleterious, inhibiting to growth and masculine potential, once a youth approaches or reaches puberty. This ambivalance, to be sure, is a generic characteristic of female or maternal blood, not a trait in which the blood of one progenetrix differs from that of another. One of the main purposes of the male initiation rites—as well as of successive male rites—is in fact to rid the body of maternal blood and reduce or eliminate its influence. As an inheritance, thus, maternal blood would seem to be not merely unwanted—though a transitional necessity—it is also subject to deliberate mitigation, since it admits of ritual and magical intervention to minimize or nullify its influence.

As a substance intrinsic to procreation, to be sure, maternal blood compares with semen in the making of a Northern Tairora child. It is inevitable and at least in that sense essential. But the indigenous view of semen is not ambivalent: there is no belief in the need for a subsequent ritual muting of its influence on the individual. The very idea might seem outrageous. Such an attribute scarcely makes maternal blood an appropriate basis on which to substantiate, as it were, the linkages of descent. Like semen, moreover, maternal blood is a simple substance, undifferentiated from one protogenetrix to another. It carries *human* information, so to speak, not an explicitly individual inheritance. In Northern Tairora society, furthermore, the progenetrix is an outsider to the sib or descent group to which her progeny will usually be assigned. As a powerful physical link to her, thus, maternal blood would tend to negate the main descent emphasis of Northern Tairora personnels.

Notwithstanding the ambiguity of the maternal procreactive role, ancestresses are sometimes recognized in Northern Tairora genealogies. It is possible in the present context to dismiss this fact as anomalous or perhaps as mythical rather than bearing on the historical sense of genealogy. It may be worthwhile, however, to consider what bearing the acceptance of ancestresses, taken literally, might have on the immediate argument. If female

First lesson in archery from his mother. The bow is the right size for a small boy, but the arrow seems to have been borrowed from an adult.

(*Above*) String figures (''cat's cradles'') with partner on call. Some figures call for two pairs of hands. The third party has not yet acquired the necessary skills. (*Below*) Young girls wearing the bare thighs of all females until marriage. The right leg, left foot, and one hand reveal the presence of a smaller sibling astride the back of the girl on right.

links are possible in a Northern Tairora descent chain, a logical inference is
that the procreative role of the male cannot therefore be an invariable precondition of descent. Otherwise female links would not be valid, no matter
how infrequent. It might equally be argued that because of the occurrence of
ancestresses, the maternal role cannot be an invariable disqualification to
intergenerational linkage or descent.

Together, these two propositions suggest that the sense of procreation in
Northern Tairora descent dogma is a rather general one. This, indeed, is the
gist of my argument: in Northern Tairora dogma neither semen nor maternal
blood—nor indeed any other prenatal influence or information—is primary
or exclusive, a specific validation or a specific disqualification, respectively,
in the linkage of generations. The positive meaning of semen surely legitim-
izes a normally and predominantly patrilateral emphasis in descent, which
the negative meaning of maternal blood (for males, at least) confirms. But
the heart of the descent metaphor, so to speak, is prior to the issue of laterality and is more general. It is, namely, a *parental* metaphor—one that is
also paternal in emphasis. However, the physical components of procreation
symbolically serve to resolve the issue of laterality, placing the emphasis on
fathers or progenitors, rather than constituting an essential and specific part
or precondition of the descent of particular personnels. In this interpretation, then, the sense of intergenerational linkage is only generally related to
the physical fact of semen or, even if ambivalently, maternal blood. It is related in the sense that the intergenerational link is in the first place one between parent and offspring, and semen is (like maternal blood and several of
the other kinds of information previously listed) a part of the information
parents normally transmit to offspring—indeed, a part which, in contrast at
least to maternal blood, is wholly positive and unbeclouded with ambiguity.
That these two components of intergenerational information so obviously differ in value should alert us to inquire about the relative standing of the remaining components. We may also find that some are more specific than
semen or blood in transmitting to progeny information of particular personnels.

The acknowledgement of occasional ancestresses appears to mean that semen, however essential to the begetting of every individual, carries no specific linkage considered essential or sufficient in the Northern Tairora dogma
of grouping according to descent. Then the salience of semen argues mainly
for the salience of paternity as compared with maternity. It asserts that the
strength and vigor of a human being is intrinsic in the procreative contribution of the male, while the female contribution, intrinsic in maternal blood,
is in some respects the opposite. The salience of semen does not assert a
linkage of children through their father to the single sib of a line of fathers
indefinitely, physically continued in the substance with which he made
them. It rather asserts that, as their father, he made them (with his semen
among other things, as will presently become clear). From this it may follow

that children are linked to the personnels of those, normally including their fathers, who made them.

To give exclusive emphasis to the symbolism of maternal blood and its ritual eradication (in the initiation rites of both sexes) hardly projects the full Northern Tairora view of the female and maternal role. Ritually, as well as in more quotidian ways, the female role in bearing children is strongly and positively recognized. When the young male initiates are returned from their drubbing and bloodletting at the water to be installed in the men's house, for instance, the women of the group demonstrate maternal concern by arming themselves with sticks with which to attack the men. This is to warn them against a too severe treatment of the boys. Subsequently the women dance and mill around the men's house, shouting and making noise. At Batainabura they ritually simulate impregnation by lifting or removing their skirts for female partners, holding penises of banana sprouts or sticks to "copulate" with them. In theory, the men inside the men's house may not know this and do not see it; but in fact some watch through cracks, so that it is for them not hearsay. They regard the performance as proper and good, a wholly acceptable statement by the women, as mothers, of their pride in the ritual advancement of the children they have borne.

Nor can one overlook the salient role of the mother's brother in Northern Tairora society. As in many others in this part of the world, he and his sons play an active, often lifelong part in the lives of his sister's children.

It would require a substantial digression at this point to deal more fully with the ambivalence of Northern Tairora culture concerning the female role. One would need to explore such matters, for instance, as the theft of the sacred instruments, now the secret property of men, from a mythic female, their original and once exclusive owner; or the moon with his "cold" and feminine qualities (obviously a complement to those of the very masculine sun), but who is nevertheless said to be a "male" because he penetrates women, causing menstruation. In less formal ways, it seems to this observer, there is a substantial gap between the public theory and the private practice, so to speak of Northern Tairora womanhood. Northern Tairora women appear to be more forceful and less subdued than the women of some neighboring peoples with whom they share much the same basic theory of manhood and womanhood. Indeed, some Batainabura observers make a similar observation of the women of Phratry Tairora in comparing them to their own daughters and sisters.

Perhaps the best way to put it briefly is that the ritual and symbolic position on womanhood (the "culture" or the dogma) is not in perfect harmony with the behavioral position or performance ("society"). One may further point out that there is at least a logical parallel here with the immediate problems of the present chapter, the dogma of descent and fraternal solidarity compared with the historical performance of Northern Tairora personnels. Nor does dogma alone in either case possess a monolithic self-consistency, though internal ambivalence seems more marked regarding femaleness than it does with respect to descent. Unless one is prepared to believe that ambivalence amounts to a noncommital or perfect neutrality, it seems necessary to take dogma as a structure of premises and qualifications, without total or perfect resolution but with tendency, strain, or leaning that can nevertheless be read. To shift to more abstract terms, neither "culture" nor "society" has the stillness of death. Both display the fact of life and process and hence of contradiction or dialectic. One is not describing a lifeless perfection in the dogma of sexuality and inheritance, then, but reading an ever-changing imperfection.

The tainted blood of Northern Tairora women is something like the Stain of Eve. It must be lived with—and ritually treated in each generation; and of course it colors the view of woman. That it does not color the view totally and unequivocally, while relevant to the present discussion, is not contradictory to the view of inheritance and descent that is under consideration.

NURSING

In the context of descent and inheritance, the significance of woman's milk appears considerably more positive, to say the least, then that of maternal blood. The Northern Tairora—more than we, of course, with formula and bottle feeding—consider woman's milk an indispensable substance in the making of a human being. It is food and almost the only fit food for growth for at least the first two years of life. There is some supplementary feeding of premasticated solid foods such as sweet potatoes; but no one supposes that this could take the place of milk. Indeed, Northern Tairora nursing may continue for longer than bottle feeding among us.

So far is milk from being a specific inheritance from the uterine parent to her child, however, that the child can be nursed by other women. Even when a child is still in the keeping of its own mother and she is healthy and has ample milk for it, other women may sometimes give it the breast. Being nursed establishes a bond between the infant and the given woman, a secondary bond if she is not the principal nurse or the only one, but a primary bond if she is.

Adoption is instructive. An ideal is for an adoptive mother, recently bereaved of her own infant, to receive a nursing child whom she is herself capable of nursing. Something is made, especially with adopted children, of the nursing bond, sometimes even to the point of feigning such a bond. The significance of nursing is exactly opposite to the linkage of offspring with progenetrix or progenitor. Like other forms of nurture, nursing can either reinforce or qualify that linkage. Through a woman's milk the adopted nursling may be linked to the household of the husband—progenitor or not—whose wife suckles him. The nurse is, in other words, *his wife*. Her milk, hence, links the child to him, to his descent group.

The nursing relationship, clearly a social linkage through nurture, is in sum, explicitly valued. It is not confined in its linkage to the nursling-nurse dyad, or even to the triad of nursling-nurse-nurse's husband. It is potentially the collective nurturance of "mothers" in a generational sense. The principal responsibility is assignable or discretionary in that it is transferable, as in adoption, to a woman other than progenetrix, other than wife of progenitor. And nursing is effortful, qualifying as an expression of the "hard work" that is thematic in the Northern Tairora stereotype of the parental role.

FOOD AND WATER

The Northern Tairora meanings of food and water make them profoundly a part of the parental legacy and assign them a central significance in intergenerational linkage. Food and water are not only the fruit of the land and the bestowal of the community; no gifts in Northern Tairora culture are more distinctive of a land or people than their food and water. The sense of a topical identity is much clearer with respect to food or water, for example, than with respect to the semen, blood, or milk of group members. Indeed, the distinctiveness is an active property, conferring on those who consume these substances an identity with the land and people wherein they originate.

As may easily be guessed from such claims, the Northern Tairora meanings of food and water are extensive and complex. The Northern Tairora meaning of food, however, is indivisible and unanalyzed—not surprisingly in a culture given far more to implication than explication. While the sense of food may therefore be changed in the present telling, there is no choice but to attempt to recognize analytically its several aspects, some of which overlap those of water. Simply for convenience, therefore, let me subdivide the indigenous meanings of food (and to a degree those of water) into three aspects: the local distinctiveness of food and water; their place as product and gift; and their role as indigenizing substances.

The foodstuffs and the water of a particular phratric territory are probably always considered by the Northern Tairora in some degree or detail locally unique. Though their actual distinctiveness may sometimes seem fairly minor to the outsider, especially as between adjacent territories with similar horticultural traditions, possible differences in food include greater emphasis on growing yams or *Pueraria;* or the use of more numerous varieties of a crop; or, here and there, the planting of a variety uncommon or unplanted in other territories. In some cases, a group claims its territory as the "home" of a certain crop. Batainabura people make such a claim with respect to winged beans. Accordingly, they explain, other peoples of the surrounding area consider them the preferred source of bean seed, making this an item of exchange. A few territories appear to possess some quite distinctive variety of a cultigen, perhaps because of being at the limit of its present distribution. Such a territory may come to be known for this crop, especially if the crop reputedly will not grow elsewhere or if scions are thought best obtained from the original source. Once established, such a tradition, like the bean seed of

Batainabura, can outlast the circumstances that gave rise to it, leaving as a residuum the notion that the local seed or settings have special virtue.

Given the range of crops and the numerous recognized varieties of many of the main crops of this area, it is almost inconceivable that there will not be something distinctive about the garden foodstuffs of a territory, not to mention the wild food sources. Any such variation thus provides objective support for the belief in the distinctiveness of different territories. It would be hard to imagine, moreover, that local differences of food production go often unnoticed by such avid gardeners as the Northern Tairora. And a belief in the distinctness of the personnel who sustain themselves with a distinct array of foodstuffs is a logical inference, given that personnels also differ.

The soils in which crops grow are almost invariably ascribed local virtues or limitations. Dwellers of the grassland regularly explain that there are differences between themselves and those of the bush, with different foodstuffs—not just crops proper to each. Indeed, some foods acceptable to bush-dwelling Northern Tairora, such as python meat, are disgusting or frightening to at least some Northern Tairora *kunai* dwellers. But even bush foods that are acceptable to the latter such as bush fowl eggs, may be an infrequent part of their diet. Not merely between grassland and forest soils, however, but even between nearby soils covered in virtually the same vegetation the Northern Tairora profess to recognize significant differences. Some soil has much "grease," other soil little or none; hence the virtues of even the same plants are seen to vary accordingly.

In a similar context, the springs and streams of different territories are recognized as different. Water from one source may be considered superior to that of another, even within the same territory. The human palate is undoubtedly capable of fine enough discriminations in the taste of water to give credence to this belief, and the different color of waters from different streams is often also quite discernible. Such differences are not taken simply as matters of taste. Nor is the point limited to one of clean versus contaminated sources of water for drinking.

For people of Batainabura, and, so they claim, for other local groups of their vicinity, the water of a large pool in the lower part of their territory is so efficacious for the growth of pigs that friendly groups come from afar to fill bamboo tubes, with the permission of the local owners, administering the water like a tonic to their animals. In the bush above the settlement there is a spring, too distant for daily use, whose water is considered especially potable and salubrious for humans. Visiting that vicinity to collect other bush materials, parties of villagers, despite heavy burdens of posts and lianas, regularly return also carrying bamboo tubes of this virtuous "forest water." It is often shared as a favor with friends and kinsmen.

Not every territory can be as well supplied with distinctive waters as Batainabura, perhaps, but few, probably, are without special claims of some kind. A local stream, even one not used for drinking, may have value simply to stand and wash in at the end of a long journey. It cleanses the legs and feet of any contact they may have had with hostile magic—the contamination of alien pathways or sorcerers' traps. The property of neutralizing or cooling the potency or "heat" of magic is generic to water, and even rain is effective. Home waters may be especially good, however, suggesting that the distinctive products of the land are not merely favorable to the indigenes but antithetical to influences harmful and alien to them. Of this more presently.

Food, and, in some of the same senses, water as well, are products of both a territory and a community. Indigenous products not merely from the standpoint of their source or creation, however, they contain properties of the territory and the community. Food as a class is multiply communal. It is produced from land collectively defended, occupied, and identified with the group, for whom the land is also usually named. It is produced by members of the group, albeit with individually managed holdings, in land collectively owned. It is locally distinctive, as previously noted, not precisely resembling the food of any other territory. And the knowledge and skill, including the magical power of a particular producer, enter into the production of the food, surely placing beyond question one sense in which food contains the properties of its producers.

As a product of the land and of the community, food is certainly the most deeply indigenous class of objects available to the Northern Tairora to use or allocate in a discretionary way, above all to present to others. The fact of feeding others is a common, perhaps an invariable source of comment; and the feeding of children by parents is certainly no exception. Furnished to children, food is not merely symbolic of the concern of parents for their nurture but is Gift in the Maussian sense (Mauss 1967, orig. 1924). More than the hand of the giver is in this gift, morover, for the giver's hand is also the producer's—and the very land has much of him in it, as he has of it.

As furnished by one generation to the next, or as given to the guest, food in Northern Tairora society shares the universal power of such prestations among men; and the prevalence and explicitness of its meaning in local ritual must also be a match for these themes elsewhere. There is scarcely any Northern Tairora ceremony not accompanied by feasting, and in nearly all the commensal act is itself central to the rites. Food is accordingly a gift of singular significance in Northern Tairora culture, its bestowal in any given case gaining from the importance of the various circumstances in which it is bestowed.

Turning from these fairly well recognized connotations of food, we may look at it from the point of view of its effects. As many ethnographers have pointed out and Sahlins has expanded (1972:215-19), food is a special type of good, its utility directly defined—and by the shortest of all cycles—by its necessity for life itself. That food is instrumental in the promotion of growth in the young, obvious to all men, is amplified in the salient and explicit emphasis of Northern Tairora religion and by the "hard work" stereotype of the parents' role in feeding and promoting the growth of their children.

In Northern Tairora culture the hand and the land, joined in meaning to the substance of food, make it not only indigenous to a particular local source but, as substance, indigenizing to the recipient or consumer. A statement of Aukwa of Batainabura provides an epigraph for this chapter. It is to the effect that those who eat our food will understand us. Aukwa is employing no metaphor of his own here, but is being quite literal in evoking what amounts to a metaphor of Northern Tairora culture. He is referring to the linkage of food with land and with the producer's hand in which as substance the food conveys to the user a terrigenic identity of a highly local and specific sort. The principle underlying this linkage is magical.

Implicit in the linkage of the hand, the land, and the consumer of food is the principle of *pars pro toto*. In the present context, specifically, a given land and its inhabitants are held to contain or express power in various forms and degrees, some of them locally distinctive. The individual denizen, including human denizens, derives his growth and strength from certain aspects of the power that are beneficial; but in some of its forms or expressions local power is potentially harmful as well. Demons such as *wera* are a common example of dangerous local power. Such forms are least harmful, or in some cases actually harmless, however, to those who have derived their own power and gained their strength from the same land and from the hand of the same local group, who themselves are of this land and who both know and embody some of its power. The power is transferable, in other words, as an influence on human beings—and possibly on other creatures. Transfer can be effected, in part, through some of the forms of life, including crops, game, wild plants, and water, that may be taken physically into the body. Such influences will naturally affect most intensely those who regularly are exposed to these forms of power, for example, in foodstuffs and water. By extension, the influences may also reach those who, as guests and visitors, are occasionally exposed to the foodstuffs or the water, along with other local influences.

In the exposure is the indigenizing effect of food and water, reminiscent in some respects of inoculation. In this guise, the indigenized person shares with his fellows both a knowledge of and a relative immunity to some of the places, denizens, or conditions of his own land, whereas exposure to them can endanger the outsider.

The practical effect of indigenization can be illustrated by the familiar folktale of the grassland visitor who dies in a bush territory from ignorantly meddling with a snake. His local host, on the other hand, both knows of the danger (to outsiders) and is, he declares, immune to it himself, because he is native to the same place as the snake. To be sure, the local man has not obtained his knowledge or his immunity to the snake's dangerous power solely from eating the product of the land. No more does the strong man attain his growth and strength solely from the food he eats, nor exclusively from his group's growth-promoting rituals. But in each case the food, or ritual, is an essential and potent factor.

The most explicit applications or proofs of the neutralization principle of

Northern Tairora culture appear to be defensive. They concern instances in which measures are taken to produce a protective rapport between a power source and a person who is endangered by it; or they are episodes of sickness or death that occur because the individual or group lack rapport with the source of the danger. The proliferation of peril and the multiplicity of defensiveness are doubtless an element in Schwartz's view of Melanesians as "paranoid" (Schwartz 1973). Yet rapport by ingestion need not be seen as purely defensive. Aukwa speaks, after all, of understanding; and the indigenization of children is a positive expression of group and territorial rapport, not just a protective one. Positive and negative, to be sure, are the opposite sides of the same rapport; but the positive value of indigenization is no doubt demonstrated more dramatically by instances in which it is lacking. Such instances are sharply defined and poignant, whereas, in a smooth-flowing stream of well-being, unpunctuated by troubles, specific instances of rapport do not tellingly stand out.

Positive or negative, the implicit principle is the same. It is that, with rapport, a source of power can be neutral or favorable which may otherwise be harmful. Thus a man who regrets having injured another can scrape his fingernails or sometimes deliver other exuviae to provide the injured party materia medica with which to counter the injury. In a mixture known as *heba*, from one of its botanical ingredients, these exuviae of the author of the injury, properly ingested, will lessen or nullify the harm, hastening recovery or preventing death.

Forest leaves, festooning the Batainabura polling place in the fearful first parliamentary balloting in Papua New Guinea in 1964, were quickly seized as the voting was completed. They were apportioned among all who had been exposed to the danger of balloting. Required for making *heba*, their efficacy was that, as a part of the voting booth itself, the leaves contained some of the dangerous power or "heat" of this frightening new activity. With suitable preparation, the leaves could be eaten to provide a controlled introduction of the dangerous power and accordingly protect those exposed from sickness or death.

It is doubtful if there is, in the realm of Northern Tairora magic, medicine, or ritual, any more fundamental principle for establishing rapport with a source of power or for countering its danger. The indigenizing effect of eating local food and drinking local water rests, in fine, on a broad cultural base, being in no sense an isolated or *ad hoc* application peculiar to these substances or to this end alone.

In the imagery of intergenerational linkage food and water appear to be a communal heritage from parent to offspring. The provision of food is crucial to the parental stereotype, explicit in the shibboleths of "hard work" and growth, and familiar in the rhetoric of one generation's legacy from, or debt to, its predecessor. Parental nurture in the form of local food and water is unique. It cannot be matched in any other group or territory, and its uniqueness is immediately related to the security and health of the group and territory from which it comes. It is indigenizing. Feeding the young is a major means of imparting to them the power of a group and a land, and thus it constitutes a legacy that is specific, one providing group identity and a profound sense of being in place and at home. In contrast to such other elements in the formation and growth of the individual as semen or blood, food and water thus have a clear, collective, and direct relation to the parochial identification of members of a group. Among the various efforts of their forebears that influence them, in other words, this one places the stamp of a descent-group legacy and in part through the magical power of the land establishes membership in a way particular to a given personnel.

RITUAL AS A COMMUNAL STAMP

Among the influences that control an individual's maturation, rituals constitute a major share. If one includes with positive rituals those whose intent and effect are detrimental, the role of ritual overall may be preponderant. Negative rituals can cause early death; or they can stunt, cripple, or weaken an individual. On the positive side, communal ritual, especially the initiation rites, are considered indispensable for growth. Without them the individual would not reach his full potential manhood or—with less cultural salience and less enterprise—womanhood. In addition to the role assigned them in promoting the growth and strength of community members, rituals are more dramatic by far, and the power they are thought to have is more intensely concentrated than any power to be found in the quotidian business of rearing children.

Sorcery is the ritual form of danger to an individual's health or strength. Three other sources of danger are supernatural intervention, accidents and magical miscalculations, and hostile action—the last two, in fact, not inevitably distinguished, in the Northern Tairora view, from sorcery itself. Sorcery against an individual is private and covert and in principle most often originates with hostile outsiders. In a negative way it is relevant to the linkage of generations, since the community defends its members—especially the young—or avenges them against the perpetrators of sorcery.

We may usefully compare sorcery and other negative effects of magic to rituals intended for positive effect. Whereas sorcery is private, covert, and typically selective in the individual targets it finds (if not always in those to which it is directed), growth and strength-promoting ritual, notably initiation rites and *ihálabu* or *órana*, are communal, public, overt, general in intent, and efficacious for all their intended beneficiaries. Positive rites are uniform in intention and in principle beneficial to nearly all who participate or are subject to their influence. Positive rituals are one component, albeit a major one, of a larger, positive program for promoting growth and strength. The rites and the program, moreover, are continuous, as distinct from the intermittent, *ad hoc*, focused attack of sorcery ritual, limited to a particular time, an immediate target, and usually to alien aggressors.

The community's positive ritual efforts on behalf of its young ideally express parental concern and nurture. Just as with terrigenic influences, the collective emphasis is clear. Both have a communal authority. Both consist of information distinctive of the local group or its territory, as well as information collective and uniform for all the children influenced. The community's claims and its sense of reponsibility for the maturation of its young future members thus appear amply to justify the collective reference commonly used in speaking of the making of the social person. When a Northern Tairora speaks of the fathers and mothers who have made him, it need be in no vague or general sense but to these very contributions that he refers. In effect, the nurturant collectivity is a generationally defined group of parents. This is the same definition we see in the conventional assumption that coresident forebears were all siblings. The generational set of the Northern Tairora kinship system, previously noted, further accommodates this convention with Iroquois terms and a prevalently parento-local residence.

Vital and essential to the self-realization of every individual, community rites must weigh heavily in any comparison between the parental contribution of the community and that of the individual's immediate family and kinsmen. That there is a difference of intimacy and intensity between the community and the family is obvious. A less obvious difference is that, unlike the family, the larger community accepts responsibility and claims credit almost solely for a *beneficial* effect, uniformly advantageous to all of its children. The community is not accountable for variation, least of all for individual failures or misfortunes. When a child is sickly or a youth unpromising, the result is beyond the community's control. They have at least done all they could do. The same allowance is not always made for the family's part.

The source of an individual's damage may not, to be sure, be internal to the group. Sorcery and physical attack by enemies, or the influence of ghosts or demons, are often not internal matters. The strangeness of a microcephalic youth in Noreiqera, a Northern Tairora personnel to the south of Phratry Tairora, is attributed to his being actually the child of a *wera* covertly substituted by its *wera* mother for a human infant. The latter was stolen by the demon while the human mother was busy in her garden. Though more extreme than many, this attack suggests a kind of supernatural intervention that is widely credited and one for which the community—and usually the family—are blameless.

When no outside source is indicated, however, blame is apt to be assigned to some individual with a grudge against parent or child; or else it is ascribed to an unfortunate incident. The parents or immediate kinsmen may themselves sometimes be held to blame for a child's deficiencies or misfortunes, on account of ignorance or negligence. The family has failed the child by not sufficiently cautioning him about some danger, perhaps, or not showing him the correct path to personal security or success. Someone near him may have violated a prohibition that should have been observed on his behalf. Hazards tend to be selective in both source and victim, and risk is individualized. The cause of harm may therefore be close and specific to the victim, and in the case of juveniles, the family is sometimes accordingly held culpable.

That the family is potentially culpable, in some cases thwarting the community's best efforts at positive nurture, does not support an inference that the community is the real parent, the family but the sometimes negligent nurse. That might carry the thread of the present argument past the breaking point. The ease and familiarity of adoption and fosterage and frequently their purely optional character, again do not suggest that adopted children are but the wards of the community. The placement of children with other parents is after all at the discretion of specific parents or close kin. And the bearing or rearing of children is a specific credit—and usually an asset—to specific parents. It seems sufficient, in assessing the balance between immediate parents and the parental collectivity—that is, family and community—to recognize how large and essential and how invariably positive is the role of the latter, and equally important, to recognize how uniform is the community's stamp compared with that of the parents. It is these qualities of the collective nurture that as legacy should be compared with those of the familial role. For the latter, we have now noted the potential transferability of the role, the risks of negligence and error that accompany a family's more quotidian responsibility, together with the parents' rather nonspecific procreative role. A fair assessment must surely be that the community legacy is at least central and constant, whether or not one would claim that the specific family, as distinct from *some* family, is almost arbitrary or incidental. In the range of logical possibilities, however, one could justly say that the Northern Tairora family is more arbitrary and incidental than is the case in numerous other societies.

CHILD-REARING AND THE DOGMA OF DESCENT

The Northern Tairora purport to have means wherewith to assure, even accelerate, maturation; and they profess to employ these means constantly and to their fullest effect on behalf of the entire personnel. Indeed, members of the group, as well as an individual's more immediate kin, often speak as if it were their most urgent responsibility to "grow" him—growth proceeding apace with the effort given to it. In linking strength and character intimately with nurture, Northern Tairora theory points toward the corporate and individual nurturance of successive generations, above all the former, as the essential social pedigree, in effect as the core meaning of inheritance in their dogma of descent.

It becomes clear that postnatal influences, which vary from group to group and place to place, far more than the uniform procreative facts, account in Northern Tairora eyes for the shaping of the individual. The beneficial influences—food, water, ritual, parental instructions—are seen as costly and prolonged. They are deliberate, very powerful in influencing the person, and, as they vary from group to group in their quality, they make each person locally identifiable. The legacy of the community-as-parent, these influences are the principal intergenerational link. These transfer the information that makes the individual one among particular sib mates, a kinsman—child, son, daughter—of a particular local group, not to mention an inhabitant of a particular land. So he speaks as they speak. If they excel in making arrows or net bags, in controlling forest magic, or in burying their dead in caves rather than in trees, in the rocks, or in the ground, or in performing *hampu*, he comes to share in that distinguishing mark of his group.

While not to be included as a part of a collective legacy to the members of a group, the negative component previously noted adds scope and weight to the significance of postnatal influences as distinct from prenatal and procreative ones. Sorcery, supernatural interferences, and the mistakes and miscues of oneself or one's associates not only bring a person misfortune but may produce a lifelong disability. Ghosts may afflict him, confusing his mind. His wife may be barren, or he sickly. An enemy may ensorcel him, perhaps because of some vulnerability his fellows do not have, perhaps unaccountably. His days may be shortened, his hearing impaired, his eyesight dimmer than others', his undertakings meager. This negative component, while defeating the community's intention in making all of its children strong, forceful, and effective, must nevertheless be set down as a part of the postnatal influences that predominantly inform the person—to his benefit or not.

It seems persuasive that the postnatal influences as seen by the Northern Tairora are far more significant than the prenatal ones, including procreation. Nothing of his specific destiny or character indeed, has been imparted to the newborn by his begetting. His strengthening, individuation, and his distinctiveness as a member of a particular sib, local group, and phratry are stamped on him in the course of his subsequent development as a person. What particular, prenatal "stuff that he is made of" could he show? For the most part it would probably only show him potentially human, with eyes and hair, organs, bones, and muscles, and with whatever attributes of temperament constitute the Northern Tairora definition of generic human nature. It is not his race or his blood or the seed of a certain father that is displayed by the hunter or sorcerer, the warrior, yam gardener, or pig breeder, the strong man or the rubbish man, or the speaker of a peculiar dialect; it is the mark of his peculiar education—that is, the mark of his education, in the broad sense, by and in a particular personnel.

While in the Northern Tairora view procreative influences could certainly not be called insignificant, they are merely initial and undifferentiated. They are inaugural in a fundamental but at the same time a narrow sense. The job of making a person is barely begun at his birth. Such a view, it seems inescapable, stamps the Northern Tairora as profoundly nonbiologistic in a Mendelian sense. While this is to put the matter philosophically, as it were, a dogma of descent is equally a "philosophical" matter. How much can such a culture take intergenerational linkage as reflecting foremost the facts of procreation? How much can the linkage be identified in a narrowly substantive sense with body stuff of some kind, such as semen? Can the intergenerational tie be considered primarily that to a particular progenitor because his progeny received from him in particular a body stuff that differs in no explicit way from the body stuff of other progenitors? In fine, it does not appear compatible in such a culture to conceptualize descent as an intergenerational succession of begetting. More compatible is a succession in which each generation makes the next by imparting its competence and art and its local and sacred knowledge and, through the magical power it summons to the task, by literally growing each person each generation to the fullest possible size and capacity.

Perhaps the broadest point to make in the context of the present chapter is that Northern Tairora thought is radically environmentalistic in many of its basic assumptions. In the maturation of the person, physical, literally consanguineal linkages do not loom large. The person becomes what he is made to become; life shapes him, not some destiny assigned him before he was born. The positive, beneficial, and indispensable part of the shaping, moreover, is claimed for the group, a collective responsibility, a collectively authored achievement. Where—if anywhere—one might think to find an emphasis on consanguineal linkage, is in the Northern Tairora theory of procreation. Yet here we find weak claims indeed, hardly suggesting the parochial "consanguinity" of Western custom, thought, and law. Given the need for large and elaborate intervention in assuring the individual's maturation, and given the vagueness and generality of the somatic inheritance from the procreator, it seems inevitable that social identity should be so heavily subject to a situational shaping, one based on nurture and the effects of the social and supernatural milieu.

If a group grows its members, it can also conceivably make members of newly born humans with relatively little regard for their somatic inheritance. Whatever outsiders might consider "blood lines," in the Northern Tairora view the "blood" has little or no color that is not imparted to it by deliberate intent—at the discretion of the inducting personnel. Descent in such a case need be no less genealogical, but it may easily be less consanguineal. Here I take "genealogy" as implying a record of intergenerational linkages and that of an ancestral legacy—a record, that is, of whatever is inherited and whoever is linked across generations by the inheritance. Just as the inheritance could not be seen as genes and chromosomes before the rise of such ideas, neither must it be seen as "blood" or anything akin to physical blood except in cultures where such a concept is found. Nor in Northern Tairora, where a substance we term "semen" is found to be a significant element of the masculine mystique, need it have the differentiating force and significance assigned to semen in some other culture. Inheritance and the linkage of generations in some dogma of descent is not necessarily, in other words, a singular and universal concept. Nor even as a complex concept is it one in which somatic or substantive elements will inevitably outweigh all others.

The time lag in incorporating outsiders into a recruiting group might be taken to show a somatic sense of lineage acting as a brake on full acceptance. The process tends to last a minimum of two or three generations—an interval that is surely not surprising, unless for its brevity. But there are at least two possible interpretations of the time lag in indigenizing an immigrant personnel. Their contrasting premises are of interest. The more familiar interpretation is that it takes a while to extinguish the knowledge of an immigrant group's extraneous origin, tantamount otherwise to a disqualification. This view is implicit, for example, in the familiar concept of "genealogical amnesia," and similar suggestions are to be found in recent ethnographic explorations in the Central Highlands of New Guinea. Extinction or oblivion, which might be called the negative view, places emphasis on the negation of an existing, alien inheritance. Only after a vacuum is created, it presumably follows, can a more convenient (if less valid) claim of local inheritance be confected for the newcomers or their descendents.

A more positive interpretation is that, given the Northern Tairora dogma of descent and their meaning of inheritance, it would take more than a generation or two for membership in a new lineage to be affirmed. If in the first generation both immigrant parents lack an indigenous inheritance, they could only be considered alien. It will not be until the third generation, at the earliest, that children of their sib (hence the sib collectively) can be born of a male parent who has lived all or most of his life in the present group, who has attained his growth through their common efforts, drunk of their water, eaten of their food, and learned their distinctive speech and other practices, all of this in contrast to every other ritual, water, food, and set of distinctive practices.

In the affirmative view, people will recognize or claim the indigenous in those who possess it. It is not that memories of the past must first become dim. The Pore name, for instance, is still current in an Abiera sib, and elsewhere a modern gloss of "Pore" is "Auyana," the present designation of a country, a series of peoples, and a language, all of which are well known but alien to Phratry Tairora. As the name still stands, remembrance of origin could hardly be an issue, but this meaning—or perhaps better the relevance of such a meaning—is denied. Would it be relevant to "remember" that the Pore, taking their name literally, must be considered an immigrant people? That they are, in other words, forever foreign? All living Pore, all of their male parents and many female ones, and perhaps no few of their deceased grandparents have in them only Tairora magic and Tairora "mud," so to speak, or at least as much of these essences by now as any other sib of the phratry. Rather than the gradual extinction of a relevant truth in favor of a more palatable fiction, the second interpretation sees acceptance as a form of naturalization in which one truth replaces—or extinguishes—another.

Neither view is wholly exclusive. The negative view of indigenization as much as the affirmative presupposes that inheritance is terminable and replaceable. The negative view seems to suggest, however, that the replacement is de facto and somewhat bogus by definition. It therefore, begs the question of what sort of inheritance, including a somatic one, is genuine. In the affirmative view the replacement may be as genuine as what it replaces; but while a Northern Tairora inheritance is less indelible than a somatic tie, it is no less legitimate. Nor is it set as swiftly as if by conception.

In Northern Tairora, as may be the case in other parts of the Central Highland of New Guinea, if not farther parts of Melanesia and beyond, descent concerns a social pedigree. It is this sense of genealogy that prevails in the culture, not the somatic sense of blood or consanguinity. This sense of genealogy, much better than a consanguinity of substance, justifies the extensive use of kinship terms and the frequent allusion to ancestry. If he fails to recognize the meaning of inheritance in a culture like Northern Tairora, the ethnographer will be left with the impression of a dogma of lineage between which and social reality there are large and frequent gaps—"gross discrepancies." But if descent is recognized to mean to those asserting it what I have argued here that it means to the Northern Tairora, the "discrepancies" will take on a different value.

In organizing their personnels, the Northern Tairora, like other known societies, make a metaphorical use of parentage and develop its close corollary, lineage: the members have a common parentage or ancestry. The root of the metaphor undeniably lies in human breeding. With the development of such a metaphor by and its use in the midst of a biological community, therefore, there will be an appreciable degree of correspondence between the two, with metaphor and its metaphorized, organic basis always in some approximate harmony. Usually this is harmony enough to make it easy to overlook that a metaphor as metaphor does not precisely match its model either in form or principle. It is selective and additive as far as concerns the original nature on which it is based. The parochial question—that is, the ethnographic question—must therefore be what is selected for emphasis, what is added, and by implication what is omitted. The metaphor in use by the Northern Tairora is expectably peculiar to them, though probably shared in some degree by their ethnic congeners. They stress certain social attributes of parentage, and, by extension, of ancestry, much more than these may be stressed elsewhere; and they stress some of the somatic attributes of the parent-as-particular-progenitor much less. We have epitomized the aspects of parentage most stressed by Northern Tairora as "nurture," those less stressed by them (less than by ourselves) as "nature." We have suggested that, in consequence of these emphases, the Northern Tairora are a profoundly environmentalistic people, as opposed to a biologistic one They are, as it were, Lamarckian, if one means to contrast their premises to the heavily Mendelian bent of Western premises. As one consequence, the roots of racism—or, perhaps better, the soil, since there may be nothing yet to call "roots"—seem shallow in aboriginal Northern Tairora culture.

Our chapter began with a concern to show the sense of "descent" and of "kinship" in Northern Tairora culture and with how Northern Tairora peoples use the dogma in assigning descent to particular personnels as distinct from others. Special problems emerging from the discussion and the data are how a frequent and substantial migration is rationalized in the local terms of descent; and how an apparent attachment to territory is symbolically fitted into genealogical claims. Does Northern Tairora descent dogma have a good fit with the performance of personnels said to be joined in common descent? How does this dogma compare with other conceivable descent dogmas, including any with which other Central Highlands of New Guinea societies may have been identified? How well does an intergenerational continuity of parental nurture and the indigenizing effects of territory and tradition resolve the contradictions apparent between claims for continuity and the actual performance of personnels? Is it possible by these or any other means to assert the continuity of descent and kinship without contradiction in the patent fission of personnels?

Answers to these questions can only be qualified. To assert intergenerational continuity and lineal succession with emphasis on the parental nurture of cultural men, rather than on a somatic succession of animal procreators, appears, as it were, a step in the right direction. The tradition does continue, like the territory, well beyond some of the generations that claim in it their continuity. The torch is passed, the homeland inherited, the communal myths remembered, whether by exclusively agnatic heirs or by the grandchildren of chosen affiliates.

After the fact of immigration, certainly, the Northern Tairora dogma provides a means for doing more than clothing reality in a merely cosmetic sense. It provides an ideological basis for the assimilation of the indigenized descendants of outsiders, and there is neither need nor room for any acknowledgment that outsiders are assimilated. Indeed, no real outsider is, for real outsiders remain what they are: immigrants. It is their children and children's children who, being neither immigrants nor outsiders, can in the fullest sense be native.

While this is to say that the recruitment and affiliation process of Northern Tairora society, specifically in its dogmatic aspects, has a perceptible efficiency, it is not to deny that the retention of kinsmen falls well short of what, in another respect, the dogma tacitly and ideally purports to be the case. In other words, if positive and effective means exist to promote the growth of groups through grafting, decay is nonetheless real and it is neither prevented nor wholly rationalized by existing dogma. In this respect, it is impossible to deny that social fact affronts belief; the departure of kinsmen contradicts the norm of fraternal solidarity.

That kinsmen, having moved out, sooner or later cease to be kinsmen, however, affirms the Northern Tairora dogma of descent. In becoming indigenized to a different land and a distinct set of terrigenous influences, as the dogma surely predicts, they are alienated from their former kinsmen. (It is only that the dogma does not predict alienation). Not those of the first generation but their unborn children will be ritually received, nurtured, initiated, strengthened, and brought to manhood or womanhood by a different community, becoming intimate with its magic, familiar with local supernaturals, native to its soil, and hence a part of its continuity.

Is this saying anything more than the obvious? Recognizing that peoples who separate drift apart is something like recognizing that smoke rises. Where is the local coloration of Northern Tairora dogma in such a recognition? To this skeptical challenge I can only comment that Northern Tairora dogma is differently colored at least from any in which "blood will tell" or in which some comparable assertion is made of somatic indelibility. It is differently colored as well from any dogma that neglects the magical and the terrigenous or assigns them a minor role. An environmentalist dogma, in stressing nurture as a crucial encoding of intergenerational information, may be more accurate—as we now see things—than any dogma of Mendelian stamp; but its local color is not less for that. It is a distinctively Northern Tairora environmentalism, including, for instance, a magic of the land.

Taken at its broadest, Northern Tairora dogma predicates ideological grounds for creating fraternal solidarity and promoting continuity, doing so in the face of a rate and scale of fission that might seem menacing to any dogma of continuity. It coexists with a type of social fission that ideology alone apparently cannot abate, much less banish. The dogma, however, uses terms and metaphors in which continuity is not flatly contradicted, even by the intermittent and substantial disruption of personnels. It can survive claims of fraternity that must often be forsaken. The dogma is thus practical; it passes certain tests. Its grounds are well suited to the real conditions of Northern Tairora life; under those conditions they are credible or irrefutable, as noted, to a degree that could scarcely be matched by any familiar form of somatic continuity.

The grounds of the dogma are also profound. They make central use of meanings and sentiments that common human experience shows to be powerful, all but generic themes in mythmaking. Northern Tairora sense of continuity blends magical, ethnic, and terrigenic elements. The land and the cultural legacy are the continuity—these and not the soma of the people in whom they are carried, the people by whom (for a given time) they are transmitted. A given people are identified not by their physical likeness (physically the Northern Tairora are a fairly diverse population), whether overt or invisible. Foreigners are foreign because of their different lands and cultural legacies, whatever their soma. Ideas of intergroup somatic differences are less denied, perhaps, than undeveloped. Ideas of interpersonal differences of physique or temperament are poorly related, if at all, to shared, collective traits. For that matter, interpersonal differences themselves seem more connected to substances and influences external to the body than to any arising with or within it, such as original body stuff. The progeny of foreigners, therefore, can become veritably indigenous as they come to have the same land and the same cultural legacy—and to have no other. The sense of recruitment is clearly "become one of us;" there are no inherent barriers. It is one of naturalization.

It may be worth noting once more that the solidarity of personnels is often spoken of in fraternal rather than lineal terms. The generational emphasis stresses brothers, brothers-in-law, and sisters and their respective children. The lineal and ancestral theme, to be sure, provides the rationale for fraternity, but it is evidently (and understandably) of less intrinsic interest, in strict consanguineal terms, than in the general sense of those who give their "story" to a certain, fraternally construed personnel, thereby making the latter part of the story.

In local parlance, to "have the same story" is a locution for common descent or ancestry. It is a figure that strongly suggests—or supports—our present view of the Northern Tairora concept of descent. In this connection we may note the Northern Tairora term, *báriqa* (cf. Agarabi: *mani*). Ancestors, especially those who figure in any such account, may be referred to as *báriqa*, the term also used for origin stories. A rough gloss of the twin usages might thus be "origin-people stories" and "origin-story personage(s)." Sometimes, to stress that he is referring to the personage(s), a speaker will say *"báriqabáinti,"* the last being the word for man (men) or person (persons). The most widely known *báriqa*, not surprisingly, portray the oldest episodes in the history of man—the first discovery and naming of things, the getting of fire, the theft by a male *báriqabáinti* of the sacred instruments from the female *báriqa* who originally owned them, and the like. These stories seem hardly connected to any particular phratry—let alone sib or local group— and in one version or another some are known all over Northern Tairora or beyond. Stories or personages that are more immediately identified with the particular forebears of contemporary personnels may also sometimes be called *báriqa*. This apparently depends on how close to the myths in time the phratric ancestors or incidents in question are considered to be.

To this observer, the dim past appears to hover not far beyond the portals of the Northern Tairora present. Time, in other words, is telescoped remarkably. This apparent advantage permits the persons and events of a local account of phratric ancestors to follow closely on the original establishment of the world and of human life, imbuing what otherwise might seem mere "clan legends" with some of the force and authority of the most ancient myths. To have the "same story," then, may constitute as deep a sharing, or connote as enduring an heritage, as if, by scrupulous rendering, Northern Tairora could demonstrate in full detail that each member had the same progenitor in the N-th ascending generation as his phratric mates.

The "shallow genealogies" often noted in the Central Highlands of New Guinea enthography seem in retrospect less a cause than an unavoidable concomitant of fission too frequent and migration too large in scale for deeper genealogies. Keeping scrupulous genealogical records of presumed begetters and begotten and their collateral kin under such conditions might be quite beyond the power of a nonliterate people, even if they had better reason to be dedicated to the task. For the local genealogists would be called on to record a moving field considerably exceeding the phratric limits that at present mark the genealogies of most concern. Then what of the familiar theme of genealogical carelessness or omission? It is developed in some eth- nographic writings about the Central Highlands of New Guinea almost as if it were a device or ploy of the open society to conceal the fact of its openness. This interpretation appears to overlook the sheer cost of consanguineal punc- tilio under open-society conditions. Rather than as cause or as a factor facili- tating the bootleg admissions of aliens into "agnatic" groups—that is, by suppressing the real truth of their extraneous origin—it seems more reason- able to consider the genealogical practices of Northern Tairora and perhaps of other Central Highlands of New Guinea societies as their response to ine- luctable necessities of their open social field.

As a matter of fact, local chroniclers or genealogists are outstandingly at- tentive and retentive in one respect: they can track the movement of person- nels in considerable depth and at a fair distance, delivering enough detail sometimes to make the ethnographer's notebook a morass of crisscrossing interconnections. But it is *personnels* that are tracked, not, in the first in- stance, persons. This is in harmony with a generational emphasis and cer- tainly with the idea of tracing an inheritance that is collective rather than individual or familistic. It is the record of people "of the same story." In- deed, it is an outsider's version of the very story itself. It is not the tree of begetting of individuals or individual families. This is the genealogy of rele- vant personnels.

In this light, the appropriateness of the Northern Tairora descent con- struct with its extrasomatic heritage gains by contrast with the exorbitance or unfeasibility of any dogma that would anchor fraternity in a detailed, somatic genealogy of individual particularity and multigenerational depth. Linkage by common story, by the history of personnels, in the circumstances of Northern Tairora far transcends any feasible linkage by sequentially remem- bered ancestors. It embraces all of time from the mythical beginning until the ethnographic moment.

In the final analysis it is probably too much to ask of Northern Tairora dogma that it should be, on the one hand, an assertion of permanence and continuity, of endlessness, order, and undying fraternal bonds, while at the same time explicitly predicating and rationalizing the conditions under which purportedly solidary personnels are split, their segments drifting apart, any or all of them falling into the orbit of a different fraternal and terri- torial set. Coping ideologically with a world of movement and revision, even on a stage less turbulent or less acutely affected than Northern Tairora by its smallness of scale, is coping with a great deal. If the key to recruitment and to such solidarity as can be attained amid such transience is the tacit denial that solidarity is ever breached, then Northern Tairora dogma, which obvi- ously cannot have it all ways, has it at least in a way that evidently resolves much.

8. Magic: The Transitive and Instrumental World

To describe the difficulty of locating the religion of the Northern Tairora is already to describe somewhat the object of the search. The object is elusive, no doubt, for several reasons. The Northern Tairora themselves trace no boundaries about any such comprehensive domain as "religion." They outline a series of essentially ritual spheres on the basis of timing, form, or purpose. "Ritualism" would embrace these various Northern Tairora practices, but it would not match a Northern Tairora domain, as far as I know, and it would cut out a part of the observer's "religion." Locating the "religion," thus, is tantamount to constructing a Northern Tairora gloss for our term or concept. Inherently subject to distortion, like all translations, this translation must reflect an original that is neither compact nor internally ordered in any explicit way. For those who know it best, that is, in practice, it does not have the unitary character it may seem to get in an observer's synthesis. I do not know all the Northern Tairora beliefs, values, or symbols to which the label "religion" might on some ground be applied, but that is less of a handicap than that *they* do not know any of them as such.

Individual ideas of many of the elements of Northern Tairora religion vary substantially. Some men say that for help the sun is invoked; others deny such a practice. Such divergence is a fact of the religion as much as is a description of the beliefs, values, or symbols that are general. To be sure, it is a part of the overt design of Northern Tairora religion that certain categories of persons know much or know little of the sources and nature of extrahuman power or the means men have to avail themselves of powers. Older males are knowledgeable in ritual and kindred matters; younger males and females are not. It is not as clearly recognized by Northern Tairora, however, that among individual men and between groups the specific quality of supposedly common knowledge also sometimes diverges. Such divergence strongly suggests not only a loosely organized body of beliefs but an active, growing religion, apparently susceptible of adjustment to needs or pressures. If new needs develop, belief or practice can apparently be modified accordingly.

There is at times a sense of inquiry, even of the use of discovery procedures. Evidence bearing on an event of current concern must be weighed in light of all seemingly relevant knowledge, and some knowledge is firmer than other knowledge. In this quasi-clinical procedure, the dreams and divinations and the diagnoses of some persons come to prevail more often than those of others. If there were no room for doubt, such differences of conviction and evaluation would not develop. The recent history of Northern Tairora religion, as far as can be reached, bears out this openness to interpretation and change quite as much as interviewing or observation bear out the variable commitment of individual views of present beliefs, values, and symbols.

What then are the uniformities of Northern Tairora religion? Beings comparable to what are called supernaturals in the treatises of numerous other religions figure in Northern Tairora belief. Of these some can be called celestial, some terrestrial; and there are consistent differences between the two classes. The sun is vaguely deified, as is a moon that is also masculine, despite some remarkably feminine characteristics. Personalized celestial bodies are few, however, and their involvement with humans is so faintly developed in some cases that it is not clear whether two names are synonyms or refer to different beings.

The paucity of celestial supernaturals and their scant definition is set off against a vast array of forms or sources of magical powers. Many of them are so specific as to invite the opinion that the realm of magic is purely mechanistic, having for the practitioner the finiteness of a cookbook.

Ritual forms are numerous. The largest number are performed by individuals, like the many forms of sorcery and everyday acts of protection or prudence, designed to avoid illness or failure or to promote health and success. Another class consists of rituals requiring the collaboration of several persons—more than one but fewer than a whole community. Family or kindred-sized affairs such as first-child rituals, first menstruation, and exorcising ghosts or their influence illustrate this intermediate scale of participation, as does *hampu* and certain kinds of sorcery requiring several practitioners. Finally there are the community-wide or intersocietal ceremonies such as *ubára* or male initiation, intergroup peacemaking, and *ihálabu* or *órana*, a renewal ritual. The staging of the latter, not surprisingly, is a significant part of the politics of Northern Tairora, and the ritual gatherings constitute the expression of the widest polity known in this social field.

Many substances have special significance, such as barks and leaves for magicomedical purposes; a large number of objects and places also have special significance, such as monoliths and certain trees; and there is a substantial and overriding lexicon of symbolism, notably the hot-dry versus cold-wet antinomy, in which substances, objects, activities, persons, and places are assigned a polarity.

One can approach Northern Tairora religion as a domain through an enumeration of supernaturals, rituals, substances, objects, and places, the ordering of their qualities, and the beliefs and practices that link them with human purposes. The foregoing sketch suggests the form of such a description. Explanatory value would be measured by how informative is the taxonomy: whether the grouping of beliefs, values, and symbols reveals more than a knowledge of the separate items, one by one, thus increasing our recognition of relations among items, as the inventory lays bare their implicit order.

The value of a suitable framing for the facts of any field of experience is well recognized and underlies taxonomies both naïve and deliberate. In this respect the folk and the scientific are implicitly one. The mapping principle, based on criteria of form, meaning, or relationship presumably deserves a place in our discussion of Northern Tairora religion, however intuitively that domain of indigenous thought and action may be held. Some mapping has already been done, of course, in the paragraphs immediately preceding.

To supplement a taxonomic strategy in describing Northern Tairora religion I propose also to theorize the domain by inferring its implicit rationale. So doing, one can test its wholeness as well as the theory. This is not primarily a partiality for one theory of religion over another, however, let alone an attempt to devise an original theory. It is primarily the choice of an approach for its expected fit and convenience in the immediate instance. It is an ethnographic choice, dictated by the needs of describing a sector of Northern Tairora beliefs, values, and symbols that may have discoverable coherence or which, at the very minimum, becomes more accessible to our understanding if the elements ascribed to it are treated together than if they are treated separately and randomly. We have already anticipated that task in speaking inclusively of "religion."

I believe, in fine, that the following approach will be helpful in understanding the Northern Tairora as having organized activities that reflect organized views of their experience. We may thus see a set of beliefs, values, and symbols that describe for them a world, particularly including that which transcends immediate or relatively unmediated control. "Immediate control" presumes the short-term application of an individual's own energy or his efforts to move others immediately to apply their energy. The direct physical manipulation of the environment or the making of demands on one's fellows stand central to the realm of the immediate. This provisional definition will be touched on again in the ensuing discussion.

In principle a version of the whole experienced world, the religion, is demonstrably more emphatic about the aspects of human purpose that seem least responsive to or least comprehended by unaided human action. By attitude (such as pride, awe or fear, or anxiety), or by emphasis (such as special respect for sources of power or for a practitioner's competence), the beliefs, values, or symbols of some parts of the experienced world may be seen to stand apart from others. This difference of emphasis, quite understandable in its own terms, sometimes leads to the view that the concern of religion is uniquely with matters considered (whether indigenously or by the observer is not always clear) as transcendant and extraordinary. Such, at any rate, is not the view I take, though I shall reflect as far as possible the points on which Northern Tairora themselves concentrate, be they viewed as quotidian or extraordinary.

Finding the Northern Tairora religion, then, is like finding the Northern Tairora economy. It is not to isolate a segment or component of a whole, making possible, as it were, a separate listing of elements. It is to view the whole of Northern Tairora experience from a particular standpoint—the economic standpoint or the religious one. If the economic standpoint is that of provisioning, the religious standpoint in Northern Tairora life is that of understanding human differences and extrahuman sources of power and knowing the uses to which some power sources may be put. The beliefs, values, and symbols that order the individual's experience of the world give a sense of what is ordinary and easily known and what is less ordinary because it is less easily or less well known. Beliefs, values, and symbols are most emphatic in connection with those experiences that seem larger than the individual, impalpable, or beyond the scope of his unaided influence, hence from his standpoint often precarious of outcome. These are matters such as procreation and birth; growth and generation; health and illness; strength and weakness; aging and death; fortune, and misfortune, wealth, and fruitfulness; psychological states such as dreaming, imagination, psychotic and neurotic experience, startle, and mental disorders; and sensory disorders such as deafness.

Magic is the sense or principle that touches the widest range of Northern Tairora beliefs, values, and symbols of the experienced world. As I am using the term here, the sense of magic in Northern Tairora culture consists at base in taking the experienced world as an array of many particular, rather finite and distinct kinds of power. Some of them overlap in efficacy or application. Others are capable of interacting and may mutually influence each other. Of these, some intensify and some attenuate or reverse others in their effects.

How much does magic as a premise of multiple and particular powers preclude the development of a centralized world field? Magical belief requires no single focus or prime mover—as distinct from common principle. There need be no common denominator, hence, for reducing multiple discrete types of power or numerous, specific forms of practice to a single field of force, as opposed to fields of forces. No focus of source or origin is implicit in Northern Tairora magic, let alone a focus of purpose. Their magic is neither hierarchical nor eschatological. It is ethically neutral, though its uses and users are not.

Were there a prime source of all powers in Northern Tairora thinking, it would most likely be the sun. The sun is an acknowledged power greater than any other. Its role in the growth of plants is recognized as well as its powerful effect on men. In too large amounts it is seen as literally sapping human will and strength. Among plants, many are credited with an unusual power for some specific purpose, but the power they afford to those who can avail themselves of it is not seen as deriving from the sun. It is not the same kind of power. Not only is it not the same in potency, which is obvious, but it is not the same in form or efficacy. The sun works though its "light"; it "shoots" a man, for example, in overpowering him and producing exhaustion, preventing him from continuing a task or a journey. Plants work through being eaten, "aimed," brought into contact with a targeted object or its surrogate, or simply combined in a ritual manner with other elements to produce a desired effect. The sun's power, however, is not available to humans to direct and use. For those who claim to ask the sun's intercession an exception must be made.

Without an abstract or common denominator such as "power" or "energy," plant powers are not translatable into sun-power terms. It is possible, moreover, that even with such an abstraction, no translation would follow, nor would the idea readily gain acceptance that the source of all powers, despite the singularity of each, was the sun. The same sun shines on all plants, it is true, but some are highly significant and some are not. Yams or taro are not more significant in rituals than sweet potatoes, nor ginger more potent than pepper leaf because the sun shines more or less on them but because of differences intrinsic to the plants themselves. Neither the most insignificant herb nor the superlethal and almost legendary bamboo, believed to kill any animal or person on mere contact, derives its efficacy from other sources or combinations of power. Some powers, moveover, are to be found in substances such as water or the muck of swamps. Far less easily could *their* power be thought to be derived from the sun.

The very use here of abstractions such as "efficacy," "magic," "potency," or "power" demands caution, accordingly, for these terms tend to misrepresent the Northern Tairora view of the world, implying some general and uniform sense or quality, some explicit dimensional attribute that is shared or apportioned in varying amounts in varying forms. Such a singular or concentric idea of the substances, activities, and beings of the world is not well developed.

The plurality of Northern Tairora magic and its lack of an abstract common denominator like power may appear to be challenged in the indigenous concepts of "heat" and its opposite, "cold." It is a limited challenge, I believe, but an examination will nevertheless be worthwhile in order to recognize the implicit logic of Northern Tairora magic.

Like certain other New Guinea peoples, Northern Tairora classify a considerable number of activities, substances, demons, and deities, as well as individual persons, in a hot-dry/cold-wet scheme. The antinomy describes a complementary power interaction or efficacy associated with the respective items of the classification. A partial list will suggest what is involved, and may be compared with the classifications drawn for numerous other New Guinea peoples. Barrau has called attention to a widespread wet-dry dichotomy of cultivated plants in Oceania, which may be related (1965).

Hot-Dry	Cold-Wet
Sun (masculine)	Moon (though nominally mascu-
Male	line)
Father	Female
Patrilineal kin	Mother
Sorcery	Matrilineal kin
Fighting	Water
Anger	Peace
Vigor	Quiet
Dry (sunny) season	Gentleness
Hunting (?)	Wet (rainy) season
Ritual occasions, rituals	Gardening
Ritual paraphernalia	Ordinary occasions
Sacred instruments like flutes,	Everyday costume
bullroarer	
Vigorous, forceful persons	
(e.g., strong men)	Quiet, unassertive persons
Extraordinary events, alien or	(e.g., "garden men")
powerful, such as balloting in	Etc.
1964 parliamentary elections	
The sea (as represented in	
cargo myth)	
The Cargo (activities, portents,	
paraphernalia)	

At least two points can be made about these antinomous items. The first concerns the implicit criterion of the classification. The items in the hot-dry column are active by nature, the moving causes of events in which they are involved, the sources of initiative and change. The items of the cold-wet column are not so much passive or impotent as they are complementary or secondary. They are reactive or in some cases counteractive in relation to their opposites. Water, for instance, is not an energizing or initiating substance, but it is capable of bringing to a halt undertakings, such as sorcery, that are hot or that generate and require heat to succeed. Surely, then, water has a high degree of efficacy. Or, to take a more obvious case, females are essential in the production of children; but the Northern Tairora see the initiative and principal role of procreation as that of the male. The female is necessary, obviously, but is not the prime mover. (Semen exists, but ova are not recognized.) Nor, certainly, could one consider the mortal danger of female pollution for the male a lack of efficacy! It is rather an opposite (and in that context wrong) efficacy, that of sickness or death.

The second point to be made about the symbolic antinomy of hot-dry/cold-wet is that it is not drawn, even implicitly, according to a scale of relative power. That is, it does not presuppose an abstract common denominator such as "power," in relation to which the items on the one side are the powerful, those on the other the powerless. The antinomy does not, then, suggest that Northern Tairora culture contains a realized abstraction of power, singular and general, in relation to which the numerous, specific kinds of power are all interconvertible.

To counter that "heat" (or "cold") implies some kind of common denominator among the items so classed is fair enough. Yet, to repeat, "cold" is not the absence of power. The term describes rather a polarity of action or relationship. There is a further sense of balance or imbalance, one that explains or predicts certain outcomes in human affairs. The balance of male against female—their juxtaposition, at any rate, because it appears to be a precarious balance—is necessary for producing children. The cold moon is a balance for the overpowering and debilitating heat of the sun. Cold matrilineal kin balance the patrilineal kin, whose "hot" discipline makes kindness and sympathy necessary when the children feel oppressed. The role of matrilineal kin in tempering the severity of initiation, or in harboring and defending the runaway bride, unready for the match her father has made for her, are specific illustrations.

It thus appears that the hot-dry and cold-wet opposites recognized by Northern Tairora do not support an inference of a well-realized single denominator or single dimension of magic. The distinction between the two sets of items is not primarily one of degree, with less potent items arrayed against more potent ones. All items do not have the same potency. The magical potential of any given item, body, or substance is qualitatively distinct. Nor does all potency have a common derivation. Hot-dry items are a multiform class each member of which shares with the others only a similar complementarity to one or more items of the multiform cold-wet class. If I have belabored this point, it is because of the risk, previously noted, that in a synthetic depiction it is easy to impute forms of ordering that are in fact extraneous to Northern Tairora beliefs.

THE MÁRAQÚRA, INVISIBLE COUNTERPART OF EVERY ENTITY

The particularity and uniqueness of items is further expressed, I suggest, in the concept of *máraqúra*. This Northern Tairora term glosses as "nature," "spirit," "essence," "self," "counterpart," "life force," or "inner" or "other" self. Since humans are notable among the many beings and things of the world endowed with *máraqúra*, one may be tempted to consider "soul" a suitable gloss. To be sure, a person's *máraqúra* departs his body at death but assertedly to disappear. Indeed, departure is the mark or cause of death. It is not the *máraqúra* that survives the body, according to informants, but the *bana*, or "ghost," which comes into being at that time. They deny that *bana* are transformed *máraqúra*.

Not just humans but animals, objects, substances, demons, deities—each

of these entities has, in principle, a *máraqúra*. Nevertheless, one hears
much less of some *máraqúra* than of others. The *máraqúra* of men or pigs
are frequently referred to, but not the *máraqúra* of demons—*wera, naabu,
aigega*. To hazard a guess about the latter circumstance, it seems likely that
the demonic "person" already incorporates all possible capacity and knowledge, so that, unlike men or pigs, there is nothing more that a demonic
máraqúra might be or do. It thus suffices to speak only of the demon itself.
Since the death of these beings is a rather nebulous possibility, moreover,
ascribing a *máraqúra* may seem dubious.

Then why ascribe *máraqúra*, even in principle, to all such items? Although I do not have this from Northern Tairora informants, I would suggest
that anything capable of being encountered in a dream must in principle be
assigned a *máraqúra*. That is, since the dream experience consists of the
encounters of the *máraqúra* of the dreamer with other *máraqúra* (the beings
or entities dreamed of), any entity one may dream of must possess such a
counterpart. The single—or the clearest—exception is ghosts, for it is the
bana themselves that one meets in dreams, not their *máraqúra*. This might
seem to suggest, contrary to informants' claims, that ghosts may in fact be
the post-mortem transformation of *máraqúra*. I rather doubt it. Ghosts
themselves probably do not have *máraqúra*, for one thing, because they are
not mortal. And as for transformation, the ghost is a very different being
from its mortal antecedent, whose *máraqúra* would therefore make an unlikely ghost. These views, like any others not closely anchored in physical
experience, may change with time.

Máraqúra are as differentiated as the beings or things whose counterparts
they are. For living things, especially for men, they represent a sensitivity to
the invisible forces or events of the world that is higher or more acute than
the conscious understanding or perception of the wakeful person or creature. If the Northern Tairora had the expression "eyes in the back of his
head," I suspect they would unhesitatingly attribute this sense of the unseen
to the individual's *máraqúra*, for it is in one respect a kind of sixth sense that
the *máraqúra* affords. The *máraqúra* is the individual's potential for contact
with what is inaccessible through his direct, sensory responses to balance,
touch, taste, temperature, sight, smell, or sound.

The *máraqúra* has physical manifestations that demonstrate to the Northern Tairora its potential separateness and independence of movement in relation to the position or movement of its host. The shadow of a being or thing
and its image on a reflective surface are among the most obvious manifestations. In living beings the breath is a manifestation even closer to the active
potential of a *máraqúra*, so much so that the word *máraqúra* is frequently
glossed in Pidgin as "win" or breath. What we consider inanimate objects,
without breath, are also ascribed breath in the sense of influence unseen but
felt or demonstrated in its effects. Thus, in a modern example, it was the hot
and dangerous "breath" or influence of the activity or paraphernalia of voting, in the first Papua New Guinea parliamentary election in 1964, that

could cause sickness or death in those it touched if unprotected. The movement of air about such an object is possibly its "breath," as distinct from the respiration of an animal. It is to this "breath" that the magical efficacy of beings, activities, or substances is often apparently ascribed. Yet informants object strongly to any inference that the *máraqúra is* the breath, the shadow, or the reflection. These are among its manifestations, along with the experience of *máraqúra* in dreams.

Dreaming is for humans probably the most keenly felt experience of their own *máraqúra*. Dreaming makes the physical person a witness to the existence, the separateness, and the powers of knowledge of the *máraqúra*. The dream experience arises from its rapport with hidden events or intentions and persons or things at a distance. A closer rapport with the magical forces of the world is implied. The truth of dreams is beyond question. Indeed, it is a profound sort of inner vision with prophetic power, creativity, and revelation simply transcending the wakeful consciousness of a person. Facts can be known at great distance—such as the impending death or moment of death of a kinsman. The hidden truth of the 1964 parliamentary election was both more significant and more potent by far than the public version presented by the electoral commission. This was revealed in a dream to one of the candidates, who came from a local group adjacent to Northern Tairora. As a warning it was credible enough to him to cause his withdrawal from campaigning.

Dreams have been vital to Cargo. Inspiration for the design of dancing regalia is also obtained in dreams. For this and the other values of dreaming, there is accordingly great emphasis on awakening at once from a dream and whenever possible repeating the details to a trusted person in order to capture as much as possible of the information or insight of one's *máraqúra*. Reflecting again the different individual characteristics of persons is the different quality of the revelations of their *máraqúra*. Some individuals are known as dreamers of significant and valid dreams, while the dreams of others are accorded little importance. Having a *máraqúra*, in other words, does nothing to change a person's status relative to anothers. It rather matches his visible self. To put it differently, no matter how small he is, his *máraqúra* does not dwarf him by being equal to the *máraqúra* of others.

The *máraqúra* of a victim of most kinds of sorcery can know of the deed and its perpetrator. The conscious person, through his direct senses, cannot possess or provide such knowledge, unless through his dreams his *máraqúra* reveals it to him. It is thus the influence of the victim's *máraqúra* that guides the hand of those who would divine the cause of his death and the identity of the killer. The *máraqúra* sometimes takes possession of a kinsman's body, its own native will suspended and wholly given over to the will of the possessing *máraqúra*, to point out or confront the sorcerer. Indeed the possessed may perhaps be killed as a consequence of his involuntary and imprudent appearance in the midst of enemies, irresistibly conducted there, that is, by the intrusive *máraqúra*.

Fright is another psychic verification of the presence and independence of the *máraqúra*. The startle sensation is perceived as being the sudden leap of the *máraqúra* in departing the body. *Máraqúra* are highly sensitive, as has been noted.

The *máraqúra* of different entities are inevitably different. There is no mention of dreaming by plants, for example. The "breath" of a polling booth or election activity is potent and can cause harm. This description does not fit the *máraqúra* of a person, however, even that of a strong or "hot" man. For what a strong man can do to affect one is direct and physical. If he means to ensorcel his adversary, for example, he will do so through the use of suitable ritual and magically potent material. He does not send his *máraqúra* to carry out his wish. Indeed, his *máraqúra* will enter the case at most only generally or indirectly. Given a strong man with the capacity to succeed in his undertakings, he presumably is matched in having a strong *máraqúra*. Conceivably, his *máraqúra*, through dreams, could provide guidance and suggest the means for effecting his purposes.

It does not appear, on the whole, that a human *máraqúra* acts as the direct agent of good or harm to others. A magical specialist known as *bure* is a possible exception, apparently using his *máraqúra* to retrieve the lost *máraqúra* of victims of sorcery. Human *máraqúra* are not an additional form of earthbound beings like *wera*, *naabu*, *aigega*, or ghosts, to make life more hazardous or uncertain. The possession of another's body, previously mentioned, is done by the *máraqúra* of a recently dead man, which is soon to disappear. I know of no instances of a "living" *máraqúra* leaving its normal abode to take up long-term residence in the body of another. Indeed, such a departure would mean the "owner's" death. In a case that bears on this assertion a child of Noreiqera was reportedly stolen from its mother by a demon, probably a *wera*. The accounts I heard, though ambiguous, suggest that the demon may actually have stolen the *máraqúra* of the human child, not the body itself, replacing it with the *máraqúra* of one of its own *wera* children. This purportedly explained the strange (microcephalic) look and behavior of the child, now a grown man. Humans deal with each other consciously in the main and not with each other's *máraqúra*. They know each other, as it were, in person. Any sense of the presence, activity, advice, or intentions of the *máraqúra* of other persons is normally obtained through one's own *máraqúra*. That sense, however, can be acute. A dream of illicit copulation with a desired partner is assumed to be adulterously shared; and it is accordingly claimed by some that the pair involved will exchange guilty looks if they meet the next day.

Ultimately, as far as I can judge, the question of *máraqúra* is not a tidy one. The best-known *máraqúra* are one's own and those of which one has witness or report in his fellow humans. To be sure, the same sense of an essence or spirit supervening the visible and physical properties of beings and objects is in principle ascribed at large to all other beings and objects. It is easier, however, to speak of the *máraqúra* of some beings and objects than of others. Those palpable creatures and entities that have significant activity or effect or weight or meaning in the experienced world, those that count in the affairs of men—it is they, naturally, who have the significant *máraqúra*. While every creature or thing in principle has a *máraqúra*, "principle" cannot ensure a *máraqúra* that is any better defined than its visible counterpart. So the shades of some things must be more shadowy than those of others. In effect, then, the contents of the spirit world, no less than those of the immediate world of the senses, shade off into things that, even if named, are of little consequence.

It appears that the *máraqúra* of efficacious things is in fact their essence—that is, their potency. It is the "breath" of magicomedicinal leaves, for example, that cures, or heals, or brings illness or confusion to those touched by it. But I am frankly unsure of the full breadth of this generalization, even as I suspect many Northern Tairora may be unsure. This ambiguity is probably most disturbing to the ethnographer, anxious that he has left some stone unturned; or it is disturbing to the reader who, having been apprised of the reference points and underpinnings of indigenous dogma, may expect their single and mutual implications to be traced out logically and finally. It is least of all disturbing to those who find it credible that, in the realm of Northern Tairora beliefs, values, and symbols of the experienced world, there are dark areas beside the well-lighted ones, and there are connections which, though we may draw them out in logic and consistency (or *generate* them by our eliciting questions), will not be drawn thus or drawn at all by Northern Tairora. They may simply have failed to notice inconsistencies, or to generalize consistencies to the utmost, or to formulate some questions. The gaps in logic do not mark gaps in life.

The claim that false leads and loose ends to a certain degree characterize indigenous belief can be supported without reference to the frustration of the ethnographer. I interrupted a conversation one day between two Northern Tairora men, already in progress before I arrived. Its subject was surprising to me and did not arise—at least not directly—from any questions I had lately been asking. The two were considering whether human feces could serve as valid exuviae for the purpose of sorcery. After all, they agreed, a person regularly drinks water, which is obviously then mixed in his body with the food he eats. Because water, as a "cold," neutralizing agent, is absolutely inimical to effective—"hot"—sorcery, they theorized, feces should thus be rendered useless for sorcery. A loose end in indigenous theory was apparent to some who lived by the theory; moreover, it was of interest to them. I dare say that neither man, whatever his intellectual pride or curiosity in recognizing this inconsistency of traditional belief, was prepared to act on or test it. I doubt that either man began defecating carelessly where anyone wanting it could collect this conventionally perilous substance—for use or for exchange. Furthermore, granting the aquafication of feces would only lead to further questions of logical consistency that they evidently had not perceived. For in drinking water constantly, could humans not believe that *all* of their exuviae were rendered neutral? I do not attempt to predict an appropriate answer to this question in Northern Tairora theory but only to note that the question itself was not raised, even in the course of the skeptical discussion of a closely related matter.

It is the prolonged separation of an individual's *máraqúra* from his physical person that defines illness or death. The ministrations of a *bure*, or specialized medical practitioner, focus on the location and retrieval of a *máraqúra* that has strayed or one that has been lured or driven from the victim by some compelling power. Often but not always the power will have been brought to bear on the victim in a deliberate attempt to ensorcel him by recognized means. But the attraction or estrangement of a *máraqúra* can also be produced by the presence of other powerful circumstances, perhaps circumstances unfamiliar to the given individual.

In 1954 I heard from two different Northern Tairora men the story of a flight each had independently made, years before, in a small aircraft that landed at nearby Kainantu. Among the first aircraft ever to use the airstrip newly cleared there, early in the 1930s, these were the first aircraft ever locally to be seen on the ground, let alone approached or entered by any local man. Out of friendly curiosity or camaraderie, probably, the pilot had grabbed a "local" and taken off with him, to show him the sights. To a naïve hearer, either of the two individual accounts I recorded could easily suggest hysteria, but the rationale of each version accords closely with the points here under discussion.

Each man independently told me he had never before recounted the experience of his flight—nor had either been pressed by fellow residents to do so. Having narrowly managed to return to his village still in possession of his *máraqúra*, hence able to move normally again among the living, he would be foolhardy to court separation once more by recalling the strange, powerful circumstances of that journey to the sea. For each of them there was still—or there had been for much of twenty years—the peril of dying, the risk that his *máraqúra* could be drawn back to that great magical site where the aircraft had conveyed him. The magic of the aircraft itself could be estimated only in the images of wild dreams. No doubt contact with it—indeed, entry into the very interior of it—posed dangers incalculable in any lesser terms than life and death; but this was not death from falling to the earth or flying into a cloud with a steep mountain inside of it. For a Northern Tairora in the 1930s, such physical hazards were simply inconceivable in so manifestly powerful a thing as an aircraft. The risk lay rather in whether the aircraft would return its passenger, *máraqúra* intact, to his point of boarding.

It was the place, however, the Martian destination, whose wonder and power evoked the ultimate excitement and displayed the ultimate gravity. Truth beyond previous conceiving lay all about the sojourner as he walked among the supernatural scenes, met and spoke to people who were at home there. According to each informant independently, the flight alone took a long time, for the wondrous place lay beyond the remotest settlement known even by name to the Northern Tairora. The entire journey lasted weeks or months, or perhaps far longer. Neither traveler knew how long, for in a dream one has no track of time. Taken to Salamaua, probably, each man saw the pre–World War II administrative headquarters of the Morobe district, at the east end of mainland New Guinea. Each of them saw, too, the mythical sea shining and hot, the unbounded, the endless source. Its horizon, was smooth, unindented, like none ever seen in the familiar world, the mountain valleys of the Tairora; and this was because the sea was interminable. It was the beginning and perhaps it was also the end.

Small wonder at the fear of death from spirit separation. In dreams is many a journey made, but, incredible, in making this journey to the other world, both body and spirit beyond doubt traveled together. Otherwise, the impressions were too vivid, the parting gift knife and the gift clothing too tangible. There were no sensations to suggest that the body had remained outside the dream, moreover, and the witness of one's fellow villagers confirmed its entry into the aircraft, its departure, and its absence. It was further proof of the transcendant adventure, if further proof were needed, to learn that those who did not go thought the traveler gone but a single night and a day. The long visit, the many encounters were realized in one setting of the sun. Time had stood still in the course of his absence. Inevitably it was beyond ordinary power to impart such experience to those with none to compare. (The ethnographer, presumed familiar with such things, was hence an exception.) The return to the living was—fortunately—within the competence of the aircraft. Having been introduced to death now meant that death still beckoned in the lethal allure of those scenes and incidents if they should be too vividly recalled.

The reality of separation from one's spirit is often confirmed for wakeful Northern Tairora by the experience of being startled. They describe the *máraqúra* as suddenly taking flight from the person. Normally, as in dreams, the *máraqúra* returns in good time; but in the face of extreme power—like a flight to Salamaua amid fantastic circumstances, or when overpowered by the attack of supernatural beings or by sorcery—the departure may be final, hence, fatal, to the person.

As these various aspects confirm, the *máraqúra* of a human has a more direct rapport than the physical person with the magical powers of the world. It is through his *máraqúra* that the individual is affected by magical power, his fate in extreme cases dependent on the response of the *máraqúra*. It is through his *máraqúra* that the conscious person may sometimes learn of events that he does not, could not, know from his usual senses. It is the meeting of one person's *máraqúra* with those of others that may give reassurance, provide warning, bring tidings, or reveal the inner truth of events imponderable on their surface.

Between the *máraqúra* of persons—and perhaps of other animals—and that of inanimate things a major difference seems implicit. The role of the human *máraqúra* as a receptor or channel, for one thing, seems much more fully figured. The equation of death with the separation of individual from *máraqúra* is also, to be sure, an aspect specifically appropriate to animals and men. Neither of these points was explicitly made, to me, however, though assent might readily be obtained from Northern Tairora informants if the question were posed.

The *máraqúra* of objects or substances of known efficacy, on the other hand, seems to reflect the involuntary and ineluctable quality of sources of power. There is little or no room, apparently, for caprice or arbitrariness. A lethal substance or ritual is lethal, not deviating in its effect in respect of one given target as distinct from another. Only the strength of a stronger target—its *máraqúra*—or the deterrence of adequate countermeasures—and efficacy equally undeviating—can produce that result.

DEFINING THE OPEN FIELD OF POWERS

The plurality of forms of magical power is reflected in the respective *máraqúra* of various known beings and substances. These would not fully define or exhaust the field of magical powers, however, even if fully enumerated. The field of the known is open-ended. The enumerable powers are only a portion of what may exist. No single person, nor possibly all persons together, knows more than a part of all the powers that are in the world. Some of the powers are local, peculiar to one people or territory and unknown, strange, inaccessible, or alien and harmful to others.

Magical power is as vast as the world, so to speak, for in sum it is the powers of the world. Its scope or vastness is implicitly subdivided, a major division being that between powers that are known and recognized and powers that are not. I do not know the relative proportions of these two areas. I doubt the question has an answer. It seems closer to the Northern Tairora sense of things simply to say that the field of magical powers is not bounded by the present knowledge of them. This belief is not merely hypothetical, in any case, for the Northern Tairora do not hesitate to credit the discovery of new forms of magical power earlier unknown to them. The revelations of "cargo" through rumor and dream may constitute the greatest sphere of newly discovered powers of recent years. From all indications, moreover, far from being resisted, these innovations were accepted with a striking speed and degree of conviction. Nor did such acceptance apparently break precedent. This is true at least for believers. There were—and are—doubters, persons never seized by the excitement. Possibly the most innovative aspect of the belief in cargo is that the newly recognized powers relate to each other—and to men—in a systematic way. Indeed, the clear eschatology of cargo beliefs provides a remarkable integration of these ideas and one that contrasts sharply, in my opinion, with the eschatological indeterminacy of much of the older knowledge of magical power. The eschatological quality of cargo belief, value, and symbol, it seems clear, is a reactionary development. With indigenous magic as the fertile seedbed for the recognition of new forms of power, the focal experience and massive impact of alien contact united the power newly recognized with a purpose wider, in a social or political sense, than any previously known. This purpose is surely longer-range and more radical in the character of its goals for the projected modification of life than any other within memory.

Receptivity to new cargo beliefs, values, and symbols, is not the only evidence of the ability of Northern Tairora religion to grow and change. Innovation in sorcery and countersorcery materials and techniques follows close behind. Here, too, postcontact conditions have played a large part, foremost by introducing New Guinea peoples who were previously remote and unknown to each other and whose repertories of magical knowledge and technique hence differed in detail, offering the chance for active, large-scale diffusion. Postcontact conditions have surely favored the intensification of magical concerns, especially sorcery, by suppressing warfare, hence restricting control of enemies to magical means, and by raising anxieties in some cases unparalleled in precontact circumstances, such as by the relative freedom of strangers to move through one's territory.

In addition to diffusion, however, wholly new magical forms have been discovered. One of these, reported to me in 1963, will illustrate the open-endedness of the Northern Tairora magical world view, its receptivity to diffusion and the validity of discovery.

A form of sorcery related to the widespread *sangguma* of many parts of New Guinea became known and feared in Northern Tairora and neighboring areas in the years since contact, for the most part, probably, since World War II. A particulary frightening aspect of this form of killing magic was that although the victim could be directly accosted by his attackers in broad daylight, so great was their power and skill, that, at their bidding, he would quietly submit to the acts that were to produce his early death. These consisted in surgically entering his body and removing key organs, particularly the liver, while completely concealing the marks of intrusion. A further source of awe in the new sorcery was that the victim's *máraqúra* was rendered helpless to reveal, either before or after death, what had befallen him. His sensate self, of course, was rendered oblivious to the encounter. Once released by the sorcerers, he returned to his normal haunts and habits for a short time. The time itself was usually assigned by them, such as "three days hence." Then, suddenly and without warning he expired. He had not seemed ill to any of his fellow residents, so nothing was suspected until the end. After death, moreover, none of the traditional techniques of divination was of any avail in indicating the authors of the sorcery or even their local identity, since all forms of divination appear to require the assistance of a victim's *máraqúra*. The new form of sorcery, moreover, was reported and was accepted as being absolutely without remedy. Even if in a given case this particular sorcery were known or suspected, in other words, nothing could be done to help the victim. There was simply no specific.

Cut off from the possibility of either remedy or retaliation, those who felt themselves the possible targets of such an attack felt singularly impotent.

Stages in the burning of certain trees to make lime from the ash. The branches and limbs are piled into a rough crib and fired. The lime, with pepper leaf and areca nut, becomes betel in the mouth. The trough of bark is used for slaking the ashes to produce the lime.

They could only be apprehensive of the approach of all strangers on the "government road" and particularly wary of persons thought to be from a certain Auyana-speaking local territory reputed for its mastery of sorcery and for the wantonness of its attacks. It was said that sorcerers like those were quite capable of selecting random victims, wholly unknown to them, simply in order to test their power and perfect their skill—and perhaps to flaunt their prowess to outsiders. And since a part of the power consisted in compelling the victim, prior to surgery, to follow the sorcerer wherever he indicated, there was no doubt of the ability to take him quietly from the security of the "government road" to whatever cover they required for their deadly purpose.

All of this belief, it must be remembered, was without any specific precedent in Northern Tairora; yet it was credible. It was generally accepted as valid in light of the local understanding of magical principles and powers.

During my stay at Abiera in 1963, however, word of a still newer discovery reached the village. Contract laborers employed in a coffee plantation nearby reported that a specific had lately been found for the terrible new sorcery. It had been found in the Gimi ethnolinguistic area to the southwest, where a man had been ensorceled and killed by the awful *sangguma*. To the consternation of his survivors, he reappeared some days later in the village. Once convinced that it was not his ghost but himself they were seeing, they were told the means of his return from the dead. His grave was at the base of a particular tree whose bark, it turned out, was a specific for the sorcery of which he had died. Through the ground the influence of the tree had reached him in his grave and restored him to life. (Implicitly, the bark had the power to reunite the victim's corpose with his *máraqúra*.) With this knowledge, the Gimi were now not only relieved of the hopelessness of an attack against which no measure could prevail; they were also possessed of a valuable magical substance, unknown (and perhaps unavailable even when known) in the lands of many potential victims who might thus desperately now want to buy it.

Credibility was evidently assured once more, above all since the Gimi live in a well-forested country. They thus share with other bush folk like the Fore, located to the south and southwest of the Northern Tairora, a convincing reputation for knowing magical substances and for proficiency in their use. With this authority they had every chance of commanding the high prices they were reportedly asking for the small amounts of the bark that were received from the home country. A fairly steady and lucrative traffic exists in such, largely botanical, substances, in which forested areas are naturally much better supplied than the grassland.

The implication seems clear: the magical world is larger than what men of a given time or place may know of it. Beyond one's own country other men may have other knowledge. Sometimes such special knowledge is limited to a single area. The form of sorcery to which *kuru* is ascribed is peculiar, for example, to the Fore area to the southwest. New knowledge can also be obtained by discovery, as we have just seen, and perhaps other circumstances than those of the Gimi case can produce it.

It is possible that the revival of one taken for dead is a recurrent circumstance in the discovery of new magic. (A widely esteemed new form of sweet potato was discovered, according to the Northern Tairora, growing from the grave of a woman in a land to the west.) Revival itself is not rare, thanks to the local view of death; and revival is also a fairly telling validation, obviously, for any means of reuniting a flown *máraqúra* with its "dead" physical counterpart. The authority of the dead and the afterworld is clearly a theme of Northern Tairora belief. While the great sweep of cargo beliefs in recent years may have accentuated the world of the ancestors beyond its aboriginal importance, the belief in a significant intercourse of the living with the dead is more general and almost certainly of long standing. This avenue leads to the discovery of much that is not known. The dead or their ghosts are frequently encountered by the *máraqúra* of a dreamer on its journeys; and the ghosts of important ancestors may give warning or provide protection to the living through their *máraqúra* when the latter is in danger of being separated from the person. Not all of what is learned from the contact of *máraqúra* with ghosts is knowledge of new forms of magic, to be sure, for some of the information is quite circumstantial and limited—as when an individual learns of the impending death of a kinsman. The implication is nonetheless strong that, once dead, the individual in the form of his ghost will be a party to much knowledge of the powers of the world that is not available to the living. (Into such a milieu there came the Christian message of eternal life in the afterworld.) There must, then, be many other such powers of which mortals are unaware.

THE ACCESSIBLE AND THE INACCESSIBLE

In the subdivision of the world of magical power into the known and the unknown, as just sketched, the known is implicitly subdivided into the accessible and the inaccessible. Not all sources or forms of power, in other words, even those conventionally known and named, are susceptible of human intervention, manipulation, or control. What we would regard as the greatest and broadest powers of the world, those that could be thought of as expressing its regularity or which are essential to its regulation, are mostly inaccessible to human will or manipulation. The sun, moon, sky, and stars all illustrate such powers in the Northern Tairora inventory. These celestial bodies are visible, remote from the quotidian concerns of men, regular in their movement, and are presumed regular in their effects on men. Viewed as essential to the necessary order of the world, they are named and assigned personality, and typical behavior is attributed to them, although, except for sun and moon, the personality is so vague as to stretch the meaning of the word. Each is referred to by name. Each is singular except for stars, which seem to be collective; and invocation of each is possible in principle, though in practice the commonest invocation is that of *kiyário* or *náruba*, the sky or heavens, or *kuwári (bano)* the sun.[1] Some men say they appeal to the sun before a battle, for instance, to ask for safety or success. Others, however, consider this eccentric or alien, attributing the behavior in one case at Batainabura to the individual's mother, an outsider, who must have influenced him. (In fact she was from Barabuna, an adjacent Northern Tairora territory and people, partly composed of refugee elements of the former Batainabura cluster.) *Kiyário* again is known differently to different individuals. Only for some, for example, does the figure appear in dreams or issue prophetic observations as to an individual's life career.

The remaining forms or sources of power that are largely or wholly beyond reach of human influence appear to be earthbound. They are the earthly demons, *wera*, *aigega*, and *naabu*, or *bana*, the ghosts of humans. They include the vaguely defined being(s) that control the lightning. Lightning is seen as capable of separating the *máraqúra* of men or especially pigs from their physical being, hence is lethal.[2] There is even more vaguely a being (or beings) who supports the earth on his shoulders and who, in shifting his burden, causes it to shake, resulting in earthquakes. A vague claim is made by some men of rain beings, identified respectively with various mountains whence come the rains of recognized provenience. The control of rain and the consequent flooding of streams is not entirely beyond the competence of magical specialists, however, and this circumstance, or the confusion with powers that are essentially local mountain demons, may explain the vagueness of such rain beings.

Wera and *naabu*, already described, refer to classes of demons, each with innumerable local representatives that tend to exhibit common characteristics. As noted earlier the *aigega* is variously reputed to be a single being or a pair but it is not in any event a class like *wera* or *naabu*. *Aigega*, along with *wera* and *naabu*, are assertedly used as bogies to frighten unruly children into obedience. It would be quite out of keeping with the general attitude toward demons to take them lightly. Yet there was unmistakably an undercurrent of amusement when the *aigega*'s sexual activity—surely the ultimate promiscuity—was described. I found a more detailed concern with *aigega* among Batainabura informants than at Abiera. If this is a real difference between the two peoples, it may be relevant to note that the Batainabura consider that the path of ghosts to the afterworld passes through their very territory. There is thus a sense that the *aigega* may be stationed at no great

---

1. *Kiyário* appears to be a vocative form. Northern Tairora informants consulted denied that *kiyário* and *náruba* are anything but different names for the same being.

2. Lightning comes up from the earth to meet the sky, as the Northern Tairora perceive it. The hole in the ground often noted, where we would probably say the lightning has struck, is the point of issue of the bolt. The difference between up and down here, interestingly enough, is not perfectly resolvable by empirical tests, for lightning sparks jump both ways. The naked eye is unable to discriminate direction, apparently, making the perception of it a purely cultural convention.

distance from Batainabura itself. It is furthermore claimed—even though the Batainabura, in contrast to the Abiera, profess little detailed knowledge of ghosts or contact with them—that the sounds of passing ghosts on their way to *bánamáqa* ("ghost land") are frequently heard and are frightening.

At Abiera ghosts or *bana* are in many ways the most feared of earthbound beings. They have a reputation for mischief and they can and do return from *bánamáqa* to move among the living. This often has unfavorable effects on those whom they contact, including sickness or even death. The ghosts in question usually know their human contacts, moreover, and this tends to make their relationship personal and even partisan.

At Batainabura I found no informant able to describe a ghost nor any report of a human who had ever directly encountered one—or been affected by ghostly contact. The question itself produced surprise in Batainabura informants. For Abiera people, ghosts are vividly depicted as having glowing eyes, "like fire," and nostrils trailing long strings of mucus. Reports of sickness or loss of sanity—a syndrome suggesting "wild man behavior" (Newman 1964)—are fairly common, and deaths from ghosts within recent memory could be readily enumerated.

Ghosts are also sometimes reported at Abiera as helping their living descendants. The case of an Abiera man, lost in the bush above the settlement, illustrates this positive side of ghosts. As the victim stumbled helplessly about, he was bewildered by voices that later proved to be hostile ghosts of Arogara, an enemy people. They bade him descend a certain ravine and enter there a beautiful place. He was on the verge of doing their bidding when the ghost of none other than Mátoto spoke sternly to him. This most famous strong man of memory in Phratry Tairora held him back, saving him. (What may be implied, but taken for granted, is that the ghost of Mátoto spoke to the *máraqúra* of the hysterical man.) Mátoto told him to resist the deceit of the voices, which were their Arogara enemies, attempting to beguile him and lure him into the afterworld to his death.

Most waking encounters with ghosts are fearful and dangerous, however, as the impulses of ghosts to greed, lust, or aggression are seen to resemble those of living persons in practically all respects but restraint. The behavior of ghosts is unconstrained, in other words, in pursuit of largely selfish purposes at whatever cost to the living. The identity of marauding ghosts may often be known or suspected, but in my experience it is not common to speak of it openly unless one is pressed. Up to a certain point, moreover, identity is almost irrelevant, since all ghosts are feared and need not be known by name to be recognized as potentially harmful.[3]

3. The contrast between grassland Abiera, with its prevalent ghosts and few *wera*, and forest Batainabura (notably Sib Airiná), with just the opposite culture, suggests a possible functional equivalence in Northern Tairora of ghosts versus demons—grasslands with ghosts, woodlands with *wera*—and that with few of one there can be expected more of the other.

CELESTIAL AND TERRESTRIAL BEINGS COMPARED

As we have seen, the character of personified sky beings shows a certain suggestive uniformity—for example, in their involvement with large-scale effects and with the visible, the impersonal, and the fairly regular. What can be said in general of the character of demons and ghosts? That they are earthbound, in contrast to the sky beings, is obvious. They are seldom seen, being invisible or not steadily visible. But visibility is not necessary to demonstrate either their existence in general or the presence of a specific ghost or demons at a particular place or time. Unlike the sky beings, again, they are not (except for *aigega*) singular. Nor are they collective like the stars. They are very numerous classes of individual beings. Most of all, they intervene directly in human affairs. Although each class has characteristic looks, haunts, and deeds, the acts of individual members are not wholly predictable in whom they may touch or how. (Again the *aigega* seem to be the exception, having their regular sexual duties.) There is an indefiniteness about *aigega*, too, however, in that the remaining possibilities of their role are not explicitly limited. They may do other things besides raping fresh ghosts. In a single and literal word, ghosts and demons are uncanny; that is not the case with the sky beings, even though they are remote and virtually unreachable. Uncertainty is mixed with fear in the feelings of men toward the terrestrial beings.

To point to the obvious, demons and ghosts contribute to the major uncertainties of the world. Their influence is undeniably capricious and variable, if not perverse, as compared, for example, with the sun's. In behaving with forbearance toward persons with legitimate claim to the stretches of forest they inhabit,however, *wera* do regulate access and the exercise of rights to these resources. Indigenous themselves, they have a more tolerant relationship at least with indigenous mortals. Territorially, the range of power of any given demon is quite small, though his power within his own precinct is sufficient to cause illness, insanity, or death to individuals on whom it is brought to bear. (*Wera*, and probably other demons, incidentally, often use means in attacking men that resemble the methods of human sorcerers.)

Ghosts, by implication, range more widely than local demons. The passage of ghosts of remote peoples, is sometimes noticed, and encounters with them are considered possible, at least in theory.[4] In coming and going from *bánamáqa* to the territory of their origin, moreover, ghosts appear to cover a rather large territory. Despite their range, nevertheless, it is far more common to assume that ghosts are concerned not with men at large but with members of the group in which they spent their mortal lives. So for practical purposes they are local, too, like demons.

---

4. The ghosts of Auyana, a distinct ethnolinguistic group, are unusually audible as they pass. In the opinion of Batainabura informants, this is because of a peculiar device or extension of their "bodies" that loudly strikes against grass and branches along the path.

Demons are easily and vividly imagined. First instilled in children, the imagery receives sufficient confirmation and hence credibility from the psychic experience of persons or their hysterical reports. Demons are plausible, helping to account for incidents or for a person's sensations in reacting to situations in which he feels apprehensive and unsure. Demons are responsible, then, for some of the irregularities of personal experience that are beyond one's power to manage or control, except by prudence or avoidance. Demons both express and reinforce the feeling of awe, especially awe of the woods and waters, where men feel less the masters and may more easily meet with mishaps. Thus does the office and influence of demons and ghosts differ from the rising and setting of the sun, the growth and death of the moon, the menstruation of women, the procreative power of semen, or the fertility of females. Demons and ghosts rather account for some of the good or ill luck of humans, the portion of it that occurs apart from the will and skill of other humans, and the portion that occurs despite one's own best efforts to regulate and control outcomes through the use of those magical powers that are accessible.

Thus, among the known forms or expressions of magic of the world, those that are largely or wholly inaccessible to human control are divided into two parts. One set of powers is in the keeping of a small number of predominantly benign and remote beings with visible and regular manifestations. These are associated with large celestial bodies or spaces. The other set of powers is in the keeping of predominantly but irregularly malign or unpredictable beings, associated with terrestrial places, generally unseen, and beyond numbering. Each of the latter has great power from the point of view of a given target he may choose, but the being is normally active only within a small range; and his actions affect only one or a few persons at a time.

Apart from the celestial bodies or spaces, there is substantial uncertainty for the human actor in confronting his world. For one thing, as noted, many magical possibilities are simply not known, some of them possibly in the hands of men of another locality, who may use their greater knowledge and access to one's disadvantage. The number if not the variety of demonic agents that may attack the individual, added to the number of humans with means and motive to do so, the presence (for some Northern Tairora) of ghosts, and the potential activity of vaguer beings, such as the lightning being, the upholder of the earth, or the causer of landslides capable of burying men, all combine to make a world full of numerous and various perils.

It goes without saying, probably, that in such circumstances speculation about cause and agency has much room in which to range. Following an affliction or misfortune, there is often among those concerned an intense discussion of possible source. The need for firmer knowledge through dream and divination is frequently acute. Otherwise, the verdicts reached are reached by stages and by consensus, rather than deriving at once from hard or incontrovertible evidence and unmistakable criteria.

However capricious the interpretation of magical indications may seem, in the face of most misfortunes the attention of men is concentrated on the actions or suspected actions of other men. So much so that an ethnographer's impression—mine at any rate—was frequently that of a world of strikingly human scale, one in which even large-scale outcomes were treated as being within reach of human intention. Not only thwarted purposes—broken fences, failed gardens, or lost pigs, individual deformity or death—but floods and landslides could occur at the wish of men with the necessary competence. The millennial promises of cargo need only be recalled to underscore the extent of power humans consider it credible for men to wield. The open-endedness of the world of magical powers means that men may wield new and even wider powers, conceivably, than they have previously done.

   The vast magical competence claimed for men in Northern Tairora belief recalls the familiar characterizations of "bizarre," "superstitious," "absurd," or "childish." "Prescientific" may be no better than a euphemism, now justly discredited as the ethnocentric stereotyping of "primitive religion." Indigenous claims to power demand to be acknowledged and to be understood in their own right. It gives a better sense of proportion and perspective to remember that Northern Tairora wishes and events are played against a world scale that is minuscule. It is smaller by far than the island of New Guinea. In a tiny earth it is a tiny race of mankind—probably fewer than twenty-five thousand people—that is held to be subject to the human control of magic. More people than that are simply unknown. The waning moon and the setting sun descend to earth not at some vast distance from the intersection of the perpendicular of the zenith but perhaps no more than thirty or forty miles. It is presumably in part from this dimension, more than from an overweening claim of competence, that men's mystery and purported mastery, hence their notions of magic, may seem grandiose. If men seem to move the world, it is a small world they move.

MAGICAL POWER ACCESSIBLE TO HUMAN USE

   To turn to magical powers accessible to human manipulation is to exchange a domain tenanted by a handful of sky beings and a mere three or four kinds of earthbound demons and ghosts for one in which the expressions of magic are exceedingly numerous and diverse. The magical powers accessible to man are objectified rather than personified. Their efficacy is not localized but can be brought to bear on a suitable objective at any place or time. Magical powers are abstract, neutral, impersonal, and intrinsically unattached to any purpose. The manipulator supplies the purpose. The power may escape his purpose, furthermore, like a lighted fuse, finding whatever may be its own innate course and outcome if the manipulator is unknowing or inept. Unintended persons or objects can be damaged, that is, simply by being in the way of a power. Thus in fact do men sometimes explain the sickening of pigs near a large settlement whose herd may be overpressing its forage, or where endemic disease rises through crowding. Too much magic is being loosed, whether or not deliberately against pigs. Manipulable magic tends to be quite specific, moreover; and when well chosen, its forms are in fairly precise relation to a particular purpose. This is easily understood once it is recognized that the choice of magical materials, and especially the choice of ritual, is governed by certain fairly clear principles.

There is probably no magical ritual of Northern Tairora that is not named, but I did not attempt to catalogue all the rituals or record the names. There are several classes of sorcery at present, for instance, such as *uqai*, sorcery using exuviae of the intended victim; *uhi*, sorcery in which ginger is used and ancestors are (in one variant) invoked against the targeted person; and *ailai*, a more elaborate form of exuvial treatment involving several practitioners. A type or class of sorcery in the foregoing sense is generally a single main pattern within which one or more options (often local or individual versions) are known or accepted. The basic pattern may consist of an essential material or technique as well as being partly defined by its potential or intended result. Variations on the basic pattern appear minor to the outside observer and are not usually accorded much importance by the Northern Tairora. When new forms of sorcery are introduced, they tend to constitute new classes with separate names. This fact is consistent with the point made earlier that magic is perceived as a multiple domain with numerious, distinct forms not to be reduced to a single abstract principle such as "power." Not only does the domain of magical knowledge have an open frontier, in other words, but the present charting of types of sorcery is transitory and insufficient to encompass future developments.

RITUAL AND MAGIC: FORM, PURPOSE, AND PERSONNEL

Magical practice is ritualized activity, though not all of ritual is magic. Greeting etiquette, dancing, oratorical form, and much else in Northern Tairora life is more or less ritualized behavior in which magic plays at most a secondary part. Magic, on the other hand, consists of more than its ritualized application, for there is a body of underlying knowledge and principle.

Rituals vary with the *number and kinds of individuals participating*, whether they are required to be specialists, whether there is more than one role to be performed, or whether they are all of one sex or not. The least rituals of all in this regard would be the observance of simple taboos, in which a single individual, unspecialized and acting alone, is frequently the sole participant as well as the immediate beneficiary of the ritual. Various precautions and avoidance procedures illustrate rituals with a sole participant. One defecates or expectorates, for instance, in a safe place—ideally where these substances will not reach hostile lands. At the other extreme are community-wide, even phratry-wide, rituals, such as male initiation with near total participation of coresidents, roles differentiated both by sex and seniority and by relationship to the initiate. *Ihálabu*, a renewal ceremony which I did not observe, would nearly match initiation for breadth of participation and perhaps for diversity of roles.

Magical rituals vary also according to their targets or beneficiaries. There are some in which target and beneficiary are the same, as in magical protection through a kind of inoculation; but in others, like sorcery, target and beneficiary are opposites. In short, the reasons people have for bringing magic to bear, the number of persons sharing the interest, the distribution of competence among them, and the number of ritual operators called for or permitted in a given mobilization of magic—all of these vary. When a ritual must be carried out covertly, for instance, as in sorcery against an enemy group, a small number of operators may be mandatory, though the intended beneficiaries be the originating community at large.

In view of this range of rituals and the absence of a Northern Tairora category as broad as "magical ritual," what is the justification for such a grouping? The justification is analytical. Cutting across these several rituals, and for the most part common to them all are a number of features that appear to warrant recognizing the larger set, "magical rituals." Among these features are (1) the common use of substances of special efficacy to promote the ritual purpose, (2) behavioral forms common to various rituals, (3) the expression of common ritual principles, and (4) the recognition of extraordinary purposes in which the relation between ritual act and purpose, as a rule, is relatively indirect, in contrast to the relation of ordinary acts and their purposes;[5] outcome is typically delayed, often following act by substantial interval (the "feedback loop" is longer); and outcome is often diffuse and complex, success relative, achievement highly susceptible of interpretation, and some actors are considered more apt or authoritative than others for interpretation ("feedback" is frequently ambiguous).

Recognizing a sphere of magical ritual, the foregoing features do not, however, separate magic as a principle of efficacy from some other domain of human purpose or activity where magic plays no part. I can find no basis in Northern Tairora for two such domains—say, an extraordinary magical domain and an ordinary, nonmagical one. Finding such a device, of course, would mean that "magic" or "religion" is conceptualized by the people as a distinct domain—a concept I have previously suggested is lacking. Magic is itself "ordinary"—an everyday, practical fact of life. It is ultimately as relevant to the commonplace as to the ritual part of the spectrum of human purposes and activities. The foregoing features, then, help identify what makes the ritual part of the spectrum—the most overtly "magical"—intuitively

5. "Indirect" operations are those in which the intended effect is produced by means other than the physical manipulation of the given object. A blow on the head by a man wielding a club is more direct, for instance, than a ritual the same man performs to cause a tree limb, or someone else's club, to fall on the same head. Giving suitable food is somewhat more direct—though not more critical—in promoting the growth of a child than is the *ubára* initiation.

special and different. It is not that magic in the indigenous sense of the word is limited to what is difficult, ritualized, or diffuse or difficult of outcome, requiring to be achieved by indirect means. Certainly both the means and the intended outcomes of magical ritual are more salient than, say, roasting a tuber or kindling a fire. But magic is wider than the outsider's intuitive sense of it as being confined to only the most dramatic, salient, or ritualized purposes and activities.

Common elements of form and common principles are to be found in rituals, from the briefest and smallest acts, of interest primarily to the single actor, to community-wide ceremonies. The hot-cold opposition can serve as an illustration of a principle common to quite distinct rituals. Despite their distinct native categorization, both covert sorcery for killing enemies and public ceremonies for promoting the growth and health of one's own group are considered "hot." In order to succeed, the ritual in each case must be carried out with a scrupulous concern for the exclusion of critical "cold" elements. In each case sexual continence is required of the participant or practitioner. A common legend of Batainabura, for instance, has a man dying because his wife, eager to copulate, deliberately conceals from him that the *ihálabu* (renewal) ceremony has begun. Sorcerers must also be continent for a period prior to and during their manipulations. The cold, female contact could endanger them and nullify their "hot" efforts.

Many of the same materials—ginger is a good example—crop up in various ritual contexts. Spraying food with a chewed mixture, typically including ginger and native salt, is a part of a number of rituals in which the consumption of food, especially pork, is also a central feature. A principle such as inoculation has multiple applications in ritual form.

The public ritual of betrothal is replete with the symbolism of wifehood, of separation of the bride from her brothers, of her conveyance by them to the groom's group, and of a new role and changing obligations. The sense of these admittedly rather stock ritual acts, I believe, is magical. At a certain point in the proceedings pig grease is smeared on the body of the betrothed woman, a measure so common in other Northern Tairora contexts as well that it, too, may seem "stock" and possibly therefore "ordinary" and nonmagical. To push such a distinction, however, would be ironic, denying a magical character to the most ubiquitous elements of the repertory for the very reason that their magic is widely and diversely employed.

There is a recurrence of purpose, principle, or rationale, of material sources of power, and again of ritual forms or procedures across the field of magical practice. It is the various combinations of such magical elements, some like the foregoing quite common, that fill the field with such a number of distinct, named practices. One by one, many of the elements are common, that is, but their various combinations are thought of as unique. A full knowledge of these combinations—of the elements, too, of course—would be very large. It is large enough, certainly, to distinguish various categories of the Northern Tairora people from each other according to the extent of their mastery—male from female, adult from immature, and adept from nonspecialist.

Unifying not only all rituals that are significantly magical in intent but at the same time showing the integrity of the Northern Tairora sense of magic is its rationale. The rationale of Northern Tairora magic includes several principles that are implicit either singly or in combination in rituals that otherwise vary widely. These principles are all more or less well known in the contexts of other cultures. Most basic of all is what might be called the transitivity model, the paradigm of magical practice. The ritualized practice of magic consists in bringing a known power to bear on an intended object or in keeping such a power from coming to bear on an object when that object may be favorably or adversely affected by the power. A simple diagram will indicate the point. Ritual forms are one of the four essential elements of the transitivity model:

I	II	III	IV
Efficacious source	Ritual form appropriate to given source-object-purpose	Target or object(s)	Desired state or condition of object to be affected

Or more briefly:

$$\text{Magic} \times \text{Object} = \text{Purpose}$$

or $M \times O = P$. The purpose, as noted, is to change a given state of an object either for the better or for the worse, or to guarantee the continuation of a desired state if it is thought to be in jeopardy of being changed. The ritual part of magical application, then, is an appropriate means of juxtaposing some magical power and a given object to a predetermined purpose.

A full description of the Northern Tairora theory of magical practice consists in determining what makes a substance efficacious for a particular end, what governs the appropriateness of a certain ritual as a means of juxtaposing suitable substance to the object of some intention, and what constitutes an object. To take the last point first, it is not only a question of what objects a practitioner may feasibly attempt to affect but of whether proxies or substitutes may be used in directing magical power toward or away from those objects, and if so, what constitutes a suitable proxy. For some purposes, bodily contact with the object may be required; for others, exuviae may be used in proxy for a person; and for still others, a substitute object like a dead rat or a banana may be named for him. All exuviae are not equal, however, in affording access to the ultimate target, and thus not all are suited to every intention in which the person-object is targeted. Food leavings give lesser access to a person-object, for example, than his feces; and, in the case of a male, give less access than semen. With lesser exuviae, more strenuous ritual effort and perhaps more potent magical substances may be required to accomplish the same effect—but the same impact is less likely than with greater exuviae.

The rationale of Northern Tairora magical practice does thus consist in a description of efficacy, of ritual, and of objects, as well as of purposes that are considered attainable. The principles or generalized rules that may be found in analyzing the rationale will be the principles that appear to underlie efficacy in substances, appropriateness in ritual form, and validity in objects. As sketched below, a number of principles are discernible in Northern Tairora magical theory. In the succeeding paragraphs and pages some of these principles of Northern Tairora magic will be discussed.

1. Principles Defining Efficacy in Material Substances

Innateness: Many of the known substances are efficacious to some degree for some purpose, and of those not known to be efficacious some may conceivably be discovered to be so.

Pragmatic rule: That which is productive is efficacious. That which is not palpably counterproductive may be productive.

Similarity: A substance having some property (such as color, texture, shape, weight, or flavor) perceived to resemble the object or an intended state of the object may be efficacious toward producing that state.

Authority: Efficacies proclaimed by persons or groups considered authoritative are probably as proclaimed.

2. Principles Defining Appropriate Ritual Form

Sympathy: Like produces like. Therefore, simulation or imitation of a desired state in the object may define appropriate ritual form.

Targeting: Type of ritual follows targeting in relation to (a) the form of efficacious substance employed and (b) the mode of its employment, such as aiming at a distance; pervasive emanation, as in large public rituals; ingestion; inoculation; contact; invasion of body's interior; and so forth.

3. Principles Defining the Object

Directness: The object itself can be reached through potent substances concealed in its vicinity.

Pars pro toto: The use of a person-object's name or a substitute object, or of exuviae of greater or less validity is required when concealment is out of the question. Exuviae have greater validity the more intimate they are to the person-object or the more proximate to the seat of his vitality, or, generally, the more internal to his body (feces, semen) as opposed to superficial exuviae (clothing, food scraps).

Vulnerability: Different classes of objects do not have the same vulnerability. Children and women, for example, are more vulnerable than men to many kinds of power. Ordinary men are more vulnerable than strong men.

PRINCIPLES DEFINING EFFICACY IN SUBSTANCES

Fundamental to Northern Tairora magic is a belief in the innate, specific power or efficacy of various known objects or substances. In this basic premise, the magical theory is rather similar, so to speak, to the theory of substances and efficacies of modern Western culture. Ginger is a substance with specific power. As a commonly used "hot" substance, ginger is the principal material in one form of ritual attack on an enemy, while in other ritual contexts it is the main power in combating illness. The power of substances like ginger, native salt, several kinds of bark, certain leaves, pig grease, cassowary fat, or pig's blood, is intrinsic to them. Traditions of long standing affirm their efficacy. To those with the rightful knowledge of its existence and of the proper ritual application for specific purposes, such power is always accessible.

We may call the known or potential uses of each substance its valence. The range of possible applications or the valence of a given material may be wide or narrow. The valence of ginger is rather broader, for example, than that of many other materials, some of them limited to a single known efficacy or application. Some substances are useful only for protective purposes, some for curative, and and some for inflicting damage, injury, or death. Pig's blood is primarily a protective and curative material, as when it is smeared on the body of a person or the posts of a house, while ginger, as mentioned, fits into both attack and healing ritual contexts. Different materials that overlap in their range of applications may also differ in potency—that is, the degree of certainty of the outcome of their use, or the amount of change they are thought capable of producing in the state of an object.

In principle, substances that common sense prompts one to call "magical" belong to the same main universe in Northern Tairora as all other substances. They do not differ from others in having valence or potency, but only in having a certain *kind* of valence or a certain *degree* of potency. It is this, in effect their efficacy, that gives some substances a special character: they are useful in effecting certain puposes. Among foodstuffs, for example, each has its particular valence, its own potency. Some foods are "strong," perhaps too strong for some persons. Every food is good for certain purposes, not for others; but some foods are also harmful for certain purposes. Certain Northern foods are considered fit to be eaten only at certain times. Although they are substances capable of feeding the body or allaying hunger, some foods are tabooed for use by one sex or the other, or by persons of a certain age, or by individuals currently in a certain condition, such as fatherhood, pregnancy, lactation, or involvement in fighting, sorcery, or ceremony. The taboos against some foods, in other words, arise from the assignment of a distinct potency and a particular valence to which individuals in the proscribed categories are considered vulnerable. Yet commonsensically one would not call such foods "magical." This common belief about foodstuffs, nonetheless, seems consistent with the Northern Tairora view that every substance has its particular potency and valence. The substances we would call magical—because they are strong or deadly or because they have potent curative power—differ only in their particular efficacy from any other substances, such as string for making net bags or fuel for making fire.

Very well, but how is their efficacy different? The shortest answer would be to say that the efficacy of "magical" materials is less ordinary, more salient, for example, than the string for knotless netting. Magical substances are those of the world's materials whose specific efficacy gives them a strategic importance for purposes whose outcomes are, on the one hand, crucial and, on the other, insecure or indirect—requiring ritual care. Attack sorcery or curative applications are clearly spheres of more intense concern and spheres in which one's means are more indirect or uncertain of control than, say, the making of fire or the knotless netting of burden bags. Success or failure, nevertheless, is determined in all cases by the choice of appropriate materials and by the use of appropriate techniques.

To speak of "magical substances," thus, is to recognize materials whose particular valence and potency prominently recommend them as instrumental for purposes that humans achieve by indirect or ritual means. This view of the magical aspect of materials (as well as of acts and situations) seems faithful to the numerous indications that the Northern Tairora world is continuous. The sense of efficacy within it is not isolated or circumscribed but is, to the contrary, pervasive of and intrinsic to all of it. It is at best but a matter of convenience if we consider some materials and situations or some activities "magical." Whatever our convenience in so doing, the fullness of the Northern Tairora world—"the pervasiveness of magical principle"—seems self-insistent. Its notion of materials, interestingly enough, could be styled as a sort of chemistry, with catalysts, reagents, and neutralizers. Abstractions like "potency" and "valence" accordingly prove useful in speaking of the implications of Northern Tairora beliefs and their uses of materials.

The nourishing qualities of food, in Northern Tairora principle, are as much their potency and "valence" as are the curative or the death-dealing virtues of ginger, appropriately administered. It is only that the purposes for which foods are primarily used are more secure—not that they are less crucial—than the purposes for which ginger is used. They are quite literally *ordinary* purposes. It is also worthwhile noting, perhaps, that a wide variety of foods can serve the same purpose in satisfying hunger, probably making it easier to see a given foodstuff as less singular than, say, ginger. The act of eating is common and frequent, with consequences both immediate and predictable. Satisfying hunger by the act of eating could hardly thus be described, at least in the short run, as the management of an outcome characterized by unusual difficulty or uncertainty, or one requiring special competence or ritual performance.

There is hardly a question that the commonsensically "magical" has greater drama and salience than the "nonmagical," nor is there any doubt about the reason for it. Though for us a poison is no more "chemical" than a potato, it is more considerable by far. Because of its potential and because of the ways in which a poison may be used—covertly, secretly, stealthily, aggressively and with intense effect—we are more concerned to know whose hands hold the poison. The salience of some Northern Tairora forms of magical power similarly arises not from their being uniquely magical but from their unique potency, their promise or threat to the interests of anyone within reach. Naturally men will speak in awe of the "wild bamboo" whose lethal power is held to be boundless. A small scrap of this plant, a single leaf in the stream from which a local group drink, will eliminate them all in a day. Mere possession—or suspected possession—of such a substance would produce admiration or alarm; but a child would probably toss a banana in the air to its heart's content without risking comment or reproach—certainly not consternation. Naturally one does not speak of bananas and the lethal bamboo in the same breath, but the difference is not between the "magical" and the "nonmagical." It is not, that is, between substances with potency and valence and others lacking them.

Rarity or remoteness, such as that of the lethal bamboo, is certainly not characteristic of all potent substances. Ginger is not rare. It grows in many gardens, probably, in every local territory. The scarcity of a substance will no doubt affect its availability or price, or the frequency of its use, or the familiarity of knowledge about it; and it can surely add to the awesomeness of a substance like the fabulous bamboo. (Indeed, were it not so rare, it perhaps could not be considered so lethal!) Many materials used magically are not in themselves either exotic or unfamiliar.

The paramount test in establishing the potency and valence of specific items must be much the same for Northern Tairora as for the rest of mankind. It is the testimony of experience, the pragmatic criterion. In netting a burden bag, building a house, trenching a garden, or spewing ginger and salt on pork, to catalyze its strength or the health of those who eat it, the constant confirmation of expectation by outcome is decisive, in the long run if not the short. The results of different efforts and applications by men vary within ranges that my be quite narrow in some cases, much wider in others. There must accordingly be a gradient or coefficient of confirmation between purpose, or what is expected, on the one hand, and variability or controlability of outcome, on the others.

The pragmatic rule does not demarcate a distinct class of human judgments, leaving all others to fall into a sharply different "nonpragmatic" category. Rather, there is a continuum of expectations with respect to the degree of control an actor can manage. Some purposes admit of more control—a narrower range of possible miscue or a lesser likelihood of countervailing intervention, hence less uncertainty of outcome—than do other purposes. Once again—and only in a slightly different context—one confronts the holistic Northern Tairora world: the means for determining the valences of its various elements do not operate discontinuously. The principle of applicability or suitability is in force across the entire range of items. To take the contrary view would be to say that "magical" items are exempt from the test of experience, that forms of sorcery or medicine are simply untested—in effect, that anything goes.

The most one can say about the continuous relevance of the pragmatic rule is that its criteria may be satisfied as long as experience does not grossly contradict expectations. Conviction may be stronger still, naturally, if experience confirms expectations. In this area, the physical world intersects with human experience to precipitate a "cognized world," as Rappaport calls it (1967:237-42). Experience both builds and prunes the cognized. Recurrent, nonproductive efforts—even more, recurrent, counterproductive efforts— will not for long be perceived as productive. Efforts that are apparently productive, or which are not counterproductive, may come to be or continue to be perceived as productive. Productive efforts are normally apt to be recognized for their value.

In this literal and simple form, these statements misrepresent reality. They disregard the size and complexity of some feedback loops, such as the fullest possible perceptual context of "productive." A ritualized bit of magical application, for example, may produce a lowering of stress in an anxious person. His "doing *some*thing" is quite likely a part of the productivity that contributes to the continued life of the belief and the practice. The insight is commonplace. Not as generally accepted, perhaps, is that the same fundamental principles underlie the valence of all acts or substances, and not just those that we may call nonmagical,. Experience confirms, reassures, establishes, validates belief and practice. The more direct the experience—the shorter the feedback loop—the more a clear experiential confirmation will make a belief or practice quotidian and ordinary, like eating or netting burden bags.

Under what conditions does the pragmatic rule require supplement? It is well to speak of supplement or reinforcement, for, unless we are mistaken, the pragmatic rule, the test of experience, is not itself suspended. However, it rules less uniquely, so to speak, in some cases than in others. The longer the feedback loop, the less directly experience can provide a crucial test of belief or practice; and the less often or regularly it can do so, the more the pragmatic rule is apt to be supplemented in Northern Tairora magic by other principles, such as similarity (e.g., ginger and "heat") or the authority of credible originators or instigators.

Of the four parts of the model of magical practice, ritual form appears to be the most subject to the others. Objects, such as persons, pigs, or garden plants, have at base a form given by their nature, and culture may enter only in attributing vulnerability or in establishing the validity of a symbolic substitute. Purposes arise from social interaction or from other needs external at least to the magic itself that serves a given purpose. The magical efficacy of certain substances is likewise ruled in part by the natural form, texture, flavor, provenience, and so forth of the substance, as well as by ascribed properties that stand or have stood the test of the criteria perviously discussed.

As behavior or movement, manipulation and act, ritual form is a locomotor linkage supplied by operators between a magical source or potential and an object in which some change (or continuity) is defined by a purpose. Ritual is, in other words, plastic and adaptable, presumably shaped by what the given objects, purpose, and available efficacy jointly require. If the magical efficacy employed requires to be brought into direct contact with the targeted object for the purpose sought, the ritual act must of course be shaped by this fact. If the magical efficacy is such that it can be projected line-of-sight at a targeted object, and if direct contact is neither required nor possible, the ritual act will differ accordingly. If the object need not be within sight of the operator but the direction of the power to the object is controlled by other means, such as invoking the object by a name, then ritual form will include such an invocation and may thus differ once more from the form required in other circumstances.

Invisibility magic is an essential standby for the professional magician who would safely move among enemy houses, for example, in order to overhear the act of copulation and collect semen at the site from a known man who may later be a target. Invisibility is attained by means of a certain leaf that is interposed between the sorcerer and those from whom he must remain concealed. Ritual form is thus prescribed in the use of the leaf by affixing it to the forehead of the sorcerer or in plastering it against the open palm of one hand, which he extends as necessary in the direction of any unwanted eyes that might observe him.

As the least autonomous element in the formula of magical practice, ritual is nevertheless indispensable. A commonplace example is the insertion of a scrap of a targeted person's food between two tightly entwined or overlapping branches of a tree that abrade each other when the wind moves them. The purpose is to produce a sore or constricted throat in the victim, or sometimes a seizure to prevent his breathing. The exuviae here stand in place of the object—the victim or his throat. The abrading branches are—through a sympathetic resemblance to the desired change in the object—the substantial source of power. The ritual of capturing and inserting the food scrap between the branches is thus the essential link between magical source, object, and purpose. It must therefore be concluded that the achievement of purpose arises no less from the ritual act than from the source of power and the object-substitute employed. In its form, however, the ritual is unquestionably dictated by Northern Tairora ideas of efficacious substances or situations and of accessible objects or object substitutes.

It is perhaps in the postcontact introduction of *sangguma* that ritual form most nearly becomes the autonomous source of magic, possibly obviating the employment of specific powerful substances. One is not on wholly sure ground, however, in taking this ritual form as an expression of the Northern Tairora theory of magic. At the time of my observations *sangguma* was probably, for many if not all Northern Tairora, more a matter of hearsay than of firsthand knowledge. In any case, in their view, it appeared to be the surgery itself—the invasion of the body cavity and the interference with its living organs—that mainly defined *sangguma*. This is not to say that they completely denied the use or need of any magical substances but only that they were much vaguer about substances than about the surgery. The modern development of *sangguma*, once it is fully established in indigenous Northern Tairora sorcery, may thus prove a break from the primary involvement of magical materials. It is surely a rather complex undertaking, on the other hand, involving not only surgical techniques but probably some source of immediate power, as yet unknown to the Northern Tairora, whereby the victim is rendered obedient to those who will victimize him, even before surgery begins. Thus even *sangguma* may have, or come to have, a component substance.[6]

Possible objects of Northern Tairora magical practice include men and their products, equipment, and enterprises. Gardens and pigs may be made to prosper or fail, journeys to succeed or be difficult, and fights to go in favor of or against one's own. But a list of all the objects that potentially may be targeted in Northern Tairora magical theory suggests a frequency and intensity of resort to ritual magic that I did not find, as well as failing to suggest that both the practice and the concern with magic are most heavily concentrated on people as objects. It may be the case that in theory almost any irregular event known to the Northern Tairora can be ascribed to or produced by magic: death or injury from falling trees, landslides, stolen or lost pigs, barren sows, washed out gardens, burned houses, adulterous wives, sickly or obstreperous children, unproductive gardens, and so forth. It may be that at one time or another every such event has been ascribed to magical intervention, perhaps correctly. Yet the people with whom I lived were in practice far less inclined to suggest deliberate magical intervention than theory might permit. Perhaps the reason was that since all magical practice was difficult and greater power was ever within reach, it did not often seem reasonable to suppose that competent magicians would delicately restrict themselves to lesser purposes. Consequently, one heard more of magic in connection with the more drastic and dramatic misfortunes, more in connection with misfortunes than with successes, and more in connection with injuries or deaths to humans than with regard to damage to their property or failure in their enterprises.

Lesser magical purposes have their principal place among one's own coresidents. Here grievances prevail often enough, but either the motive may be

6. Others will know better than I could know it from Northern Tairora the history and development of *sangguma* within New Guinea and perhaps beyond. For what it is worth, there is to me a haunting resemblance between the sense of *sangguma* in Northern Tairora and the procedures of modern surgery. The initial inducement of submission in the victim, for example, resembles the administration of an anesthetic. His oblivion concerning what has been performed on his body resembles the state of anesthesia. The victim's death a short while after treatment (but an interval whose duration is set by and known only to the practitioners) suggests any death of a former patient that might easily—and sometimes correctly—be attributed to his surgery by peoples unfamiliar with Western medicine. Even if this resemblance between the Northern Tairora idea of *sangguma* and Western surgical practice is indeed more than an accident, it need not have been a part of the inception of *sangguma*, however and wherever that was first developed. The convergence could occur as the idea of *sangguma* spread among peoples simultaneously exposed to surgical techniques but not yet familiar with either.

lacking or the risk too great to warrant, say, killing as opposed to causing sickness. Lesser purposes thus show the constraint that would be expected of a kinsman or coresident, albeit perhaps no resort whatever should in principle be made to sorcery against one's own people. Lesser purposes, on the other hand, serve to restrain those who are tempted to take advantage of their fellows, and sorcery in this role, as has often been recognized, can serve as social control. As far as the apparent contradiction of even admitting sorcery against coresidents is concerned, that is easily answered: it would not be used wantonly or without cause; and if cause has been given, the fraternal obligations have already somehow been violated, so that one who then resorts to sorcery cannot be blamed as instigator.

As previously noted, an object is anything whose state is considered to be alterable or conservable by appropriate magical means, and the broad variety of potential objects has just been sketched. In divination, however, the object is less readily defined. Divination is usually if not invariably practiced to learn the identity of an individual who has perpetrated some injury against one's own, or more often to learn the group of the perpetrator. A variety of forms of divination exist, the majority being variations on one of a few main themes. Rats named for various local groups may be exposed to cooking heat: the one with the culpable name remains uncooked. An arrow with a fiery tip may be discharged from a ridge or hilltop against a dark sky. Its flaming path leads directly to the local group that originated the sorcery in question. There it is believed to strike the center post of the men's house with a shower of sparks. This, incidentally, will advise the sorcerer his stealth has not succeeded and will terrify him. Still another form of divination involves the participation of a group of kinsmen close to the deceased victim. In unison they hold a long pole, bamboo, or spear with which they repeatedly stab down at a banana, sometimes placed on the shield of the deceased. With each stroke a possible group or individual thought capable of the attack is named. Until the right name is called, however, the blows continue to miss or stop short of the target; but with the name the thrust of the spear hits home, soon mashing the banana to a pulp. As blows come faster and faster with mounting excitement, the hands of the kinsman are helpless to resist, and conviction is likewise overpowering.

While the purpose of divination is clear enough in the terms we are using, a word or two may be needed concerning the object. In the proposed formula of Northern Tairora magical practice, it seems correct to focus on the banana itself as the key to the object. It is physically present in the ritual—in fact the immediate target on which physical change is to be effected in the course of a successful divination. Like the rats in cooking divination, moreover, or like the men's house center post in flaming arrow divination, the banana fits the logic of Northern Tairora magic as a substitute object. The banana or the rat, or even more directly the center post of the sorcerer's men's house, is the symbolic substitute of the intended object—the sorcerer or his group. The identity of the banana, like that of the sorcerer, must be discovered. The changed state of the object which is purposed, then, is the discovery of the sorcerer-object's identity, which he has heretofore concealed.

One could probably take the divination ritual, moreover, as a part of larger ritual in which it is the prelude. It is the intelligence phase, so to speak, for the countersorcery that will be directed at the target, once that is properly specified. The sorcerer-object, thus, will be the same throughout both the divination phase and the subsequent attack in which the object becomes the target of hurtful powers. Whether with divination as a discrete ritual or as a ritual phase of a larger magical undertaking, the suggested formula of Northern Tairora magical theory appears to be an adequate model. The recognition of divination ritual as essentially consistent with general magical principles helps in recognizing the full breadth of the Northern Tairora theory of objects and their symbolic substitutes.

Exuviae, a major category of objects, involves the principle of *pars pro toto*. The exuvial substance is selected for some physical association it has or has had with the object—for example, food scraps, scrapings from a doorpost, nail parings, hair, clothing, spittle, feces, or semen. Here the substitute is identified with the object innately and before ritual is begun. Its identity has in fact influenced the selection of the substitute, which must be correct lest the magical power strike an unintended object. A mistake would be committed if the wrong substitute were used, for the connection between a substitute and an object is intrinsic.

Exuvial object substitutes are graded, furthermore, according to the intimacy of their association with the object. The amount of power that can be brought to bear on an object through the manipulation of a substitute differs from one substitute to another. As previously noted, semen is the surest and amplest, hence the most lethal substitute of the foregoing list. It is the one through which the maximum injury can be inflicted in exuvial sorcery. The implicit reason seems to be that semen (as is true to a slightly lesser degree of feces) is from deep inside the body—and semen is furthermore close to the seat of a man's maleness.

In a second order of substitutes the association with the object is not intrinsic but rather a linkage established when the magician-operator names the substitute for the object. This is illustrated by the rat that is named before placing it in a swamp where its decay will pace the decline of the targeted victim-object. The operator's decision is not entirely free, however, since the substitutes for a given object are limited to certain things, such as rats. Additional criteria like similarity or resemblance may have a bearing on the validity of object substitutes. A rat, for example, is a warm mammalian body when alive, cold when dead, and its body is capable of rotting like a human's when placed in the ground. Incidentally, the swamp, being both cold and wet, could be said to be even more strongly associated with death than other burial places, in addition to which animal flesh may decay faster in local swamp soil.

In some forms of divination there appears to be a third order of object substitutes. Here there is neither an intrinsic association with the object nor, in some cases, a specific identity established by assigning a name to the substitute beforehand. The name is rather sought. The ritual of divination is, in essence, an interrogation. It is intended to ascertain (with the help of the victim's own *máraqúra*) an identity not previously or certainly known. In all observed forms of divination an object substitute is a given. In the case of banana-stabbling divination the ritual itself will establish the proper name of the substitute. For the practitioner, the banana substitute is already a substitute person or group, to be sure, with the identity, let us say, of a "party or parties unknown." This is true, at least, from the moment a particular banana is selected for use. What specific person or group the banana represents will be revealed to the participants in the course of the ritual. In effect, then, an unknown person substitute is linked to an unknown person-object, the mutual identity of both substitute and object being simultaneously revealed in the ritual. In other divination rites a prior linkage exists or is established. With cooking divination, the identities of the respective rats are assigned by the practitioner, as is done in certain magical rituals besides divination. Each rat is now known, but what remains to be known is which of them is the sorcerer—which, that is, responds uniquely to the fire by remaining uncooked. In the case of flaming-arrow divination, the object substitutes are intrinsically given, once more, after the principle of *pars pro toto* or synecdoche. The center posts of the men's houses of neighboring local groups cannot fail to be associated with the sorcerers of each or with the local group of the sorcerer.

Nonobjects and nonsubstitutes for objects of magic have at least been implied. Nonobjects are seen in the parts of the world that are inaccessible to human agents. It is less easy to deal with items that are not substitutable for objects. The question of object substitutes has been touched on in connection with the principles that define acceptable and valid substitutes. What principles may define a substitute as unacceptable or invalid is not easy to say, once one has passed one or two fairly obvious deductions. For the purposes of this monograph, I will confine myself to illustrating what deductions I consider to be "fairly obvious" and to examining the case of blood and urine, which, unlike a number of other body substances, are not clear and valid object substitutes for the purpose of magical attack.

It seems fairly obvious that remoteness from or lack of resemblance to objects tends to invalidate conceivable object substitutes. Remote or dissimilar items are less apt to be accepted as substitutes for given objects of magical attack, protection, or promotion than items that are similar or near to the given objects. Such a flat statement, not surprisingly, needs qualification. Indigenous precept and symbolism betray the naïve outside observer often enough. The resemblance of rats to humans has been suggested, although I suspect there may be a deeper resemblance here than the externalities I have mentioned. As for bananas, they are a crop of explicitly masculine cultivation, which might suggest why they and not sweet potatoes are used in divining the provenience of magical attack by sorcerers, who are doubtless masculine. This is hardly enough to permit one to say, however, why yams are not used, since they are explicitly likened to men's bones, their testicles, or their penises. I am prepared to believe that there may be a gap in my knowledge of Northern Tairora culture in this sector (as well as in many others). It may be the case, however, that some reason now forgotten governed the original selection of bananas over other crop items.

Urine, as far as I was able to discover, does not figure in magical attack by human agents as a valid or common object substitute. If some exception escapes my notice, it would still be safe to say that urine is a far less prominent substitute than several other exuviae. The ones mentioned most often in these pages are so conventional and stereotyped as to seem almost a litany, even when recited by Northern Tairora persons of no special magical knowledge. Yet urine comes from inside the body and is surely a more intimate substance than sweet potato skins, bits of clothing, or scrapings from a doorpost where the occupant of a house may have left his sweat. The invalidity of urine would appear to be at least partly attributable to its watery nature. Water, it will be recalled, is a specific counteragent. it is a "cold" substance as opposed to the necessary "heat" of successful magic. The case is imperfect at best, however, because while one often hears that falling rain or water deliberately poured on a sorcerer's materials can bring his efforts to naught, the possibility of urinating on them to the same end is not cited. Nor is urine entirely useless for magic, albeit not the magic of humans. In an unfamiliar bush, men are said to be anxious about the disposition of their exuviae. A resident *wera*, resentful of their trespass, or offended by some breach of etiquette even by legitimate visitors, might capture such substances and use them magically to the detriment of their owners. A bit of soil on which a man has urinated is specifically noted as being useful to a *wera* in confusing his victim's mind. It does not seem reasonable that urine should be of lesser validity than spittle, about which there is at least some exuvial concern. One is as "watery" as the other. I have seen men take great care to dispose of their spittle by placing it in a hole in the ground when attending a large gathering sponsored by the subdistrict office. There, to be sure, they were in the midst of a greater number of nearly total strangers than they would normally encounter in a lifetime in their own territories. In other contexts, as anyone who has traversed the roads and pathways of Northern Tairora must have noticed, men spew with great abandon the saliva that betel-chewing brings to their mouths. They leave this highly visible expectorate on rocks, fences, logs, clay banks, or on the beaten path, with no show of concern, where even the clumsiest of sorcerers could capture it if it were of value. Possibly it is thought that the betel invalidates spittle for magical purposes, even as defecating in water robs feces of their magical value.

Among exuviae invalid for magical use, blood is if anything more complex than urine. Blood has ample ritual use and a powerful significance, particularly for sexuality. As a specifically maternal legacy, it is a substance whose influence must be mitigated as far as possible to permit masculine qualities to develop. Menstrual blood is a major pollutant, potentially lethal to men not properly protected from its influence. Men deliberately shed their own and each other's blood through ritual nose bleeding, not only in initiation but subsequently in adulthood. Ideally, when preparing for battle, a group of men collect blood from each of them, intermix it with salt and other substances, and serve a share to be eaten by each participant. *Esprit de corps* is powerfully expressed in this act but possibly also the principle of a common inoculation against a common weakness.

Blood was never cited to me as valid for ordinary exuvial purposes. A malicious woman is conventionally credited with sometimes using her own menstrual blood to harm a husband she resents. While this declares the dangerous potency of (female) blood to males, it is certainly not a claim that blood affords a valid magical access to its erstwhile owner. On balance one can note the marked symbolism of blood in contexts other than magical attack. Although possessing several prime qualities of exuviae, its meaning in other symbolic contexts is perhaps too distinctive and too contradictory to permit the acceptance of blood as a valid object substitute.

The Open Nature and Innovative Potential of Northern Tairora Religion

The foregoing arguments are unrefined and probably are based on an incomplete statement of indigenous belief, value, and symbol. The two cases considered surely do no exhaust the anomalies of Northern Tairora theory, nor do the considerations presented above exhaust the theory of objects and substitutes. The cases rather illustrate one of the less well lighted areas of Northern Tairora magical theory and practice. A number of dimly lit areas surround the familiar parts of both theory and practice, parts that are known by rote and can be delivered by rule to an inquiring ethnographer. While the foregoing discussion suggests that the ethnographer has unfinished business, I trust it will also suggest that Northern Tairora theory has unfinished business of its own. Such is probably the perennial condition of Northern Tairora belief, value, and symbol. My particular uncertainties, I believe, do not simply reflect an incomplete knowledge of linkages and consistencies that must be presumed to be fully enclosed. The existence of such perfect dogma and praxis rather remains to be shown, and I suspect it cannot always be shown.

It has already been emphasized that tension and open-endedness, with consequent variability and disagreement of knowledge from individual to individual, seem to be among the defining attributes of Northern Tairora religion. In effect, there is uncertainty in those who live by the religion as well as in those who, like the ethnographer, wish to know it. It is commonly asserted that religions afford their adherents certainty in the midst of a world that must appear uncertain. So be it. But this familiar axiom should not, in a case like the present, blind one to the existence of uncertainties in the very means for providing assurance. In some ways, it seems fair to view Northern Tairora religions—or Northern Tairora magic—not only as assertive but as interrogative. Perhaps one should see it as a frame for asking questions as well as one for grounding answers. The essentials of power or powers are granted; but their infinitude, as against the existential finiteness of human competence, surely implies a question mark.

This philosophizing of Northern Tairora religion might suggest in its tone that the Northern Tairora themselves are philosophical in addressing the uncertainties implanted in their beliefs. Such is not the case. Northern Tairora religion is not codified. Its rationale is in large part covert, and discussion, even elicitation, is ordinarily difficult. Surely none of this suggests a philosophical bent.

In response to the questions that Northern Tairora religion frames of the world, the answers typically sought—or those obtained—are immediate answers. They deal with matters close at hand. Even when theory is used deductively, as in the discussion of the validity of feces for magical attack, the argument is quite practical and material, close to the surface of things. It seems to be in confrontation with the surface of things, with direct experience, that the openness of Northern Tairora ideas is most pronounced—the ready acceptance of new plants, the desire for new technical devices, the accommodation to the new authority of the administration, the interest in the new word of Christian missionaries, the ready authority of the new world of cargo cult and the credibility of its spokesmen, the new sorcery of *sangguma* and *kuru*, and the new countersorcery of *sangguma*.

The openness of the Northern Tairora and their neighbors to rumors of very large scope, and the speed with which such rumors appear to course the breadth and length of the country, once more bear out the impression of a system of ideas that is the very opposite of being closed. I myself have been stopped on a cross-country path by persons I did not know well and without preliminaries asked whether I agreed with the millennial interpretation given to some word allegedly emanating from a local mission. Nor should it be thought for a moment that this is entirely a postcontact development. Postcontact evidence of the tendencies of which I am speaking is naturally much more plentiful and accessible. This circumstance may well lead to the assumption that these are the abnormal responses of a people shaken to their ideological roots by the momentous changes through which they are passing. But a rumored impending plague of serpents and a period of landslides reached and took firm hold of the Northern Tairora long before the first white men or their New Guinea emissaries arrived; and the large houses especially built for protection against this threat had tumbled down or been dismantled even before contact—leaving people uncertain whether there was any connection between the earlier excitement and the subsequent arrival of astonishing newcomers.

There is a greater depth to the "pragmatism" often attributed to New Guinea peoples like the Northern Tairora than is usually recognized. Its surface is so familiar to those who know the area that they are apt to look no further. It may seem but a practical willingness, however marked, to adopt new things. To be sure, when they are listed, the new things adopted prove remarkably numerous for so short a time. Take crops alone: well before the more viable cash crops of the present—coffee, tea, pyrethrum—the Northern Tairora area had passed, one after the other, through a series of new-crop experiments. Most of these attempts were associated in the minds of the people, however vaguely, with a promise in fact too great to be fulfillable. Tobacco, manioc, and maize were adopted in late precontact times. Since then cinchona (for its bark), citrus, a variety of truck-garden produce, passion fruit, white potatoes, and cabbages have been tried, each as a separate attempt to fulfill still another promise. Ultimately came the coffee, which, though in 1964 still far from fulfillment, has come closest to the understood promise. To be sure, these postcontact developments have each been conceived and projected for mundane, "commercial" purposes by those who instigated them; but it must not therefore be supposed that they are unrelated to our present religious theme.

In the Northern Tairora theory of the world and its contents, as we have seen, "magic" is not a closed compartment lying across a chasm from the immutably ordinary. The credulity of local peoples in accepting the advantages claimed for growing cinchona, garden truck, passion fruit, or white potatoes may have seemed to Europeans the obvious and natural utilitarian recognition of their own superiority, or a kind of childlike obedience, or a manifestation of simple "ignorance." As between different cultures, such abstractions have a truly amazing breadth and opacity. With no lack of benevolence on the European part, there was surely a profound lack of understanding of the difference between what the one side said and what the other side heard.

I am suggesting that the repeated—and repeatedly successful—European persuasion of local peoples to plant new crops, however much it was cast in terms of ordinary sale for cash and of simple utility and self-interest, was not always (if ever) perceived in any "ordinary" sense by the local peoples, in widely and quickly acceding to one such proposal after another. For one thing, the nature of commerce with the white man was hardly ordinary. There was simply no precedent for it in local experience. For here were people who proposed to become one's trading partners and as such to commission the planting of crops—wholly new crops at that; to pay for them in unique and unprecedented goods; to collect them in jeeps and lorries; to take them not to use but to put them aboard aircraft, which left for distant and unknown places; and ultimately to refuse to accept the very crops they themselves had commissioned. While much of this unmistakably provides ample undertones for cargo beliefs, that is not my point. It is rather the existence in the local people of a view of the world—their magical view, of a

credence about *things* (in the present instance, crops)—such that those possessed of this credence may readily suppose, in a case that might otherwise
be unconvincing, that momentous possibilities may indeed inhere in the
new things or in the recommended use of them. How else explain their readiness to adopt? How else explain in them the profound disappointment, the
sense of deception, when they speak of unfulfillment? How else account for
the willingness to try again, and again?[7]

It is tantalizing to speculate how much the openness of regional systems of
belief and practice may have abetted the rapid adoption and adaptation of
sweet potatoes and the ensuing large-scale revisions in the life systems of the
Central Highlands of New Guinea (Watson 1965a, 1965b). In a similar spec-
ulative vein, one might also wonder how much the startling success of sweet
potato innovations may have affirmed or enhanced indigenous beliefs in a
world whose powers are indeed thought numerous, vast, widely unknown,
and potentially discoverable. It may be related—though it is certainly no
answer to these questions—that I was avidly pressed by some Agarabi
neighbors for seeds of okra which I had brought along with me to plant in a
kitchen garden. My neighbors quite thoroughly questioned me about the
plant, which parts were edible, and so forth, and were keen to try it. I felt
rather awkward in telling them that the uses of okra known to me were much
less than their enthusiasm seemed to imply. The simplest account of my
neighbors' interest would stress their being dedicated gardeners; and that is
doubtless correct at one level. What might be called the experimental willingness displayed on this small occasion, however, is common to the trial
acceptance of the many other kinds of things suggested in the previous paragraphs.

Here, then, if the argument is sound, is a religious tradition that is far
from immobile, however much the conventional wisdom may predicate religious stability and immobility in "traditional" peoples like the Northern
Tairora. It is a flexible, adaptive religion whose flexibility, moreover, demands no radical change in underlying principles, these in fact the very
source of flexibility. The surface pragmatism and flexibility of religion finds a
nice match, moreover, in the ideology of membership, descent, and group
identity. There, too, the ease of incorporating outsiders and of indigenizing
them is in keeping with underlying principles that, far from being under-
mined or falsified, are for the most part revitalized in the very process. In
the light of both membership ideology and the ideology of powers, thus, we

7. Dr. Ben Finney has explored the ready adaptation of the Central Highlands of New
Guinea peoples to cash-crop entrepreneurship, attributing it ultimately to an achievement syndrome in which both old and new cultures are compatible (1973). I believe he may be right as to
this compatibility but would point out at the same time that the innovativeness of which we are
speaking here predates any exposure to modern entrepreneurial models in the Northern
Tairora area and has broad ideological roots, whatever may be the more recent linkage to personal status-seeking, money, and prestige.

appear to be dealing with groups whose culture is well suited to the ready acceptance of new people and new practices.

A final comment about religion is in order concerning the seeming fragility of indigenous New Guinea belief and ceremony in the face of organized, intensive, Christian missionization. It is usually emphasized that religions like the Northern Tairora lack explicit dogma, are uncodified, and are not expounded, rationalized, or defended by any spokesmen of special authority or commitment. The beliefs live most effectively in their observance and not in formulation. These features, which commonly define the religious life of small-scale societies, are widely considered to place a religion at a disadvantage in the face of the militant proselytism of an organized faith. In areas undergoing missionization it may therefore be plausible to look to such features in accounting for the rapid introduction of new religious themes or practices, or for the rapid loss or confusion of indigenous themes and practices.

In 1964 it was quite possible to talk to men still in their fifties, as I did one day at Batainabura, who could open one's eyes about some remembered ceremony never brought up before. A particular ceremony was remembered fondly on this occasion, with much drawing of breath through the teeth in pleasure and much shaking of the head in puzzlement over why so fine a custom had been allowed to die. Its death in the boyhood of this man in his fifties, however, would either have predated Christian missionization in the area or would have come almost with the first missionaries. The loss of the ceremony is hardly attributable to missionization, in other words, although Northern Tairora informants of the 1960s tend to use "the mission" as stereotyped explanation for many waning customs.

Old customs were abandoned, including customary religious observances, and new customs were adopted at an appreciable rate before any impact of Christianity. In addition to the ceremony just mentioned (which involved sequestering youths in the forest), one may note the annual renewal ceremony called *ihálabu*, previously referred to. It seems certain that Christianity cannot be credited with the abandonment of *ihálabu*. If anything, it is rather the adoption (by some Northern Tairora) of an Agarabi or Gadsup ceremony, *órana* or *órande*. *Órana* appears to have somewhat the same purpose as *ihálabu*, occurs at the same time of the year, marking the harvest of winged beans, and emphasizes renewal. Such, at least, is the conventional explanation offered today by older informants at Abiera as to why *ihálabu* is no longer enacted: they adopted *órana* instead. And *órana* itself is now a pale facsimile of its former expression.

While no previous Northern Tairora ceremony may have been displaced by it, the adoption of the *hampu* (Agarabi: *ámpu*) ceremony by local groups of Phratry Tairora (and perhaps by others) is once again indicative of a receptivity to change in ceremonies. The spread of *hampu* can hardly be ascribed to Christian missionization either in time or in its character as a device for circumventing normal courtship and betrothal.

The point is threefold. First, as noted, these examples of ceremonial change are prior to and distinct from the influence of Christianity and represent precontact conditions, nearer to normal, presumably, than those of the postcontact period. Second, even from ethnohistorical inquiries that were not exhaustive or systematic one can compile in one small area this number of instances of substantial ceremonial change—omitting both cargo and Christianity. It does not seem far-fetched in this light to speak of a significant rate of ceremonial change or to speak of a marked degree of receptivity to ceremonial change. Finally, the changes mentioned surely did not come about through the influence of an organized religion with deliberate proselytism. Whatever additional momentum of change may arise from such differences of institutionalization, in other words, there appears no reason to attribute recent changes in Northern Tairora religion entirely to the special circumstances of organized Christianity. It rather appears to be a characteristic of long standing, native and indigenous, to be highly receptive to novelty and change, albeit primarily changes at the ceremonial surface.

9. On the Edge of Change

During the first year I lived among the Northern Tairora and their neighbors I formed an impression of unstable societies fluctuating in a turbulent sea. By a decade, thus, this idea antedated my published proposition that the Central Highlands of New Guinea at the time of first contact were undergoing a series of rapid and extensive changes (Watson 1965a, 1965b). Local manifestations of this movement, in other words, were sensed even when I could identify no clear cause. Now that causes are identified and their local impacts are increasingly clear, it is not easy to appreciate that in 1954 the reasons for precontact turbulence and change were anything but obvious or that a proposition formulating such causes and effects would meet with immediate rejection.

I believe that anyone who thought about it in 1954 knew or could have known that the sweet potato was an exotic crop whose adoption must be recent in the Central Highlands. In fact, that point had already been made (Brass 1941). But no one, seemingly, had connected the New Guinea case with the impact of the sweet potato in China and parts of Indonesia or the Philippines. The main thrust of research, for the social anthropologists, at least, left such "historical" questions aside, even though anthropologists are well equipped to recognize the institutional implications of ecological change. In the fifties, moreover, the outsider's impression of the region—mine, too—was one of great isolation and separateness. There was much that seemed to support this impression, not least the late entry of the outsiders themselves, only well into the twentieth century. From great isolation it presumably followed that regional history had been one of slow change and gradual evolution, marked principally by the occasional diffusion of goods or ideas from outside. Here of course is a prejudice: the notion that great change comes from the direct and intensive intervention, in some sense, of the outside. That the new crop might itself be such an impingement was simply not apparent, in part because, although necessarily entering the interior of the island from the outside, sweet potatoes left no change in their

326

wake such as to match or foretell the changes they would occasion in reaching the Central Highlands. As has been the case elsewhere, in fact, the transmission of the plant was quite unobtrusive.

Ethnohistory received only the most casual attention during my first field trip to Kainantu, 1953-55. I had not set out to "study New Guinea" so much as to find in that likely and wonderful place the right setting for a natural experiment, specifically the contrasting responses of two different peoples to virtually the same contact experience. I hoped to measure and perhaps account for the diference by referring to the cultural and psychological differences between the two groups. Not until my second field trip, about ten years later, did I come with the intention of doing a fully rounded ethnographic study. It was during the course of this visit that I paid closer attention to the precontact history of Kainantu peoples.

In any case, during the 1954 Christmas break, with far more conviction than proof, I stated to an Australian friend long resident in the area my doubt that the Kainantu peoples could long have been living as they were when first seen by outsiders. Later, when I thought about it, my pronouncement seemed bold, being based on little more than a feeling I had about the two Kainantu peoples I had briefly known. But to me the turmoil that lay within their immediate recall strongly suggested a reaction or response to some important change in the pattern of life, and it seemed likely that the area had not yet settled down again before European contact commenced another series of far-reaching changes in the lives of local peoples. I could more easily think of cultures in transition than of a stable, precontact tradition that had long stood or could conceivably stand in the terms reported.

There were unmistakable suggestions of late precontact events, to be sure: an epidemic of some kind, the arrival of *kumukumu* (large cowrie) shells in unprecedented quantity, a possible shift in the siting of settlements from swamps or cane brakes to higher ground, and a disturbing prophesy of landslides, preceded or followed by a plague of serpents.

This last rumor was credible enough to lead many if not most of the peoples of the vicinity to construct a prescribed new type of large house (to be referred to by a novel name rather than by the conventional word for "house"). In these stoutly made houses they were to take shelter from both the shifting earth and the impending snakes. But I did not see these incidents as fully or directly responsible for what I sensed as the turbulence of local life and the improvisation of local organization. Fortunately, perhaps, my friend did not press me for the particulars of my loose case. I was inclined to believe what I had said to him, but I had got off quite lightly in saying it. It may have been an omen.

I later argued in print that the cultures of the Central Highlands at first contact could not be of great antiquity. By then I thought I had far better reasons than in 1954, and I had had time to compose what seemed a coherent and plausible case for far-reaching changes and for their apparent cause (Watson 1965a, 1965b). This time, however, I was not to get off lightly. A seminar, including experts of various national and disciplinary provenience, was in due course convened in Canberra to deal with the proposition. It reached what were at the time represented almost point for point as sharply divergent conclusions (Brookfield and White 1968). While the interest was flattering, it was disappointing to have suggested almost nothing that my critics found convincing.

With further evidence and the passage of time, however, the specific views of the seminar rejoinder, one by one, seem to have dissolved into but a single point, a lingering insistence by some on the use of a certain vocabulary—such as "gradual," "evolutionary"—in describing late precontact Highlands history. With the substantive issues progressively less in dispute, it seems doubtful whether terminological nuances like these greatly sharpen the discussion.

As far as the historical development originally projected some ten years ago is concerned, most of the central elements can be more firmly asserted at this writing than in 1964, when I first wrote. Indeed, additional facts or indications have been recognized, conjectured, or thought likely, expanding and refining the original hypothesis. There now seems to be considerable agreement that the following developments have probably occurred since the advent of the sweet potato in the Central Highlands (at some time since 1600) and directly or indirectly on account of it:

1. A major crop innovation, the sweet potato (*Ipomoea batatas*), with a greatly enlarged potential for both food and fodder and an adaptability to a wider range of slopes and altitudinal niches than older staple crops.

2. Changes in agricultural technology, such as emphasis on an open field system and fencing of fields against pigs, or other measures for controlling those voracious animals. Possible disappearance of the pond-field system for growing taro, still (in 1964) remnant in one or two places in the Central Highlands.

3. A population surge.

4. Substantial migratory movement, including the peopling of pioneer or sparsely settled lands, especially forested land, hillsides, and higher elevations unsuited to taro.

5. In some cases the abandonment of older lands, including some that were hydraulically engineered for crops no longer cultivated, notably taro.

6. With an expanding supply of fodder a sharp increase in the regional pig herd, registered archeologically.

7. A concomitant intensification of ceremonialized intergroup exchange and systems of credit and debit, inferable from the fact that these are the major contexts in which pigs or pork are distributed nearly everywhere throughout the region.

8. Changes in labor and production intensity, inevitable with the raising of more pigs and the growing of more fodder.

9. An inflation in the value of women as the main labor force in an intensified agriculture and husbandry, predictable from the foregoing changes.

10. Probable development or increase of gradients, that is, differences of supply/demand, between the peoples of one vicinity and those of another; various gradients of wealth, women, and warfare, with areas of relative scarcity in one good or service intensifying their traffic with areas of complementary scarcity and demand. Gradients are notable in reference to pigs, shells, and women, and the traffic they generate serves as a major means of spreading the new economy to virgin populations.

11. Probable intensification of warfare partly on account of the crowding of the most desirable cleared and arable lands, with more people whose per capita demand for land is increased because of the rising consumption of pigs. This effect presumably follows the initial migration to virgin lands as core areas become densely settled.

12. Variable consequences in social structure, ritual, and ideology, where change is inherently less easily recognized or inferred. This monograph deals with some relevant aspects of social structure and ideology.

The same assumptions and methods that underlie the foregoing propositions broadly describe what are now known as "impact studies." A certain innovation is predicated. The task is to identify the particular, typically multiple consequences that will follow from placing the innovation in a given system or setting. The student of impacts may be obliged to consider different scenarios wherever there are options and the decisions of actors or factors cannot be limited to a single possibility. Dealing with an initial event (or set of events) that has not yet occurred, the standard impact study is of course predictive.

The retrodictive form of impact study is often called "evaluation" or "case study," and such researches are commissioned when some innovation has had an outcome considered worthy of attention, avoidance, remedy, or replication. The retrodictive impact study, like that of sweet potatoes in the Highlands, though no more guaranteed against flaws than the predictive study, has the obvious advantage of a known outcome, and sometimes all important factors are known or knowable. The ipomoean hypothesis (from the generic name of sweet potato) quite simply represents a retrodictive evaluation of the impact of the adoption of the new crop by peoples of the Central Highlands.

This volume is ethnographic, however, not regional. Probably the largest single point to make about the ethnographic relevance of this regional development is that to attempt to account for the pattern of life and society in Northern Tairora without acknowledging the probability of a regional transformation would leave one with a stunted view of the locality. Without the larger perspective, it would be possible only to say about the warring of the Northern Tairora and their neighbors, perhaps, that these were "warlike peoples," "given to aggression," and "committed" to it by such institutions as the initiation of young males to make them strong and forceful, watchful, and quick to suspect and react to a challenge. Plain facts of local life, to be sure, these no more explain themselves than does the absence of such facts among other peoples. Neither are the contingency and improvisation, the flexibility, opportunism and pragmatism of the social order an explanation. They are—if I am right—facts to be explained. Why, for instance, do people circulate in substantial numbers through a system that at one point pulls them into a new local group as protokinsmen, "kinifying" their progeny in rather short order, only to "dekinify" some of the descendants of the same progeny one or more generations later? What makes new blood so often better than the old, which, in the local rhetoric of kinship and fraternity, should be preferred? If it explains anything to say that people stress fighting because they are "warlike," it should be equally satisfactory to say that people tolerate the short-term creation and extinction of kinship relations because they are not at heart inclined to genealogical continuity.

One will not explain every detail of Northern Tairora life, every nuance of culture, by referring to events of perhaps a hundred years or more earlier, events that perhaps first occurred hundreds of miles away—wherever in the Central Highlands the sweet potato first took hold. Yet the intensification of intergroup exchange and rivalry plainly attributable to increased fodder and pig production, based on the adoption of the sweet potato, has been a powerful drive not only at the point or points of first inception but in spreading irresistibly across the partnership networks of the Highlands, as group has been linked to group, as far in any direction as intensive sweet potato and pig production are ecologically feasible and as far as pigs are a valuable and principal asset (e.g., as a part of bride wealth and affinal payments) of intergroup partnership.

When fodder and pig production are increased in one part of a network, there are several effects. Immediately there is an advantage to the parties who initiate the increase. They are better able than previously to demand of their partners the goods and services of intergroup exchange. Almost as rapidly those partners are in turn obliged to increase their own production of fodder and pigs, in order to continue in reasonable parity with the group or groups that initiated the intensification.

It follows from an intensification of production that there is an increase of work and that the value of the worker, above all women, thus rises. The means to make affinal payments—notably pigs—for brides are thus increased at the very time that the value of women is rising. The circumference of this vicious circle rather completely encloses the options of empartnered local groups so far as whether they dare resist the change or must follow suit.

The local gradient of supply/demand whereby brides move unilaterally against pigs cannot often be satisfactory for long. Fodder and pigs are far more readily increased than female children; and perhaps only where a clientship can develop between the poorer, weaker party and the wealthy and powerful one, offering a reliable refuge to the bride-supplying partner, can such complementarity long survive. If, here and there, there were circumstances favorable to such client groups, permitting them the shelter of a supply/demand gradient, it is equally clear that the presence of too many separate groups would often render such unilateral arrangements undependable if not unattainable. There is also a question whether groups traditionally organized for reciprocal parity, each with roughly equal control over its own destiny, would be able to offer or, as the case might be, accept clientship.

Given a swiftly escalating exchange parity, supply/demand gradients cannot support long-term security for very many based on complementarity. The simple rivalry of contending equals must therefore occupy a good number of peoples. Thus does the dynamic of exchange ultimately engulf peoples like the Northern Tairora, even far removed in time or space from the first arenas of ipomoean innovation. The scenario is replicated in a moving wave as what are today known as the "core" areas of the Central Highlands progressively radiate outward their influence on a widening "fringe." The notion here is obviously epidemiological, the vectors those of political economy. Parity is raised and competition intensified whether or not a given local habitat is short of important natural resources. For rivalry in the first instance concerns security, and competition develops as groups struggle to retain the means by which to remain competitive. Those means are manpower—productive women, fighting men, and elders astute in the rapid maneuvering of small groups engaged in making peace and war. Recruitment of a sufficient body of basically loyal coresidents is requisite—as is, if possible, the retention of such a personnel.

It takes success to make success, and the fact of success must be accompanied by its unmistakable appearance, stated as overtly as possible within the acceptable limits of style and etiquette. The successful group must prevent or mask failure in every possible way, for it needs the ablest possible allies as well as ones who will find good reason to remain constant. Competition, in a word, is in part for partners such as these, and any group must consider that its best friends may cool if denied the support they need, even as on its own behalf any group must turn from partners insufficient to help it meet its own needs.

These tensions are stated and adjusted through a complex network of individual enterprise and opportunism usually phrased as—and in fact partly being—*pro bono publico.* The strongest or "biggest" men are those with the most to win or lose in operating from a given social and political base. Like their failures, their successes tend also to be those of the given collectivity, and thus the members of a local group may be called upon to display a certain tolerance for the self-dramatization and excesses that overtly supplement and express the successful strong man's personal power.

The closest friendships are, as noted, contingent on the ability of the given parties to meet each other's needs. It must be so in the long run if not in the short, for where enemies have allies, no one can be without equally capable allies of his own. The same is true of the fraternally bonded coresidents of the local group. Although some diversity of loyalties is inescapable, in view of differences of intermarriage and indigenous or exogenous origin, the final test is where an individual feels his own best interests lie. A successful group has less to worry about on this account than one whose fortunes are fading. At some point, the latter group must begin to lose its adherents—outside allies and coresident members. If there are in addition ineradicable sources of disaffection or rivalrous local leaders, or if one leader moves to recruit refugees who as clients will owe him a greater loyalty than his own long-time coresidents, then the departure of some of the community may well ensue.

Against these harsh realities claims of kinship might still prevail if the process of estrangement always required an initial and unequivocal denial of kinship. For such a blatant denial might not at first be possible. But estrangement need not begin with the ultimate denunciation of kinsmen or kinship claims. It often begins with a change of residence for some of the kinsmen. At first the change may be small, but over time kinship and friendship are redefined as the cumulative outcome of the viable and the necessary. Life is often conducted at a rather shrill pitch and always with the recognition that anyone's failure will be someone's triumph and no one's triumph can occur without at least a threat to someone else.

Why so? Obviously it is not simply because of the adoption somewhere in the Highlands of the sweet potato as fodder for an expanding pig herd. Basically it is because of the proximity and exchange redundancy of numerous small groups committed to a small-group political order and lacking immediate means of widening their polities. Such a description fits the Northern Tairora better than it fits some areas to the west of Kainantu, areas more populous than Kainantu. I have suggested elsewhere (1965a, 1965b) that the sweet potato played a role in increasing the regional population, and I remain unpersuaded by the arguments I have so far seen against it (Brookfield and White 1968). I know of no grounds on which to suppose that the population density at contact would have been possible or necessary without the adoption of the sweet potato.

In any case, small-group polity with relatively dense population means numerous small groups. If this condition is of many centuries standing, then we must wonder about some of our views of social structure and its evolution. For it would then seem to follow that the turbulence and instability of Northern Tairora life and life elsewhere in the Central Highlands have had a long history. One would have to conclude that the accommodations that over time produce the stable social orders repeatedly shown in ethnographic literature for some reason did not produce them here.

Social fields in which small groups are present, each closely replicating the next in its exchange capability, are by nature turbulent. While every group may need one or more partners, no group uniquely needs a specific other group as partner or military ally. Various conceivable partners, that is, can meet the same demand. Such a condition mirrors Durkheim's mechanical solidarity, the same notion that Bateson (1958) was later to dub "symmetry" in analyzing the forces that draw together or push apart the parties of a dyad. When independent proximate peoples can serve each other in no way that is unique as well as positive, yet are capable of harm and will actually find advantage in inflicting harm, there warfare is endemic. This description also fits the Northern Tairora and their neighbors. Lacking the means to be uniquely useful to every other group within effective range, each will always find good and sufficient reasons to be actively hostile to some of those groups. Some but not all groups have more to gain from each other's enmity than from friendship, for in fact friendship between some groups requires hostility to others. A part of the price of friendship, that is, is making common cause against some of a friend's enemies. The friendship of some thus feeds on the enmity of others—a fateful momentum stopped or slowed only by the evolution of wider polities or by the intervention of a powerful third party bent on hegemony.

If this was the long-standing history of precontact Kainantu, then the post-ipomoean intensification of exchange may only have exacerbated a prior condition by increasing competition and placing heavier burdens on the work force of the typical small groups. Because of their small size, moreover, the greater and more critical the burden of each, the more often must groups falter in supporting the load, vulnerable as they are to the scale effect. With the possibility of faltering partners must come an increasing need for the close monitoring of partnerships, hence the opportunism of friendship and enmity. This is at the heart of the turbulence of which I speak in referring to Northern Tairora society. It is no defect of the kinship system, no defect of memory such as is implied in the concept of "genealogical amnesia." And— surely it is not necessary to say—it is no defect of morality or attribute of personality, save in the secondary sense that personality presumably has some congruence with the immediate options and contingencies of life and death.

If, as I am convinced, regional and local populations of the Central Highlands surged following the adoption of sweet potatoes and the settlement of a wider zone, then turbulence may have increased even faster in the last century or so than it would otherwise have done. The foddering of a rising number of pigs and the consequent inflation of this quasi-monetary commodity, that is, would produce an effect but a lesser one than if accompanied by an expanding population.

The more pronounced and recent effect seems better to accord with the state of Northern Tairora society, specifically in accounting for the contingency features that permit an opportunistic handling of genealogical claims. Granted that I have made a case for the compatibility of Northern Tairora recruitment with ideas of birthright, identity, descent, and fraternity, this has not at the same time been an argument that the dismissal of kinsmen and the incorporation of outsiders is essential in sustaining these cultural conventions. The accommodation potential of Northern Tairora cultures does not require a recurrent loosening or negation of proclaimed bonds, nor does flexibility demand a recurrent testing.

The ethnographies and ethnographers of New Guinea have in several ways been greatly aided if they wished to depict local cultures as isolated and unique developments—islands within an island quite as much as the sea-girt peoples of farther Oceania. Mead displayed three examples of the impressive variegation and self-enclosure of New Guinea cultures in a single book (1950). But this is not likely to be matched in the realm of social structure nor especially that of intergroup exchange. Barring the very rare Crusoe community, intergroup exchange is surely everywhere a primary factor in determining the structures of human societies. The lives of the Northern Tairora are what they are largely because of whom they have for neighbors and who, accordingly, they must themselves be as neighbors. A related fact is of course long familiar in the guise of "diffusion," the notion that local culture—indeed, culture more than society—assumes a coloration reflecting the influence of other cultures according to proximity. It is not the imitative absorption of neighborhood ways that is stressed in the present study of ecology but the structural accommodation—"defensiveness" is acceptable—of social groups and polities in coping with others of their kind, their neighbors. I have tried to sketch some of the main internal consequences of that external coping as well as suggesting the history of coping in its present form. As of the present writing, this is how I see the late history and recent development of the Northern Tairora area. I am keenly aware that much remains to be known and said about that area and about the region at large. I therefore hope that this study may contribute to those yet to come.

Bibliography

Allen, M. R.
  1967   *Male Cults and Secret Initiations in Melanesia.* Melbourne: Melbourne University Press.
Barnes, J. A.
  1962   "African Models in the New Guinea Highlands." *Man* 62:5-9.
Barrau, Jacques
  1965   "L'Humide et le Sec: An Essay on Ethnobiological Adaptation to Contrastive Environments in the Indo-Pacific Area." *Journal of the Polynesian Society* 74:329-46.
Bateson, Gregory
  1958   *Naven: a Survey of the Problems Suggested by a Composite Picture of the Culture of a New Guinea Tribe Drawn from Three Points of View.* Second edition. Stanford: Stanford University Press. First published 1936.
Berndt, Ronald M.
  1964   "Warfare in the New Guinea Highlands." In *New Guinea: The Central Highlands,* edited by James B. Watson. Special publication of *American Anthropologist* 66 (no. 4, pt. 2): 183-203.
Brass, L. J.
  1941   "Stone Age Agriculture in New Guinea." *Geographical Review* 31:555-69.
Brookfield, Harold C.
  1962   "Local Study and Comparative Method: An Example from Central New Guinea." *Annals of the Association of American Geographers* 52:242:54.
Brookfield, Harold C., and J. Peter White
  1968   "Revolution or Evolution in the Prehistory of the New Guinea Highlands: A Seminar Report." *Ethnology* 7:43-52.
Brown, Paula
  1962   "Non-agnates among the Patrilineal Chimbu." *Journal of the Polynesian Society* 71:57-69.
Dixon, Roland B.
  1916   *Oceanic Mythology: The Mythology of All Races,* vol. 9. Boston: Marshall Jones.

du Toit, Brian M.
    1962   "Structural Looseness in New Guinea." *Jouranl of the Polynesian Soci-ety* 71:397-99.
    1964   "Filiation and Affiliation among the Gadsup." *Oceania* 35:85-95.
Eggan, Fred
    1950   *Social Organization of the Western Pueblos.* Chicago: University of Chicago Press.
Finney, Ben R.
    1973   *Big Men and Business: Entrepreneurship and Economic Growth in the New Guinea Highlands.* Honolulu: University of Hawaii Press.
Heider, Karl G.
    1970   *The Dugum Dani: A Papuan Culture in the Highlands of West New Guinea.* Chicago: Aldine Publishing Company.
Hogbin, H. Ian, and Camilla H. Wedgwood
    1953-54   "Local Grouping in Melanesia." *Oceania* 23:241-76, 24:58-76.
Howlett, Diana
    1967   *A Geography of Papua and New Guinea.* Melbourne: Thomas Nelson (Australia) Limited.
Langness, L. L.
    1964   "Some Problems in the Conceptualization of Highlands Social Structures." In *New Guinea: The Central Highlands*, edited by James B. Watson. Special publication of *American Anthropologist* 66 (no. 4, pt. 2): 162-82.
    1967   "Sexual Antagonism in the New Guinea Highlands: A Bena Bena Example." *Oceania* 37:161-77.
Lawrence, Peter
    1955   *Land Tenure Among the Garia.* Social Science Monograph 4, Australian National University. (Reprinted in H. I. Hogbin and P. Lawrence, eds., *Studies in New Guinea Land Tenure.* Sydney: Sydney University Press, 1967.)
Leininger, Madeleine M.
    1964   "A Gadsup Village Experiences Its First Election." *Journal of the Polynesian Society* 73:205-9.
Linton, Ralph
    1936   *The Study of Man.* New York: D. Appleton-Century Company.
Littlewood, R. A.
    1972   *Physical Anthropology of the Eastern Highlands of New Guinea.* Anthropological Studies in the Eastern Highlands of New Guinea, vol. 2. Seattle and London: University of Washington Press.
Lowman, Cherry
    1968   "Maring Big Men." *Anthropological Forum* 2:199-243. (Reprinted in Ronald M. Berndt and Peter Lawrence, eds., *Politics in New Guinea.* Perth: University of Western Australia Press. Seattle: University of Washington Press, 1973.)
Luzbetak, Louis J.
    1954   "The Socio-religious Significance of a New Guinea Pig Festival." *Anthropological Quarterly* 27:59-80, 102-28.
McKaughan, Howard P.
    1964   "A Study of Divergence in Four New Guinea Languages." In *New Gui-*

nea: The Central Highlands, edited by James B. Watson. Special publication of *American Anthropologist* 66 (no. 4, pt. 2):98-120.

McKaughan, Howard P., ed.
1973   *The Languages of the Eastern Family of the East New Guinea Highland Stock.* Anthropological Studies in the Eastern Highlands of New Guinea, vol. 1. Seattle and London: University of Washington Press.

Mauss, Marcel
1967   *The Gift: Forms and Functions of Exchange in Archaic Societies.* Translated by Ian Cunnison. New York: W. W. Norton & Company. First French edition 1925.

Mead, Margaret
1950   *Sex and Temperament in Three Primitive Societies.* Mentor Book. New York: The New American Library. First published 1935.

Meggitt, M. J.
1962   "Growth and Decline of Agnatic Descent Groups among the Mae Enga of the New Guinea Highlands." *Ethnology* 1:158-65.
1964   "Male-Female Relationships in the Highlands of Australian New Guinea." In *New Guinea: The Central Highlands,* edited by James B. Watson. Special publication of *American Anthropologist* 66 (no. 4, pt. 2): 204-24.
1965   *The Lineage System of the Mae-Enga of New Guinea.* Edinburgh: Oliver and Boyd.
1967   "The Pattern of Leadership among the Mae-Enga of New Guinea." *Anthropological Forum* 2:20-35. (Reprinted in Ronald M. Berndt and Peter Lawrence, eds., *Politics in New Guinea.* Perth: University of Western Australia Press. Seattle: University of Washington Press, 1973.)

Murdock, George P.
1949   *Social Structure.* New York: Macmillan.

Newman, Philip L.
1964   " 'Wild Man' Behavior in a New Guinea Highlands Community." *American Anthropologist* 66:1-19.

Oomen, H. A. P. C., W. Spoon, J. E. Hesterman, J. Ruinard, R. Luyken, and P. Slump
1961   "The Sweet Potato as the Staff of Life of the Highland Papuan." *Journal of Tropical Geography and Medicine* 13:55-66.

Pataki-Schweizer, K. J.
1980   *A New Guinea Landscape: Community, Space, and Time in the Eastern Highlands.* Anthropological Studies in the Eastern Highlands of New Guinea, vol. 4. Seattle and London: University of Washington Press.

Pouwer, Jan
1960   "Loosely Structured Societies in Netherlands New Guinea." *Bijdragen tot de Taal-, Land- en Volkenkunde* 116:109-18.

Rappaport, Roy A.
1967   *Pigs for the Ancestors: Ritual in the Ecology of a New Guinea People.* New Haven: Yale University Press.

Raulet, H. M.
1960   "Some Ecological Determinants of Social Structure in Northwest Melanesia." Ph.D. dissertation, Columbia University.

Read, Kenneth E.
   1952   "Land in the Central Highlands." *South Pacific* 6:440-49, 465.
   1954   "Cultures of the Central Highlands, New Guinea." *Southwestern Journal of Anthropology* 10:1-43.
Robbins, Sterling G.
   1970   "Warfare, Marriage, and the Distribution of Goods in Auyana." Ph.D. dissertation, University of Washington, Seattle.
Sahlins, Marshall D.
   1963   "Poor Man, Rich Man, Big-man, Chief: Political Types in Melanesia and Polynesia." *Comparative Studies in Society and History.* 5(3):285-303.
   1972   *Stone Age Economics.* Chicago: Aldine-Atherton.
Salisbury, Richard F.
   1956   "Unilineal Descent Groups in the New Guinea Highlands." *Man* 56:2-7.
   1962   *From Stone to Steel: Economic Consequences of a Technological Change in New Guinea.* Melbourne: Melbourne University Press.
   1964   "Despotism and Australian Administration in the New Guinea Highlands." In *New Guinea: The Central Highlands,* edited by James B. Watson. Special publication of *American Anthropologist* 66 (no. 4, pt. 2): 225-39.
Schwartz, Theodore
   1973   "Cult and Context: The Paranoid Ethos in Melanesia." *Ethos* 1:153-74.
Sorenson, E. Richard
   1972   "Socio-ecological Change among the Fore of New Guinea." *Current Anthropology* 13:349-83.
Steward, Julian H.
   1955   *Theory of Culture Change.* Urbana: University of Illinois Press.
Strathern, Marilyn
   1969   "Why Is the *Pueraria* a Sweet Potato?" *Ethnology* 8:189-98.
Sumner, William G.
   1906   *Folkways: A Study of the Sociological Importance of Usages, Manners, Customs, Mores, and Morals.* Boston: Ginn and Company.
Vayda, Andrew P.
   1961   "Expansion and Warfare Among Swidden Agriculturalists." *American Anthropologist* 63:346-58.
   1971   "Phases of the Process of War and Peace among the Marings of New Guinea." *Oceania* 42:1-24.
Vayda, Andrew P., ed.
   1969   *Environment and Cultural Behavior.* New York: American Museum of Natural History.
Vayda, Andrew P., and R. A. Rappaport
   1968   "Ecology, Cultural and Noncultural." In *Introduction to Cultural Anthropology,* edited by J. Clifton, pp. 477-97. Boston: Houghton Mifflin.
Watson, James B.
   1963a   "A Micro-Evolution Study in New Guinea." *Journal of the Polynesian Society* 72:188-92.
   1963b   "Krakatoa's Echo?" *Journal of the Polynesian Society* 72:152-55.
   1964a   "A Previously Unreported Root Crop from the New Guinea Highlands." *Ethnology* 3:1-5.

1964b   "A General Analysis of the Elections at Kainantu." *Journal of the Polynesian Society* 73:199-204.

1965a   "From Hunting to Horticulture in the New Guinea Highlands." *Ethnology* 4:295-309.

1965b   "The Significance of a Recent Ecological Change in the Central Highlands of New Guinea." *Journal of the Polynesian Society* 74:438-50.

1965c   "The Kainantu Open and South Markham Special Electorates." In *The Papua-New Guinea Elections 1964*, edited by David G. Bettison et al., pp. 91-119. Canberra: Australian National University Press.

1967a   "Tairora: The Politics of Despotism in a Small Society." *Anthropological Forum* 2:53-104. (Reprinted in Ronald M. Berndt and Peter Lawrence, eds., *Politics in New Guinea*. Perth: University of Western Australia Press. Seattle: University of Washington Press, 1973.)

1967b   "Horticultural Traditions of the Eastern New Guinea Highlands." *Oceania* 38:81-98.

1968   "*Pueraria:* Names and Traditions of a Lesser Crop of the Central Highlands, New Guinea." *Ethnology* 7:268-79.

Watson, James B., ed.

1964   *New Guinea: The Central Highlands*. Special publication of *American Anthropologist* 66 (no. 4, pt. 2).

1966   *New Guinea Micro-Evolution Studies*, memorandum no. 18. "Conference on the Project Monographs, July 5-15, 1966." Unpublished. Department of Anthropology, University of Washington, Seattle.

1981   "The Exchange Strategies of Crowded Partners." In *Persistence and Exchange: A Symposium*, edited by Roland W. Force and Brenda Bishop, pp. 151-53. Honolulu: Pacific Science Association.

Watson, Virginia Drew, and J. David Cole

1977   *Prehistory of the Eastern Highlands of New Guinea*. Anthropological Studies in the Eastern Highlands of New Guinea, vol. 3. Seattle and London: University of Washington Press.

Wurm, Stephen A.

1960   "The Changing Linguistic Picture of New Guinea." *Oceania* 31:121-36.

1961a   "The Linguistic Situation in the Highlands Districts of Papua and New Guinea." *Australian Territories* 1:14-23.

1961b   Map of the Languages of Eastern, Western, and Southern Highlands, Territory of Papua and New Guinea. Canberra: Australia National University.

1962   "The Languages of the Eastern, Western and Southern Highlands, Territory of Papua and New Guinea." In *A Linguistic Survey of the Southwestern Pacific*, edited by Arthur Capell, pp. 105-28. New and revised edition. Noumea: South Pacific Commission, Technical Paper 136.

1964   "Australian New Guinea Highlands Languages and the Distribution of Their Typological Features." In *New Guinea: The Central Highlands*, edited by James B. Watson. Special publication of *American Anthropologist* 66 (no. 4, pt. 2): 77-97.

Index

193-94; Batainabura, 194-98; meaning of, in Northern Tairora, 197-98, 199-200, 206-9; as security sphere, 212; instability of membership, 227; growth and fissioning of, 238-42, 243-47

Pigs: in gardens, 42; raising and use of, 49-57; wild boars in breeding of, 50; depredations of, 50-51; range and shelter for, 51-52, 70; slaughter of, 52, 56-57; at Abiera and Batainabura, compared, 52, 84-85, 87-89; attachment of owners to, 53-54, 74, 86; grasslanders *vs.* bush folk, 53; exchange of, 54-55, 72; keeping of, as compared to hunting/gathering and gardening, 58

Pigs, wild, 60, 61-62

Pine forest: at southern edge of world, 16

Place names: as relevant to group names, 79-80; as sib names, 161-68

Pleiades: as abode of sky-beings, 20

Pollution, and gardening, 42, 48, 65-66

Polygyny: comparison of Abiera and Batainabura, 100; opposition of missions and government to, 100; decline of, 101-2

Ponds and pools: magical significance of, 14-15

Population: density of, as related to exchange, 72; pyramids, 75-78; comparative statistics, Abiera/Batainabura, 89-93; significance of, 92-93; putative expansion of, 149; Ipomoean hypothesis of, 328, 332

Pore: as general term for peoples to the south, 149-50

Poreqórxntx: origin and status of immigrant sib, 149-56; proper name of sib at Abiera, 154; illustrates sib formation, 225-26, 228

Post-natal influences: *vs.* pre-natal influences in inheritance, 272-77

Power: lack of, 48; magical, 304-5

Process: norms of, mistaken for structural "discrepancies," 231

Productivity: need for, 72-73; intensification of due to sweet potato, 328, 330

Pythons: as game, 59-60, 61

Quntoqa (*quntóqa*): current name of Abiera, 79; settlement of, 110

Rappaport, Roy: concept of "cognized world," 313

Rats, 61

Refugees: significance of, 9-10; Batainabura, 128-30, 131-32; Poreqórxntx, 149-56; Abiera asylum with Óndxbúrx, 163; from Onxmantxqa among Kamáno, 168-71; JabuNka, temporarily among Batainabura, 182-83; Hararuna, at Kamunakera, 183-84; Batainabura, among JabuNka, 185; among Arau, 185-86; Batainabura, at Andandára, 187, 188; Airina, at Tompena, 188; high frequency of, 227-29

Religion: diffuseness of, 281-84; magical character of, 281-325 *passim*; uncertainty in, 320-21; innovation in, 320-25; as frame for interrogation, 321. *See also* Magic

Resources: perceived sufficiency of, 8; development of, 26-74 *passim*; use of, 59-62, 70-74

Ritual: as communal stamp, 270-72. *See also* Magic

Rumors: pre-contact inspiration for building big houses, 321; of impending landslides and plague of serpents, 327

Sahlins, Marshall: on significance of food, 267

Salamaua, 293

Sangguma (sorcery): impotence of *máraqúra* in, 295-99; as example of growth of magic, 295, 298-99; report of specific for, 298; as alien to local magical concepts, 314-15; influenced by modern surgery (?), 315n; mentioned, 321

Saruwaged Range, 15

Sash, bark: worn by women, 68

Sea: lack of concept of, 15

Semen: concept of, as genealogical link, 255, 257-59, 262-64; as primary among exuviae, 258

"Shallow genealogy": on concept of, 253-54; as consequence of frequent fission, 279-80

Shelter: forms of, 62-66

Sibs: nature of, at Abiera, 104-19 *passim*; residential patterns of, 107, 110-12; phylogeny of, 110; marital patterns of, 113-15; membership of, at Abiera, 116-19; membership of, at Batainabura, 119-22, 130-36; residential patterns of, at Batainabura, 122-25; exogamy of, at Batainabura, 125-28, 132-36; local segments of, 156; naming of, 161-68; Abiera and Batainabura compared, 190-94; place of, in Northern Tairora society, 199-200, 206-9; growth and decay of, 238-42; multiplication of, 240, especially fig. 6, 241-42

Singsings, 201-5

Site, residential: location and use of, 70-71

Skirts, women's: described, 66-68

Sky: as abode of supernaturals, 20

Snakes, 59, 60. *See also* Rumor

Social control: precarious in local society, 237

Social process, 239

Somatic differences: limited role of, in genealogical conceptualization, 278-80

Sorcery: prevalence of, 11; as secret weapon, 215; danger to growth of children, 270-72

Sorenson, Richard: on pioneering of South Fore peoples, 243

Space. *See* Landscape

Steel tools: importance of, 49

"Story": significance of having "same story" (common history), 279